AN ESSAY ON JUDICIAL POWER AND UNCONSTITUTIONAL LEGISLATION

Da Capo Press Reprints in

AMERICAN CONSTITUTIONAL AND LEGAL HISTORY

GENERAL EDITOR: LEONARD W. LEVY

Brandeis University

AN ESSAY ON JUDICIAL POWER AND UNCONSTITUTIONAL LEGISLATION

Being a Commentary on Parts of the Constitution of the United States

By Brinton Coxe

DA CAPO PRESS • NEW YORK • 1970

A Da Capo Press Reprint Edition

This Da Capo Press edition of
An Essay on Judicial Power and Unconstitutional Legislation
is an unabridged republication of the first
edition published in Philadelphia in 1893.

Library of Congress Catalog Card Number 79-99476

SBN 306-71853-7

Published by Da Capo Press
A Division of Plenum Publishing Corporation
227 West 17th Street, New York, N. Y, 10011
All Rights Reserved

Manufactured in the United States of America

AN ESSAY

ON

JUDICIAL POWER

AND

UNCONSTITUTIONAL LEGISLATION,

BEING A COMMENTARY

ON

PARTS OF THE CONSTITUTION OF THE UNITED STATES.

By BRINTON COXE,
OF THE BAR OF PHILADELPHIA.

"Does the Constitution express or imply the truth that its *jus legum*, which binds legislators in legislating, also binds judges in deciding ?"—*Post*, page 113.

PHILADELPHIA:
KAY AND BROTHER,
1893.

NOTE.

During his last illness, Mr. Coxe expressed a wish that I should see this book through the press. When it reached my hands, all the first part of the work, including the 37th chapter, was not only set up in type but electrotyped, and is, of course, now published in the same condition in which its author left it. The remaining portion of the work was still in manuscript, and unfortunately not sufficiently completed to justify its publication. This conclusion has only been reached after careful consideration, but has seemed unavoidable. Some portions of the second part of the book were almost entirely unwritten, and what was written was in parts fragmentary, and plainly not in the condition in which its author would have published it. Notes and queries in the manuscript showed that he had in mind changes which he thought ought to be made, and these can, of course, be made by no one else. This is greatly to be regretted, and the work, as it is now given to the public, lacks completeness in one sense ; the purpose with which the author began it, and which he states in his Introduction, is not fully carried out. But I think this defect is more apparent than real, for the published portion is entirely capable of standing by itself, and contains all that was intended to form a part of the Historical Commentary upon the constitution. It is, of course, much to be wished that the Textual Commentary had been completed by the author, in order to meet the views of those he refers to on page 49 of the Introduction ; but none the less the portion of the work which he did finish is complete upon the subjects which it treats of, and its great importance can not be doubted.

In regard to the second part of the book—The Textual Commentary—unfinished though it is, the outline of the author's purpose is clear ; he intended in it to treat of the two clauses of the Constitution (2.VI and part of 2.III) which read :

"This Constitution, and the Laws of the United States which shall be made in pursuance thereof ; and all treaties made, or which shall be made, under the authority of the United States, shall be the supreme law of the land ; and the judges in every State shall be bound thereby, anything in the Constitution or laws of any State to the contrary notwithstanding."

"The judicial power shall extend to all cases, in law and equity, arising under this Constitution, the laws of the United States, and treaties made, or which shall be made, under their authority." * * *

These two clauses Mr. Coxe intended to examine critically from the standpoint of historical jurisprudence ; and it was evidently upon these "twin texts" and upon the reading of them together, that he relied to establish the subject matter of that part of his work—that the Constitution contains express texts providing for judicial competency to decide questioned legislation to be constitutional or unconstitutional and to hold it valid or void accordingly.

The exact line of his argument cannot now be made out from his manuscript, and I greatly fear that any effort to make a résumè of it will fail to do justice to what he had in mind. Indeed, there is so great difficulty in one person's trying to fill out the partially completed argument of another, and there are so certain to be gaps in the reasoning, which the author would have been the first to see and to regret, that I long doubted the advisability of trying to formulate his argument. But Mr. Coxe had evidently worked a great deal upon the matter, and, to some who have been consulted, it seemed so unfortunate that all this work should go for naught, that I have made the effort. I am well aware that the sketch is very imperfect, but I believe that the imperfections are under the circumstances unavoidable.

In the first place, the author examined clause 2 of article VI and called attention to the fact that it is *legislative.* It enacts what the law shall be, as clearly as any statute ; and it must, therefore, bind all judges and all public and private persons capable of being bound ; otherwise it would not be legislation. The fact that it reads that the judges of the State courts shall be bound thereby by no means confines its operation to those officials, but simply means that even they shall be bound ; and it was inserted to avoid evils well known in public affairs at that time. The effect aimed at by this legislation was then more nearly approached by en-acting that certain things pointed out should be the su-preme law of the land, and in this connection laws unauthor-ized by the Constitution were excluded from this effect by the use of the technical words (taken almost *verbatim* from Article 12 of the Articles of Confederation) "in pursuance thereof,"* by which laws not enacted in pursuance of the Constitution were excluded from the effect given to pur-suant laws by the clause in question. The clause was finally perfected by the use of the words "anything in the Con-stitution or Laws of any State to the contrary notwith-standing." These words, also, are technical and express, and are an instance of the very well-known *non-obstante* clause, the effect of which has always been held to be to derogate to—or to repeal and make of no effect—any legis-lation that comes within its scope. This was very well known, and its operation seen in many instances familiar

---

*Pursuance and variance or departure are well defined terms in pleading ; and in the Civil law "*variare*" is equally so.

to all in 1787 ; and was applied directly to colonial laws by
the statute of 7 and 8 William III cap 22 (see *post*, page
183), by virtue of which all colonial laws violating certain
anterior British statutes were declared to be null and void.

The words "law of the land," contained in this same section have also a technical meaning, and are to be found
used in multitudes of instances as far back as our law can
be traced ; not only do they occur in the Constitutions of
nine States in 1787, but they extend back to the days
of law latin—where *lex terrae* is a frequent and familiar
term—and to those of Norman French and of "*la ley de la
terre;*" and the exact equivalent is moreover to be found on
the Continent of Europe. In all these systems, the words
had a distinct meaning, constituting a body of laws and
privileges, the right to which could only be lost by certain
offenses, *and which it was particularly the duty of the
judiciary to enforce*—their oath of office required them to
decide by it.

The term, moreover, referred to a law of the land of each
State, and not to one law of the land of the whole Union.*
It existed in nine State Constitutions at the time ; Trevett
v. Weeden shows positively that there was a "law of the
land" of Rhode Island at its date; and the then New
York Constitution (Article 33) and the United States Con-

---

*In this connection, Mr. Coxe calls attention to the error of Mr. Calhoun,
in his debate with Mr. Webster in the Senate on February 24th, 1849. (See
Curtis's Life of Webster, ed. 4, Vol. ii, p. 366) :

"Mr. Calhoun : Then the simple question is, does the Constitution exterd
"to the territories, or does it not extend to them ? Why the Constitution
"interprets itself. It pronounces itself to be the supreme law of the land.

"Mr. Webster : *What land ?*

"Mr. Calhoun : *The land, the territories of the United States are a part of the*
"*land.* It is the supreme law, not within the limits of the States of this
"Union merely, but wherever the flag goes—wherever our authority goes, the
"Constitution in part goes, not in all its provisions certainly, but all its suit-
"able provisions."

stitution are alike (the latter being evidently taken from the former) upon the subject of impeachment, except that the former provides that the person impeached shall be still liable to trial according to the laws *of the land*, while the United States Constitution reads "according to law." The words "of the land" were evidently omitted, because they could only refer to the system of each State and would, therefore, have been quite out of place in this section of the Constitution.

Finally, in the expression "and the judges in every State shall be bound thereby," *bound* is another technical and express word, the meaning of which is to be found discussed by writers treating *e. g.* of statutes which *bind* the king; and these statutes do not mean that they bind only the king but that they bind even him, as well as every one else.

The clause, therefore, will read thus, if its technical terms are especially emphasized: This Constitution and the laws of the United States made in *pursuance* thereof and all treaties made or which shall be made under their authority —shall be the *supreme law of the land;* and the judges in every State shall be *bound* thereby, *anything in the Constitution or laws of any State to the contrary notwithstanding.* By the adoption of the Constitution, the Constitution itself and the constitutional laws of the Union were engrafted upon the law of the land of each respective State in the Union as a part thereof; and the conclusion is therefore express and unavoidable that it became the function of the State judiciaries to enforce that new law; they must obey, and execute the legislative derogation of the *non-obstante* clause. It is peculiarly their function to decide upon points of the law of the land, and all questions arising thereunder are hence judicial questions.

Next, as to the express competency of the United States Supreme Court to do the same thing, that is pointed out by the clause (2.III) upon the judicial power. The judicial power necessarily extends to a judicial question and hence extends to questions arising under 2.VI, which have been shown to be judicial questions. But clause 2.III alone would not have that effect; what precedes is also necessary to it, and the conclusion is mainly to be reached by reading together 2.VI and 2.III in the view of what has already been shown. To put them together, they are as follows:

The judicial power (of the United States) shall extend to all cases in law and equity arising under this Constitution, the laws of the United States and all treaties made, or which shall be made, under their authority, (and) this Constitution, the laws of the United States which shall be made in pursuance thereof, and all treaties made, or which shall be made, under the authority of the United States shall be the supreme law of the land (in every State), anything in the Constitution or laws of any State to the contrary notwithstanding.

The Index and the Table of Contents have been prepared by me; the latter mainly by the use of the author's headlines. The Table of Cases was made by Mr. Adrian van Helden, who had rendered valuable assistance to Mr. Coxe in many ways during the preparation of the book.

WILLIAM M. MEIGS.

216 South Third Street, Philadelphia.

TABLE OF CONTENTS.

INTRODUCTION.

(ix)

TABLE OF CASES.

INTRODUCTION.

CHAPTER I.

Of the subject of this Essay and matters related thereto.

The subject of this Essay is the relation of judicial power to unconstitutional legislation according to the text of the constitution of the United States. The constitutional relation of judicial power to unconstitutional legislation is to be considered in connection with the particular texts of that instrument bearing thereupon. This Essay is thus concerned with any legislation conflicting with the constitution of the United States, whether it be such as is made by Congress or such as proceeds in any form from a state. It is concerned with the judiciary of the United States and the judiciaries of the several states, in so far as any of the courts and judges thereof have constitutional relations to such unconstitutional legislation.

The chief purpose of the writer is to show that the constitution of the United States contains express texts providing for judicial competency to decide questioned legislation to be constitutional or unconstitutional and to hold it valid or void accordingly.

Subordinate to this chief purpose are four others. The first of these subordinate purposes is to show that the Framers of the constitution, according to the extant records of their debates and proceedings at Philadelphia in 1787, expressly intended to provide for the said judicial competency as to such unconstitutional legislation.

The second subordinate purpose is to point out and comment upon certain texts in federal documents older than the constitution, which are historical antecedents of the constitutional texts concerned.

The third subordinate purpose is to examine the history of the relation of judicial power to unconstitutional legislation in certain of the states before and during the confederation, and to show that the judicial competency under discussion is an American institution older than the constitution of the United States.

A fourth subordinate purpose is to make an historical investigation of foreign laws in order to show the true place of the judicial competency aforesaid in the legal history and comparative jurisprudence of Europe and America. This investigation will include the laws of certain European states and unions of states, and an examination of the Roman and Canon laws.

The writer's purposes have been enumerated in an order which is the inverse of that in which he will endeavour to execute them. In accordance with them, this Essay will be divided into appropriate divisions and subdivisions, besides the Introduction.

Of the special reasons for a new discussion of the subject.

Discussions of the whole, or any part, of the text of the constitution of the United States may be assumed at any time to be proper. This general reason makes it perfectly proper now to discuss afresh the subject of the relation of judicial power to unconstitutional legislation according to the text of that constitution. There are, however, at the present time extraordinary reasons for a fresh discussion of the subject. Some of these relate to the judicial history of the constitution from the beginning, and are concerned with all the decisions in which the Supreme Court has pronounced against the constitutionality of legislation. Others relate especially to the recent judicial history of the constitution and are concerned with but one decision of the Supreme Court, and have their origin in it and the controversy caused by it. The decision here alluded to is that made in the case of Juilliard *v.* Greenman, or more precisely that part thereof which relates to the constructive powers of Congress.*

---

* Juilliard *v.* Greenman is reported in 110 U. S. Reports, 421–470.

The Introduction to this Essay will consider both these classes of extraordinary reasons for a fresh discussion of its subject. Before doing so, however, it is proper to make some observations in further explanation of the subject and in justification of the writer's chief purpose.

Justificatory and explanatory observations.

The chief of the writer's purposes is to show that the constitution of the United States provides in *express* terms for the judiciaries of the United States and the several states having the following competency *viz.*, a judicial competency to decide questioned legislation to be federally constitutional or unconstitutional and to hold it valid or void accordingly, whether it be made by Congress or proceed in any form from a state. Eminent professional authority has denied that the U. S. constitution contains any express mention or reference whatsoever to the subject, and has categorically asserted that, while the power of the Supreme Court to declare a questioned law unconstitutional and void is certain, it is also certain that such power is based exclusively upon implication and inference, and not upon the express import of any text of the constitution.

This opinion is not an isolated one. On the contrary, it is a representative opinion. Chief Justice Marshall's decision in Marbury *v.* Madison is relied upon to support it. As far as it relates to acts of Congress, at least, that decision can certainly be relied upon for such support. As far as it relates to state laws and state constitutions, no one of the texts, for which certain express meanings are hereinafter asserted, in order to refute such an opinion, can have the asserted express meaning without contradicting or correcting a meaning given thereto by either Marshall, Story or Webster.

The persons who acquiesce in the opinion in question are, doubtless, very numerous.

At the first sight it, therefore, may seem that the writer of this Essay is attempting an impossibility, or an absurdity, in seeking to show that the constitution contains texts of express import upon a certain subject, when others of its students think otherwise. Words which convey an express meaning to one reader must convey it to all, it will be said; otherwise the meaning will not be an express one. When a writing calls a spade a spade, there is no doubt about its express meaning to all readers. This is a very important objection and requires a full answer at the threshold of this Essay.

In the first place, it is observed in answer that, assuming the objection to be true in ordinary cases, it is not true whenever a written document contains technical terms, whether those terms belong to law, medicine, or any particular science or art whatsoever.

The constitution of the United States is written law. Unquestionably it contains many technical terms of law, *e. g.* *habeas corpus*, bill of attainder, *ex post facto*, bankruptcy, law of nations, levying war, etc. To lawyers, every one of these terms is of technical import; and so, *ipso facto*, of express import. All technical terms in all sciences and arts have an express import, and, when used, are used for that very reason. That the meaning of technical terms of the law should escape the understanding of laymen is not surprising. Whether for good or evil, the constitution of the United States can not be fully and entirely understood by minds ignorant of the science of the law. Story's Commentaries are addressed to learned readers (ed. 1, § 955, ed. 2, § 958). That lawyers should sometimes ignore or forget the true meaning of technical terms of the law, may seem to some readers surprising. It is, however, natural. Lawyers are especially warned in a decision of Chief Justice Marshall, that the words "levying war," in the definition of treason in section 3. III. constitute an ancient and technical term of law which must be understood in its technical meaning, although the natural import of the words would certainly have admitted of some latitude of construction, if the application thereof to treason had for the first time been made by the constitution. U. S. *v.* Burr, 4 Cranch, page 470.

The errors of lawyers as to the *express* meaning of the constitutional text are not confined to cases in which technical terms are used. The constitution is so frequently quoted from memory that errors must occur. Certain of its readers frequently delude themselves by imagining that they know parts of its text by heart, and therefore fail to verify quotations. In the ardour of composition, inadvertencies are often very natural. In recalling comparisons of texts in the constitution and the confederation, or in the constitution and the original draft thereof, or in a part of the constitution and a corresponding statute, errors are natural to some persons at all times and to most persons at exceptional times. In a word, to make one's self a good and precise textualist of the constitution is a difficult task. Moreover, the best textualist must keep in constant practice or run the risk of his memory deteriorating. In order that a commentator upon the constitution may be confident that he has before his mind all the texts relating to a given subject (whether they be technical terms or not), he must feel that he is so well prepared as to know and to command everything apt, which is written in the whole text of the document. He must likewise be confident that his memory has not been too active and injected words into the constitution which belong to other instruments. To be always up to such a standard, is in practice difficult. Practically, it demands a circumspection depending upon the memory as well as the eye. Errors will be made even by the most distinguished commentators, and still more by ordinary writers.

Many readers of this Essay will doubtless assent to these remarks because of their reasonableness. Those who have made a rigorous study of the constitutional text will be able to reinforce them by reasons derived from their own experience. There may be readers, however, who will be skeptical as to such errors being possible, unless in other cases similar ones have been made. They may demand examples of errors, on the part of distinguished commentators, as to constitutional texts other than those involved in the subject of this Essay.

In the first appendix to this Essay will be found a collection of instances of actual errors, as to such other texts, which have been made by distinguished commentators.

The texts relied upon by the writer for his own chief purpose will, it is contended, be proved, in every case except one, to be technical legal terms, whose express meanings have been inadvertently overlooked. In the excepted case, no term merely a legal one is used. The exception is a word used in a special logical sense, which can be so used on the highest kind of authority in any branch of learning whatsoever. The iterative use of the word in this sense by the constitution is so marked, that its logical and authoritative meaning is, in fact and in law, its express meaning in the constitution.

CHAPTER II.

Of the reasons for a fresh discussion of the subject, which are derived from the judicial history of the constitution from the beginning thereof.

No. 1. Of the reasons aforesaid, which will be considered in the form of a review of the final paper in the Appendix to 131 U. S. Reports.

No. 2. Of the cases in which the Supreme Court has decided acts of Congress to be unconstitutional.

No. 3. Of the case of Dred Scott v. Sandford.

No. 4. Of Hayburn's case.

No. 5. Of the case of the United States v. Yale Todd.

No. 6. Of the case of —— v. the Secretary of War.

No. 7. Further consideration of the latter case.

No. 8. Of the case of Marbury v. Madison.

No. 9. Of the cases of the United States v. Ferreira, and Gordon v. the United States.

No. 10. Of the case of Ex parte Garland.

No. 11. Of the case of the United States v. De Witt.

No. 12. Of the foregoing cases in general.

No. 13. Of the cases in which the Supreme Court has decided state legislation of any sort to be (federally) unconstitutional with a detailed statement thereof.

No. 14. Of the latter class of cases in general.
No. 15. Conclusion from the foregoing review.

This chapter will be devoted to the first class of extraordinary reasons for a fresh discussion of the subject. They relate to the judicial history of the constitution from the beginning. They are concerned with all those decisions of the Supreme Court in which it has pronounced against the constitutionality of legislation.

No. 1.

Of the reasons aforesaid, considered in the form of a review of the final paper in the Appendix to 131 U. S. Reports.

The reasons aforesaid can best be explained in a review of the contents of an important paper by Mr. Davis, the official reporter of the Supreme Court. In the year 1889, there appeared the 131st volume of the reports of cases adjudged in the Supreme Court of the United States. This official volume contains a remarkable appendix of some 280 pages by the reporter, which is most appropriately published on the occasion of the Supreme Court completing the first century of its existence. The elaborate papers contained therein are of great value and interest to the constitutional law and judicial history of the Union. One of these papers relates to the subject of this Essay. After describing the other contents of the Appendix, the reporter observes on page XVIII:

"In addition to these papers I have added, at the end of "the appendix, a list of cases in which statutes or ordi-"nances have been held by the court to be repugnant, in "whole or in part, to the constitution or laws of the United "States. The period covered by this table begins with 2 "Dall. and ends with the present volume.

"It only remains to say that all this matter has been laid "before the justices of the court individually; and it is now

"respectfully submitted to the judgment of the members of
"our common profession."

This table of cases occupies some twenty-two pages of the
Appendix. It is divided into two parts, A. and B. Part A.
is a list of cases in which statutes of the United States have
been "held to be repugnant to the constitution or laws of
"the United States, in whole or in part," by the Supreme
Court of the United States. Part B. is a list of cases in
which acts of states and territories (including some ordinances of municipalities) have been "held repugnant to
"the constitution or laws of the United States, in whole or
"in part," by the Supreme Court of the United States.

The mere publication of such an important paper invites
and suggests further discussion. An examination of it will
do more, it is contended, and will show the urgent necessity
of further discussion. The writer will, therefore, proceed
at once to comment upon a sufficient portion of this table of
cases, to establish the proposition that it shows that there
are special reasons for a new discussion of the subject of the
exercise of judicial power in decisions concerning legislation
questioned as unconstitutional according to the constitution
of the United States.

No. 2.

*Of the cases in which the Supreme Court has decided acts
of Congress to be unconstitutional.*

Part A. of the table contains twenty cases arranged chron-
ologically. The first eight are as follows:

"1. *Hayburn's Case*, August T., 1792, 2 Dall. 409.
"Whether the act of March 23, 1792, 1 Stat. 243, conferring
"upon the United States courts jurisdiction to pass upon
"claims for pensions, was unconstitutional, was not decided
"by the court; but the judges were individually of that
"opinion, as appears by a note to the case reporting deci-
"sions in circuit made by every justice except Mr. Justice
"Johnson. See *United States* v. *Todd*, No 2, *post*.

"2. *United States* v. *Yale Todd*, February T. 1794, 13
"How. 52 *n*. In this case the court held the act of March
"23, 1792 (considered in *Hayburn's Case*, No. 1, *ante*), to

"be unconstitutional, as attempting to confer upon the "court power which was not judicial.

" 3. *Marbury* v. *Madison*, February T., 1803, 1 Cranch, " 137. The provision in the Judiciary Act of 1789, c. 20, " § 13, 1 Stat. 80, 81, conferring upon the Supreme Court "original jurisdiction to issue writs of mandamus directed " to 'persons holding office,' is not warranted by the con- "stitution.

" 4. *United States* v. *Ferreira*, December T., 1851, 13 " How. 40. The acts of March 3, 1823, 3 Stat. 768, c. 35; "June 26, 1834, 6 Stat. 569, c. 87; and March 3, 1849, 9 "Stat. 788, c. 181, confer upon the District Court powers " which are not judicial, and they are therefore void.

"5. *Gordon* v. *United States*, December T., 1864, 2 Wall. "561, sections 5, 7, of the act of March 3, 1863, 12 Stat. 765, "conferring jurisdiction of appeals from the court of claims, "are void. No reasons are given. But see, 117 U. S. 697, "and *United States* v. *Jones*, 119 U. S. 477.

" 6. *Ex parte Garland*, December T., 1866, 4 Wall. 333. "The act of January 24, 1865, c. 20, 13 Stat. 424, respect- "ing the oath to be administered to attorneys and counsel- "lors in courts of the United States, was *ex post facto*, and " in the nature of a bill of pains and penalties.

" 7. *Hepburn* v. *Griswold*, December T., 1864, 8 Wall. " 603. The legal tender act of February 25, 1862, c. 33, 12 " Stat. 345; the joint resolution of January 17, 1863, 12 " Stat. 822; and the act of March 3, 1863, 12 Stat. 709, so 'far as they made the notes of the United States a legal "tender for debts contracted before their respective enact- " ments, were unconstitutional. This ruling was reversed " in *Knox* v. *Lee*, 12 Wall. 457; *Dooley* v. *Smith*, 13 Wall. " 604; *Railroad Co.* v. *Johnson*, 15 Wall. 195; *Maryland* " v. *Railroad Co.*, 22 Wall. 105; and *The Legal Tender* " *Case*, 110 U. S. 421.

"8. *United States* v. *De Witt*, December T., 1869, 9 " Wall. 41. Section 29, c. 169, act of March 2, 1867, 14 Stat. " 484, so far as it applies to the offence described by it when " committed within a state, is in excess of the powers con- " ferred upon Congress."

The remaining twelve cases of Part A. are all dated in 1869 or subsequent years.

No. 3.

Of the case of Dred Scott v. Sandford.

Part A. is a remarkable list, both for what it contains and for what it does not contain. The reader will be surprised when he scrutinizes it and fails to find the case of Dred Scott v. Sandford, which should have its place therein between No. 4 and No. 5.

In that case the opinion of the court said, on page 452 of 19 Howard:

"Upon these considerations, it is the opinion of the court "that the act of Congress which prohibited a citizen from "holding and owning property of this kind in the territory "of the United States north of the line therein mentioned, "is not warranted by the constitution and is therefore void; "and that neither Dred Scott himself, nor any of his fam- "ily were made free by being carried into this territory; "even if they had been carried there by the owner, with "the intention of becoming a permanent resident."

That the Dred Scott case should have been omitted in the list aforesaid, is a circumstance which suggests many grave reflections. Such an omission in such a list is a fact, which is, of itself alone, a sufficient reason for further discussion and investigation of the relation of judicial power to unconstitutional legislation. If the Dred Scott decision can escape recollection, anything legal or historical relating to the subject may be forgotten. Even if a writer's usefulness be restricted to increasing the attention given to the subject, he may feel that he has written something needful.

The Dred Scott case was a remarkable one in many ways, one of which should be mentioned now. Unless the list be still further defective, the Dred Scott decision was the first in which an act of Congress was decided by the court to be unconstitutional for reasons *not* relating to its own judicial department of the government. In all the previous cases concerned, Congress was decided to have legislated unconstitutionally concerning the judiciary. In the Dred Scott case, the act of Congress related to a subject not peculiar to the judicial department, but affecting every department of the U. S. government, especially Congress itself. It is unnecessary to enlarge upon this distinction. None will deny its historical importance, although all may not agree in opinion as to its legal effects.

No. 4.

Of Hayburn's Case.

The first case on the list is Hayburn's case. As it was never decided, it is not properly entitled to a regular place and number in the list of cases. It is, however, useful and edifying that it should be added thereto, without a number. It is suggested that the same kind of addition may be made of the letter of the judges of the Supreme Court to President Washington, in answer to his letter to them dated April 3d, 1790. This paper is extrajudicial, but *quasi*-official. It comments upon the then recent act to establish the judicial courts of the United States, and says: "On com-"paring this act with the constitution, we perceive devia-"tions which are important." It then comments on these "deviations," which relate specially to the judicial department. The text of this letter is found in Story's Commentaries, Ed. 1, vol. 3, § 1573, pages 438–441.

No. 5.

Of the case of the United States v. *Yale Todd.*

The second case on the list is that of the United States *v.* Yale Todd. If it be certainly entitled to a place therein, it is remarkable as being the first case in which the Supreme Court made a negative decision upon the questioned constitutionality of an act of Congress. No written opinion deciding the case is extant, nor is there any statement of the contents of such an opinion by any writer claiming to have read it. The question whether the case is entitled to be placed in the list, is one which may be raised with utility.

The authority for United States *v.* Yale Todd being a case

in which an act of Congress was decided unconstitutional, is the note found at the end of the report of United States *v.* Ferreira, in 13 Howard, 52, which was written by Chief Justice Taney, and was inserted in its place by the order of the court. This note is intimately related to the report of Hayburn's Case in 2 Dallas, 409, and to the comment thereupon in 13 Howard, 49, with both of which it must be considered.

The case of United States *v.* Yale Todd was this. The act of Congress of March 23d, 1792, required the circuit courts to examine and report upon the pension claims of disabled officers, soldiers, and seamen, and to certify their opinions to the secretary of war, who should thereupon place the persons so certified and reported upon the pension list. The 2d, 3d, and 4th sections of the said act were repelled as unconstitutional by the circuit courts, because the duties imposed were not judicial. In the New York circuit, however, the judges, while refusing to act judicially, agreed to construe the act as conferring on them power to act as commissioners for pension claims, and did act, report and certify as such, in a number of cases. The parts of the act, which were so impeached, were repealed, and another pension procedure was established by an act of February 28th, 1798. The third section of this act excepted all rights to pensions, under the repealed part of the act, that had been favourably passed upon by the judges acting as commissioners, and provided that the secretary of war and attorney general should take the necessary measures to obtain an adjudication of the Supreme Court upon the validity of the said excepted rights. In pursuance of this act, the amicable action of the *United States* v. *Yale Todd* was brought before the Supreme Court in original jurisdiction. It was an action upon the case, brought to recover $172.91 paid to Todd as one of the pensioners whose claims had been determined by judges acting as commissioners. Judgment was rendered by the court in favour of the United States for the above-mentioned sum. While the record of the case is otherwise complete, no opinion is found on file. It is known that Chief Justice Jay and four other judges were present at the decision. In his note,

Chief Justice Taney thinks that the opinion of the court must have been unanimous. He considers that Hayburn's Case and United States *v.* Yale Todd, taken together, show that, in the opinion of the then judges, the pension power given to the circuit courts was not judicial power, and, therefore, was unconstitutional, and could not be exercised by the courts; that the act of Congress intended to confer a judicial function and could not be construed as an authority to act out of court as commissioners; and that the money paid under a certificate from such unauthorized persons could be recovered back by the United States.

It would seem, therefore, that, if Chief Justice Taney be correct as to the contents of the opinion, the court must have decided part of the act of 1792 to be unconstitutional and held it therefore void. This is, however, only an inference, for no opinion is extant. It seems strange that no public journal should have published anything relating to an opinion deciding a pension act to be unconstitutional. If such be the fact, times have changed much, and men more. At the present day, many persons will deem it incredible that the U. S. Supreme Court should have rendered its first negative decision upon the constitutionality of an act of Congress, and that act a pension law, without a printed record being somewhere made of such an opinion. Moreover, the judgment for the United States and against Yale Todd may, perhaps, be accounted for otherwise. It certainly meant that the acts of the judges sitting as commissioners upon pension applications, were void. It is, however, possible, in the absence of a written opinion, to surmise that the Supreme Court held that the circuit judges refused to proceed judicially as a court; that they actually proceeded extrajudicially as commissioners; that, in so proceeding, they acted outside of the statute and not under it; that in acting as commissioners, they assumed to create and usurp new offices, unknown to that or any other statute; and that their acts as commissioners were, therefore, illegal and void. Assuming this conjecture to be true, it follows that the constitutionality of the statute was not drawn in question, for nothing was done under it, and the acts performed by the commissioners were not authorized by it, even if it were constitutional and valid.

If the weight due to these considerations make it the more probable presumption that no act of Congress was decided unconstitutional in the lost opinion in United States *v.* Yale Todd, then that case should not be inserted in Part A. of the table of cases, as one fully entitled to a place therein.

If, however, the foregoing considerations have properly no such weight, then the case of United States *v.* Yale Todd is entitled to remain in the table. This is, however, by no means an end of the matter. Another branch of it then begins. The question is immediately raised, whether the case of United States *v.* Yale Todd is not one of a pair of pension cases, in which the three sections of the act of 1792 were decided to be unconstitutional. If an affirmative answer must be given to this question, the other case is that of ——— *v.* the Secretary of War.

No. 6.

Of the case of ——— v. *The Secretary of War.*

The case of ——— *v.* The Secretary of War must now be considered. All that is known of it is to be found on pages 171 and 172 of 1 Cranch, in the opinion of the Supreme Court in the case of Marbury *v.* Madison delivered by C. J. Marshall. On the previous pages of the same, the chief justice expresses the opinion of the court as to the cases in which, on legal principle and English authority, the writ of *mandamus* may issue to an executive officer. He immediately adds :

" This opinion seems not now for the first time to be taken "up in this country.

" It must be well recollected that in 1792 an act passed "directing the secretary at war to place on the pension "list such disabled officers and soldiers as should be re-"ported to him by the circuit courts, which act, so far as "the duty was imposed on the courts, was deemed uncon-"stitutional ; but some of the judges, thinking that the law "might be executed by them in the character of commis-"sioners, proceeded to act and report in that character.

" This law being deemed unconstitutional at the circuits,
" was repealed, and a different system was established ; but
" the question whether those persons who had been reported
" by the judges, as commissioners, were entitled, in conse-
" quence of that report, to be placed on the pension list,
" was a legal question, properly determinable in the courts,
" although the act of placing such persons on the list was
" to be performed by the head of a department.

" That this question might be properly settled, Congress
" passed an act in February, 1793, making it the duty of the
" secretary of war, in conjunction with the attorney gen-
" eral, to take such measures as might be necessary to obtain
" an adjudication of the Supreme Court of the United
" States on the validity of any such rights, claimed under
" the act aforesaid.

" After the passage of this act, a *mandamus* was moved
" for, to be directed to the secretary of war, commanding
" him to place on the pension list a person stating himself
" to be on the report of the judges.

" There is, therefore, much reason to believe, that this
" mode of trying the legal right of the complainant, was
" deemed by the head of a department, and by the highest
" law-officer of the United States, the most proper which
" could be selected for the purpose.

" When the subject was brought before the court the de-
" cision was not, that a *mandamus* would not lie to the
" head of a department, directing him to perform an act
" enjoined by law, in the performance of which an individ-
" ual had a vested interest ; but that a *mandamus* ought
" not to issue in that case—the decision necessarily to be
" made if the report of the commissioners did not confer
" on the applicant a legal right.

" The judgment in that case is understood to have decided
" the merits of all claims of that description ; and the per-
" sons, on the report of the commissioners, found it neces-
" sary to pursue the mode prescribed by the law subsequent
" to that which had been deemed unconstitutional, in order
" to place themselves on the pension list.

" The doctrine, therefore, now advanced is by no means "a novel one."

The resemblances between the cases of United States *v.* Yale Todd and ——— *v.* the Secretary of War are more remarkable than the differences between them. It is true, that one was an action upon the case, brought against a person on the pension list to recover pension money paid him, and that the other was a proceeding for a *mandamus* against the secretary of war moved on behalf of a pension claimant to get a place on the pension list. On the other hand, both litigations were pension cases that were adjudications of the Supreme Court in original jurisdiction. Both were adjudications directed to be obtained by the third section of the act of 28 February, 1793. In both, the decision was against the validity of rights to pensions that had been determined favourably by the circuit court judges acting as commissioners. The opinions of the Supreme Court in both cases are not extant. Inference and tradition are the only possible sources of knowledge as to the contents of both opinions. Consequently, if it be supposed true that in the case of United States *v.* Yale Todd the court decided the three sections of the act of 1792 to be unconstitutional, there is great reason to presume that it did likewise in the case of ——— *v.* the Secretary of War. Therefore, if the first case be supposed properly inserted in Part A. of the table of cases under consideration, the second case ought also to be inserted therein.

It will be observed that Chief Justice Marshall says nothing one way or other, as to the act of Congress being decided unconstitutional in ——— *v.* the Secretary of War. If this silence be deemed an argument against any such question being decided therein, it must also be taken as militating against the same question being decided in the lost opinion in United States *v.* Yale Todd. It is a two edged sword and militates against both cases being admitted in Part A. of the table. The conclusion that both cases should be admitted or both excluded is, therefore, the most reasonable one, *provided both cases actually existed.*

No. 7.

Further consideration of the case of ——— v. the Secretary of War.

This proviso, however, is a very grave one and raises the question whether the case ——— v. the Secretary of War ever existed.

The case of United States v. Yale Todd certainly existed. The records of the court adduced by Chief Justice Taney prove this proposition. Only the contents of the lost opinion can be questioned. The judgment is duly recorded. On the other hand, recollection or tradition is all the evidence that Chief Justice Marshall adduces for the existence of the case of ——— v. the Secretary of War. Doubts must suggest themselves affecting the correctness of the tradition detailed, and raising the question whether the case of ——— v. the Secretary of War be not apocryphal. It may be that these doubts can only be settled upon the hypothesis that there was but one adjudication made in pursuance of the third section of the act of February 28th, 1793, and that the case of the United States v. Yale Todd was that adjudication. If this view be true, no such case as ——— v. the Secretary of War ever existed, and no *mandamus* was ever moved for in the Supreme Court in original juris-. diction on behalf of any pension claimant.

If this conclusion be thought, or assumed to be, correct, everything said by Chief Justice Marshall concerning the case of ——— v. the Secretary of War must be discarded in investigating the nature of the opinion in United States v. Yale Todd. The moment this is done, however, a very serious question necessarily arises as to another effect of the non-existence of any such case as ——— v. the Secretary of War. If no such case ever existed, what is the effect of such a fact upon the opinion in the great case of Marbury v. Madison?

No. 8.

Of the case of Marbury v. *Madison.*

This brings the discussion to the third case on the list, which is Marbury *v.* Madison.

It is certain that the opinion in the case of Marbury *v.* Madison proves that the court assumed that such a case as ——— *v.* the Secretary of War existed, and that it pondered seriously upon the relation thereof to the case before it. It must, therefore, be true in point of fact that the court thought thus, *viz.*, that there were two cases as to a *mandamus* in original jurisdiction which were known to it as actually existing; that in the first case, it had refused to issue the writ because of a decision on the merits, not because of any doubt as to the jurisdiction; that it had not questioned its original jurisdiction in that case, and so had recognized the constitutionality of the involved portion of the judiciary act; that in Marbury *v.* Madison, or the second case, its action contradicted its former action in the first, because it refused to take jurisdiction and decided that the said involved portion of the judiciary act was unconstitutional.

Thus, in Marbury *v.* Madison, the court must have thought that it was virtually overruling the therein mentioned case of ——— *v.* the Secretary of War. It could not, indeed, have formally overruled it, because it had neither a report nor a record of the case before it. Only a tradition of the case was before it, and mere traditions can not be formally overruled. In point of fact, the tradition detailed is not free from doubt as to its correctness.

Now, if it be true that no such case as that of ——— *v.* the Secretary of War ever existed, the opinion in Marbury *v.* Madison is not correct in all and each of its parts. If no such case ever existed, all reliance upon it to strengthen the merits of Marbury's case must be given up. Its important place in the exposition of those merits must be made a blank. This is saying something of great moment. Two-thirds of Marshall's opinion are devoted to the discussion of the merits, after which comes the discussion of the jurisdiction. It is well known that the correctness of this method has been adversely criticised. In Van Buren on "Political Parties" (pages 287 and 288), such an objection is strongly urged against Marbury v. Madison. In Mr. Patterson's essay on "The Political Crisis of 1861" (page 19), that case is coupled with Dred Scott v. Sandford, and both are commented upon as liable to such adverse criticism.

It can not be denied that in *Ex parte* MacCardle (7 Wallace, pages 513, 514), the court decided against its jurisdiction in the case, and held that therefore "it is useless, if "not improper, to enter into any discussion of other ques- "tions." Its opinion, furthermore said that, "jurisdiction "is the power to declare the law, and when it ceases to ex- "ist, the only function remaining to the court is that of an- "nouncing the fact and dismissing the cause. And this is "not less clear upon authority than upon principle." If this doctrine of MacCardle's case be the rule, Marbury v. Madison must be either an exception to that rule, or a violation of it. To be an exception, the opinion of the court must be correct as a whole. The opinion shows that the court thought that a denial of the writ would be a denial of justice, if it were competent to issue the same in original jurisdiction in obedience to the statute. Consequently, the court must have investigated the merits of Marbury's case and decided in favour of his right to the claimed office, in order to demonstrate that his case was absolutely a judicial one, and that it was, therefore, a judicial and not an extra-judicial question whether the act giving him an apt remedy was repugnant to the constitution or not.

The case of ——— v. the Secretary of War is too important a part of the opinion as a whole, for it to be struck out, without weakening the claim of Marbury v. Madison, to be an exception to the rule asserted in MacCardle's case. If it be true that no such case as ——— v. the Secretary of War ever existed, the opinion in Marbury v. Madison, considered as a whole, becomes weakened, perhaps even imperfect. Thus, is raised the question whether it conflicts with the opinion in MacCardle's case ; because, if it be not an exception to the rule laid down therein, it must be a violation of it.

The entire discussion of the merits of Marbury's case can, of course, be stricken out of the opinion, without affecting in any way the reasoning of that part of it which treats of the great question, whether an unconstitutional enactment can become a law. So doing, does not affect the logic by which a negative conclusion on that question is reached. It does, however, affect that part of the opinion in other respects. The truth in point of legal history, and in point of judicial precedent, concerning the conclusion when reached by correct logic, must be well pondered, in order to understand precisely the place which Marbury *v.* Madison occupies among the court's judicial decisions on unconstitutional legislation. If the fact be that there was no such case as ——— *v.* the Secretary of War, then the court erred in thinking (as it must have thought), that its action in the case of Marbury *v.* Madison contradicted its previous action in a former case as to a *mandamus* in original jurisdiction. It furthermore erred in thinking (as it must have thought), that its affirmation of the unconstitutionality of part of the judiciary act, contradicted a previous decision recognizing the validity thereof. Whether such errors were committed is a question here raised. It cannot be answered, until it be settled one way or other whether such a case as ——— *v.* the Secretary of War ever existed. This is not the place to settle the doubts thereupon. It is, however, the place to say that such doubts exist.

No. 9.

Of the cases of the United States v. *Ferreira, and Gordon* v. *the United States.*

The 4th and 5th cases are those next on the list in Part A. They are the United States *v.* Ferreira and Gordon *v.* the United States. In both these cases, the legislative provisions, which were decided to be unconstitutional, related specially to the judicial department of the U. S. government.

After the 4th case, that of Dred Scott *v.* Sandford should be inserted. As has been mentioned, it was the *first case in which the statute decided to be unconstitutional did not specially relate to the judicial department.* The great uproar and opposition made against this decision are well known.

No. 10.

Of the case of Ex parte *Garland.*

The case numbered the 6th, is *Ex parte* Garland. The legislation, which was decided to be unconstitutional, related to the oaths of members of the bars of the U. S. courts. It therefore specially concerned the judicial department.

The case numbered the 7th on the list is Hepburn *v.* Griswold. The legislation decided to be unconstitutional related to the legal tender of greenbacks. It thus was the second of the decisions which did not relate specially to legislation for the judicial department. Like Dred Scott *v.* Sandford, it excited great opposition. It was finally overruled in subsequent decisions of the court.

No. 11.

Of the case of the United States v. *De Witt.*

The case numbered the 8th on the list is the United States *v.* De Witt. This was a criminal case of the date of December term, 1869. It was the third case, in which the legislation decided to be unconstitutional, did not relate specially to the judicial department. At last, a decision of that sort was made, which did not excite opposition.

No. 12.

Of the foregoing cases in general.

It is unnecessary to comment upon the remaining twelve cases of Part A. Sufficient has been said to show, that further discussion of the subject of this Essay is specially invited by the history of decisions upon unconstitutional acts of Congress.

No. 13.

*Of the cases in which the Supreme Court has decided state
legislation of any sort to be (federally) unconstitutional, with a detailed statement thereof.*

The same necessity for further discussion is shown by the
history of the Supreme Court's judicial decisions upon federally unconstitutional acts of the several states.

Part B. of the table of cases in the Appendix to 131 U. S.
Reports, contains a list of cases in which acts of state legislation have been " held to be repugnant to the constitution
"or laws of the United States, in whole or in part." According to the writer's count, the number of these cases is
185. From this number, three cases must be subtracted,
viz., Kansas No. 3, Missouri No. 12, and West Virginia
No. 3, in which the statutes involved were decided to be repugnant to the constitutions of the respective states, not to
the constitution of the United States : See Loan Associa-
tion *v.* Topeka, 20 Wallace, 655 ; Cole *v.* La Grange, 113 U.
S. 1 ; Parkersburg *v.* Brown, 106 U. S. 487.. A further re-
duction of five cases is proper, that being the number of
cases in which acts of territorial legislation were decided
unconstitutional. Such cases should not be confounded,
either in principle or in any commentary upon the constitutional text, with cases in which state laws or state constitutions are involved. Thus, the number of cases is reduced
to 177.

Of these 177 cases, there are 11 in which the federal unconstitutionality pronounced by the court affected state
constitutions; and 152 in which it affected state statutes. In
the remainder, either acts connected with secession or ordinances of municipalities were involved.

It may be remarked that in 63 cases, or more than one-
third of the whole number, the constitutional repugnancy
was to the clause prohibiting state laws impairing the obligation of contracts.

No. 14.

General observations upon the class of cases contained in Part B. of the final paper in the Appendix to 131 U. S. Reports.

It is obvious from the great number and great importance of the cases in Part B., that there must be much utility in a further discussion of the constitutional relation of judicial power to unconstitutional legislation. The decisions of the Supreme Court upon federally unconstitutional state legislation alone, are sufficient for such a conclusion. This truth is proved over again by what has happened since the table of cases was published. Since then, the so-called original package decision of the Supreme Court has been made, and has caused an immense amount of discussion, both in the halls of Congress and throughout the United States.*

No. 15.

Conclusion from the foregoing review.

The foregoing review of the final paper in the Appendix to 131 U. S. Reports, it is contended, shows conclusively that that paper should be the beginning, and not the end, of a new discussion of the relation of judicial power to unconstitutional legislation according to the constitution of the United States. This important conclusion is drawn from the experience of a century. It is supported by the history of the constitution, as studied in the reports of cases before the judicial tribunal from whose decisions on constitutional questions there is no judicial appeal.

* Leisy *v.* Hardin, 135 U. S. Reports, 100.

CHAPTER III.

Of the second class of extraordinary reasons for fresh discussion of the subject.

No. 1. Of the case of Juilliard v. Greenman; of Mr. Mc-Murtrie's defence of the decision therein ; and of his doctrine as to the exercise of judicial power in declaring legislation to be unconstitutional and void.

No. 2. Of the doctrine of the opinion in Juilliard v. Greenman, concerning the constructive or implied powers of Congress.

No. 3. Of the rigorous exercise of such powers of Congress according to the said doctrine.

No. 4. Of the effect of the two foregoing doctrines, when the same are taken and applied together ; and of a supposed case of an act of Congress prohibiting the Supreme and Inferior Courts from declaring any act of Congress to be unconstitutional and so void.

No. 5. Quotations from Mr. McMurtrie's Observations showing his doctrine concerning judicial power.

No. 6. Quotations from the opinion in Juilliard v. Greenman, showing the Supreme Court's doctrine concerning legislative powers.

No. 7. Of the consequences of both doctrines being true.

No. 8. That the foregoing considerations prove the existence of a second class of extraordinary reasons for a fresh discussion of the subject of this Essay.

This chapter will be devoted to the second class of extra-ordinary reasons for a fresh discussion of the subject. They are derived from a part only, and a recent part, of the judicial history of the constitution.

No. 1.

Of the case of Juilliard v. Greenman ; of Mr. McMurtrie's defence of the decision therein ; and of his doctrine as to the exercise of judicial power in declaring legislation to be unconstitutional and void.

The second class of the said reasons is concerned with but one decision of the Supreme Court and has its origin in it and the controversy caused by it. This decision is that made in the case of Juilliard *v.* Greenman in 110 U. S. Reports, 421–470. The case is the last of the celebrated legal tender litigations, but the part of the opinion of the court herein specially concerned is that which lays down a general doctrine relating to the constructive or implied powers of Congress.

In Juilliard *v.* Greenman * the U. S. Supreme Court decided, *inter alia*, that Congress in its discretion had power to make U. S. bills of credit a legal tender in payment of all debts. Mr. Bancroft, in February, 1886, published an important essay in adverse criticism of the decision of the court. In the autumn of 1886, Mr. McMurtrie published a learned answer to Mr. Bancroft's criticisms, containing a defence of that decision and also his own views of the legal tender question. The differences between the historian and the jurist are grave, both as to conclusions and methods of reaching them.

The following are the titles of these important essays : "A Plea for the Constitution of the United States of "America wounded in the House of its Guardians. By "George Bancroft." New York, 1886.

"Plea for the Supreme Court. Observations on Mr. "George Bancroft's Plea for the Constitution. By Richard "C. McMurtrie." Philadelphia, 1886.

The writer's study of the opinion of the Supreme Court and Mr. McMurtrie's defence thereof, has resulted in a conviction that, great as is the importance of the legal tender

---

* 110 U. S. Reports, 421–470. Decided March 3d, 1884. Reported under the name of "Legal Tender Case, Juilliard *v.* Greenman."

question, *another and still greater one* has become involved
in the controversy. That question relates to the competency
of the U. S. Supreme Court to decide a legal tender act or
any other act of Congress to be unconstitutional and to
hold that the same is void, if the opinion in the case of
Juilliard *v.* Greenman be law as to the constructive powers
of Congress. The decision of the court might anyhow suggest a re-study of the grounds of its exercise of judicial
power in this respect. Mr. McMurtrie's essay has, however,
directly re-opened the whole of that subject ; and in this
wise. Persons denying the power of making greenbacks a
legal tender, are reproached by him with thorough inconsistency. He contends that they maintain that the court
should declare the legal tender laws to be void, on the
ground that the legal tender power is based exclusively on
implication and inference ; that in so doing they at the same
time ignore that the court's power of "declaring void a legislative act" is based exclusively on implication and inference ; and that the judicial power of so declaring was never
heard of, before tacit implication and inference originated in
this country.

This doctrine, coming from a jurist of so high a rank, can
not be ignored. Its scope is vast ; for, if true, it applies
to all questions of constructive powers in Congress, and not
merely to the one in debate. It amounts to a warning to
every lawyer, in every case, to take heed how he argue that
the court should decide against any claim of constructive
legislative power in Congress, for the judicial power of the
court itself only constructively extends to cases involving
any such questions at all.

The gravity of this doctrine is such that it must be disposed of in some way, either by refutation, or limitation,
or precise ascertainment; otherwise, the discussion of most
constitutional questions may be embarrassed, by its being
vouched at any moment.

The presentation of this doctrine is certainly a very serious move on the logical chessboard of any legal controversy
concerning the implication of a legislative power. If the
existence of the judicial competency under discussion de-

pended solely upon implication, it would have to be answered by a move different from that which the writer will make. His view is that the constitution provides for such a judicial competency in express terms and he will proceed accordingly.

The connection of Mr. McMurtrie's doctrine as to the exercise of judicial power in declaring legislation unconstitutional and void, with the doctrine of the U. S. Supreme Court in Juilliard *v.* Greenman concerning the constructive powers of Congress, makes the matter a very extraordinary one in point of law. It is true that Mr. McMurtrie makes no allusion to any connection between these two doctrines. He may, perhaps, admit no connection between them. To the writer's conviction, however, the connection is intimate and remarkable, and so, most important.

The doctrine of Juilliard *v.* Greenman upon the constructive powers of Congress will now be examined.

No. 2.

Of the doctrine of the opinion in Juilliard v. *Greenman concerning the constructive or implied powers of Congress.*

In the case of Juilliard *v.* Greenman* the U. S. Supreme Court, in its decision, proceeded upon a certain general doctrine therein laid down, concerning the relation of the powers of Congress to the powers belonging to sovereignty in other civilized nations, which the national legislatures thereof habitually exercise. According to this doctrine, it follows as a legal and necessary consequence of the expressly granted powers of Congress that it has constructively, as incidental thereto, all the powers *which the national legislatures of foreign sovereign and civilized governments have and use, as incidental to powers identical with the express powers aforesaid ;* provided only that such constructive powers are not "prohibited" to Congress by the constitution. The same doctrine holds that Congress, as the legislature of a sovereign nation, has certain great

*110 U. S. Reports, 421.

powers expressly granted to it ; and that therefore all other powers, which are powers belonging to sovereignty in other civilized nations that are used incidentally and similarly by their national legislatures; are necessary and proper means of carrying into execution the powers vested in Congress, and are in consequence constructively granted to Congress ; provided only that such constructive powers be not "expressly withheld" from Congress by the constitution.

No. 3.

Of the rigorous exercise of such powers of Congress according to the said doctrine.

This important constitutional doctrine is a far reaching one. It is laid down in ample terms. It maintains that no such constructive power is defeated, or restricted, by the fact that its exercise may affect the existing rights of individuals. It maintains that, if upon a just and fair interpretation or construction of the whole constitution, a particular power exists. such power may be exercised in cases in which the existing rights of individuals are incidentally affected, as much as in cases in which those rights are not so affected.

This scope of the doctrine is asserted in the opinion without any mention or consideration of the ninth amendment of the constitution in connection with such constructive powers. That amendment provides that "the enumeration "in the constitution, of certain rights, shall not be construed "to deny or disparage others retained by the people." Nevertheless, if the constructive or implied power exists as asserted, it must do so to the denial or disparagement of all existing rights retained by the people, which are not expressly enumerated in some part of the constitution. There is no proviso in the opinion withholding the exercise of the constructive power in the cases of rights, the denial or disparagement of which is not expressly prohibited by the enumeration thereof. If the people have retained a right to free elections, or a right to an unimpaired obligation of their contracts, the power can reach either when rigorously exercised, because neither is enumerated in the constitution. The only provisos are: (1) that the power be not prohibited (that is to say, not expressly withheld); and (2) that it be one which belongs to sovereignty in other civilized governments and is exercised by the sovereign legislatures thereof as incidental to powers identical with those to which it is incident under the U. S. constitution.

The doctrine is not laid down with any limitation that Congress must expressly say that it proceeds in derogation of existing rights. Hence, in the absence of any declaration to the contrary in an act of Congress, the rule for construing it must be as follows: the *presumption* is that Congress does not proceed according to the good right of its power, but proceeds according to the strict rigour thereof, regardless of all existing rights aforesaid. It has itself no right to respect those rights, unless it expressly declares that it proceeds rightfully in legislating. No matter how exorbitant or odious the rigorous exercise of a power may sometimes be, the presumption in favour thereof must be made in all cases in which the act of Congress contains no express disclaimer. Such presumption is not limited to the particular cases of debased coin and greenbacks, but extends to those of all existing rights within the reach of the rigorous exercise of sovereign powers by sovereign legislatures as aforesaid.

If the opinion in Juilliard *v.* Greenman be correct as to the constitutional law of legislation, Congress can proceed in a rigorous and not rightful exercise of a legislative power, without expressly declaring that it so proceeds. *A fortiori* it can proceed in a rigorous exercise of a power, when it expressly declares that it legislates with rigour. Such a rigorous exercise of a constructive power of legislation is as legal as a rightful exercise thereof, whenever the power is not prohibited, (that is to say, not expressly withheld), and is one which belongs to sovereignty and is exercised by sovereign legislatures abroad as aforesaid.

When construction has gone so far in either revealing or ampliating the powers of legislation, the most natural question possible for a critical observer to ask is: What next? The next thing has been already mentioned. It is Mr. Mc-

Murtrie's doctrine concerning judicial power and unconstitutional legislation.

No. 4.

Of the effect of the two foregoing doctrines, when the same are taken and applied together; and of the supposed case of an act of Congress prohibiting the Supreme and Inferior Courts from declaring acts of Congress to be unconstitutional and void.

The court's doctrine in Juilliard *v.* Greenman, concerning the implied or constructive powers of Congress, and Mr. McMurtrie's doctrine, that the U. S. Supreme Court proceeds upon a purely implied power in declaring acts of Congress to be unconstitutional and void, when taken together, seem to undermine the foundations of the judicial power as hitherto understood.

According to its decision in the case of the State of Georgia *v.* Stanton, Grant and Pope (6 Wallace 50–78), the U. S. Supreme Court is competent to declare a questioned act of Congress to be unconstitutional and void in certain cases ; namely, those in which the rights in danger are not merely political rights. In cases, in which the rights in danger are merely political rights, the court, by its own decision, is *not* competent to declare any act of Congress whatsoever to be unconstitutional and void.

Article 113 of the Swiss Federal constitution prescribes that the Federal Tribunal shall apply in all cases all laws enacted by the Federal Assembly. If, in admiration of such Swiss ideas, the U. S. Congress were to enact a statute prohibiting the Supreme and Inferior Courts from declaring any act of Congress in any case to be unconstitutional and void, it seems impossible to understand how such a statute would not be valid, supposing the doctrine in Juilliard *v.* Greenman and Mr. McMurtrie's doctrine to be both wholly correct. If they both be wholly correct, the power to enact such a law can not be expressly withheld, must be unknown in every other civilized country, and must be incidental to the express legislative powers of Congress, among which is that of making all laws necessary and proper for carrying its *other* powers into execution.

Mr. McMurtrie maintains that the existence of a judicial power of declaring acts of Congress to be unconstitutional and void is ascertained solely by tacit implication and inference, is not expressly granted and is not expressly mentioned or expressly referred to in the constitution. It is clear, therefore, that such a power can not either be mentioned or referred to in any express text forbidding Congress to pass any law prohibiting the Supreme and Inferior Courts from exercising the same. A power of passing *ex post facto* laws is twice expressly mentioned in the constitution ; once, in forbidding Congress, and again, in forbidding the states, to pass such laws. This shows, that it would be impossible to prohibit or withhold that or any other power expressly, without mentioning it expressly. The power of passing a statute prohibiting the exercise of judicial power as above supposed, cannot, therefore, be expressly withheld by the constitution.

Mr. McMurtrie furthermore maintains that a judicial power of declaring legislation to be void has always been unknown in any other country. Hence, it is clear that in all other countries, present or past, having constitutions of any sort or kind, the legislature of each government can or could bind the courts to obey and apply all its laws, and has or had, as incident to its legislative powers, the power of prohibiting the courts from declaring any law to be unconstitutional and void.

Recurring to the question raised by the case put, it is contended that the foregoing observations show that an affirmative answer should be given to it ; that is to say, if the Supreme Court's doctrine and Mr. McMurtrie's be both wholly true, Congress has power to pass a law prohibiting the Supreme and Inferior Courts from declaring any act of Congress to be unconstitutional and void.

To make the evidence of the correctness of this answer to the question as complete as possible, it is requisite that the foregoing statements of the respective doctrines of the Supreme Court and Mr. McMurtrie should be verified by re-

producing the actual language used by both. This will now
be done.

No, 5.

*Quotations from Mr. McMurtrie's Observations, showing
his doctrine concerning judicial power.*

Mr. McMurtrie's doctrine is found in the following passages from pages 13, 14 and 15 of his Observations :

"Let me ask, whence is derived this power that we are
"now discussing, that of declaring void a legislative act?
"Was such a political power ever heard of before? Did
"any state before ever grant to its judicial functionaries the
"power of declaring and enforcing the limits of its own
"sovereignty? What state before conferred on a court of
"justice, in determining the rights of two suitors as a mere
"incident, and without a hearing on behalf of the state, the
"power to determine that its legislative acts, approved and
"sanctioned by all its statesmen for thirty years, had al-
"ways been mere nullities—nullities *ab initio*?* But
"granting this to be covered by the constitution, what are
"we to say of the thirteen independent sovereignties who
"thus surrendered to a tribunal they were to have no part
"in constituting, the absolute and uncontrollable power of
"deciding between themselves, and the power that appointed
"the court? Is there any such grant in the constitution,
"or any allusion to it? Since C. J. Marshall's judgment in
"Marbury *v.* Madison, I should have said, but for the facts
"contradicting me, that no one probably has been able to
"question that the power does not exist, and that it was
"created by the constitution. But it is a mere deduction
"of logic. Impossible (to my apprehension) for a sane
"mind to question,† but still derived by *tacit implication,*
"a process which one of the most conspicuous members of

---

* These powerfully put observations make a most interesting contrast with
Iredell's remarks on page 147 of Vol. 2 of his Life, being paragraphs 4, 5 and
6 of his paper reprinted in Chapter 26 of this Essay.

† The emphatic form of expression here used recalls Marshall's sentence on
oaths of office at the end of the 1st paragraph of page 416 of 4 Wheaton, beginning: "Yet, he would be charged with insanity, who should contend," etc.

"the Convention assured the most important of the com-
"munities that enacted the instrument, could not be a ground
"for asserting a grant.

          *   *   *   *   *   *   *

"It is certainly true that before the adoption of the
"constitution Mr. Hamilton asserted this power was
"placed with the Court, but he limited it to the determi-
"nation of the extent of the powers granted by the in-
"strument;* and if the makers of that instrument really
"foresaw what they were doing, and the consequences in-
"volved, and yet left such questions to be determined as
"they have done, with no provision for what might occur
"while the legislation was undisputed, anything more un-
"finished than their work can be scarcely mentioned. But
"intended or not, is it not a power that is to be ascertained
"to exist by reasoning, and reasoning only? Why is the
"judiciary the only branch of government, whose views as
"to the powers they possess by the grant, are to be regarded?
"If this be not implication and inference, and the exact
"converse of an express grant, I am at a loss for a meaning
"to these words.

"Therefore it seems to me plain that as it has been dem-
"onstrated for seventy years, and acquiesced in by all,
"that one of the most important functions of the govern-
"ment, nothing less than a control over legislatures, execu-
"tives and the sovereignties which formed the United States,
"has been created and lodged by inference, and by inference
"only, in one branch of that government, uncontrollable
"by the united powers of the imperial state and of the
"states which constituted the *imperium*, and this has been
"done without any reference to the subject in the constitu-
"tion, and probably as to one branch of the subject (the
"right to determine the illegality of state legislation), with-
"out any person concerned in the matter, seeing that it
"had been done, is it impossible that other high powers may
"be found to have been similarly granted?"

---

*This is understood to be an allusion to observations in the Federalist,
which will be found on page 541 *et. seq.* of Dawson's edition.

In the foregoing it is, among other things, distinctly maintained :

(1). *That the power of declaring legislation to be unconstitutional and void has been created and lodged by inference, and by inference only, in one branch of the government, viz., the judicial :*

(2). *That there is no reference whatsoever to any such power in the text of the constitution :*

(3). *That no such exercise of judicial power has ever been heard of before in other civilized countries.*

No. 6.

Quotations from the opinion in Juilliard v. *Greenman, showing the Supreme Court's doctrine concerning legislative powers.*

The language of the court, which it is necessary to quote, will be found on pages 447 and 449 of 110 U. S. Reports, and is as follows:

"It appears to us to follow, as a logical and necessary "consequence, that Congress has the power to issue the ob-"ligations of the United States in such form, and to impress "upon them such qualities as currency for the purchase of "merchandise and the payment of debts, as accord with the "usage of sovereign governments. The power, as incident "to the power of borrowing money and issuing bills or notes "of the Government for money borrowed, of impressing "upon those bills or notes the quality of being a legal ten-"der for the payment of private debts, was a power univer-"sally understood to belong to sovereignty, in Europe and "America, at the time of the framing and adoption of the "constitution of the United States. The governments of "Europe, acting through the monarch or the legislature, "according to the distribution of powers under their re-"spective constitutions, had and have as sovereign a power "of issuing paper money as of stamping coin. This power "has been distinctly recognized in an important modern "case, ably argued and fully considered, in which the Em-"peror of Austria, as King of Hungary, obtained from the

"English Court of Chancery an injunction against the is-
"sue in England, without his license, of notes purporting
"to be public paper money of Hungary. (Austria *v.* Day,
"2 Giff. 628, and 3 D. F. and J. 217.) The power of issu-
"ing bills of credit, and making them, at the discretion of
"the legislature, a tender in payment of private debts, had
"long been exercised in this country by the several colonies
"and states; and during the Revolutionary war the states,
"upon the recommendation of the Congress of the Confed-
"eration, had made the bills issued by Congress a legal ten-
"der (see Craig *v.* Missouri, 4 Pet. 435, 453; Briscoe *v.*
"Bank of Kentucky, 11 Pet. 257, 313, 334–336; Legal Ten-
"der Cases, 12 Wall. 557, 558, 622; Phillips on American
"Paper Currency, *passim*). The exercise of this power not
"being prohibited to Congress by the constitution, it is in-
"cluded in the power expressly granted to borrow money
"on the credit of the United States.
"   *   *   *   *   *   *   *   *   *   *

"Congress, *as the legislature of a sovereign nation, being
"expressly empowered by the constitution to 'lay and col-
"'lect taxes, to pay the debts and provide for the common
"'defence and general welfare of the United States,' and 'to
"'borrow money on the credit of the United States,' and
"'to coin money and regulate the value thereof and of for-
"'eign coin;' and being clearly authorized, as incidental
"to the exercise of those great powers, to emit bills of
"credit, to charter national banks, and to provide a na-
"tional currency for the whole people, in the form of coin,
"treasury notes, and national bank bills; and the power to
"make the notes of the Government a legal tender in pay-
"ment of private debts being one of the powers belonging
"to sovereignty in other civilized nations, and not expressly
"withheld from Congress by the constitution; we are irre-
"sistibly impelled to the conclusion that the impressing
"upon the treasury notes of the United States the quality
"of being a legal tender in payment of private debts is an
"appropriate means, conducive and plainly adapted to the

---

*110 U. S. Reports, p. 449.

"execution of the undoubted powers of Congress, consist-
"ent with the letter and spirit of the constitution, and
"therefore, within the meaning of the instrument, 'nec-
"'essary and proper for carrying into execution the powers
"'vested by this constitution in the Government of the
"'United States.'"

No. 7.

*A restatement of the consequences of both doctrines being
wholly true.*

If the doctrine concerning the constructive powers of Congress contained in the above quotations from the Supreme
Court's opinion be true, and if the doctrine concerning judicial power contained in the foregoing quotations from Mr.
McMurtrie's Observations be true, the series of propositions
contained in the following six paragraphs A, B, C, D, E
and F, must likewise be true as to the case above put, that
is to say, the case of a law enacted by Congress prohibiting
the Supreme and Inferior Courts from declaring any act of
Congress to be unconstitutional and void. Previously to
putting them before the reader, it is requisite to refer to
parts of the opinion in McCulloch *v.* Maryland, found on
pages 416, 417 and 418 of 4 Wheaton.

According to those parts of that decision, the following is
law. Among the *incidental* powers belonging to Congress
as a *sovereign* legislature is that of legislatively prescribing
punishments for crimes in all rightful cases except the
limited number of cases expressly mentioned in the constitutional text, which are those of treason, counterfeiting,
piracy, felonies on the high seas and breaches of the law of
nations. The magnitude of the incidental power of punishment inferred by Marshall in the cases of unexpressed
crimes and misdemeanors is not greater than that of the
incidental power of legislation inferred by the case put in
the cases of endangered non-political rights. In the first
instance the jurisdiction of the judiciary is enlarged, and
in the second it is restricted, by the same means, namely,
by inference.

The following proposition is asserted upon the authority of Chief Justice Marshall in the opinion of the court as aforesaid. It is therein distinctly laid down: (1), that the power of punishment exercised in the penal code of the United States in cases not expressed in the constitution is one appertaining to *sovereignty;* and (2), that whenever the sovereign can rightfully act, that power is *incidental* to the sovereign's constitutional powers. As examples of unexpressed cases in which the power is incidental, the following are specified: Stealing letters from postoffices, robbing the mails, perjury in U. S. courts, falsifying U. S. judicial records, and stealing such records.

It will be observed that the propositions contained in the following six paragraphs are expressed in language which adheres as closely as may be, *mutatis mutandis,* to the language of the Supreme Court in Juilliard *v.* Greenman.

A. By the constitution, Congress has expressly certain great legislative powers, among which is the power to make all laws which are necessary and proper for carrying into execution all the *other* powers vested in itself. These powers are *sovereign* powers and must be construed as such, according to the usages of *sovereign* legislatures and lawgivers at the time when the constitution of the United States was framed and adopted.

B. As *incident* to the *sovereign* powers of every legislature and lawgiver, the power of binding judicial courts to obey all laws and of prohibiting them from criticising any law and declaring it void, was a power, universally understood to belong to sovereignty in Europe and America, at the time of the framing and adoption of the constitution of the United States.

C. The governments of Europe acting through the monarch as lawgiver or a collective body as legislature according to the distribution of powers under their respective constitutions, had and have as *sovereign* a power of binding judicial courts by all laws and of prohibiting them from criticising any law and declaring it void, as of binding private individuals by all laws and of prohibiting them from disobeying the same under penalties of punishment.

D. The power of binding judicial courts to obey all statutes and of prohibiting them from criticising any statute and declaring it void, was a power exercised by parliament in England, and in the American colonies, and in all other parts of the British empire during the whole colonial period.

E. The exercise of the legislative power in question is *not prohibited to Congress by the constitution.* It is, therefore, *included* among the *legislative powers* of Congress, one of which is to make all laws which are necessary and proper for carrying into execution all the *other* powers vested in itself.

F. Congress as the legislature of a *sovereign* nation, being expressly granted certain great legislative powers relating to civil and military, national and international, subjects of a sovereign nature, one of which is especially the power of making all laws necessary and proper for carrying into execution all the other powers vested in itself, and being clearly authorized as incident to those great powers to bind private individuals to obey all its laws and to prohibit them from disobeying the same under penalties of punishment; and the power to bind judicial courts to obey all laws and to prohibit them from criticising any law and declaring it void, being *one of the powers belonging to sovereignty in other civilized nations and not expressly withheld from Congress by the constitution;* it follows as an irresistible conclusion that binding all judicial courts to obey all congressional laws and prohibiting them from criticising any law and declaring it void, is an appropriate means conducive and plainly adapted to the execution of the undoubted powers of Congress, consistent with the letter and spirit of the constitution, and, therefore, within the meaning of that instrument necessary and proper for carrying into execution the powers vested by the constitution in Congress as the legislative department of the government of the United States.

No. 8.

That the foregoing considerations prove the existence of a second class of extraordinary reasons for a fresh discussion of the subject of this Essay.

If then the respective doctrines of the Supreme Court and Mr. McMurtrie be wholly true, it is also true that the constitution gives to Congress the power to make a law prohibiting the Supreme and Inferior Courts from declaring any acts of Congress to be unconstitutional and void.

Few American lawyers will accept as true any conclusion affirming such a proposition. It is safe to say that the Supreme Courts both of the United States and of the several states would, without exception, deny the truth thereof.

The proposition is certainly a great error; but the greater its error, the more strongly does it support the contention of the present chapter as to the existence of a second class of extraordinary reasons for a fresh discussion of the subject of this Essay. The erroneous proposition is a conclusion correctly reached in reasoning from the premises. The premises consist of two germane doctrines relating respectively to legislative powers and to judicial power under the constitution. The doctrines are of the highest interest, both theoretically and practically, to the United States. Both pronounce upon the constitutional law of all other civilized governments besides that of the United States. Some part or parts of one or both these doctrines must be error, if the conclusion be error. If the conclusion be absurd, there is a *reductio ad absurdum* of some part or parts of one or both the premised doctrines. But whether the conclusion be error only, or downright absurdity, its correct deduction from the premises fully sustains the writer's present contention ; namely, that there are extraordinary reasons for a fresh discussion of the subject of this Essay, which are concerned especially with the decision in Juilliard *v.* Greenman and have their origin in it and the controversy caused by it.

Some lawyers may be surprised that the decision in Juilliard *v.* Greenman and Mr. McMurtrie's defence thereof should, when taken together, be capable of producing such consequences. Others, however, will not be surprised that so strong a decision as Juilliard *v.* Greenman should produce strange results. The following will elucidate this observation.

Hepburn *v.* Griswold, 8 Wallace 603, was a strong decision. It declared that Congress could issue bills of credit and did not deny that it could make them a legal tender for future debts. It denied only that it could make them a legal tender for pre-existing debts. Knox *v.* Lee, 12 Wallace 457, was a stronger decision. It held that Congress could make bills of credit a legal tender in payment of pre-existing debts, in certain cases like that before the court. Next came Juilliard *v.* Greenman, 110 U. S. Reports 421, the strongest decision of all. It invoked generally all the legislative powers belonging to sovereignty in Europe and decided particularly that Congress can make bills of credit a legal tender, for both future and pre-existing debts, in all cases whatsoever.

This series of decisions thus gained strength as it proceeded, until either very great or too great progress was made and more invited. Now, Juilliard *v.* Greenman places great reliance on the English case of Austria *v.* Day. The following remark of an eminent English judge upon English decisions progressing in a series like the legal tender cases is, therefore, in point.

In 1861, Lord Chief Justice Erle said to Nassau W. Senior, then a master in chancery, when they met in travelling on the continent:

"A great part of the law made by judges consists of "strong decisions, and as one strong decision is a precedent "for another a little stronger, the law at last on some matters "becomes such a nuisance, that equity intervenes or an act "of parliament must be passed to sweep the whole away."

These are the speaker's precise words, the manuscript report being corrected by himself.*

---

* See Conversations during the Second Empire by N. W. Senior (London, 1880), I. 321.

The decisions, which Lord Chief Justice Erle condemned, were remarkable for strong will, not for strong reason. He would have agreed with Lord Mansfield in praising decisions remarkable for strong reason: see Lord Mansfield's letter to Chief Justice McKean, prefixed to 1 Dallas.

The strong decisions criticised by Lord Chief Justice Erle were made by an abuse of the proceeding to similars expounded in *Dig. lib. 1. tit. 3. l. 10, 12.* There the cases are explained in which, *is, qui jurisdictioni praeest, ad similia procedere, atque ita jus dicere, debet.*

Long and strong steps in legal theory have been made in proceeding from the express power of borrowing money to an *implied and similar* power of forcing private parties to make loans because the party borrowing is sovereign. How many more long and strong steps in legal theory are required to proceed from the various legislative powers expressly granted, to an implied and similar power of prohibiting courts from declaring void any legislation, because the legislature is sovereign? The answer need now surprise no one. Not more such steps are required in theory than are possible, if the respective doctrines of the Supreme Court and of Mr. McMurtrie be both wholly true.

It is in point here to quote the following passage from Madison's debates of the convention which framed the constitution of the United States (5 Elliot's Debates, 429). On August 15th, 1787, he records that:

"Mr. Mercer heartily approved the motion. It is an ax-"iom that the judiciary ought to be separate from the leg-"islative; but equally so, that it ought to be independent of "that department. The true policy of the axiom is, that "legislative usurpation and oppression may be obviated. "He disapproved of the doctrine, that the judges, as ex-"positors of the constitution, should have authority to "declare a law void. He thought laws ought to be well "and cautiously made and then to be *uncontrollable.*"

CHAPTER IV.

Of the plan of this Essay and its division into Historical and Textual Commentaries.

No. 1. Of the Historical Commentary.

No. 2. Of Part 1. of the Historical Commentary.

No. 3. Of Part II. of the same.

No. 4. Of Part III. of the same.

No. 5. Of Part IV. of the same.

No. 6. Of the Textual Commentary.

No. 7. Of the relation of the Textual Commentary to the exposition of the Framers' intentions.

No. 8. Further observations upon the Textual Commentary.

No. 9. Of the opinion in Marbury v. Madison in connection with the Textual Commentary.

This Essay will be divided into two branches, the Historical Commentary and the Textual Commentary. The former will treat of the history of the judicial competency which is the subject of this Essay, in so far as is necessary. The latter will examine the texts of the constitution which are especially concerned. It is intended to be an exposition of the law of the subject, according to the express and precise meaning of those texts.

No. 1.

Of the Historical Commentary.

The Histórical Commentary will be divided into four parts. It will discuss the subject in connection with: (1), foreign laws existing before and after 1787 ; (2), the laws of certain states of the Union in and before 1787 ; (3), the historical antecedents of the constitutional texts; and (4), the intentions of the Framers of the constitution.

No. 2.

Of Part I. of the Historical Commentary.

The foregoing chapters show that there are two classes of extraordinary reasons for a fresh discussion of the subject of this Essay. The reasons belonging to the second class show the necessity of an investigation of foreign laws for light on the subject. Such an investigation should include the laws of certain European states and unions of states and an examination of the Roman and Canon laws. It should discriminate between the different periods in the history of the different laws investigated. Especially, should it distinguish between what was law abroad before, and what after, 1787, the date when the U. S. constitution was framed in Philadelphia.

Such an investigation of foreign laws is imperatively necessary since the making of the decision in Juilliard *v.* Greenman. Since the opinion in that case, foreign laws may be freely appealed to to decide constitutional questions. In it, a Hungarian case of royal power is appealed to in order to support an implied power of making U. S. bills of credit a legal tender, and French law is relied upon in order to extend such legal tender power to previously existing as well as future contracts.* Thus an implied power of making a law impairing the obligation of contracts is obtained for Congress. This climax of implication is reached by grouping a Hungarian case with a French authority.

In defending the decision of Juilliard *v.* Greenman, Mr. McMurtrie cites Vattel and invokes the authority of a Polish case upon the law of coined money to support one of the links of his argument.† This is done in defence of a legislative power. In discussing the nature of judicial power, he maintains that a power of declaring laws to be void for any reason whatsoever is utterly unknown to all foreign laws. The weight of foreign laws upon this matter is so great that

---

* See pages 447, 449, of 110 U. S. Reports.

† See his page 23. Contrast Poor's Charters and Constitutions, page 1890, paragraph 2 from bottom.

it must have decided his judgment against such a power at
any time before Marshall wrote his opinion in Marbury *v.*
Madison.   Marshall's reasoning is held to be pure implication, but its force is declared to be so great that it triumphs
over all arguments from foreign laws to the contrary.   Before Marbury *v.* Madison, therefore, the judicial power and the
legislative powers delegated by the constitution were in the
same predicament, as far as foreign doctrines were concerned.
Implication against implication, the foreign doctrines then
predominated as to the latter as well as to the former.   It is
only the force of Marshall's extraordinary genius which
has made the change, if Mr. McMurtrie be correct.

Both the court and Mr. McMurtrie abstain from going into
detail, in appealing to foreign laws relating to the legislative
powers discussed by the former and the judicial power expounded by the latter.   Both group foreign laws together
and generalize from the mass.   This is going too far, if
foreign doctrines be objectionable.   If they be unobjection-
able, it is not going far enough.   No appeal to foreign laws
can be final, unless such laws be investigated in detail.   If
foreign doctrines are to decide, or to have a share in deciding
constitutional questions, the different foreign laws should be
examined *seriatim.*   English law, Roman law, French law,
German law, and other laws should be investigated separately.   When necessary, different periods in each law and
different branches thereof should be discriminated.   By so
proceeding, when truths are ascertained, they can be stated
with precision.   When errors are committed, they can be
attacked in detail.   The best of methods can not afford security against error in so wide a field of investigation.   But
a method of detail can prevent confusion and bring the in-
vestigator nearer to the truth : *citius emergit veritas ex
errore quam ex confusione.**

Such a method will be that followed in Part I. of the Historical Commentary, which will investigate the most important foreign laws bearing on the subject.   These will be
studied in detail.   Each law will be examined with refer-

---

* Bacon : Novum Organum, II. aph. 20 ; Bacon's Works, Spedding's edition,
I. 260.

ence to the relation of judicial power to legislation impeached as contrary to constitutional or other right, written or unwritten. Each law will be examined in order to ascertain whether therein can be found a constitutional or other fundamental rule of binding right, which is of such a nature that the question of contrariety may become a judicial one. The investigation will include the further question, whether, according to any foreign law, legislation judicially ascertained to be contrariant to a constitution or other rule of binding right, should therefore be judicially regarded as null or void.

The result of such an investigation of foreign laws will, it is contended, show that, when Americans invented written constitutions in the last century, they did not create an unprecedented novelty in framing them upon a principle that judiciaries might decide questioned legislation to be contrariant to a constitution and hold it therefore void : that is to say, that it might be a judicial and not an extrajudicial question whether such legislation was so contrariant or not. But on the contrary, that there were then important precedents in Europe for such a judicial institution. Long before American independence, there were in Europe unwritten systems of public law, according to which legislation might sometimes be judicially decided to be contrariant to a binding right of superior strength to the legislative power exercised. Thus, whether legislators had or had not proceeded *secundum jus potestatis suæ*, and, whether challenged legislation was consonant or accordant to binding right, might sometimes be judicial and not extrajudicial questions.

No. 3.

Of Part II. of the Historical Commentary.

The next part of the Historical Commentary will relate to American legal history. It will discuss the relation of judicial power to unconstitutional legislation in certain of the states before and during the confederation. The legal history of certain of the states has an important bearing on the subject of this Essay. It will show that the men who framed the U. S. constitution did not lead the way to the judicial competency under discussion, but followed the route indicated by judicial decisions in certain of the states.

No. 4.

Of Part III. of the Historical Commentary.

An historical investigation of the constitutional texts concerned does not begin with the meeting of the Framers in convention. It must examine the public historical antecedents of those texts. These antecedents are other texts, which were printed and published before the Framers met, and with which they were familiar. Under existing circumstances, this Essay would be actually incomplete, if this branch of constitutional history were forgotten.

The investigation of the historical antecedents of the texts of the constitution, which are herein concerned, will be Part III. of the Historical Commentary.

No. 5.

Of Part IV. of the Historical Commentary.

This Essay maintains that the text of the constitution expressly establishes a certain judicial competency relating to unconstitutional legislation, and does so by using words and phrases which are technical terms of law with one exception only. If this be so, the Framers of the constitution must have expressly intended what such language expressly means. To deny this, would be contrary to common sense. It is true that suggestions have been quite often made in print that men have built wiser than they knew in building structures less visible than stone houses. But nobody has ever thought that the framers of a written constitution could build wiser than they knew, if they used technical terms of law without knowing the meaning thereof.

The recorded evidence of the debates and proceedings of the Framers must, therefore, be examined to ascertain what light they throw upon the relation of judicial power to constitutional legislation. A full examination will be made and the result will, it is contended, show that the Framers expressly *intended* what is expressly imported by the constitutional text, as the writer reads it. That is to say, his two contentions as to the express meaning of the text and the express intentions of the Framers thereof, are in full harmony with each other. Those jurists who maintain that the judicial competency under discussion is implied, but not expressed, by the text, must do one of two things. They must either show that the writer misunderstands what the Framers intended, or prove that the latter did not select apt words for expressing their acknowledged intentions.

No. 6.

Of the Textual Commentary.

The second branch of this Essay will be the Textual Commentary. The observations, which are now in place upon it, have been anticipated to a great extent in previous remarks. In the Textual Commentary the texts of the constitution, which are especially concerned, will be considered in detail. It is the most important portion of the work, and the one to which the other parts lead up.

This branch of the Essay will consider the relation of judicial power to unconstitutional legislation in a commentary upon the particular texts concerned. It will endeavour to show that the constitution contains express texts providing for judicial competency to decide questioned legislation to be constitutional or unconstitutional and to hold it valid or void accordingly. This Textual Commentary is thus concerned with any legislation conflicting with the constitution of the United States, whether it be such as is made by Congress, or such as proceeds in any form from a state. It is concerned with the judiciary of the United States and the judiciaries of the several states in so far as they have any constitutional relations to such unconstitutional legislation.

Whether impeached legislation be constitutional or unconstitutional, is a question which can be asked according to any constitution, written or unwritten, American or European. But the second question,—whether the previous question is a judicial or an extrajudicial one, can never be asked according to some constitutions. According to them, any judicial tribunal attempting to decide the previous question would certainly proceed *extrajudicialiter*. The Textual Commentary will endeavour to show that the U. S. constitution contains express terms providing that the previous question may be a judicial and not an extrajudicial one.

It is an opinion that has received the greatest amount of acquiescence that the constitution implies, but does not express, the existence of judicial competency to declare legislation unconstitutional and so void. The writer's most important contention is that such a competency is expressly provided for by constitutional texts. This expressage of meaning is due to the fact that the constitution legislates upon the subject by using technical legal terms. The meanings of technical terms in all sciences are express ; and it is for that reason that such terms are selected by those who decide to use them. This head of the subject has been enlarged upon in Chapter 1. (see p. 4). What is there said, is again called to the reader's attention in connection with the nature of the Textual Commentary.

It may seem strange at this date, when the constitution is more than a century old, that it should be possible to contend that the express meaning of any portion of its text is not universally recognized. Strange as the fact may be, it is not as much so as a very ancient fact well known throughout all Christendom. Eastern and Western Christians have been divided for more than a thousand years as to the express meaning of a text of a common creed. The former hold that the insertion of the *filioque* contradicts the express meaning of the text. The latter deny any such contradiction. Thus, the East of Christendom asserts an express meaning for a fundamental text, which the West denies.

The Textual Commentary will proceed upon the basis that the written text of the constitution can not be altered, either

directly by corruption, or indirectly by misinterpretation.
No matter how inveterate and universal an erroneous interpretation may be, it can not overcome the express meaning
of the text of the constitution. That text is a thing which
can never become obsolete ; *quia per non usum etiam per
mille annos nunquam tollitur.*

No. 7.

*Of the relation of the Textual Commentary to the exposi-
tion of the Framers' intentions.*

The exposition of the meaning of the constitutional text
in the Textual Commentary harmonizes with the exposition
of the intentions of the Framers in the Historical Commentary. The writer's method will, however, be to establish
the truth of both expositions separately and independently
of each other. Readers will not be asked to rely upon his
views of the Framers' intentions in order to be convinced of
his understanding of the constitutional text. His object is
to convince readers of every school of opinion. He, therefore, must have regard to the scruples of those jurists who
refuse to be influenced by anything in the proceedings and
debates of the Framers, either because they were kept secret
for many years after the adoption of the constitution, or because they are held to be without authority in expounding
its text. These gentlemen are a very important class of constitutional lawyers, whether they be few or many in number.
They include Mr. McMurtrie, and it is necessary to meet
them on their own ground. Nowhere else can they be convinced. The Textual Commentary will, therefore, avoid introducing anything which they may feel bound to object to.

There is another class of constitutional lawyers, who regard the intentions of the Framers as matters of great weight
in expounding the constitution. They must be numerous ;
for they include Story, who did not hesitate to make free
use of the Journal of the Convention. Madison's Debates
he could not use ; for they were made public after the first
edition of his Commentaries, which was the only one published in his lifetime. The gentlemen of this school of

opinion naturally expect that the debates and proceedings of the convention should be carefully studied. Their expectations can not, under the circumstances, be disappointed. They will find that the writer's exposition of the Framers' intentions, and his exposition of the meaning of the text, are supplementary to each other. While both are separate from and independent of each other, they are in harmony and are so written that they may be readily compared together and fitted to each other. The hope of meeting the requirements of two such different classes of readers is, therefore, entertained.

It is also hoped that those readers will be satisfied, who regard the proceedings and debates of the Framers as, it would appear, the U. S. Supreme Court regards them. In Juilliard v. Greenman, on page 444 of 110 U. S. Reports, the court only goes so far as to maintain that "too much weight" should not be given to the debates and votes in the convention upon such a question as that before them. In Hauenstein v. Lynham in 10 Otto, 489, the court says, in discussing Ware v. Hylton, 3 Dallas, 199:

"We have quoted from the opinion of Mr. Justice Chase "in that case, not because we concur in everything said in "the extract, but because it shows the views of a powerful "legal mind at that early period, when the debates in the "convention which framed the constitution must have been "fresh in the memory of the leading jurists of the country."

This is said of Judge Chase's opinion, although it was delivered before the proceedings and debates of the Framers were published in any form, and although he was not a member of the convention.

No. 8.

Further observations upon the Textual Commentary.

According to Mr. H. C. Lodge, there were formerly two modes of interpreting the constitution, but now one of them has become obsolete.* According to Judge Baldwin, there are three modes.† Possibly there are four or more. It is,

---

* In the preface to his edition of Hamilton's Works.
† Constitutional Views, 36, 37.

however, unnecessary here to enter into so general a question. Remarks upon certain particular points are alone necessary.

First. This Essay is a legal treatise. It is intended for "the learned reader," to whom Story addresses his Commentaries : see his volume 2, page 430, first edition.

Secondly. The frequent reference to foreign laws herein made is absolutely necessary in a work so intimately related to the opinion in the case of Juilliard *v.* Greenman as hereinbefore mentioned. That opinion appeals to foreign notions of powers belonging to sovereignty, in order to interpret the constitution upon a disputed question of the greatest moment. The writer is compelled to do likewise. Unknown quantities of sovereignty introduced from abroad must become *known ;* for, under the circumstances previously mentioned, they cannot be disregarded. Whether writers upon all other heads of constitutional law are, or are not, bound to do likewise since Juilliard *v.* Greenman, is a question which need not be discussed.

Thirdly. Some remarks will be made as to the words, " constitutional," and " unconstitutional," the last of which is on the title page of this Essay. Neither adjective is found in the constitution. The adverb, " constitutionally," is, however, found at the end of the 12th amendment : " no " person *constitutionally* ineligible to the office of President " shall be eligible to that of Vice President of the United " States." A collation of this text with paragraph 5 of section 1. II. shows that the use of the adverb " constitutionally " is not to be restricted to the cases arising under the constitution which are of a judicial nature. It must also be used in cases whose nature is extrajudicial. What is true of that adverb ought consequently to be true of the adjectives " constitutional " and " unconstitutional."

In the following pages the words " constitutional " and " unconstitutional " are applied, in a federal sense, both to congressional legislation and to state legislation. In these two cases, the precise meanings of the words, according to the strict text, are not identical. The use of the two words, as general terms applicable in both cases, is, however, prac-

tically indispensable in discussion.   It is theoretically unob-
jectionable, if the precise differences of meaning in each case
be ascertained in the course of the commentary upon the
text.   Although the word " unconstitutional" is of English
origin, and was applied in America to acts of parliament
during the colonial period, such as the stamp act,—these circumstances have not prevented its general use since then,
under political systems very different from the English, but
called also by the name of constitutions.   There is, however,
no difficulty about such a use of the word " unconstitutional."   At least there is none, as long as a word like
" extraconstitutional," is not contrasted with it.

No. 9.

*Of the opinion in Marbury v. Madison and its relation
to the Textual Commentary.*

The view maintained in the Textual Commentary is directly opposed to that of Mr. McMurtrie and those who
agree with him.   Mr. McMurtrie categorically asserts that
the power of a judicial court to declare a law unconstitutional and void, is based exclusively upon inference and implication.   At the same time, he maintains that such a power
is so fully and thoroughly proved to be constitutional and
legal by the opinion in Marbury *v.* Madison, that no sane
man can doubt the correctness of Chief Justice Marshall's
reasoning therein.   It is, therefore, here necessary to ask
the question whether it is correct to say that Marshall's
conclusion in favour of such a power is based exclusively
upon inference and implication, and not upon the express
import of texts in the constitution ?

To this question, it is first answered that Mr. McMurtrie's
opinion is the general one.   Thus, Kent evidently takes
it for granted that Marshall's reasoning is of the nature
attributed to it by Mr. McMurtrie.   Kent's view of the
Chief Justice's reasoning on the judicial competency in
question is certainly that it consists of inference and is not
based upon expressage of constitutional texts.   The case of
Marbury *v.* Madison is reviewed twice in his Commenta-

ries, Ed. 1, Vol. 1, 424 and 301. On page 424, he observes :

" In Marbury *v.* Madison, the subject was brought under
"the consideration of the Supreme Court of the United
"States, and received a clear and elaborate discussion. The
"power and duty of the judiciary to disregard an unconsti-
"tutional act of Congress, or of any state legislature, were
"declared *in an argument approaching to the precision*
"*and certainty of a mathematical demonstration.*"

The precision and certainty of a mathematical demonstration, of course, means inference and not a reliance upon express texts.

After careful study of Marshall's reasoning, the writer
fully assents to Mr. McMurtrie's proposition, that that reasoning is exclusively based on implication and inference.
So far, at least, he fully agrees with Mr. McMurtrie. The
relation which such a proposition bears to the plan of this
Essay is, however, too important for it to be accepted as true,
without a new and special examination of the reasoning of
Marshall. Moreover, another consideration exists, which
of itself is more than sufficient to justify any reader in refusing assent to Mr. McMurtrie's proposition, without a
special investigation of its truth. This second consideration
is based upon an observation of Marshall's at the bar in
Ware *v.* Hylton, on page 211 of 3 Dallas.

In that case, as counsel for the defendant, Marshall said :
"The legislative authority of any country can only be re-
"strained by its own municipal constitution : This is a
"principle that springs from the very nature of society ;
"and the judicial authority can have no right to question
"the validity of a law, unless such a jurisdiction is *expressly*
"given by the constitution." Thus, at a date anterior to
Marbury *v.* Madison, if Marshall's words be taken literally,
he held that the jurisdiction in question could not be implied ; and thought, as, it seems to the writer, Mr. McMurtrie must have thought, if the opinion in that case had
never been written.

It is, therefore, doubly necessary to make a careful and
detailed examination of Marshall's reasoning in that part

of the opinion in Marbury *v.* Madison, which relates to the constitutional question. This task will be undertaken in the next and final chapter of this Introduction.

CHAPTER V.

Of that part of the opinion in Marbury v. Madison, which treats of the constitutional question.

No. 1. Review of that part of the opinion
No. 2. Continuation.
No. 3. Continuation.
No. 4. Conclusion drawn from the foregoing review.
No. 5. A further consideration of Marshall's observation in Ware v. *Hylton.*

This chapter will consist of a review of that part of the opinion in Marbury *v.* Madison, which is devoted to the consideration of the constitutional question involved in the case.

No. 1.

Review of that part of the opinion in Marbury v. *Madison, which treats of the constitutional question.*

That part of the opinion in Marbury *v.* Madison, which is now reviewed, is found on pages 176–180 of 1 Cranch and begins thus:

"The question, whether an act repugnant to the consti-"tution, can become the law of the land, is a question deeply "interesting to the United States ; but, happily, not of an "intricacy proportioned to its interest. It seems only nec-"essary to recognize certain principles. supposed to have "been long and well established, to decide it."

Here Marshall puts what he holds to be the question at issue. As he states that question, it is whether an act of Congress repugnant to the constitution can become the law of the land. He does not say one of "the laws of the Union," which words are used in clause 15 of Section 8, I. The words "law of the land" are only to be found in paragraph 2, VI.* He then proceeds to the general portion of this part of the opinion.

" That the people have an original right to establish, for "their future government, such principles as, in their opin-"ion, shall most conduce to their own happiness, is the "basis on which the whole American fabric has been erected. "The exercise of this original right is a very great exertion; "nor can it nor ought it to be frequently repeated. The "principles, therefore, so established are deemed funda-"mental. And as the authority, from which they proceed "is supreme, and can seldom act, they are designed to be "permanent.

"This original and supreme will organizes the govern-"ernment, and assigns to different departments their re-"spective powers. It may either stop here; or establish "certain limits not to be transcended by those departments."

The above propositions are postulates to be used in making the inferences following. They do not contain quotations from the text of the constitution. Their only relation to that text is that of things presumed or presupposed thereby. Such presumptions are not things expressly mentioned in the text of the constitution.

" *The government of the United States is of the latter* "*description. The powers of the legislature are defined* "*and limited; and that those limits may not be mistaken* "*or forgotten, the constitution is written.*"

This is a postulate to be used in making the inferences following. No text of the constitution is quoted. That it depends upon inference, and not upon the express meaning of texts, is shown in No. 2 of this chapter.

---

* Is an act of Congress repugnant to the constitution in the following case? Its contents are not repugnant to the constitution. It is, however, a question whether it has been passed according to the forms prescribed by the constitution. If this question be answered in the negative, the act of Congress is certainly unconstitutional ; but is such unconstitutionality covered by the phrase "repugnant to the constitution."

"To what purpose are powers limited, and to what pur-
"pose is that limitation committed to writing; if these lim-
"its may, at any time, be passed by those intended to be
"restrained? The distinction between a government with
"limited and unlimited powers is abolished, if those limits
"do not confine the persons on whom they are imposed,
"and if acts prohibited and acts allowed are of equal obli-
"gation. It is a proposition too plain to be contested, that
"the constitution controls any legislative act repugnant to
"it, or, that the legislature may alter the constitution by
"an ordinary act.

"Between these alternatives there is no middle ground.
"The constitution is either a superior, paramount law, un-
"changeable by ordinary means, or it is on a level with or-
"dinary legislative acts, and like other acts, is alterable
"when the legislature shall please to alter it."

This is a dilemma, at which the reasoning has arrived, by
proceeding through a series of inferences from the postulates above mentioned.

"If the former part of the alternative be true, then a leg-
"islative act contrary to the constitution is not law: if the
"latter part be true, then written constitutions are absurd
"attempts, on the part of the people, to limit a power in
"its own nature illimitable."

That is to say, if the first horn of the dilemma be assumed
to be true, it must be inferred that an unconstitutional act
of legislation is not law; but if the second horn be assumed
to be true, a conclusion must necessarily be inferred, which
reduces such an assumption to an absurdity.

"*Certainly all those who have framed written constitu-
"tions contemplate them as forming the fundamental and
"paramount law of the nation, and consequently the
"theory of every such government must be, that an act of
"the legislature repugnant to the constitution is void.*"

This passage first asserts a fact, and then infers a theory
therefrom, upon which comment will be made presently.

"This theory is essentially attached to a written consti-
"tution, and is consequently to be considered by this court as
"one of the fundamental principles of our society. It is
"not therefore to be lost sight of in the further considera-
"tion of this subject.

"If an act of the legislature, repugnant to the constitu-
"tion, is void, does it, notwithstanding its invalidity, bind
"the courts, and oblige them to give it effect? Or, in other

"words, though it be not law, does it constitute a rule as "operative as if it was a law? This would be to overthrow "in fact what was established in theory; and would seem, "at first view, an absurdity too gross to be insisted on. It "shall, however, receive a more attentive consideration."

That is to say, the inference so made is one which seems an absurdity. In the passage immediately following, he proceeds to demonstrate that this absurdity is not merely apparent, but real and certain.

" *It is emphatically the province and duty of the judic* "*ial department to say what the law is.* *Those who ap-* "*ply the rule to particular cases, must of necessity expound* "*and interpret that rule.* If two laws conflict with each "other, the courts must decide on the operation of each.

"So, if a law be in opposition to the constitution; if "both the law and the constitution apply to a particular "case, so that the court must either decide that case con-"formably to law, disregarding the constitution; or con-"formably to the constitution, disregarding the law: the "court must determine which of these conflicting rules govern "the case. This is of the very essence of judicial duty.

"If then the courts are to regard the constitution; and "the constitution is superior to any ordinary act of the leg-"islature; the constitution, and not such ordinary act, must "govern the case to which they both apply.

"Those then who controvert the principle that the con-"stitution is to be considered, in court, as a paramount law, "are reduced to the necessity of maintaining that courts "must close their eyes on the constitution, and see only the "law.

"This doctrine would subvert the very foundation of all "written constitutions. It would declare that an act which, "according to the principles and theory of our government, "is entirely void, is yet, in practice, completely obligatory. "It would declare, that if the legislature shall do what "is expressly forbidden. such act, notwithstanding the "express prohibition, is in reality effectual. It would be "giving to the legislature a practical and real omnipotence "with the same breath which professes to restrict their "powers within narrow limits. It is prescribing limits, and "declaring that those limits may be passed at pleasure."

That is to say, the apparent absurdity above mentioned is, after full consideration, inferred by demonstration to be actually the gross absurdity that it seemed to be, at the first view of it. "That it thus reduces to nothing what

"we have deemed the greatest improvement on pol-
"itical institutions—a written constitution, would of itself
"be sufficient, in America where written constitutions have
"been viewed with so much reverence, for rejecting the con-
"struction."

No. 2.

Continuation of the review.

So much for the first or general part of Marshall's reasoning, which relates principally to the nature of written constitutions in general. No text of the U. S. constitution is
quoted, cited, or named. His successive conclusions and
final decision are reached only by inference. The three
passages which have been italicized in the above abstract,
are the only ones requiring additional remarks in this connection. The first passage reads thus : "The government of
"the United States is of the latter description. The powers
"of the legislature are *defined* and limited." This is a
postulate from which inferences are made. The postulate
is itself an inference from the constitutional text, as is proved
by the following collation of two passages of Marshall's in
different judicial opinions. Here, he says that "the powers
"of the legislature *are defined and limited.*" In Gibbons
v. Ogden, in 9 Wheaton, 189, after quoting the clause beginning, "Congress shall have power to regulate com-
"merce with foreign nations," he adds : "The subject to be
"regulated is commerce ; *and our constitution being, as*
"*was aptly said at the bar, one of enumeration, and not*
"*of definition,* to ascertain the extent of *the power* it be-
"comes necessary to settle the meaning of the word."

This collation proves that neither of such contradictory
propositions can be expressly laid down in the text. Both
must be inferences therefrom, and one or other an incorrect
inference.

The second italicized passage is the following sentence :
"Certainly all those who have framed written constitutions
"contemplate them as forming the fundamental and para-
"mount law of the nation, and consequently the theory of
"every such government must be, that an act of the legis-
"lature repugnant to the constitution is void."

The first part of the above is the assertion of a fact relating to the point of view from which framers of written constitutions, in general, have regarded their work. On the other hand, it is the fact that men have undertaken to frame or amend written constitutions and yet denied that they are always fundamental and paramount laws. In certain European states, those framing written constitutions upon the *octroyé* or *auctorata* theory, must have done so. According to that theory, a written constitution is held to be granted as of grace by an hereditary monarch, vested with sovereignty by right and law antecedent to, and independent of, such constitution.* Examples of men so proceeding are not confined to Europe. The statue of Seward, recently erected in Auburn, represents him as asserting the existence of a higher law than the constitution.† Most of those opponents of the fugitive slave law, who asserted a law higher than the constitution, did not think that that belief should be abjured by such of their number as undertook in Congress and state legislatures to make amendments to that instrument.

Conceding, however, the fact to be as Marshall states it, the theory held to be a consequence thereof (*i. e.* that a law repugnant to a written constitution is void), is purely a matter of inference. It is not only an inference, but an erroneous inference, according to the case of Rutgers *v.* Waddington, which was decided in New York in 1784, under a written constitution. This was a recent and important case when the Framers met in Philadelphia. It is reviewed hereinafter. On page 41 of the opinion in Rutgers *v.* Waddington,‡ it is said :

" The supremacy of the legislature need not be called into " question ; if they think fit *positively* to enact a law, there " is no power which can control them. When the main ob- " ject of such a law is clearly expressed, and the intention

---

* *Cf. H. A. Zachariæ: Deutsches Staats-und Bundesrecht*, Ed. 3, Vol. 1, pages 257, 287, 291, 292; *Welcker's Staatslexikon*, Ed. 3, Vol. 10, pages 735–738.

† See, the New York Times for November 16, 1888, on the Seward Statue.

‡ Pamphlet Report : New York, 1784, page 41. See *post*, chapter 24, on this case.

"manifest, the judges are not at liberty, although it appears
"to them to be *unreasonable*, to reject it: for this were to
"set the *judicial* above the legislative, which would be
"subversive of all government."

The doctrine of Blackstone's tenth rule for construing
statutes, as laid down in his Commentaries, I. 91, is thus
applied to acts of the legislature under a written American
constitution.

An important postulate of the opinion remains to be considered.

Marshall lays down that "it is emphatically the province
"and duty of the judicial department to say what the law
"is. Those who apply the rule to particular cases, must of
"necessity expound and *interpret* that rule."

This proposition may be deemed by some to be a correct
general inference from the judicial institutions of civilized
nations in all times and places. Proper investigation will,
however, show that such cannot be the case. The proposition is, indeed, a proof that, in writing this opinion, the
institutions of lands of the Common law could only have been
clearly in the Chief Justice's contemplation. In the
countries of the Civil law there are two methods of interpreting written laws, the authentic or authoritative, and the
doctrinal or judicial. Authentic interpretation is made by
the lawgiver or legislature, upon the principle of *ejus est
interpretari cujus est condere.* Merlin's Répertoire in the
article on Interpretation observes:

"C'est au législateur qu'il appartient naturellement
"d'interpréter la loi: *ejus est legem interpretari cujus
"est legem condere.* C'est une maxime tirée du droit ro-
"main. *Quis enim* (disait l'empereur Justinien, dans la
"loi 12, C. *de legibus*), *legum ænigmata solvere et aperire
"idoneus esse videbitur, nisi is cui soli legislatorem esse
"concessum est ?*

"En France, nos rois se sont toujours reservé l'interpré-
"tation de leurs ordonnances."

Authentic interpretation by legislators overrules the doctrinal interpretation of the judiciary and binds them in all
future cases, whether they involve previous acts and con-

tracts or not. It is liable to be abused, but lawgivers and legislatures are not the only authorities who have interpreted laws abusively. Upon the two kinds of interpretation, see Von Mohl on Unconstitutional Laws in his *Staatsrecht, Voelkerrecht und Politik*, Vol. 1, pages 77, 78, 79 ; Merlin, Ed. 1827, Vol. 8, page 562, col. 2 ; Dupin's *Opuscules de Jurisprudence*, Ed. 1851, page 389.

Bowyer, in his Commentaries on the Modern Civil Law page 27, observes :

"The law is to be interpreted either by judicial or by the "legislative power ; and Domat shows that the legislative "power should be called upon to interpret the law only in "those cases where the rules of construction, which the "courts are bound to follow, prove insufficient to remove "the difficulty. This was the original and sound doctrine "of the Roman law, though after the legislative power be-"came vested in the emperors, legislative interpretation far "exceeded those limits."

It is probable that most civilians, after perusing the decision in Chisholm *v.* Georgia (2 Dallas, 419), would pronounce the 11th amendment to be an authentic interpretation of the text of the constitution concerning controversies between a state and citizens of another state.

The postulate in question is thus certainly an inference, and furthermore, an incorrect inference, if the powers belonging to sovereign legislators and legislatures in other civilized nations be appealed to. This conclusion must be admitted to be correct by all ; even by those who believe that Marshall's idea of judicial duty is the true conception of *jus dicere*, and that the ordinary interpretation is in all cases judicial, while legislative interpretation is extraordinary in all the cases in which its existence is possible. The question is not whether Marshall's postulate ought to be law everywhere, but whether it is and has been law everywhere, especially in the countries of the Civil law.

No. 3.

Continuation of the review.

The first or general part of Marshall's reasoning nas now been fully considered. Next comes the second or special part. It relates chiefly to "the peculiar expressions" of the constitution of the United States which furnish "additional arguments" for rejecting the doctrine that a law, which is unconstitutional and therefore void, nevertheless binds the courts, and compels them to read it only and close their eyes on the constitution. Here, if anywhere, must be found meanings derived from texts, which are not derived from inference, but from express words. Six texts of the constitution are commented upon or referred to.

"But the peculiar expressions of the constitution of the "United States furnish additional arguments in favour of "its rejection.

"The judicial power of the United States is extended to "all cases arising under the constitution.

"Could it be the intention of those who gave this power, "to say that, in using it, the constitution should not be "looked into? That a case arising under the constitution "should be decided without examining the instrument un- "der which it arises?

"This is too extravagant to be maintained."

That is to say, the truth of part of his meaning of the said text is inferred, because, if the contrary be assumed true, an absurdity must be inferred. The text so understood may or may not show that the question, whether an act of Congress be constitutional or not, is a judicial and not an extrajudicial one. If it do so, the conclusion must be based only on inference.

"In some cases then, the constitution must be looked into "by the judges. And if they can open it at all, what part "of it are they forbidden to read, or to obey?"

That is to say, the truth of the remaining part of his meaning of the said text is inferred, because, if the contrary be assumed true, an absurdity must be inferred.

"There are many other parts of the constitution which "serve to illustrate this subject.

"It is declared that 'no tax or duty shall be laid on arti-
"cles exported from any state.' Suppose a duty on the
"export of cotton, of tobacco or of flour ; and a suit instituted
"to recover it. Ought judgment to be rendered in such a
"case? Ought the judges to close their eyes on the consti-
"tution, and only see the law ?"

That is to say, the truth of his meaning of another text
is inferred, because, if the contrary be assumed true, an absurdity must be inferred.

"The constitution declares 'that no bill of attainder or
"'*ex postfacto* law shall be passed.'

"If, however, such a bill should be passed, and a person
"should be prosecuted under it, must the court condemn to
"death those victims whom the constitution endeavours
"to preserve?"

That is to say, the truth of his meaning of another text,
or rather two other texts, is inferred, because, if the contrary be assumed true, an absurdity must be inferred.

"'No person,' says the constitution, 'shall be convicted
"'of treason, unless on the testimony of two witnesses to
"'the same overt act, or on confession in open court.'

"Here the language of the constitution is addressed es-
"pecially to the courts. It prescribes directly for them, a
"rule of evidence not to be departed from. If the legisla-
"ture should change that rule, and declare *one* witness, or
"a confession *out* of court, sufficient for conviction, must
"the constitutional principle yield to the legislative act ?"

For this purpose, this text is the strongest of those adduced. The answer to its concluding question, however,
makes the reasoning a *reductio ad absurdum*. Thus, it is
upon inference only that he relies, to prove that courts are
bound to say that an act of Congress is void because conflicting with the constitutional text under consideration.
In other words, his proposition that the judicial courts are
especially addressed by the text, is affirmed as inferred from
the text itself, not as expressed in it. He confines his attention exclusively to the contents of the clause, without alluding to its location in the whole text, or its relations to
other clauses. The contents of the clause include no mention whatsoever of the judges of the United States courts,
while paragraph 2. VI. after mentioning the constitution
and certain other written instruments, expressly mentions

state judges as bound thereby : "and the judges in every "state shall be bound thereby." This present clause does not contain any words such as "the judges of the courts of "the United States shall be bound thereby." In the case of this text upon treason, the question whether it does or does not bind the judicial department as against an act of Congress decides whether the violation thereof results in constitutional grievances to be redressed by petition to the government, or in legal wrongs to be redressed by judicial proceedings.

On this point, Iredell's argument, reprinted in chapter 26 of this Essay, may be consulted as to any written constitution whatsoever.

Marshall's observations on the text in question are of much importance as a very early example of the theory of the address of clauses in a written constitution. The memorable *habeas corpus* controversy, in which Binney played a leading part, will be recalled in this connection. Whether the *habeas corpus* clause of the U. S. constitution was addressed to Congress or to the executive power, was regarded by many persons as an open question.

Divisions B., C. and D. of chapter 9 following, are also of interest in this connection, and show how two German supreme courts differed as to what a disciple of Marshall would call the address of a clause in the written constitution of the State of Bremen. That clause prescribed that well-acquired rights should not be injured. The late Hanseatic Court of Upper Appeal decided that certain legislation conflicted with the said clause, and held it therefore void. Subsequently, the new Imperial Tribunal of the German Empire decided that the same clause was to be understood merely as a rule for the legislative power itself to interpret, and did not mean that a command of that power could be disregarded by the judiciary, because injurious to well-acquired rights. It thus held that the clause was exclusively addressed to the legislature, a proposition which must be denied by any one affirming the truth of the Hanseatic decision. Compare Georgia *v.* Stanton, 6 Wallace 50.

The cited text upon treason can not bind any judicial

court in a case of conflict between it and an act of Congress, unless it be a judicial question whether a challenged act of Congress be constitutional or unconstitutional and valid or void accordingly. If it be an extrajudicial question no court can, of course, decide it. The said text may imply, but certainly does not *express*, the proposition that the said question is a judicial and not an extrajudicial one. Neither does any one of the other texts expounded by Marshall expressly assert that proposition, if his exposition thereof be correct. According to Marshall's reasoning, that question can only be inferred to be a judicial, and not an extrajudicial one. The cited text upon treason could, therefore, be only inferred by him to bind the judicial department in the said cases of conflict. The writer, of course, maintains that it binds the judiciary in all cases; but at the same time contends that the said question is expressly made a judicial one by other texts of the constitution.

"From these, and many other selections which might be "made, it is apparent that the framers of the constitution "contemplated that instrument as a rule for the govern-"ment of *courts* as well as of the legislature."

This language imports, *inter alia*, that the constitution is a rule for the government of courts, to the extent that it is a judicial and not an extrajudicial question, whether an act of Congress be repugnant to the constitution or not. Such a proposition is correct, but as far as Marshall is concerned, it is purely an inference from the constitution as commented upon by him.

All the previous conclusions from texts actually selected, have been shown to be inferred therefrom, not expressly imported thereby. None of the "many other selections "which might be made" from the constitution, are mentioned. What texts they may be, can only be conjectured. They are omitted quotations, and this last conclusion is merely matter of inference like its predecessors.

" Why otherwise does it direct the judges to take an oath "to support it? This oath certainly applies, in an especial "manner, to their conduct in their official character. How "immoral to impose it on them, if they were to be used as

"the instruments, and the knowing instruments, for violat-
"ing what they swear to support ?"

That this is merely inference, is clear from a collation of
the text of paragraph 3. VI. with that of the end of section 1. II. There is nothing special to his office expressed
in the constitutional oath required of a judge, while the only
special oath of office prescribed by the constitution is the
President's. The former text requires senators and representatives, members of the state legislatures and the executive and judicial officers of the United States, and of the
several states, to be bound by oath "to support this consti-
"tution." The latter text requires the President to swear
that he will faithfully execute his office, and will to the best of
his ability " preserve, protect and defend the constitution of
"the United States."

"The oath of office, too, imposed by the legislature, is
"completely demonstrative of the legislative opinion on this
"subject. It is in these words : ' I do solemnly swear that
" ' I will administer justice without respect to persons, and
" ' do equal right to the poor and to the rich ; and that I
" ' will faithfully and impartially discharge all the duties
" ' incumbent on me as ———, according to the best of my
" ' abilities and understanding, agreeably to the constitution
" ' and laws of the United States.'

" Why does a judge swear to discharge his duties agree-
"ably to the constitution of the United States, if that con-
"stitution forms no rule for his government ? if it is closed
"upon him, and can not be inspected by him.

"If such be the real state of things, this is worse than sol-
"emn mockery. To prescribe, or to take this oath, becomes
"equally a crime."

The above conclusions are merely inferred from an inference made by Congress.

" It is also not entirely unworthy of observation, that, in
" declaring what shall be the supreme law of the land, the
" constitution itself is first mentioned ; and not the laws of
" the United States generally, but those only which shall
"be made in pursuance of the constitution, have that
" rank."

It is of the highest importance to observe that the above
comment upon the text of paragraph 2. VI. is said to be only
" not entirely unworthy of observation." The lesson can

only be inference, for, if he held it to be the express import of the words, he would certainly have thought the comment entirely worthy of observation.

"Thus, the particular phraseology of the constitution "of the United States confirms and strengthens the principle, "supposed to be essential to all written constitutions, that "a law repugnant to the constitution is void, and that courts, "as well as other departments, are bound by that instru-"ment."

That is to say, his essential principle of all written constitutions is supposed only ; supposed, it is true, because it is contrary to reason to do otherwise. There is, however, nothing in the text of the constitution, as he expounds it, expressly asserting it. The peculiar phraseology of the constitution "confirms and strengthens" the principle, but does *not express* it.

No. 4.

Conclusion drawn from the foregoing review.

The foregoing review, it is contended, makes it evident that Mr. McMurtrie is correct in his emphatic assertion as to the nature of Marshall's reasoning on the constitutional question in Marbury *v.* Madison. That is to say, he is entirely correct in affirming that the said reasoning proceeds exclusively upon implication and inference in drawing the conclusion that a judicial court can declare a law to be unconstitutional and void.

It is a consequence of this conclusion being true, that any writer who maintains that such a judicial competency is matter of express import according to the constitutional text, must proceed otherwise than Marshall, and must reason upon a basis different from the opinion in Marbury *v.* Madison.

No. 5.

A further consideration of Marshall's observation in Ware v. Hylton.

It is another consequence of the foregoing conclusion that Marshall changed his mind between the dates of Ware *v.* Hylton and Marbury *v.* Madison, if his observation at the bar in the former case is to be taken literally. If that observation be so taken, he then thought that in every country the judicial power had no right to question the validity of a law on constitutional grounds, unless such a jurisdiction was *expressly* given by the constitution.

Whether Marshall's language in Ware *v.* Hylton is to be taken literally is a very interesting question in legal history. It is one which ought not to be answered without further consideration.

In the first place, Dallas, in the note on his page 207, expressly says, that he was not present at the argument, that he was disappointed in obtaining from counsel their briefs, and that he used the notes of a member of the bar who had been in court when they spoke. These volunteer notes, it may, perhaps, be presumed, were not made with a view to reporting the case in print. Anyhow, the reporter's printed foot-note shows that Marshall was not bound by the letter of the printed report of his argument on any point on which a more probable statement can be presented.

Can such more probable statement be presented? The answer to this question depends upon the history of the North Carolinian case of Bayard *v.* Singleton, which is the first reported case under a written constitution in which a law was decided unconstitutional and held therefore void. It is involved in the discussion of the present question in this wise. Among the judges whom Marshall addressed in Ware *v.* Hylton, was Iredell. That eminent jurist, as counsel in Bayard *v.* Singleton, led the way to the court's decision therein. His important place in the judicial history of written constitutions will fully appear when Bayard *v.* Singleton is rehearsed in chapter 26 of this Essay.

Marshall said, according to the report of Ware *v.* Hylton : "The legislative authority of any country can only be re-"strained by its own municipal constitution. This is a " principle that springs from the very nature of society ; and "the judicial authority can have no right to question the " validity of a law." So far there is no difficulty in under-standing or interpreting the words. As reported, he then added : "unless such a jurisdiction is *expressly* given by " the constitution." Now the history of Bayard *v.* Single-ton will show that he must have contradicted Iredell's his-torical position in constitutional law, if he meant: *unless such a jurisdiction is given by the constitution expressly saying that the judicial authority has the right to question the validity of a law when it is made in contradiction to constitutional restraints of legislative authority.* But he agreed with Iredell's historical position, if he meant : *unless such a jurisdiction is given by the constitution expressly restraining the legislative authority so as to make it a limited and not an omnipotent one.*

It must be assumed that Marshall knew who the judges were whom he addressed, and what their legal biographies were. He could not have differed with Iredell on such a question, without knowing that he did so, and meaning to do so. If he did not mean to differ with him, he thought that when a written constitution expressly restrained the legislative authority, such *express* restraint of legislation was the basis of an *implied* judicial right to question the validity of a law made in contradiction thereof. A legisla-tive authority *expressly* limited by the constitution *implied* a corresponding jurisdiction in the judicial authority. This is what Iredell meant by the term, "*express constitution*," used by him in 1787, in a letter addressed to a Framer of the constitution, while the convention was in session. Accord-ing to Iredell's view of the law of constitutions, the consti-tution of North Carolina *was*, and the British constitution was *not*, such "an express constitution."*

---

* See Life of Iredell, vol. 2, page 172, line 9 from bottom, and page 146, line 1 from bottom, both of which texts are reprinted in chapter 26, *post*, in the ac-count of Bayard *v.* Singleton.

If the words actually used by Marshall were not those of the report, and were such as agreed with Iredell's position, he must have used language like the following: "unless "such a jurisdiction is given by the constitution expressly "restraining the legislative authority," or, "unless such a "jurisdiction is given by an express constitution." If Marshall used such words, or others of identical meaning, he did not change his mind between the dates of Ware *v.* Hylton and Marbury *v.* Madison. It is for the reader to decide whether any such conjecture is good ground for an emendation of the report of Marshall's argument at the bar in the former case.

Certain it is that Iredell actually denied the truth of what is written in the first column below, but not the truth of what is written in the second.

Marshall's words as reported.	*Suggested emendation of the report of Marshall's words.*
"The legislative authority of any "country can only be restrained by "its own municipal constitution: This "is a principle that springs from the "very nature of society; and the judic-"ial authority can have no right to "question the validity of a law, *unless* "*such a jurisdiction is expressly given* "*by the constitution.*"	"The legislative authority of any "country, can only be restrained by its "own municipal constitution: This is "a principle that springs from the very "nature of society; and the judicial "authority can have no right to question the validity of a law, *unless such* "*a jurisdiction is given by an express* "*constitution.*"

By "express constitution," Iredell meant one which was the direct opposite of the British constitution, because it restricted the legislature in express terms; see chapter 26, *post,* and Life of Iredell as cited in previous note.

HISTORICAL COMMENTARY.

PART I.

INVESTIGATION OF FOREIGN LAWS ON JUDICIAL POWER AND ITS RELATION TO LEGISLATION CONTRARIANT TO A CONSTITUTIONAL OR OTHER RULE OF RIGHT.

PART II.

INVESTIGATION OF THE LAWS OF CERTAIN OF THE STATES ON THE RELATION OF JUDICIAL POWER TO UNCONSTITUTIONAL LEGISLATION BEFORE AND DURING THE CONFEDERATION.

PART III.

OF THE HISTORICAL ANTECEDENTS OF THE TEXTS OF THE CONSTITUTION, WHICH ARE CONCERNED.

PART IV.

OF THE INTENTIONS OF THE FRAMERS OF THE CONSTITUTION ON THE RELATION OF JUDICIAL POWER TO UNCONSTITUTIONAL LEGISLATION.

(71)

HISTORICAL COMMENTARY.

–.–.––.–.–.–.––.–.–.

PART I.

Part I. of the Historical Commentary will consider the subject in connection with certain important foreign laws past and present. It will include an investigation of the laws of certain European states and unions of states, and an examination of the Roman and Canon laws.

CHAPTER VI.

Preliminary.

No. 1. Preliminary as to England.
No. 2. Preliminary as to continental Europe.

This chapter will be concerned with considerations preliminary to the investigation of foreign laws.

No. 1.

Preliminary as to England.

It is correct to say that it is now law in England, and that it was law there long before 1776, that the judges of the courts are bound by acts of parliament in all cases according to the clear and clearly expressed intent of the legislature. When that intent is clear and clearly expressed, the judges can not explain it away by any interpreting device or defeat it by that or any other means whatsoever.

Blackstone is now and, when the Framers met, was sufficient authority for the foregoing proposition. On page 160 of his first volume, he speaks thus of the authority of parliament:

"It hath sovereign and uncontrollable authority in the "making, confirming, enlarging, restraining, abrogating, "repealing, reviving, and expounding of laws, concerning "matters of all possible denominations, ecclesiastical, or "temporal, civil, military, maritime, or criminal."

Parliament has thus an absolute and unlimited plenitude of power. The relation thereof to the judiciary is explained by him in another passage. Where the meaning and intent of parliament is clear, the courts, he holds, must obey the statute no matter how unreasonable it may be.

Blackstone's words are the following (I. 91) in his tenth rule for construing statutes:

"Lastly, acts of parliament that are impossible to be per- "formed are of no validity: and if there arise out of them "collaterally any absurd consequences, manifestly contra- "dictory to common reason, they are, with regard to those "collateral consequences, void. I lay down the rule with "these restrictions; though I know it is generally laid "down more largely, *that acts of parliament contrary to* "*reason are void. But if parliament will positively enact* "*a thing to be done which is unreasonable, I know of no* "*power in the ordinary forms of the constitution, that is* "*vested with authority to control it: and the examples* "*usually alleged in support of this sense of the rule do* "*none of them prove, that, where the main object of a stat-* "*ute is unreasonable, the judges are at liberty to reject* "*it;* for that were to set the judicial power above that of "the legislature, which would be subversive of all govern- "ment. But where some collateral matter arises out of the "general words, and happens to be unreasonable, there the "judges are in decency to conclude that this consequence "was not foreseen by the parliament, and therefore they "are at liberty to expound the statute by equity, and only

"*quoad hoc* disregard it. Thus if an act of parliament
"gives a man power to try all causes, that arise within his
"manor of Dale; yet, if a cause should arise in which he
"himself is party, the act is construed not to extend to
"that, because it is unreasonable that any man should de-
"termine his own quarrel. But, if we could conceive it
"possible for the parliament to enact, that he should try as
"well his own causes as those of other persons, there is no
"court that has power to defeat the intent of the legis-
"lature, when couched in such evident and express words,
"as leave no doubt whether it was the intent of the legis-
"lature or no."

The proposition laid down at the outset is thus fully supported by authority.

Blackstone's doctrine concerning the relation of the judiciary to acts of parliament was accepted in the colonies as
well as in England, when the American revolution broke
out. Those American lawyers and public men who have
doubted, hesitated or wondered concerning a judicial competency of deciding legislation unconstitutional and holding
it therefore void, or have denied the existence of such competency, have done so under the influence of English law
as expounded by Blackstone. If there are any, who have
done so for other reasons, they must be exceptions to the
rule.

For the purposes of clearness, this statement is made in
the beginning. Due examination and consideration of the
English law bearing upon the subject at different periods
of English history will be made subsequently. Two remarks only are now necessary:

First; that the English constitution is not a written, but
a consuetudinary constitution, which is of great antiquity;
and that part of what was true in 1776 may have only become so since the discovery of America.

Second; that Blackstone teaches "that acts of parliament
"that are impossible to be performed are of no validity;"
and that this proposition requires investigation both as to
its previous history in England and its subsequent history
in America.

No. 2.

Preliminary as to continental Europe.

It is also correct to say that, as a rule, it is law in the civilized states of modern Europe, that the legislature can bind the judiciary to obey and apply all statutes in all cases, and can restrain courts from declaring any statute to be either unconstitutional or void. Upon this head, it is remarked by Bluntschli, in his General Public Law (*Allgemeines Staatsrecht*), ed. 1863, I. 550, 551 :

"In most modern states there is, however, no legal "remedy against the validity and applicability of a law al- "lowed upon the ground that the contents thereof stand in "contradiction to the constitution. The authority of the "legislative body, so far as its functions reach, is valid as "the highest and as an incontestable authority. Hence "the courts are not empowered to touch the contents of a "law and, by their own authority, to declare the same to "be invalid."

These principles are stated to be of "general validity in "England as well as on the European continent." On the other hand, the United States are mentioned as being remarkable for the existence of a contrary system in their public law.

"In North American public law," Bluntschli further remarks, "we find another and opposing system. According "to that system, the courts are authorized and obliged, "when they are convinced that a law conflicts with the "constitution, to refuse recognition thereto, and prevent "the execution thereof, because it is invalid."*

It will be observed that while the foregoing observations are limited to "most modern states," they include such states, without regard to their constitutions being written or unwritten. Most of the states of continental Europe now possess written constitutions ; and every European written constitution, past or present, is dated after the establishment of the constitution of the United States. Between

---

* Translation.

that date and the date of the opinion in Marbury v. Madison, however, at least twelve written constitutions were promulgated in Europe.* They are manifestly ignored by Chief Justice Marshall in that opinion, as has been before noted.

CHAPTER VII.

Of French law in connection with the subject of this Essay.

No. 1. *Of French written constitutions. Of their relation to the previous unwritten polity in the matter of judicial power.*

No. 2. *Of the regency cases in the reigns of Lewis XIII., Lewis XIV., and Lewis XV.*

No. 3. *Considerations upon the French parliaments.*

No. 4. *Of the pragmatic sanction of Charles VII. and the concordate of 1517.*

No. 5. *Conclusions from the foregoing examination of French law.*

This chapter will investigate French law for light upon the subject of this Essay. It will begin with the modern law, brought into existence by the French revolution, and then discuss the law of the old monarchy.

---

* See the collection published by F. A. Brockhaus at Leipsig, in 1817, entitled, *Die Constitutionen der europäischen Staaten seit den letzten 25 Jahren,* vol. 1, pp. 58, 114, 137, 209, for France ; p. 325 for the Netherlands ; vol. 2, pp. 6, 16, for Poland ; vol. 4, pp. 365, 387, 395, 409, for Switzerland ; vol. 4, p. 813, for the Cisalpine Republic ; vol. 3, p. 469, for the Italian Republic ; vol. 3, p. 515, for Lucca ; vol. 3, p. 457, for Genoa. Compare vol. 3, p. 530, as to the Roman Republic.

No. 1.

Of French written constitutions. Of their relation to the previous unwritten polity in the matter of judicial power.

Excluding the ill-fated document known as the Polish constitution of May 3d, 1791, the French constitution of September 3d, 1791, was the first written one in Europe. Article 16. of its declaration of the rights of men and citizens, is thus translated :

" Every society in which the guarantee of rights is not " secured, or the separation of powers is not fixed, has no " constitution."

Articles 1. and 3. of chapter 5. of the constitution provide :

" The judicial power can not in any case be exercised by " the legislative body or by the king.

" The tribunals can not interfere with (*s'immiscer dans*) " the exercise of the legislative power, nor suspend the exe- " cution of the laws, nor encroach upon administrative func- " tions, nor cite any administrators to appear before them " on account of their functions."*

The general relation of the French constitution of 1791 to the past was revolutionary, and its continuance was of brief duration. Its above restriction of judicial power had, however, a future and a past. That restriction has unquestionably prevailed in France from 1791 to the present day under all forms of government. Neither can it be doubted that it had historical antecedents in connection with a great question of French polity then requiring settlement. In France, for centuries, the kings and the judiciaries called parliaments, had been periodically in conflict upon the right or claim of the latter to criticise acts of legislation, to refuse registration to legislative acts deemed wrongful, and to ignore them in judicial decisions. The question had been settled too recently and too arbitrarily against the parliaments to be considered an issue incapable of revival by a

---

*F. A. Hélie : *Les Constitutions de la France,* 270, 288

new judiciary on a fitting opportunity. An explicit provision, upon the competency or incompetency of the judiciary to criticise legislation, was certainly proper, if not unavoidable. The decision of the constituent powers in the
new constitution was against the competency. This determination of the question must have been largely due to the
peculiar idea of the separation of powers then prevailing in
France.

The quotations above given show that the greatest importance was attributed to a real separation of powers. As
a matter of fact, the varied functions of the old parliaments
had been connected with a confusion of powers of government and a division of classes of Frenchmen, which other
critics besides the revolutionists of 1791 have objected to.*

The influence of French historical associations, therefore,
led to the principle of the separation of powers being deemed,
in France in 1791, to be hostile to any judicial competency
to criticise legislation for unconstitutionality. This is extremely curious, for the weight of American opinion is now
and always has been the other way upon the effect of the
separation of powers, ever since Americans began to write
constitutions. In the last century, Montesquieu and other
writers upon that subject were deeply pondered by political students both in America and in France. Frenchmen
did so, under the dominant influence of French history.
Americans did so, under no such dominant influence. The
former seized the opportunity of a written constitution to
restrict the French judiciary as aforesaid.† On the other
hand, Americans wrote the U. S. constitution upon the principle that in judicial cases arising thereunder it was necessary for courts to criticise legislation.

---

* See Gneist on English and German Administration, Justice and Legal
Methods : (*Verwaltung, Justiz, Rechtsweg*, etc.); Berlin, 1869. page 161.
† See Solon : *Répertoire des Jurisdictions*, Paris, 1843, vol. 1, pages 25 to 28.

No. 2.

Of the regency cases in the reigns of Lewis XIII., Lewis XIV., and Lewis XV.

While the Framers of the constitution of the United States were not dominated by French history on this subject, it would be a mistake to say that they were ignorant of it.

The generation, which made the French alliance, could not have been ignorant of the great facts in the then later history of France. Certain of these facts have an important bearing upon the history of judicial power or jurisdiction to criticise acts of legislation.

In France under the old monarchy the parliaments were judicial courts, of which the parliament of Paris was the chief (the Estates General corresponding to the parliament of England).* It is true that they had powers some of which were extrajudicial, but this did not prevent them from being judicial courts. The courts of Pennsylvania do not cease to be judicial tribunals, because they have extrajudicial powers as to certain matters.

The parliament of Paris, upon the accession of the minor king Lewis XIII., in 1610, made a judicial decision declaring the queen mother to be regent, thus ignoring any claims of any prince of the blood. Martin, in his History of France, XI, page 4, thinks that there was no law "which "attributed this exorbitant right to this court of justice." It was, however, a precedent for two great cases in which the parliament declared legislative acts of kings of France to be null and void. The first of these cases was that of the regency during the minority of Lewis XIV. His father, Lewis XIII, by a formal declaration of his last will, made in view of approaching death, enacted that the queen consort should be regent with powers greatly restricted by those of a council of regency, which he therein appointed. After the king's death (1643) the parliament of Paris declared the queen to be sole regent without any council, thus

---

* Fortescue on Monarchy, ed. 2, pages 16, 17.

partially annulling the enactment of the late king, on the
ground "that the queen once recognized as regent by
"virtue of the last wishes of the late king, consented to by
"the grandees of the kingdom, had, of right, the plenitude
"of the royal power."*

The second case is that of the regency during the minority of Lewis XV. By the testament of Lewis XIV., it
was enacted that the regency should be vested in a council,
of which the next prince of the blood, the Duke of Orleans,
should be president. Upon the king's death, the Duke of
Orleans successfully opposed the registration of the testament by the parliament of Paris. The duke claimed that
the testament was contrary to the laws and usage of the
kingdom, and prejudicial to his right to be regent. This
claim was sustained by the parliament, which adjudged the
regency to the Duke of Orleans.† The session of the parliament which did this was held on September 2d, 1716.
When it was ended, there was, according to Martin,‡ nothing left of the wishes of Lewis XIV. except the parchment
upon which they were written. The minor king was not
present at the session. The new regent therefore required
a further ceremony, the name of which recalled that the
parliament was a judicial body. A "bed of justice" was
held on September 12th, when the king sat in parliament
on the cushioned throne of justice. The previous action of
the parliament was then recorded with great solemnity in
the royal presence.§

In making a comparison of these cases in the old French
public law with cases in constitutional law on this side of
the Atlantic, it is not asserted that it runs upon four legs,
for there was no such distinct division of powers in the
former, as exists in the latter. The parliaments, although
judicial courts, were competent to decide many extrajudicial questions. These French cases, however, suffice to show
that the idea of a judicial court holding legislation to be

---

* *Martin: Histoire de France*, XI, 588.

† See the Historical Register for 1716 (London, 1717), pages 35 to 45.

‡ *Histoire de France*, XV. 7; *cf*. XI. 6.

§ Same Work, XV. 8.

void because contrary to binding right, was known in France before the time when the constitution of the United States was framed. This is remarkable, and peculiarly so, when it is remembered that the then constitution of France was unwritten.

No. 3.

Considerations upon the French parliaments.

The whole history of the French parliaments is of great interest in this connection. For several centuries before the French revolution, conflicts between the crown and the parliament of Paris were constantly occurring. Legally, the main question of public right in these contests was the extent of the powers of the parliament concerning its registration of the king's edicts and ordinances. The full claim of the parliament was that, for proper reasons, it had " the right to refuse *registration* to a royal ordinance, and " thus to strike the same with nullity by paying no regard " thereto in its decisions." See *Chéruel: Dictionnaire Historique des Institutions de la France* (Paris, 1855), articles, *Parlement* and *Enrégistrement.* See also *H. Martin: Histoire de France,* XI., 3, 4, 5.

This power, if exercised by the parliament to the full extent of the claim, could be made an effective restraint upon the king's legislative power. Many judicious thinkers in France are of opinion that the parliament opposed a useful resistance to absolute power. It must not be forgotten that the French monarchy fell because the meeting of the Estates General had ceased to be habitual. The kings had secured practically a monopoly of legislation by refusing to convoke that assembly. Those who have thought that the parliaments were fully liable to a charge of usurpation must have failed to appreciate the fact that such a charge would have been impossible, if the Estates General had been in the habit of meeting at proper intervals on the summons of the crown.

No. 4.

Of the pragmatic sanction of Charles VII. and of the concordate of 1517.

The next example is rather a series of cases than a single one. It should be premised that the registration of the bulls of the popes by the parliament was necessary to the legal promulgation thereof. By refusing registration, a check upon the exercise of spiritual power might be made as long as the refusal could be kept up. This was sometimes a matter of difficulty.

A pragmatic sanction was issued by king Charles VII., concerning ecclesiastical affairs, which was registered by the parliament of Paris on July 13th, 1439. This pragmatic sanction provoked continual papal remonstrances. In consequence, the succeeding king, Lewis XI., issued letters patent of November 27th, 1461, abolishing the pragmatic sanction. The parliament of Paris refused to register these royal letters patent. A serious conflict between France and Rome resulted from this refusal, which lasted formally as well as substantially until 1517. In that year a concordate was made between the king and the pope then reigning. It was actually registered in the following year by the parliament of Paris, but the registration was unwillingly made. The court accompanied their act with a declaration that the registration was made by the express order of the king, and formally protested against the concordate two days after. See *André: Cours du Droit Canon*, I. 585, 603, 605, II. 842. Thus, for over fifty years the parliament of Paris resisted the pressure made by royal power to force it to overrule itself. A tribunal which, for more than half a century, could so restrain a legislative authority within disputed limits on so great a matter can not be overlooked by American students of constitutional law at the present day. Neither can it be assumed to have been overlooked by American students in the last century.

No. 5.

Conclusions from the foregoing examination of French law.

From the above cases two lessons are to be learned :

First ; that long before 1787 a French judicial court criticised legislation and, in two constitutional instances, declared legislation to be void because contrary to binding right ascertained by itself.

Second ; that the history of France shows clearly that the court got into extrajudicial affairs in so doing, a thing which in the end produced disastrous results to all the parliaments in France.

The Framers of the constitution of the United States must certainly have known the first lesson. In the subsequent pages that discuss the Framers' intentions as to the Supreme Court of the United States, reasons will be given for thinking that they also profited by the second lesson.

It is contended from the foregoing that the history of French public law shows the following remarkable results :

First ; that under the constitution of the old monarchy, a judicial power or right to hold legislation void because contrary to binding right, was well known :

Second ; that the first written French constitution in 1791 prohibited any judicial power or right to criticise laws for unconstitutionality or other cause, or to hold them void for any reason ; which provision has continued to be public law in France until the present day :

Third ; that the constitution of the old monarchy was *unwritten*, while that of 1791 was *written*, and that the said judicial power or right existed under the former, but was prohibited under the latter, and has been prohibited under various subsequent written constitutions. French public law upon the subject is thus in direct contradiction to Marshall's view of written constitutions. French legal history is also in curious contrast with the prevailing idea among Americans of the present day as to the relation of judicial power to written and unwritten constitutions.

CHAPTER VIII.

Of Swiss public law in connection with the subject of this Essay.

No. 1. *Of Swiss public law and the present federal constitution and federal government.*

No. 2. *Of the Federal Tribunal and federal laws conflicting with the federal constitution.*

No. 3. *Of the relations between cantonal constitutions and the federal constitution.*

No. 4. *Of the relation of the judiciary of a canton to a cantonal law conflicting with the cantonal constitution.*

No. 5. *Of cantonal laws conflicting with the Federal constitution.*

No. 6. *Of a cantonal law conflicting with the federal guarantee of the cantonal constitution.*

The next topic for consideration in connection with the subject of this Essay is the public law of Switzerland.

No. 1.

Of Swiss public law and the present federal constitution and federal government.

Swiss public law has long naturally attracted American attention. In 1789, the subject of Swiss institutions was not neglected by the men who framed and ratified the U. S. constitution. In the Federalist (Dawson's ed., 302), Swiss public law and Swiss political history are appealed to in support of the excellence of "the domestic violence" provision of section 4. IV., of the new constitution. A parallel is made between Shays' rebellion in Massachusetts and similar events in Swiss Cantons.

Swiss publicists and legislators of the present day have given great attention to American constitutional law. An elaborate work by Prof. Rüttiman is a striking proof of this assertion. It compares in detail the law of the two federal systems, besides adding much relating to the constitutional law of the respective states of the two unions. It is entitled: The Public Law of the North American Federal Republic compared with the Political Institutions of Switzerland: Zurich, 1867, 1872, and 1876. (*Das nordamerikanische Bund sstaatsrecht verglichen mit den politischen Einrichtungen der Schweiz; von Professor Rüttiman.*)

The example of the constitution of the United States has been followed by the Swiss in what C. J. Marshall has declared to be its most marked characteristic. The federal constitution of the Swiss *Eidgenossenschaft* is a written one. It provides for a federal government capable of directly operating upon individuals and not restricted to indirectly doing so through the medium of the cantons or states. This system was introduced by the constitution of 1848 and continued by that of 1874. It is avowedly copied from the constitution of the United States.*

The federal government has three branches. The legislature is the Federal Assembly, which consists of two chambers. In one chamber the several cantons are equally represented, in the other the people of the several cantons are represented according to their respective numbers. The executive is the Federal Council, which consists of seven members. The judiciary consists of one supreme court, the Federal Tribunal. There are no inferior federal courts. The judges of the Federal Tribunal are appointed by the Federal Assembly for six years. They are nine in number. Care is taken that they represent the three legal languages. There are also nine substitute judges.†

---

* See 6 Wheaton, 388; *Von Orelli: Das Staatsrecht der schweizerischen Eidgenossenschaft*, p. 25, (in Marquardsen's series) Freiburg i. B., 1885.

†Adams and Cunningham on the Swiss Confederation, London, 1889. Chapters 3, 4, 5.

Sir F. M. Adams and Mr. C. D. Cunningham observe on their page 48:

"The separation of powers is not very strictly observed "between the Federal Assembly and the Federal Council "(nor, indeed, as mentioned in our chapter upon the Fed- "eral Tribunal, between the judicial authority and the two " political federal authorities)."

No. 2.

Of the Federal Tribunal and federal laws conflicting with the federal constitution.

The Federal Tribunal has a civil and a criminal jurisdiction and "also deals with questions of public law," (same work p. 68). Its organization and authority are the subject of articles 106 to 114 of the federal constitution. The last paragraph of article 113 is thus translated:

" In all these cases, however, the laws and generally ob- "ligatory resolutions passed by the Federal Assembly, and "also the treaties ratified by it, shall be binding for the "Federal Tribunal."

The Federal Tribunal is thus bound to obey and apply all laws of the Federal Assembly in all cases coming under its jurisdiction.

To an important extent the Federal Tribunal has jurisdiction of conflicts between the authorities of the confederation and those of the cantons. Prof. Von Orelli, in speaking of this disposition, calls attention to its resemblance to the model of the U. S. Constitution. He regrets, however, that, while in North America the tribunals of the Union decide upon the constitutionality of the laws of Congress, it is ordained in Switzerland that the laws and general resolutions of the Federal Assembly must be applied, without any such qualification, by the Federal Tribunal.*

---

*Von Orelli, 26, 27, 43. Adams and Cunningham, 73.

No. 3.

Of the relation between the cantonal constitutions and the federal constitution.

Thus the Federal Tribunal is not competent to decide the question whether a federal law be constitutional or unconstitutional. There can be no such judicial question. Neither can it be a judicial question whether the constitution of a canton contain any thing contrary to the constitution of the confederation. Such a question is extrajudicial and is decided by the Federal Assembly. Before the constitution of a canton or an alteration thereof can go into vigour, it must be subjected to the criticism and receive the consent of the Federal Assembly : (compare the final paragraph of section 9. I. of the U. S. constitution, which prescribes that no state shall, without the consent of Congress, enter into a compact with another state). The action of the Federal Assembly on a cantonal constitution appears to be final and so to bind the Federal Tribunal.*

No. 4.

Of the relation of the judiciary of a canton to a cantonal law conflicting with the cantonal constitution.

The judiciary of a canton are not competent to decide whether a cantonal law is or is not repugnant to the cantonal constitution. Such a question is not a judicial one. Mr. Vincent observes on his page 142 :

" Contrary to the practice of American courts, the Swiss " cantonal tribunal does not try acts of the legislature. No " court can set aside a statute because of disagreement with " a state constitution, because the legislature is regarded as " the final authority upon its own act."

*See, J. M. Vincent on State and Federal Government in Switzerland, Baltimore, 1891, page 34.

No. 5.

Of cantonal laws conflicting with the federal constitution.

The foregoing quotations naturally lead one to suppose that the cantonal judiciaries are not competent to decide the question whether a cantonal law is or is not repugnant to the federal constitution. Such a supposition is probably correct. Should, however, a cantonal court undertake to decide that a questioned cantonal law is federally constitutional, the result of an erroneous decision would be that a conflict must arise between the federal and the cantonal authorities. Over such conflicts the Federal Tribunal has jurisdiction. *Prima facie*, it would therefore seem, to an American, that in such case the Federal Tribunal would be called upon to decide the question whether such cantonal law is federally constitutional or unconstitutional and that such question would be a purely judicial one before it. On reflection, however, a foreigner will wait for a Swiss opinion on the matter. Meantime, he will reject such a conclusion, or accept it only with modifications. Further reflection will suggest that such a question would not necessarily arise as a purely judicial one before the Federal Tribunal. The Federal Assembly can pronounce upon the federal constitutionality of the part or the whole of a cantonal constitution, and it seems probable that it is also competent to pronounce upon the federal constitutionality of the whole or a part of a cantonal law. Supposing a resolution of the Federal Assembly to have decided that a cantonal law is or is not federally constitutional, such resolution must bind the Federal Tribunal according to article 113 of the constitution.

No. 6.

*Of a cantonal law conflicting with the federal guarantee
of the cantonal constitution.*

A law of a canton violating the constitution of the canton may raise a federal question. Such a law may be repugnant to the federal guarantee of the cantonal constitution provided for in articles 5 and 6 of the federal constitution. Both the Federal Council and the Federal Assembly have important powers and obligations relating to such guarantees: (Von Orelli 31, 34). It seems, therefore, possible that, before the Federal Tribunal could proceed in a case under such guarantee, the Federal Assembly might pronounce by federal resolution upon the question at issue. Such resolution would bind the Federal Tribunal according to the said article 113.

CHAPTER IX.

Of German law in connection with the subject of this Essay.

DIVISION A

Of conflicts between the laws of the German Empire and those of the several German states.

DIVISION B.

Of conflicts between the constitution and the laws of a German state.

DIVISION C.

Of the case of Garbade v. the State of Bremen.

DIVISION D.

Of the case of K. and others *v.* the Dyke Board of Niedervieland.

DIVISION E.

Further observations upon the two foregoing cases.

DIVISION F.

Of the court of the Imperial Chamber under the old German Empire.

Chapter IX. will be devoted to an investigation of German public law for light upon the relation of judicial power to unconstitutional legislation.

DIVISION A.

Of conflicts between the laws of the German Empire and those of the several German states.

No. 1. *Of the constitution of the present German Empire.*

No. 2. *Statement of the law concerning conflicts between the laws of the Empire and those of the several states.*

This division of this chapter will discuss one of the two kinds of conflicts of laws, whose constitutional nature has been ascertained according to German public law.

No. 1.

Of the constitution of the present German Empire.

The constitution of the German Empire is a written one, as was its predecessor the constitution of the North German *Bund*. The former was promulgated in 1871 and has been translated by Prof. James.* The latter was promulgated in 1867. A translation will be found in the Executive Documents of the U. S. Senate, cong. 40, sess. 2, no. 9.

Article 2. of the constitution of the Empire prescribes that "the Empire shall exercise the right of legislation accord-"ing to the provisions of this constitution; and the laws "of the Empire shall take precedence of those of each in-"dividual state;" (see James, page 18). This latter provision may be compared with the heading in lib. 1. tit. 3, § 4 in Lancelot's Institutes (often printed as an appendix to the Corpus Juris Canonici): *Inter discordantia concilia præponitur sententia ejus, quod est majoris auctoritatis.*

No. 2.

Statement of the law concerning conflicts between the laws of the Empire and those of the several states.

Conflicts between the laws of the German Empire and the laws of the several German states will now be considered. The following view of this head of German public law has been taken from Prof. Laband's Public Law of the German Empire (*Das Staatsrecht des Deutschen Reiches*); II, 119, 120, 120 notes, I. 266 note.

Every authority, either judicial or administrative, which has to apply points of law in the course of its official duties

---

* The Federal Constitution of Germany, with an Historical Introduction, translated by E. J. James, Philadelphia, 1890. (Publication of the University of Pennsylvania).

must ascertain what point is applicable to the particular case actually before it. If conflicting legal rules are contained in the legislation or other sources of law involved, it must be decided which of these sources governs the actual case according to fundamental principles of law, such as the precedence of a *lex specialis* over a *lex generalis*, or that of a *lex posterior* over a *lex prior*. Such a conflict may arise between a law of the Empire and a law of a state or land. As the constitution of the Empire is self-evidently one of the laws of the Empire,* the provision of its article 2d is plainly decisive, wherever such a conflict arises. By it, it is provided that the laws of the Empire take precedence over the laws of the lands. That is to say, such an authority as aforesaid, in its decision of the case before it, must not apply the rule of the law of its land, but the rule of the law of the Empire. The question whether a conflict between such laws exists, belongs, however, to the authority of highest rank in the particular department concerned. There is therefore a difference between " the position of the " courts and that of administrative officials. In regard to " the latter, the decision of an administrative superior is " binding upon subordinate officials and can be decisive for " them in other like cases. As to the courts, however, the " decision of the superior judicial tribunal only makes for- " mal law for the particular case. Contradictions between " the law of the Empire and the laws of the lands may not " only occur when one of the former prescribes a different " legal rule from one of the latter, but also when the Em- " pire has expressly or tacitly prohibited a legal rule exist- " ing in one of the laws of a land." The author adds here a foot-note: " In application of this principle, the " Court of Upper-Appeal at Dresden, by its declaration of " September 27th, 1872, declared the Royal Saxon ordinance " of December 10th, 1870, to be inoperative. An abroga- " tion of the ordinance was made in consequence." The author's text thus continues: " there exists, besides, the " right of the Empire to watch over the execution of the

---

* This coincides with the view hereinafter maintained that the constitution of the United States is one of the laws of the Union.

"imperial laws and to supervise the affairs enumerated in
"article 4th of its constitution. The operation of this
"power is not by the emperor, through his minister the im-
"perial chancellor, declaring the law of the land to be null,
"or by the Federal Council doing so, or by either of them
"interfering immediately with the official business of the
"authorities of the lands. The power operates upon the
"prince of the particular land, that is to say, upon the cen-
"tral government of the particular state, by a declaration
"to such state that the law enacted by it is inadmissible,
"and by a requisition for the due withdrawal thereof."
Two cases relating to this procedure are referred to in foot-
notes. The first is as follows :

At a session of the Federal Council of the German Empire
on February 27th, 1871, the chair made a communication
that a difference of opinion had arisen between the Federal
Chancery and the Senate of Bremen as to whether an ordinance of that state was in contradiction with an act of the
Empire. After the report of a standing committee, on the
following November 12th, the Federal Council resolved that
the ordinance was not in agreement with the views which
had led to the drafting of title 3d of the imperial act in its
present shape. Whereupon the plenipotentiary of Bremen
announced that the Senate of that state would abrogate
the ordinance.

In the second case, the Federal Council recognizea by resolution that the enactment of legislation by the particular
lands or states, upon certain expressly specified matters,
was not precluded by the existence of certain imperial legislation expressly mentioned.

Two points in the foregoing exposition will attract the
special attention of American lawyers :

First, that whenever a judicial court decides that a state
law conflicts with an imperial law and must therefore yield
thereto, its decision is so limited to the particular case that
it constitutes no precedent in the American sense :

Secondly, that such decision may, nevertheless, lead the
state to abrogate its conflicting law.

Since Prof. Laband's work was printed, the German Imperial Tribunal has decided two cases involving additional matter of interest. In October, 1887, in the case of the Prussian Tax-Fisc *v.* A. G. Company, it was decided that the existing stamp-tax legislation of a state was put out of vigour by the subsequent enactment of imperial stamp-tax legislation, but that the former was not *ipso jure* revived by the repeal of the latter. See Decisions of the *Reichsgericht* in Civil Causes, Vol. 19, p. 181.

In the case of the Imperial Military Fisc *v.* the Municipality of Gotha, in 1889, the Imperial Tribunal held as follows: the question of the existence of a judicial right of decision in respect of the constitutionality of the laws of the late North German *Bund* and the present German Empire is still contestable, although the affirmative thereof has been predominantly maintained : "*Allerdings ist die Frage, ob ein richterliches Prüfungsrecht in Ansehung der Verfassungsmaessigkeit von Bundes-bezw. Reichsgesetzen besteht, bis heute noch streitig, wenn schon solche ueberwiegend bejaht wird.*" Decisions of the *Reichsgericht* in Civil Causes, vol. 24, p. 3.

It is thus certain that the law of a state must yield whenever there is legally a conflict between it and the constitution or other law of the Empire and that in such conflict a judicial tribunal can and must decide accordingly. It is, however, still uncertain whether a judicial tribunal can decide upon the questioned constitutionality of a law of the Empire.

DIVISION B.

Of conflicts between the constitution and the laws of a German state.

The next head of German public law, connected with the subject, is that of a conflict between the state constitution and a state law in one of the several states of the Empire. It is here well to recall that, while most of the states of the German Empire are monarchies, three are republics, viz., the Hanseatic states of Bremen, Hamburg and Lubeck.

The quotation from Bluntschli's Public Law, previously given,* is authority for the proposition that, in 1863, in Germany, no judicial court could declare a law of its state to be void because conflicting with the written constitution of the state. That proposition was in 1883, and is since, equally true of the judiciaries of the several states of the German Empire. Between those two dates, however, two most interesting cases have been decided, in the first of which the truth of the proposition was denied with great ability by the Hanseatic Court of Upper Appeal at Lubeck. In the second case, the doctrine of the first was overruled by the Imperial Tribunal or supreme court of the German Empire. Thus with the exception of a temporary recognition within the limited territories of the Hanseatic republics, the proposition in question has always been law in the different states of Germany possessing written constitutions, that is to say, in nearly every German state.

DIVISION C.

Of the case of Garbade *v.* the State of Bremen.

The first case was decided in 1875. It is that of Garbade *v.* the state of Bremen and is reported in Seuffert's Archives for the Decisions of the Highest Courts of the German States, vol. 32, No. 101. The following is a translation of the decision of the Hanseatic Court of Upper Appeal, there given in the original:

"Positive directions like that of article 106 of the Prus-
"sian constitutional charter sometimes prohibit an official
"testing of the legal validity of ordinances [of the sovereign]
"which have been authenticated in due form. When such
"directions do not exist, the judge has, according to general
"legal principles, both the authority and the duty of refus-
"ing to apply an ordinance of the sovereign (*Landesherr*),
"which, while its provisions are those of a law, has not
"been enacted according to the forms prescribed for making

* See chapter 6, no. 2.

"laws by the constitution of the land. For this purpose,
"the judge must, of course, first of all examine whether,
"when the law in question was published it was then ex-
"plicitly stated that the constitutionally prescribed forms
"were observed. (See case in Kierulff's collection, vol. 5,
"p. 331.) The proper decision in such a case, however, de-
"pends only upon the question as to what evidence is suf-
"ficient to put the judge in a position of ascertaining with
"certainty that the constitutional forms for making laws
"were complied with. The decision itself, therefore, takes
"for granted that the judge must have no doubt as to
"the observance of the constitutionally prescribed forms in
"making the law in question, and when the decision has
"shown a condition of things, which prevents any such
"doubt, it goes no farther.

"It is thus true that, in cases of laws which are not or-
"ganic ones altering the constitution, the judge must be
"sure that the law, which he is to apply, has been made
"according to constitutional forms. Such being so, it must
"be equally true that the same requirement must be met
"in the case of organic laws altering the constitution, for,
"either a part or the whole of their provisions may enlarge
"or diminish existing rights as hitherto constituted. For
"the judge is as much bound by the organic constitutional
"law of the land as by any other law.* If therefore the
"observance of certain forms is constitutionally prescribed
"for changing a constitutional charter, it can only be al-
"tered or abolished by observing those forms. An ordi-
"nary law exists until it is abolished by way of legislation
"according to the forms prescribed for the enacting of laws.
"So too, a constitution exists until it is abolished by way
"of organic legislation according to the forms prescribed
"for changing the constitution. These points do not in-
"clude a further and a different question as to what are the
"conditions under which the judge must feel convinced

---

* This doctrine concerning a written constitution was put in print by Judge
Iredell, in his letter of an Elector, which was published at Newbern as early
as August 17th, 1786. See Life of James Iredell, vol. 2, page 148, line 14
et seq.

"that the requisite forms for altering the constitution have
"been observed. An answer to this question is not, how-
"ever, necessary in the case before us.

"That case is as follows:

" A constitution has been made in Bremen, the 19th arti-
"cle of which reads:

" '*Property and other private rights are inviolable.*
" '*Cession, surrender, or limitation of the same for the*
" '*general good can only be required in the cases and*
" '*forms prescribed by law and upon proper indemnifica-*
" '*tion.*'

" A law has been enacted in Bremen which is an ordi-
"nance relating to rural communities dated 28 December,
"1870. It conflicts with the said constitution and is not an
"organic constitutional law. Its 15th section reads thus:

" '*All hitherto existing exemptions from communal*
" '*taxes, so far as not based on federal laws or state*
" '*treaties, are abolished without indemnification.*'

" The last named law has been enacted according to the
"forms prescribed for ordinary legislation and therefore
"ought to be binding upon the judge. Nevertheless, if the
" forms prescribed for ordinary legislation are not sufficient
"for legislation altering the constitution, such an act of or-
"dinary legislation leaves the constitution intact. The
"latter continues to exist and, as long as it does so, the
"judge must hold it to be an existing law. Hereby arises
"a conflict of legal provisions. On account of the inequal-
"ity of the conflicting laws, this conflict can not be settled
"upon the principle of *lex posterior derogat legi priori.**
"It can only be settled by an application of the doctrine
"that ordinary laws conflicting with organic constitutional
"laws can not be enacted.

"The judge is to be considered competent to make this
"decision, even without any authority having been explic-
"itly given him by any special law; because he is obliged
"to apply the laws and because the application of two ex-
"isting laws, conflicting with each other, is an impossi-

---

* Compare Life of James Iredell, vol. 2, page 148, line 16 *et seq.*, and the
Federalist, page 543, in Dawson's edition.

"bility. The recognition of the legal principle, that the
"judge is not to apply a law conflicting with the constitu-
"tion, includes therefore no assertion of a superiority of
"the judge over the lawgiver.* So doing is merely an ac-
"knowledgment of his authority, in an actual case of con-
"flict, to apply that law, which general legal principles re-
"quire to be applied. In cases of conflict between laws of the
"Empire and laws of the land, there exists a written legal
"provision for the settlement thereof. In the case of a con-
"flict between laws, which are of different import but ema-
"nate from the legislative power of the same state, there
"enters the legal principle that ordinary laws must not con-
"flict with the provisions of the organic constitutional law.
"It may, perhaps, be objected that, when the legislative
"authorities have under forms of ordinary legislation, en-
"acted a law, which the judge deems to be in contradiction
"to the provisions of the constitution, those authorities
"have themselves previously considered the question
"whether such a contradiction exists. Granting this, how-
"ever, the resulting obligation of the judge, in such a case,
"does not extend beyond weighing carefully the reasons
"on both sides of the question in a way like that which he
"must follow in another and similar case. This other case
"is that in which he is compelled to declare, in opposition
"to the legislative authorities of a particular state, that a
"law made by them contradicts the laws of the Empire.

"Now the constitutional charter of Bremen, dated Feb-
"ruary 21st, 1854, in its article 67, establishes certain for-
"malities, by observing which, alterations of the constitu-
"tion can alone be made.† The observance of these for-
"malities in enacting the law of December 28th, 1870, would
"have been considered sufficient for the adoption of any
"law altering the constitution. According to the docu-
"ments before us, it can, however, by no means be admit-
"ted that this was done; there being no indication that, in

---

* Compare Life of James Iredell, vol. 2, page 148, line 27 *et seq.*, and the
Federalist, page 541, in Dawson's edition.

† That is to say, alterations of the written constitution of Bremen can only
be made in pursuance of itself.

"the case of the law of December 28th, 1870, any thing
"other than an act of ordinary legislation was in question.
"This being so, the result arrived at in the reasons given
"for the previous part of this judgment, including likewise
"the consequences deduced therefrom, directly follow as a
"matter of course."

In concluding this account of the judgment of the Hanseatic Court of Upper Appeal, it ought to be added that it
seems probable that that tribunal was greatly influenced by
the whole of Von Mohl's treatise on "Unconstitutional
Laws," and especially by its pages 79 and 80. See his
*Monographie ueber die rechtliche Bedeutung verfass-
ungswidriger Gesetze* in his work entitled, *Staatsrecht,
Voelkerrecht und Politik*, (Tuebingen, 1860), vol. 1, pages
66–95. Von Mohl was undoubtedly influenced by American ideas and writings, as pages 69 and 71 of the above
work prove. He expressly mentions the authors of the
Federalist, Story and Kent. He does not name Marshall
but must have been influenced by his views. Elsewhere he
expresses great admiration for the Chief Justice.

DIVISION D.

Of the case of K. and others *v.* the Dyke Board of Niedervieland.

The case of Garbade *v.* the State of Bremen was expressly
overruled, some eight years later, by the Imperial Tribunal.
This was done in the case of K. *v.* the Dyke Board of
Niedervieland, which was also a Bremen case. It is reported in the Decisions of the *Reichsgericht* in Civil Causes,
vol. 9, page 233. From the original report, the following is
partially abstracted and partially translated.

The suit was originally brought in the Land Court of Bremen by K. and other interested parties against the Dyke
Board of Niedervieland in the State of Bremen. Thence an
appeal was taken to the Superior Land Court of Hamburg in
second instance. Recourse in third and final instance was

then had to the *Reichsgericht* or supreme court of the German
Empire. The original plaintiffs, who were finally defendants,
claimed that their well-acquired rights, as commoners of a
swine pasture, had been violated by the Dyke Board proceeding under section 29 of the dyke ordinance of Bremen,
a state of the German Empire. That ordinance was an act
of ordinary legislation and its section 29 was alleged to be
in conflict with the provisions of the written constitution of
Bremen which prohibited legislation impairing well-acquired
rights of property.

On behalf of K. and the other commoners it was contended,
inter alia, that the said section of the dyke ordinance was
an invalid law because it conflicted with the constitution as
aforesaid. All the questions raised in the case were decided in favour of the Dyke Board. The constitutional
questions are, however, the only ones requiring mention
here. The following extracts are translated from the portion of the decision, which relates to the constitutional
branch of the case. This final judgment in third instance
was given on February 17th, 1883. In it the court of second
instance is alluded to as the court of appeal :

"The principle is maintained by the court of appeal that,
"when two interpretations of a law appear possible to a
"judge, one conflicting and the other not conflicting with
"the constitution, the former is simply to be rejected :
"and this is laid down universally and without limitation,
"(as is indicated by the court's use of the words ' *schon*
"*deshalb* '). So laid down, this principle can not be recog-
"nized as correct.

"When both the form of a law and the procedure of
"its enactment are not those prescribed for an alteration of
"the [written] constitution, it may happen that a particular
"interpretation thereof may according to the judge's view
"be in conflict with a principle of the constitution. Prop-
"erly, this circumstance must be considered only one of the
"reasons determining the interpretation of the law. It can
"only be a decisive one when, exclusive of it, the grounds
"for one or other of the two contradicting interpretations
"are equally balanced. The court of appeal contented

"itself with mentioning that the interpretation given in
"first instance by the Land Court to section 29 of the dyke
"ordinance was not one of actual necessity, although its
"view of the constitutional repugnancy of the section was
"based upon that interpretation. The court of appeal,
"therefore, attributed too great weight and significance to
"the interpretation made by the Land Court, while not
"holding the same merely in itself to be fully satisfactory.
"In so doing, the court of appeal overlooked weighty con-
"siderations, proper in seeking to ascertain the legislative
"will. Among these was, especially, that of the question
"as to what was the purpose of the law, and what value ac-
"cording thereto one interpretation had when compared
"with the other. The omission to consider that question
"further involved the loss of an available means of assist-
"ance which would otherwise have been obtainable.

". . . . . . . There remains to be considered only
"the question left undecided by the appellate court, namely,
"whether section 29 of the dyke ordinance shall be denied
"the force of binding law, because it is only an act of ordi-
"nary legislation, while the constitution is a law of a higher
"order. In a similar case, such denial was made by the
"formerly existing Court of Upper Appeal at Lubeck. (See
"Seuffert's Archives, vol. 32, No. 101*). This view, how-
"ever, can not be acceded to. On the contrary, the cor-
"rect view on this head is that which was taken by the
"same court in another case only a few years before. (See
"Kierulff's Collection, vol. 7, page 234). This correct view
"is as follows: the constitutional provision that well-
"acquired rights must not be injured, is to be understood
"only as a rule for the legislative power itself to interpret,
"and does not signify that a command given by the legis-
"lative power should be left disregarded by the judge be-
"cause it injures well-acquired rights.† This is said with-
"out affecting the question whether the state may or may

* The case of Garbade v. the State of Bremen previously given.

† That is to say, the text is addressed to the legislature and not to the judiciary, to use language modelled after that of C. J. Marshall in Marbury v.
Madison in 1 Cranch, page 179, paragraph beginning: "Here the language."

"not be bound to grant damages ; a matter not here brought
"into consideration.   There is, therefore, no occasion to in-
" vestigate whether well-acquired rights have been violated
"or not.   The question is not whether a particular principle
" of the constitution has been altered or not ; but whether
" the law could have been enacted without an alteration of
" the constitution itself, and therefore without applying the
" forms prescribed for such alteration.   This last question,
"however, is one which can not be examined by the
" judiciary." .   .   .   .

The case above mentioned in Kierulff's collection, vol. 7,
page 234, is that of Krieger *v.* the State of Bremen, decided
by the Hanseatic Court of Upper Appeal on June 15th, 1872.
On the page cited, the court declares it to be law that the
constitutional principle, which prohibits the injury of well-
acquired rights by legislation, is to be understood only as a
rule for the legislative power itself :   that it does not signify
that a command, which is given by the legislative power, is
to be disregarded by the judiciary because it injures well-
acquired rights.   This is said with a saving as to whether
the state may or may not be bound to grant remuneration
for the injury.

DIVISION E.

Further observation upon the two foregoing cases.

In order fully to appreciate the divergence of the two
foregoing decisions, it must be recollected that in the continental states of Europe the courts of law have not, as a
rule, the power to decide upon the legality or illegality of
the administrative acts of executive officials.   Such questions
seem to be regarded as matters of public right and so properly withheld from the courts, whose jurisdiction over civil
rights should not extend beyond private right.   It can
hardly be denied that every American lawyer, who holds
that judicial courts are competent to decide questioned laws
to be constitutional or unconstitutional, presupposes that

the same courts are competent to decide questioned executive acts to be legal or illegal. Indeed, it is safe to assert, that every American must ponder long before he can understand how a judiciary which can not question an executive act, can question an act of legislation. When judicial power was in America extended to cases arising under written constitutions, which involved the unconstitutionality and resultant invalidity of legislation, that extension was partially due to originality in creating new institutions and was partially the effect of existing causes. One of the most potent of existing causes must have been that the judges in every land of the Common law could decide upon the legality or illegality of the executive acts of officials. It has been said in France that judges should not be competent to decide laws to be unconstitutional because the judiciary is a feeble power. Doubtless, it is correct to say that the judiciary is a feeble power in France and other Civil law countries. But in all the lands of the Common law, whether in the Eastern, the Western, or the Southern hemisphere, the judiciary is not a feeble power, and never has been. The Common law judiciary grew and developed together with the trial by peers and by jury, and with a law of the land that bound the ruler of the land as well as the ruled thereof. Therefore in all Common law communities the judiciary is strong. Very different were the institutions amid which the existing judiciaries of the Civil law countries of Europe took form and shape. Therefore they are feeble. Continental princes and assemblies of estates were very different from kings and parliaments in England. Above all, on the European continent, the criminal tribunals were not courts of justice, but courts of injustice ; for, trial by torture, not trial by jury, was their rule. Consequently, it is not strange that written constitutions have been established in Common-law and Civil-law communities with different results as to the constitutional rights and duties of the judicial power.

DIVISION F.

Of the court of the Imperial Chamber under the old German Empire.

The following remark is translated from Bluntschli's work above mentioned, vol. I, p. 560 :

"In composite states there is an opportunity to provide "for the legislative power of the several states being held "within bounds by the judicial system. The federal or im- "perial constitution will possess organs for the maintenance "of law throughout the whole confederacy or empire, to "which the chief authorities of the several states are to a "certain extent subordinated. Such was the significance "of the Court of the Imperial Chamber in the later period "of the [former] German Empire. The Supreme Court of "the United States has, as we have seen, an extended com- "petency of this sort."

The Court of the Imperial Chamber above mentioned is referred to in the Federalist, No. 80,* and by Randolph in argument in Chisholm v. Georgia, 2 Dallas, 425, at dates when it was still in existence. In both instances such reference was made by a Framer of the constitution. The remarks in the Federalist are interesting in themselves and also in connection with those on the then existing institutions of the old German Empire in No. 19.†

In the Tuebingen *Zeitschrift* for Political Sciences, 1888, 44th year, p. 383, will be found an account of a case in the Imperial Chamber between the Baron of Frauenhofen, plaintiff, and the Elector of Bavaria, defendant. In it, the following were among the judicial questions arising for the decision of the court : whether the lordships of the Old and New Frauenhofen were free lordships held immediately of the Emperor and the Empire : whether the Elector of Bavaria and his ancestors had unduly claimed to bring those lordships under their territorial superiority and so into

---

* Dawson's Edition, page 554.

† Dawson's Edition, p. 119.

mediate and not immediate feudal relation to the Empire. Upon these questions it depended whether the Barons of Frauenhofen were or were not subjects of the Electors of Bavaria, as lords of the land. The case was a never-ending one. It lasted through generations and was not finally adjudicated, when the old Empire, and with it, the Court of the Imperial Chamber ceased to exist.

CHAPTER X.

Of the Roman law in connection with the subject.

DIVISION A.

Preliminary.

DIVISION B.

Of the law of rescripts in the classic period of the Roman jurisprudence.

DIVISION C.

Of the law of rescripts in Justinian's time.

DIVISION D.

Of certain points in the *jus legum* of the Roman republic.

This Chapter will begin the examination of the Roman law, for light upon the subject of this Essay.

DIVISION A.

Preliminary.

In the foregoing cases it will be observed that the *written* constitutions mentioned are all junior to the constitution of the United States. Any consideration of them, therefore, regards things unknown to the Framers. When their convention met in 1787, eleven states of the Union possessed written constitutions, two of which had been adopted in 1776 before July 4th, while the constitutions of the two remaining states were unwritten. Written constitutions were then still unknown abroad. They are now the rule, and not the exception, on the continent of Europe.

The chapters following will be concerned with unwritten constitutions, and, for the most part, with laws and systems older than the constitution of the United States. With those laws and systems, the Framers were, or may be presumed to have been, familiar.

The Roman law prevails on the continent of Europe and has a certain restricted vigour in England. The principles of the Roman law bearing upon the subject will first be investigated.

DIVISION B.

Of the law of rescripts in the classic period of the Roman jurisprudence.

Under this branch of the investigation, the law of rescripts as developed in Rome during the earlier empire will first be considered.

At a period when the world-embracing legislative power of the emperors and a renowned jurisprudence existed together in Rome, the law of rescripts was as follows, if the writer has correctly understood the exposition in Weiske's *Rechtslexicon*, IX, pages 285, 286.

Rescripts were laws, but there was an important distinction between "them and other laws." In imperial edicts, as in the former republican *leges*, the legislative will undoubtedly laid down general propositions of law, and there was rarely any doubt as to who was bound thereby. The regular interpretation thereof was confined to the subject of the meaning of the law so laid down. In the case of rescripts, however, all this could be doubtful and often was so. The legal effect of a rescript, as a whole, depended upon interpretation. Whether it was to be held general legislation or not, depended upon the special interpretation of jurisconsults or *prudentes*, who could and did use freedom of judicial judgment in their official responses thereupon. A rescript was not necessarily authority for a generally binding proposition of law. Interpretation must decide whether or not the imperial disposition was based upon a legal rule of general application. Frequently, the disposition made in an act of the emperor was appropriate only to a particular case and its extension to other cases was not intended by the prince. Such acts were called personal constitutions: *Dig. lib. 1. tit. 4. l. 1. § 2.* Hence when a rescript, which might or might not be a personal constitution, was adduced as authority for a rule of law, recourse was in some cases had to legal reasons other than its authority in order to establish the rule, so that thereby all doubt might be removed concerning its vigour as an act of general legislation. In other cases, a like free judgment was exercised, in order to prove that a doubtful rescript was a personal constitution and so without vigour as general legislation. "Rescripts, which undoubtedly laid down a "generally applicable proposition of law, could be termed "*generalia rescripta* in opposition to *personalia*, and the "expression was actually used in that sense." (*Dig. lib. 35. tit. 2. l. 89. § 1; Dig. lib. 26. tit. 4. l. 1. § 3; Dig. lib. 28. tit. 5. l. 9. § 2.*)

If the above be correct, it is true that in Rome, at a certain date, official jurisconsults or *prudentes* were competent to decide the question whether an imperial rescript was a general or personal constitution, and, according to their decision of that question, a given rescript, if decided to be general, was held to be binding in all cases ; but, if personal, then to be binding only in the particular case. This last was not, indeed, holding a legislative act to be void, but it was holding that a legislative act was void of vigour in all cases except one.

The following references may be added to the above given : *Inst. lib. 1. tit. 2. § 8 ; Gaii Inst. I. 5, 7.*

DIVISION C.

Of the law of rescripts in Justinian's time.

The law of rescripts, in the shape in which it is found in the code of Justinian, next requires consideration. Normally, these rescripts were binding only in the particular cases for which they were made. A rescript of this sort had only the vigour of a law between the parties thereto. It did not have the vigour of a general law. Such is the proper interpretation of the passage in Justinian's Institutes, lib. 1. tit. 2. § 6 : *quodcumque ergo imperator per epistolam constituit, vel cognoscens decrevit, vel edicto præcepit, legem esse constat.* See Reiffenstuel's *Jus Canonicum*, ed. 1864, vol. I. page 217.

Upon this portion of the law of Justinian, two texts of the code will be examined. The first is *Cod. lib. 1. tit. 22. 1. 6.*, where it is said : " We admonish all judges of every "administration, greater or less, in our whole common-"wealth that in the trial of every sort of litigation, they "permit no rescript, no pragmatic sanction and no imperial "adnotation to be alleged before them, which seems to be "adverse to general law or to public utility : but that they "have no doubt that general imperial constitutions are to " be observed in every way." *Omnes cujuscunque majoris vel minoris administrationis universæ nostræ reipublicæ judices monemus : ut nullum rescriptum, nullum pragmaticam sanctionem, nullum sacram adnotationem, quæ generali juri vel utilitati publicæ adversa esse videatur, in disceptationem cujuslibet litigii patiantur proferri : sed*

generales sacras constitutiones modis omnibus non dubi-
tent observandas.

By this text, when any rescript of the emperor was pleaded in a court, the judge must pass upon the question whether it was or was not adverse to general law or to public utility. If it were so adverse, the judge must reject it. That is to say, the rescript was then invalid ; which term is suggested by the words *non valeant* found in another text, *Cod. lib. 1. tit. 19. l. 4.*, containing a general constitution prescribing that certain rescripts *non aliter valeant* than upon a particular condition. It will be observed that while the text requires judges to weigh well the admission of rescripts, it prescribes that they must have no doubt about observing all general constitutions.

The second text is *Cod. lib. 1. tit. 19. l. 7.* which says : " We command that rescripts which are obtained from us "*contra jus* shall be rejected by all judges unless perchance "there be something therein which injures not another and " profits him who seeks it, or gives pardons for crime to " the suppliants." *Rescripta contra jus elicita, ab omnibus judicibus refutari præcipimus : nisi forte sit aliquid, quod non lædat alium, et prosit petenti, vel crimen supplicantibus indulgeat.*

By this text it appears that a judge must pass upon the question whether or not a rescript has been obtained *contra jus*, certain specified cases excepted. If it be judicially ascertained to have been obtained *contra jus*, it must be rejected, that is to say, be held invalid.

It thus appears that, according to the Code of Justinian, an imperial judge might decide a rescript of the emperor to be contrary to general law or to public utility, or to be obtained *contra jus*. When the judge so decided against the rescript, he held it invalid. When, however, the judge's decision was in favour of the rescript, it had the vigour of a written *lex* within the legal limits restricting the operation of such legislation and was judicially applied in a case within those limits.

DIVISION D

Of certain points in the *jus legum* of the Roman Republic.

It is here necessary to repeat that this investigation relates only to cases in which a judicial tribunal consisting of either one or several judges, can hold a law to be wholly or partially void, because of reasons judicially ascertained and decided. The investigation does not, therefore, include within its limits those acts of the Roman senate by which it judged that challenged laws were nullities. Some mention thereof will, however, be useful.

A *lex* was a written law constituted by the lawfully assembled people upon the rogation of a magistrate. No private person could move the people to legislate. In certain contingencies the senate could decide whether a challenged enactment was or was not a law. When so doing, its decisions were made according to the *jus legum* or law of laws. Such decisions *de jure legum* are adverted to in Cicero's oration for his house before the pontiffs.

In his oration, Cicero maintained that the enactment by which he was banished was no law : *legem quidem istam nullam esse.** It had been abrogated,† but he maintained that it was a nullity from the beginning for divers reasons. One was that it had been passed upon the rogation of Clodius as tribune. Such a rogation was a nullity, for that pseudo-plebeian was incompetent to be tribune.‡

In chapters 26 and 27 Cicero says "for as often as the "senate said sentence concerning me, so often it judged "that that law was null, since by that writing of that man "[Clodius] it was prohibited from saying any sentence. " . . . . The senate, whose judgment is most weighty "concerning the law of laws, as often as it rendered an "opinion concerning me, so often judged that the same was

---

* Oration, cap. 26.

† Ersch & Grueber : article Cicero, 197, *cf.* 196.

‡ Oration, cap. 13 to cap. 16.

"null." *Nam legem quidem istam nullam esse, quotiens-cumque de me senatus sententiam dixit, totiens judicavit: quoniam quidem scripto illo istius sententiam dicere veta-batur. . . . Senatus quidem, cujus est gravissimum judi-cium de jure legum, quotienscumque de me consultus est, totiens eam nullam esse judicavit.*

The precedent of the nullity of the laws of Marcus Dru-sus, is mentioned by Cicero in chapter 16. The Senate had judged that the people were not bound by the laws of M. Drusus, which had been made contrary to the Caecilian and Didian law: *sin eadem observanda sunt, judicavit senatus M. Drusi legibus, quae contra legem Caeciliam et Didiam latae essent, populum non teneri.*

The *lex Caecilia et Didia* was a portion of the *jus legum* which prohibited the proposal of any law containing two or more matters not germane.* It may be compared with the similar legislations in some American constitutions, which have been caused by the so-termed "omnibus laws."†

It should be remarked that when Cicero said that the senate's *judicium de jure legum* was most weighty, he used the word *judicium* in a sense not judicial.

This power of the senate was distinct from its power of legislating by *senatus-consulta*. Ortolan observes that Maintz has shown that the pretended right of abrogating laws, which Asconius attributes to the senate, is nothing else than the right of testing the obligatory force thereof.‡

In connection with the subject of this Essay, it may be remarked that the study of the Roman *jus legum* teaches a very important constitutional lesson. It was intended to regulate the legislative power of the Roman people. There are thinkers who believe that the best polities are those that have a legislature which is governed exclusively by its own will. Such a view is at variance both with the unwritten

---

* See Smith's Dictionary of Antiquities, article *lex*, pages 559, 561.

† A colonial example of royal objection to such legislation will be found in the instructions to the Governor of North Carolina, dated December 14th, 1730. See Saunders's Colonial Records of North Carolina, vol. 3, page 94, no. 15.

‡ Ortolan : *Législation Romaine*, ed. 11, vol. 1. No. 289, text and notes.

republican constitution of Rome and with the written republican constitutions of America.

The Roman people legislated in original assembly. Representative assemblies of legislators were unknown in antiquity. The *jus legum* was the *jus populi* also.* It used
both law and religion to regulate the legislative power of
the Roman people and to govern them in the exercise
thereof. The augurs, as representatives of religion, were
habitually consulted in the course of legislation. It is said
that the Roman augurs sometimes laughed in secret on
solemn occasions. They are not the only persons connected
with legislation, that have scandalized religion. Modern
legislators have sometimes done so by violating their oaths.

There are resemblances, as well as differences, between
the legal restrictions upon the legislative power of the Roman people under the republican constitution, and the legal
restrictions upon the legislative power of a representative
assembly under a written constitution. Thus the resemblance between the *lex Caecilia et Didia* and constitutional
clauses against "omnibus laws" is quite a remarkable one.
But the differences between the Roman republican constitution and American written constitutions do not prevent
them uniting in teaching the same lesson, *viz.*, that the best
legislature is not one exclusively governed by its own will.
The generation which framed and ratified the constitution
of the United States learned that lesson well, as is proved
by Iredell's paper written in 1786 and reprinted in chapter
26, *post.* Had they not learned it, the constitution of the
United States would never have existed. Some different
instrument of union would have been made. It would have
been one adapted to a union between states having parliaments uncontrolled by written constitutions.

The constitution of the United States contains a law
of laws which binds senators and representatives in legislating as much as the Roman *jus legum* bound the Roman
people in legislating. In some cases this law of laws is expressed in clear terms by the constitutional text, *e. g.*, the

---

* See Cicero *pro Domo*, cap. XV, at the end.

Congress shall make no law for the establishmen, of religion. In other cases it is not expressly written. One of the most remarkable peculiarities of this constitutional *jus legum* is that it binds judges in deciding as well as legislators in legislating. This peculiarity is intimately connected with the subject of this Essay. Does the constitution express or imply the truth that its *jus legum*, which binds legislators in legislating, also binds judges in deciding? According to the chief contention of this Essay, the constitution expresses that truth and does not merely imply it.

CHAPTER XI.

Further consideration of the relation of the Roman law to the subject.

DIVISION A.

Of the views of the Civilian Bowyer on the constitution of the United States.

DIVISION B

Of the Roman law of mandate and the delegation of legislative power.

DIVISION C.

Of Vattel's doctrine concerning legislative power and the relation thereof to the Roman law of mandate, on one hand, and to American constitutions, on the other.

Chapter XI. will further consider the relation of the Roman law to the subject. The next matter concerning that law requiring examination is a general one. It is this : Do the general principles of the Roman or Civil law raise any presumption contrary to the propriety of judges criticising a law made under a written constitution, in order to ascertain whether it is actually constitutional or unconstitutional and valid or void accordingly ?

DIVISION A.

Of the views of the Civilian Bowyer upon the constitution of the United States.

In this connection the views of the English Civilian Bowyer may be referred to with much edification. His works contain sympathetic appreciations of the constitution of the United States which are made from the point of view of one familiar with both American works upon constitutional law and Civilian works upon public law. In discussing American views upon the " right of the courts to pro-"nounce legislative acts void, because contrary to the con-"stitution," he-is of opinion that " this doctrine is strictly "in accordance with the principles of public law. The act "of a delegated authority contrary to the commission or "beyond the commission under which it is exercised, is "void. Therefore no legislative act, contrary to the consti-"tution, can be valid." In support of this proposition, his authority is the text of the Roman law, *Dig. lib. 17. tit. 1. l. 5 :* " *Diligenter fines mandati custodiendi sunt : nam* "*qui excessit, aliud quid facere videtur.*" ("The limits "of a mandate are to be diligently preserved ; for he who "has exceeded them is deemed to do something other "than that in the mandate.") Bowyer : Universal Public Law, 343, 344.

In his Readings in the Middle Temple in 1850, pages 82, 83, Bowyer also discusses the same subject. He observes : " We may safely say that the federal government ot the

"United States could not long exist without the extraordi-
"nary jurisdiction which we are now examining. . . . .
"The act of a delegated authority, contrary to the commis-
"sion or beyond the commission under which it is exercised,
"is void. *Diligenter fines mandati custodiendi sunt: nam*
"*qui excessit, aliud quid facere videtur.* He who acts be-
"yond his commission acts without any authority from it.
"Now the judicial power can declare void the acts of the
"legislative power where those acts are beyond the dele-
"gated power of the legislature, and therefore not legisla-
"tive acts except in form only. . . . . . . These con-
"stitutional questions are cases of conflict between a funda-
"mental law and an ordinary act of the legislature, in which
"the judges must be governed by the fundamental law.
" . . . . . Thus the ordinary statutes of the United
"States are *lex sub graviori lege.*"

The grave importance of this application of the Roman
law requires it to be remembered that the text of the Roman
law in question (*Dig. lib.* 17. *tit. 1. l. 5*) relates to matter
of private right and that Bowyer applies it to matter of public right. There is, however, important authority for the
application of the rules and principles of mandate to public law. This is expressly stated by Bowyer himself, in his
work upon the Civil Law, pp. 225, 226, 227. This he does
upon the authority of publicists whose writings were familiar to the Framers of the constitution: Vattel, IV, 5,
par. 56; Puffendorf, III, 9, par. 2; Grotius, II, 2, par. 12;
II, 21, par. 1; III, 22, par. 4, No. 2.

DIVISION B.

Of the Roman law of mandate and the delegation of legislative power.

The cases from Vattel, Puffendorf, and Grotius may be
deemed conclusive as to the application of the Roman principles of mandate to public as well as to private law upon
one condition, namely, that a power to legislate is such a
one as can be given by a mandate. All the cases just re-

ferred to relate to other descriptions of public powers. The question, therefore, arises whether according to the Roman law a power of legislation could be given by mandate. To this question an affirmative answer can be given.

During the republican period, the legislative power belonged to the Roman people. By a process of revolution they lost it and the Roman emperor became lawgiver. But the legal view differed from the historical view. In notion of law, the emperor derived his title to his legislative power from the Roman people. They were held to have granted to him by a law, called the *lex regia*, the *imperium* and *potestas* belonging to themselves. See *Inst. lib. 1. tit. 2. § 6, Gaii Inst. I. 5, Dig. lib. 1. tit. 4. l. 1.* Even if no *lex regia* was in fact enacted, the notion of its existence was accepted as true by lawyers and others including the people themselves. If this notion was erroneous, it is not the only great case in history in which the official statement concerning fundamental legislation is erroneous.

Bowyer points out that, although the *lex regia* was apochryphal, yet the assertion of such a delegation of sovereign power to the emperor by the people, makes it evident that the Roman law did not attribute a divine origin to the imperial authority.[*]

The eminent historian, Prof. Mommsen, has examined the Roman law of legislation under mandate. His treatise on the *Lex* for Salpensa and the *Lex* for Malaca contains important observations relating to the emperor's power of legislation.[†] The correct legal view, he holds, is that it was based on the *lex regia* and was a power of legislation given by the mandate of the people to the emperor. Mandates delegating legislative powers had existed in the republican period. Legislation by the Roman people, he terms immediate. That made by virtue of a mandate to exercise legislative power, he terms mediate legislation.

Among the questions which Mommsen had occasion to discuss are two here requiring notice. One is whether a

[*] Bowyer's Civil Law, page 29.

[†] In the Proceedings of the Royal Saxon Society of Sciences, vol. 3, pages 390 *et seq.*

single individual could receive the delegation of such legislative power. This he answers in the affirmative. The other
is whether the term *lex* was ever applied to any of the
acts of legislation enacted by such an individual. This
second question he answers affirmatively also. Examples
of *leges* mediately enacted are stated to be found in the republican period in cases in which the Roman people granted
to a magistrate having *imperium*, (who was usually a military commander-in-chief), either the legislative power of
giving the right of citizenship to foreigners, or the power of
enacting legislative regulations for dependent communities
or provinces. A more ancient example is found in the power
of a Roman citizen to make his testament in the cases in
which the proceeding by mancipation was used.* This
power was based upon a general mandate given by the
twelve tables to every individual citizen respectively to enact mediately a *lex* in a case in which the popular *curiae*
had previously done so immediately.

That the emperor had included in the legislative power
delegated to him individually the right to legislate for a
dependency such as *Malaca* in the form of a *lex* and to do
so without innovating, is held to have been unquestionable in
point of law. "Just as a *judicium* could proceed from *im-*
"*perium* given by mandate as validly as from original *impe-*
"*rium*, so a *lex* could proceed from power of legislation given
"by mandate as validly as from original legislative power.
"The technical term for passing mediate legislation is *legem*
"*dare*, as that for passing immediate legislation on rogation
"of the people is *legem rogare:* so that our municipal law
"is termed a *lex data*. In this shape, the mediate legisla-
"tion by the emperor continued to be exercised for making
"grants of citizenship and conceding municipal rights, long
"after the immediate legislation by the people had become
"antiquated."

Recurrence may now be had to Sir George Bowyer's opinion concerning the constitution of the United States. He
holds that its system of legislative and judicial powers is

---

* See *Gaii Inst. II.* 101, 102, 103.

strictly in accordance with the principles of public law involved, which are based upon the Roman law of mandate.
It is not a good objection to Bowyer's position to say that
the principles of mandate must be restricted to cases of private law and private powers, and cannot be extended to
cases of public law and governmental powers. Ample authority has been shown to exist for the extension of the
Roman principles of mandate to cases of public law and
governmental powers, including power of legislation.

Besides general reasons, a special one exists for the foregoing defence of the application of the legal principles of
mandate to matters of public law. In the case of the State
of Georgia *v.* Stanton, Grant and Pope, 6 Wallace 50–78,
the U. S. Supreme Court decided that the judicial power
does not extend to cases arising under the constitution and
laws of the United States, in which the rights in danger are
merely political rights. It extends only to cases arising
thereunder in which the rights in danger are those of person and property. This distinction between political rights
and rights of person and property has considerable resemblance to the distinction between public and private law and
that between private and governmental powers. The resemblance is, indeed, great enough for the foregoing discussion of the law of mandate to require no other justification.

DIVISION C.

Of Vattel's doctrine concerning legislative power and the relation thereof to the Roman law of mandate, on the one hand, and to American constitutions, on the other.

Thus, according to the Roman law, the principles of mandate can, with propriety, be applied to legislative as well
as to other powers.

No objection can, therefore, be made to Bowyer's views
of the U. S. constitution on the ground that he errs in his
views of Roman law.

Some readers may, however, object that Bowyer erroneously attributes to the framers and ratifyers of the constitution certain views which have a Roman law origin and were foreign to their intentions and purposes.

Any such objection would be an erroneous one.

The legal history of American constitutions is in harmony with the foregoing exposition of the application of the Roman law of mandate to public powers.

Vattel, in discussing the legislative power of a state and the authority of those entrusted with it, raises the question whether their power extends as far as to the fundamental laws, so that they may change the constitution of the state. He maintains, "that the authority of these legislators does "not extend so far, and that they ought to consider the "fundamental laws as sacred, if the nation has not, in very "express terms, given them the power to change them. "For the constitution of the state ought to be fixed : and "since that was first established by the nation, which after-"wards trusted certain persons with the legislative power, "*the fundamental laws are excepted from their commis-*"*sion. . . . . . In short, these legislators derive their* "*power from the constitution ; how then can they change it,* "*without destroying the foundation of their authority ?*"*

This doctrine of Vattel as to the commissions of legislators applied the Roman principles of mandate to every constitution and was published before written constitutions existed.† On the one hand, thus related to the Roman law, it is on the other intimately connected with the early American decisions rejecting statutes as void because unconstitutional.

In 1786 in Rhode Island in the great historical case of Trevett v. Weeden, the Civilian publicist's words are quoted and applied by Varnum in his argument, pages 24, 25, 26, as hereinafter more fully explained.‡

---

* Vattel, book 1, cap. 3, sec. 34.

† Vattel died in 1767. As a jurist he was of course a civilian. As a pub licist, he was the fourth of a series, of which Grotius, Puffendorf and Wolff were the preceding three. See *Nouvelle Biographie Générale* and *Encyclopædia Britannica* under his name.

‡ See Varnum's pamphlet on Trevett v. Weeden, pages 24, 25, 26, and chapter 25, *post*, on the case.

In 1787 in North Carolina, in the great historical case of
Bayard *v.* Singleton, the Superior Court of that state, without naming Vattel, applies his doctrine, in saying that the
general assembly could not alter or repeal the constitution
without destroying their existence as a legislature.† In
Vanhorne *v.* Dorrance in 1795, Judge Patterson strongly
applies Vattel's doctrine in his charge to a U. S. jury but
without naming him : See 2 Dallas page 308. Judge Wood-
bury's opinion in Luther *v.* Borden, 7 Howard 66, links
Patterson and Vattel together and re-asserts their opinions.

On page 541 of the Federalist (Dawson's edition), it is
said in very general terms but without citation of authority :

"There is no position which depends on clearer princi-
"ples, than that every act of a delegated authority, con-
"trary to the tenor of the commission under which it is ex-
"ercised, is void. No legislative act, therefore, contrary
"to the constitution, can be valid."

Vattel is the link connecting this doctrine of the Federalist with the Roman law of mandate.

Thus it is shown that Bowyer was justified in attributing,
to the framers and ratifyers of the constitution, views,
which had a Roman law origin and were interwoven with
their intentions and purposes. His regarding the constitution from a Roman law point of view has not led him into
historical error as to the ideas involved in the frame of the
constitution.

Before legislation under a constitution can be held void
according to the above mentioned doctrine, it must be ascertained and decided to be contrary to the constitution. Some
jurists have maintained that the question, whether legislation be according or contrary to a constitution, must be an
extrajudicial question. Others have maintained that it
may be a judicial question. Such a difference of opinion
can only exist under a particular constitution, when its text
is silent upon the question whether the previous question is
a judicial or an extrajudicial one. When the text is not
silent and makes the question a judicial one, men may dif-

† See Martin's Reports, first division, 50, and second edition, 1. 45, and chapter 26, *post* on the case.

fer as to the wisdom of the framers of such a constitution, but not as to the *jus legum* under it.

The foregoing doctrine does not conflict with that of Mr. Cooley, according to which legislative power can not be delegated.* What is there really meant is not the delegation, but the subdelegation, of legislative power by a legislature under a written constitution. By the Roman law, whenever a *jurisdictio mandata* was given by legislation to a magistrate, he could not transfer it. Whatever inherent jurisdiction a magistrate had in right of his office, he could transfer by mandate to another proper person. That is to say, a magistrate could delegate his inherent jurisdiction, but could not subdelegate his delegated jurisdiction: See *Dig. lib. 1. tit. 21. l. 1.* Mr. Cooley's doctrine as to the subdelegation of legislative power, be it correct or incorrect, resembles this Roman doctrine as to the subdelegation of jurisdiction.

CHAPTER XII.

Of the Canon law and its relation to the subject.

No. 1. *Of the partition of power between church and state, or the division into spiritual and temporal powers.*

No. 2. *Account of a case in the Court of the Rota Romana in 1648, in which legislation of the Republic of Genoa concerning testaments was held null because judicially ascertained and decided to be contrary to the liberty of the church.*

No. 3. *Of the texts of the Corpus Juris Canonici concerning the nullity of temporal legislation affecting the rights of the church.*

---

* Constitutional Limitations, Ed. 1, 116 ; Ed. 2, 139.

No. 4. *Of a case before the Court of the Rota Romana in
1638, in which it was held that the legislative acts of two
popes, as temporal princes, were not to be accounted good
against a third party, because they were decided to be prejudicial to his well-acquired right under a contract.*

Chapter XII. will be devoted to a general consideration of
the Canon law in connection with the subject. By a general consideration is meant one not confined to the working
of the Canon law in a particular state. A special consideration of the Canon law in England will be made in the subsequent chapter.

No. 1

*Of the partition of power between church and state, or
the division into spiritual and temporal powers.*

The consideration of the subject in connection with the
Canon law is concerned with matter of the highest importance, for it involves an investigation of the partition of power
between church and state, or the division into spiritual and
temporal powers. This division of the powers by which
society was governed was the constitution of Europe for
centuries. The Canon law was thus part of the constitutional law of every land of the Roman obedience, including
England, before the Reformation.

The whole weight of the jurisprudence of the Canon law
is thrown in favour of the doctrine that a law, which is made
by a legislature or lawgiver without proper power, is null
and void. Centuries ago, in the states and countries where
the Latin church prevailed, the Canon law authorities felt
compelled to assume this position. They, doubtless, thought
it necessary in order that the partition of power between
church and state, or the division into spiritual and temporal

powers, should be a living reality, and that the Latin church in Western Europe should escape a dependency upon the state like that of the Greek church in the Greek Empire.

The following case in the Court of the Rota Romana was decided in 1648 and explains the doctrine upon the subject. It was one concerning Roman lands arising under the testament of Antonia Spinola, a citizen of the Republic of Genoa. The following account is translated and abridged from the *Decisiones Recentiores* of the Rota Romana, part 10, decision 231. As some may prefer the full original text of the decision, it is inserted in Appendix No. 2. to this Essay.

No. 2.

Account of a case in the Court of the Rota Romana in 1648, in which legislation of the Republic of Genoa was held null because judicially ascertained and decided to be contrary to the liberty of the church.

Among other hereditary property which had belonged to the deceased Antonia Spinola of Genoa were certain mountain places of pasture, which had been detained by her brother, Francis Spinola, as her heir *ab intestato*. The pastures were situate in Roman territory. Whereupon, John Baptist dei Franchi, the heir written in her testament, brought suit in the court of the Roman Rota. The cause was introduced before Cerri, Dean and one of the auditors of the Rota. John Baptist asked for a mandate of immission into possession. This, Francis contended should be denied, making the two defences following.

First, because the testament of Antonia did not have the lawful number of witnesses, having been made with only five. Seven witnesses in all were rightfully required according to *Inst. lib. 2. tit. 10. § 14*, and if one were wanting, the testament was bad by *Cod. lib. 6. tit. 23. l. 12.*

Secondly, because the statute of Genoa, in the rubrick concerning testaments and last wills in chapter 12. of its book 1., prohibited Genoese subjects from making any priest or clerical man a testamentary executor, or fideicommissary, under penalty of the testament being null *quoad hoc*. Wherefore, as John Baptist was a clerical man, the testament was of no validity as to him.

Notwithstanding these things it was resolved that the immission into possession should be given to John Baptist, because it was not controverted that the mountain pastures were the hereditary property of Antonia, and because a testament was exhibited which was neither obliterated, nor cancelled, nor subject to suspicion in any part, according to *Cod. lib. 6. tit. 33. l. 3.*

The first objection was decided to be without force, because the statute of Genoa under the same rubrick made a disposition, which prescribed that a testament, or last will, should be firm and valid, when proved by a public instrument in which five witnesses were described. Wherefore, as in the testament in question there were found five witnesses, its validity and subsistence could not be impugned. The statute could diminish the number of witnesses required by the Civil law ; a proposition for which authorities are given.

Moreover, it could not be maintained that the aid of such a statutory disposition must be excluded because the testament was made in the church of the Society of Jesus at Genoa, which was a place exempted from the jurisdiction of the enactors of the Genoese statute. This would be so, if the matter concerned " an odious statute," requiring greater solemnities than were required by the Civil law. But it was otherwise, when the question related to "a favourable statute," which diminished the solemnities of the Civil law. Authorities on these heads are given.

The second objection of the defence was also decided to fall to the ground, for the following reasons. That part of the statute of Genoa, upon which it relied, deprived clerical men of a faculty belonging to them by the dispositions of both the Civil law and the Canon law: *Cod. lib. 1. tit. 3. 56. § 1. ; Decretal. lib. 3. tit. 26. c. 9. & 19.* Its enactors spoke in restrictive, prescriptive and prohibitive words directed against persons, and making express mention of clerical men. *The statute in this part was judicially held to be null in the following remarkable words ·*

"*as contrary to ecclesiastical liberty it is null* ipso "facto et jure *from defect of the power of the laymen en-* "*acting it:* TANQUAM CONTRA LIBERTATEM ECCLESIASTICAM " EST NULLUM IPSO FACTO ET JURE EX DEFECTU POTESTATIS " LAICORUM STATUENTIUM."

Numerous authorities are given in support of this declaration of the law, which cover citations from twenty doctors of Canon law. They are classified into such as support it when the lay statutes do either of three things: (1), when they deprive clerical men of what is by law conceded to them; (2), when they are preceptive, restrictive or prohibitive as to clerical men; (3), when their dispositions make express mention of clerical men and churches, even when they so do favourably and by way of granting privileges.

Such, as well, was the law, if the active and prohibitive words of the statute should seem not to be directed against the persons of clerical men, but against the person of the testator. As had been said, there was contrariety to ecclesiastical liberty when the statute either deprived clerical men of a benefit belonging to them by law or made express mention of them as above mentioned. It sufficed that the statute, by prohibiting executory competency virtually and indirectly as against the persons of clerical men, so touched and injured them, for it to be of no strength and firmness (*ut inde nullius sit roboris, et firmitatis*). Laymen could not legislate concerning ecclesiastical persons nor concerning their property, either directly or indirectly, because the same were not under their jurisdiction. For these propositions authorities are given.

John Baptist had availed himself of the disposition of one part of the Genoese statute which made the testament valid with only five witnesses. This did not impose upon him any obligation to accept the other part of the statute which provided that clerical men should not be constituted fideicommissaries, or testamentary executors. These propositions are considered fully and authorities supporting them are adduced. Furthermore, a critical examination of the terms of the testament supported the conclusion that the testatrix must be held to have made a disposition *ad pias causas.* Such a disposition could be sustained by two witnesses only, as the adduced authorities showed.

The law of the decision as to lay statutes was that of the whole court, whose membership was large. All its members, too, agreed to the justice of the resolution giving John Baptist the mandate of immission into possession of the mountain places. In consultation, however, a minority of two lords of the court considered that the terms of the Genoese statute should be construed in a more restricted manner than had been done. They thought that it prohibited only executory competency, and should not be extended to John Baptist's case, who was heir written in the testament. Further, that the prohibitions of the statute related only to the execution of profane matters. Such a disposition would not be contrary to ecclesiastical law, which prescribes that clerical men should not take part in lay business.

In concluding the account of this decision, a selection from the editor's summary or head notes will be given.

"8. A statute contrary to ecclesiastical liberty is *ipso "jure* null" : *Statutum contra libertatem ecclesiasticam est ipso jure nullum.*

"9. A statute made by laymen even favourable to clerical "men and to the church is *ipso jure* null" : *Statutum etiam clericis, et ecclesiae favorabile, conditum a laicis est ipso jure nullum.*

"10. That a lay statute may be of no strength and mo- "ment, it suffices that it touch and injure clerical men only "virtually and indirectly" : *Statutum laicale ut nullius sit roboris, et momenti sufficit, quod etiam virtualiter, et indirecte clericos tangat, et laedat.*

"11. Laymen can not, either directly, or indirectly, leg- "islate concerning ecclesiastical persons, or their property" : *Laici non possunt neque directe, neque indirecte, de personis ecclesiasticis, eorumque bonis disponere.*

The Canon law related to a partition of powers between church and state in Europe. The constitution of the United States contains a partition of powers between the Union and the states. The constitutions of the United States and of the several states contain partitions of powers between legislative, executive and judicial departments of government.

The foregoing Rotal decision shows that it was jurisprudential for Canon law courts to decide whether temporal legislation was or was not contrary to ecclesiastical liberty and to hold it null or valid accordingly.

If it were jurisprudential for Canon law courts so to do, it is equally jurisprudential for American courts to decide whether legislation is or is not contrary to a constitution and to hold it void or valid accordingly.

American constitutions originated no unprecedented novelty in making judicial courts competent so to proceed and decide. Canon law courts had proceeded and decided in a similar manner long before the framers of the first American constitution were born.

No. 3.

Of the texts of the Corpus Juris Canonici concerning the nullity of temporal legislation affecting the rights of the church.

The foregoing decision was made in 1648, but the doctrine of the case is much more ancient. Perhaps the most frequently cited canon on the subject is the *cap. Ecclesiae Sanctae Mariae* or *Decretal. lib. 1. tit. 2. cap. 10*, which dates from 1199. It declares that every lay statute affecting churches, whether favourably or unfavourably, is of no strength, unless approved by the church: *nullius firmitatis existit, nisi ab ecclesia fuerit approbatum.* It also declares that there can be attributed to laymen no faculty over churches and ecclesiastical persons, as to whom laymen must have the necessity of obeying, not the authority of commanding: *quod laicis (etiam religiosis) super ecclesiis et personis ecclesiasticis nulla sit attributa facultas: quos obsequendi manet necessitas, non auctoritas imperandi.*

A still more ancient canon is *Decret. par. 1. dist. 10. c. 4.*, which prescribes that (temporal) constitutions contrary to the canons, and the decrees of the Roman *praesules*, or to good morals, are of no moment: *constitutiones contra canones, et decreta praesulum Romanorum, vel bonos mores, nullius sunt momenti.*

Decret. par. 1. dist. 10. c. 1. declares that the law of the emperors is not above the law of God, but under it. Ecclesiastical rights can not be dissolved by imperial judgment: *Lex imperatorum non est supra legem Dei, sed subtus. Imperiali judicio non possunt ecclesiastica jura dissolvi.*

The following points will be found in the 2d and 3d titles of the Institutes of Lancelot, sometimes printed with the Corpus Juris Canonici. A constitution is written law: *constitutio est lex scripta.* Some constitutions are civil, others ecclesiastical. The former are enactments made by the civil authorities mentioned, the latter are canons made by the ecclesiastical authorities mentioned. Civil constitutions are worthy of all reverence, if they be not contrary to evangelical and canonical decrees: *si evangelicis atque canonicis decretis non sint contrariae, sunt omni reverentia dignae.* Otherwise they are of no moment, a rule which obtains to such a degree, that even if any thing should be enacted in them, which has respect to the advantage of churches, it is of no strength unless it should be approved by the church: *alioquin nullius sint momenti, quod usque adeo obtinet, ut etiamsi quid in eis statutum fuerit, quod ecclesiarum respiciat commodum, nullius firmitatis existat, nisi ab ecclesia fuerit comprobatum.*

The Canon law upon the relation between the laws of the church and those of the state is still unchanged. Upon the death of the German emperor and king of Prussia, William I., a carefully written obituary appeared in the London Times. In it, the statement is made that the late Pope Pius IX. declared "certain Prussian statutes to be null and void." These statutes constituted the well-known Prussian legislation relating to the Roman Catholic church, which had been made during the late king's reign and which gave rise to so much friction between his government and the Roman curia.*

---

* See the London Times of March 10th, 1888.

No. 4.

*Of a case determined in the Court of the Rota Romana in
1638, in which it was held that the legislative acts of two
popes, as temporal princes, were not to be accounted good
against a third party because they were decided to be
prejudicial to his well acquired right under a contract.*

So much for the Canon law in cases of partition of powers.
Such cases were concerned with conflicts of laws emanating
from different authorities. They do not include all the
relations of the Canon law to the subject. A different class
of cases will now be considered.

The popes were temporal princes in central Italy. As such
they exercised temporal power of legislation in the pontifical
states. The law of such legislation is intimately related to
the previously mentioned doctrine of rescripts in Justinian's
time.

In a case decided in 1638, the Court of the Rota Romana
held that certain legislative acts of two popes as princes,
expressly made in the plenitude of power, *were not to be
accounted good* against a third party because they impaired
or prejudiced his well-acquired right under a contract with
the government of Bologna. This case will now be rehearsed.
The account is translated and abridged from the *Decisiones
Recentiores* of the Rota, part 8, decision 4.

In 1466, the Cardinal Legate at Bologna with the consent
and will of the members of the government of Bologna
granted to Bartholomew Ghisilardi, the elder, and his heirs
and successors the faculty of building a mill beyond the
walls of the city. All other mills within one mile were prohibited and all inhabitants were to be free to have corn
ground at the new mill. The grant was made because the
grantee had offered, in consideration of it, to buy land and
build a needed mill. After the mill had been constructed,
Sixtus IV, after diligent examination, confirmed the grant
and *motu proprio* granted it anew, in 1473. Bartholomew and
his heirs and successors continued in quiet possession of the

mill and the rights and business belonging to it until 1520. In that year the government of Bologna made a statute providing that the bakers of the city should not be permitted to have their corn ground outside of its walls. This statute was confirmed by Leo X., proceeding on his own motion, from certain knowledge and of plenitude of power, with derogation to all and all kinds of privileges by whomsoever granted. The prohibition of the statute so confirmed was one gravely injuring the business of the mill. In consequence whereof, a suit was brought by Anthony Ghisilardi, nephew of the deceased grantee, *super invaliditatem ejusdem statuti*. Pending this suit, the government of Bologna sought and obtained another and a similar confirmation of its statute from Clement VII. In its supplication or request therefor, no mention of any pending suit was made.

The auditor, or judge who heard the suit, stated a *dubitatur* to the whole court as to whether the letters patent of Leo X. and Clement VII. were to be accounted good against the Ghisilardi and it was answered that both were not to be accounted good against them : *Dubitavi, an literae Leonis X. et Clementis VII. suffragentur contra DD. de Ghisilardis, et eas non suffragari fuit responsum.*

It should be recollected that Bologna was then one of the most important of the pontifical states, and possessed a legislative power of making statutes subject to the legislative confirmation of the pope as supreme temporal prince. Such confirmations, like the English king's approval of American colonial statutes, were acts exercising legislative power. Each confirmation of the statute in question was thus judicially held not to be good as an exercise of legislative power against the mill owner.

The decision first considers the letters patent of Leo X. It was true that "they emanated from the pope on his "own motion, from certain knowledge and of plenitude of "power, with derogation to all and whatsoever privileges to "whomsoever granted, and with other most ample clauses : *quamvis emanaverint motu proprio, ex certa scientia, ac de plenitudine potestatis cum derogatione omnium, et quorumcumque privilegiorum quibuscumque concessorum, et cum aliis amplissimis clausulis.* They contained, however, matter to the prejudice of a third party, the Ghisilardi, who had a well-acquired right or *jus quaesitum* of grinding corn for all comers. The pope was ignorant of the contract between them and the government of Bologna, which gave them such a right. The presumption must therefore be made that the letters patent confirming the statute had emanated at the suggestion of one party only and that the pope had been circumvented under cover of words, for he had no intention of prejudicing a third party. Two doctors and a previous decision of the Rota were cited as authorities for this doctrine. The pontiff, although he can do such a thing, was never held to wish to destroy a well-acquired right: *pontifex enim licet possit, nunquam censetur velle tollere jus quaesitum.* For this *Decretal. lib. 1. tit. 3. cap. 3* and glosses thereupon were cited. The pope was ignorant of the contract between Ghisilardi and the government of Bologna, and it was probable that if he had known of it, he would not have made the derogation, or would have had greater difficulty in making it. For this position several doctors of Canon law are cited.

Various questions suggested by the texts of the supplication, the letters patent, and the statute, were discussed and decided in harmony with the conclusion that the letters patent were not to be accounted good against the mill owners.

The litigation had been a long one. In its previous stages the plaintiff had obtained a mandate for the manutention of his possession of his right of grinding corn for all comers. The court had also allowed his appeal from the statute, on the ground of its being issued in his prejudice as a third party, because it prohibited his said right. The previous settling of the questions relating to these proceedings made the court more easily come to the final opinion.

Every thing said concerning the letters patent of Leo X. as above, was held to apply to those of Clement VII. The latter, indeed, were decided to be subject to an additional objection. When they were obtained, the supplication made no mention of the suit pending in the Rota. They were

therefore surreptitious.   Authorities on this point, including a previous decision of the court, were cited.

This decision of the Rota thus shows that the legislative
acts of two popes, as temporal princes, confirming a statute
of a pontifical state, were by that court not accounted good
against a third party, because his well-acquired right was
destroyed.

Such being the law of the confirmations, the statute itself
was invalid against the injured plaintiff.   His suit had
been introduced in the Rota *super invaliditatem ejusdem
statuti.*

Some observations upon a point of contact between the
foregoing case and that of Fletcher *v.* Peck may be added.

On page 130, paragraph 1, of 6 Cranch, C. J. Marshall, in
delivering the opinion in that cause, observes :

"If the principle be conceded, that an act of the supreme
"sovereign power might be declared null by a court, in con-
"sequence of the means which procured it, *still would
"there be much difficulty in saying to what extent those
"means must be applied to produce this effect.*"

In saying this, the Chief Justice had particularly in mind
those cases in which persons soliciting legislation procure
it by corrupting legislators.   His observation, however, is
general as to wrongful means of procuring legislation.   It
covers cases in which legislators are not corrupted, but deceived by soliciting parties.   As to this latter class of cases,
the jurisprudence of the Civilians concerning rescripts, in
its fullest and latest development, affords, perhaps, a means
of overcoming the difficulty, as far as private legislation
and the rights of third persons are concerned.

A legislative rescript was an act written back or rescribed
in answer to a supplication.   The supplication was a request or petition for legislative relief.   It was the matrix
in which the legislative answer of the lawgiver was formed.
If the supplication deceived the lawgiver by false statements
of the case or by concealing the truth thereof and the sup-
pliant thereby procured legislation, the rescript was of no
strength in prejudicing the well-acquired rights of third

parties. It was a judicial question whether the supplication was impeachable or not. If the judge decided it to be so, he held the rescript based upon it to be of no strength against the well-acquired rights of third parties.

To appreciate fully this law of legislation, it should be remembered that the majority of legislative rescripts should be compared with private acts of parliament in England and not with public general statutes. The fact that, in continental Europe, rescripts were often called letters patent, should not divert attention from private acts of parliament.

In America, where written constitutions prevail, it may, perhaps, be possible to imitate the Civilians as far as private legislation is concerned. If it be possible to do so, the written constitution of a state might contain dispositions, of which the following is an imperfect sketch. Such a constitution might provide that all private acts of legislation should be procured on petition only; that the petition should tell the truth and the whole truth of the case, or be legally defective; that no legislation should affect the rights of third parties, when procured by a petition legally defective; that the courts of justice should be competent to decide whether a questioned petition be legally sufficient or defective; and that they should hold legislation procured by a defective petition to be void of effect upon the rights of third parties.

CHAPTER XIII.

Of the Canon law in England and the relations between it and the English law before the Reformation, in so far as the present subject is concerned.

DIVISION A.

Of the Canon law in England before the Reformation.

DIVISION B.

Of the case of the constitutions of Clarendon.

DIVISION C.

Of the case of the English statutes held void as against the church during the suppression of the Templars in England.

DIVISION D.

Of the English law before the Reformation concerning temporal legislation contrary to ecclesiastical right and liberty.
Of the case of the Prior of Castlaker *v.* the Dean of St. Stephens in the Year Book of 21 Henry VII.

DIVISION E.

Further reflections suggested by the case of the Prior of Castlaker *v.* the Dean of St. Stephens.

DIVISION F.

Further consideration of the connection between the Canon law and the English law. Of the case in Fitzherbert's Abridgment, Annuity 41, or Rous v. an Abbot.

DIVISION G

Of the Reformation and the restrictions which it removed from the power of parliament.

Chapter XIII. will be devoted to a special consideration of the Canon law in connection with England and the English law. During the middle ages, the Canon law was one general to the countries of Europe not included within the Greek Empire. Its actual operation, however, varied in the respective countries. Its operation in England was especially affected by local circumstances.

DIVISION A.

Of the Canon law in England before the Reformation.

The principles of the Canon law and those of the Civil law were constant companions. In England, fortunately for all communities now speaking the English tongue, the Common law stoutly excluded the Civil law. Thus in England there was a special dualism between the law of the church, or spiritual law, and the law of the land, or Common law.* The barons' famous "*nolumus leges Angliae* "*mutare*" was uttered against a rule, which was sanctioned

---

* *Cf.* Year Book, 10 Henry VII., pp. 9, 10, No. 22 ; p. 17, No. 17 ; 12 Henry VII., p. 18 ; pp. 22, 23, 24.

by both the Civil law and the Canon law, and urged as such
by the bishops. This was the rule of *legitimatio per sub-
sequens matrimonium.**

It is consequently necessary to ascertain how the Canonical
doctrine concerning temporal laws and statutes was regarded
in England before the Reformation, both by the church and
by the state.

The standard work of Lindwood, who wrote upon the
Canon law in England before the Reformation, affords the'
means of ascertaining the views of the English Canonists on
the subject.

Lindwood expressly asserts that the Canon law doctrine
in *Decretal. lib. 1. tit. 2. c. 10.* was in vigour in England.
In commenting upon an act "ordained formerly by the
"royal consent and that of the magnates of England, as if
"for ecclesiastical right and liberty," he says that "such
"an ordinance even though in favour of the church, when
"made upon the mere motion of the king and the two tem-
"poral estates, would *not be valid* (*non valeret*), except so
"far as it be made at the requisition of the church, or after-
"wards be approved by the church. *Decretal. lib. 1. tit.*
"*2. c. 10.*" See Lindwood's Provinciale, Ed. 1679, page
263: *prout consensu regio, et magnatum regni Angliae
tanquam pro jure ecclesiasticaque libertate ab olim extitit
ordinatum.* And gloss *consensu regio* on the same: *talis
ordinatio etiam in favorem ecclesiae mero motu regio et
duorum temporalium facta non valeret, nisi quatenus ad
requisitionem ecclesiae fieret, vel postea ab ecclesia appro-
baretur.* Extra. de consti. c. Ecclesia Sanctae Mariae; *ubi
de hoc.*

---

* See Bracton and his Relation to the Roman Law, by C. Gueterbock, translated by B. Coxe, pp. 59, 65, 127 *et seq.*

DIVISION B.

Of the case of the constitutions of Clarendon.

No. 1. *Of the constitutions of Clarendon and the successful ecclesiastical opposition thereto.*

No. 2. *Practical example of the consequences of the nullity of the constitutions of Clarendon. Of the ecclesiastical immunity called benefit of clergy.*

No. 3. *Of the resemblance between the ecclesiastical immunity claimed for clerical men in the case of the constitutions of Clarendon and the federal immunity claimed for U. S. officials in the case of the state of Tennessee v. Davis.*

That the Canon law doctrine of the nullity of lay statutes contrariant to ecclesiastical right and the liberty of the church had legal vigour in England as well as on the continent, is very fully shown by two cases memorable in English history. The first of these is the case of the constitutions of Clarendon, and the second that of the statutes conflicting with the proceedings for suppressing the Templars and annulled therein.

No. 1.

Of the constitutions of Clarendon and the successful ecclesiastical opposition thereto.

The case of the Constitutions of Clarendon will now be considered. These acts of temporal legislation were formally declared null or void by the Primate Becket, as Archbishop of Canterbury, proceeding *jurisdictionaliter* according to the Canon law.

The history of Becket's quarrels with King Henry II. is well known. Although he lost his life in consequence, his ecclesiastical action against the legislation of the constitutions of Clarendon was in the end successful.

The constitutions are called by Hale * a "considerable

---

* Hale: History, 5, 136.

"body of acts of parliament." They were enacted in the
year 1164 by King Henry II., by the advice of his council
or parliament held at Clarendon. They consisted of sixteen
articles and legislated concerning the relations between
church and state in England.* Five of these articles were
especially objected to by Becket, but all were included in
his denunciation.

One of those five articles authorized the punishment of
criminals, who were clerical men, by trial in the secular
courts. Becket's words are: *quod clerici trahantur ad
saecularia judicia.*† This provision of the constitutions is
therefore intimately connected with the history of the benefit of clergy. Its enactment was made necessary by the then
existing state of things. Numerous clerical men, who had
committed murder, had never been called to account. One
clerical murderer in Worcestershire had produced general
indignation by the heinousness of his crime, but Becket refused to consent that he should suffer more than degrada-
tion, and insisted that a degraded ecclesiastic could not be
delivered to the secular power for further punishment, because no man should be tried twice for the same offence.
His doctrine was thus not only most rigorous, but most
comprehensive, for it applied to all criminal ecclesiastics.‡

The document containing Becket's action is his letter to
his suffragans, dated 1166, and recorded by Hoveden in his
Chronicle.§ In it, he speaks officially as archbishop and
judicially as ecclesiastical judge upon several heads, among
which are the excommunications of seven persons named.
It should here be remembered that, as Archbishop of Canterbury, Becket was the legate of the pope in England.

Becket's denunciation of the invalidity of the constitutions
of Clarendon could hardly be plainer. He contemptuously
terms them "that writing." He publicly condemns and
quashes the writing and the authority thereof. He makes
invalid and quashes the authority of the writing and the

---

* Stubbs : History, library Ed., I. 526.

† Hoveden, Rolls edition, I. 238.

‡ Hume, A. D. 1163, paragraph 6.

§ Rolls Edition, I. 238.

writing itself, together with the "depravities" contained in it:
" Scriptum illud . . . . . . ipsiusque scripti auctoritatem
" . . . . . publice condemnavimus et cassavimus. . . .
" *Auctoritatem ipsius scripti, ipsumque scriptum, cum*
" *pravitatibus quae in eo continentur, in irritum duximus*
" *et cassavimus.*"

This proceeding of Becket's was not an isolated ecclesiastical act, for in the year before, 1165, Pope Alexander' II. had condemned in the strongest terms the then most important of the sixteen constitutions and anathematized all who observed them. The effect of the pope's act had been to continue, not to settle the conflict. Neither did Becket's act at first do more.

With various vicissitudes, unsettled relations between the church and the state continued until December 29th, 1170, when Becket was murdered by partisans of the king under circumstances, which made the latter fear that the pope might hold him responsible for the deed. In that age of superstition, such a danger was most formidable. As it was, Becket's power triumphed in his death, which was popularly held to be that of a martyr. King Henry immediately applied to Rome for absolution, declaring himself free from all complicity with Becket's death. On learning that legates commissioned to absolve him had arrived in Normandy, he repaired thither. On May 21st, 1172, he made his submission to them, clearing himself by oath from all complicity as aforesaid, and "renouncing the constitutions of Clar-
" endon."* *Becket's declaration of the invalidity of those temporal laws was thus made effective.* The king's loss was the pope's gain. The papal power henceforth continued to increase in England until it reached its highest point in the reign of Henry III., the grandson of Henry II.†

---

* Stubbs, library edition, I. 536.
† Gneist : *Verfassung*, 196. Ashworth's Translation, I. 240.

No. 2.

Practical example of the consequences of the nullity of the constitutions of Clarendon. Of the ecclesiastical immunity termed benefit of clergy.

The foregoing statement shows that there was a legal partition of power between church and state, the execution of which the former could secure by its spiritual weapons against any temporal opposition. The arms of the church were then, indeed, as capable of doing execution as any arms of the flesh. What is now called Boycotting affords a modern object lesson of the earthly power of excommunication. To such earthly evil was added the superstitious terror connected with untold punishment in the next world. Moreover, this partition of power was practical as well as theoretical. How practical it was, is well exemplified in the branch of criminal law, which has already been spoken of and which may be further adverted to in elucidation of the case of the constitutions of Clarendon.

The abusive condition of things as to ecclesiastics guilty of murder and other crimes against the state continued unreformed. The church continued to claim their exemption from trial in the king's courts, insisting upon their being subject only to the jurisdiction of its own courts, while it was either really unwilling or practically unable to try and punish them therein. The constitutions of Clarendon had in vain striven to remedy the evil. The church had declared those laws void because of defect of power in the lay enactors thereof and had carried its point.

The benefit of clergy, as successfully secured by Becket, was an immunity of ecclesiastics from the execution of justice by the state in cases of murder and felony according to the Common law. No king of England could admit the proposition that such an immunity ought to exist, unless it were true that all clerical criminals ought to be tried only in courts that either could not or would not punish them. A critic of the period might have said of such a proposition:

" Were the object to give felons an immunity to commit
"crime, and to provide a way for their escape from punish-
"ment, it seems to me that it would be difficult to devise
"any mode more effectual to that end than the theory em-
"bodied in that proposition."

No. 3.

*Of the resemblance between the ecclesiastical immunity
claimed for clerical men in the case of the constitutions
of Clarendon and the federal immunity claimed for U.
S. officials in the case of the state of Tennessee v. Davis.*

The foregoing medieval example of an exorbitant exemption from jurisdiction is well worth studying by all wishing
to understand the system of dual government by church
and state, which was the fundamental public law or constitution of Europe before the Reformation.

The division of powers into spiritual and temporal in the
states of medieval Europe and the division of powers into
federal and municipal in the states of the American Union
have a marked resemblance. A system of dual government
marks both. In England before the Reformation every
Englishman owed obedience to both pope and king. In
every state of the union, every citizen owes obedience to
both the union and the state. The resemblance between the
two divisions of powers is of much importance for the purposes of this Essay ; and no specially good opportunity for
illustrating it should be neglected in this examination of the
Canon law. Such an opportunity is afforded by the present
discussion of the benefit of clergy in Becket's time. The
far-reaching exemption of ecclesiastics from temporal jurisdiction, which he successfully claimed, deserves attentive
consideration by modern Americans, for they will find something strangely like it now existing within the United
States.

The government of the United States by its legislative
and judicial acts has declared that its executive officials,
who may have committed murder and other crimes against

a state while claiming to act officially, are exempt from the jurisdiction of the courts of the several states. It has further insisted that the trials of such indicted persons must be removed from the state courts to the U. S. courts, although it is and ever will be impossible to secure therein the trial, conviction and punishment of U. S. officials, who have been actually guilty of crimes against the rightful, valid and necessary laws of the states.

This observation requires a reference to the case of Tennessee *v.* Davis, in 10 Otto 257. The laws of Tennessee provide for the trial of all persons accused of crimes against the state, in the same way as is done in other states of the Union. The relation of the state laws to any plea of defence urged as a federal question by U. S. officials is the same in Tennessee as in other states. In the suit of Tennessee *v.* Davis, the indicted man claimed to be exempt from trial for homicide in the state court, because he was a U. S. official claiming to have acted officially. The Supreme Court of the United States held the laws of Tennessee to be void to the whole extent of the official's claim of immunity from trial in the state courts; just as the Roman church of Becket's time held the laws of England to be void to the whole extent of the clergy's claim of immunity from trial in the king's courts. The court decided that the suit must be removed to, and tried by, the U. S. Circuit Court. This was done in terms which covered the case of the indicted man being guilty just as much as that of his being innocent.

A benefit of removal, which secured an immunity strangely like that secured by Becket's benefit of clergy, was thus asserted for U. S. officials.

Judge Clifford, in his dissenting opinion in Tennessee *v.* Davis, regarded the contentions of the opinion of the court as tantamount to asserting the proposition that a state indictment for felony can be removed from a state court into a U. S. circuit court, although it was substantially admitted that a prisoner can not be tried there until Congress shall enact some mode of procedure. Such a proposition he regards as most erroneous and nearly approaching an absurdity. He adds:

"Were the object to give felons an immunity to commit "crime, and to provide a way for their escape from punish-"ment, it seems to me that it would be difficult to devise "any mode more effectual to that end than the theory em-"bodied in that proposition."*

Thus the conduct of the Roman church in the twelfth century and that of the U. S. government in the nineteenth strongly resemble each other ; so strongly, indeed, that Judge Clifford's language may be applied to the conduct of both.   Both endeavoured to secure what they claimed to be their own rights by usurping rights which they knew belonged to other jurisdictions.   *Both might have secured all rightful immunity for their innocent officials without wrongfully protecting the guilty.*   Both, however, insisted upon usurping immunity for their officials regardless of guilt or innocence.   The Roman church abused its spiritual power to the extent of gravely violating the rights of the English state.   The U. S. government abused its federal powers to the extent of gravely violating the rights of the states of the Union.

DIVISION C.

Of the case of the English statutes held void as against the church during the suppression of the Templars in England.

The second of the above-mentioned cases, in which the Canon law doctrine upon temporal statutes was received in England, is that of the statutes held void as against the church during the suppression of the Templars.   This was done in the reign of Edward II. and pontificate of Clement V.   It is difficult to imagine a greater case in the law of laws.   Magna Charta itself was invalidated.

The suppression of the Templars in Europe has recently been investigated by an historian whose learning and authority are of the highest rank.   What Mr. Lea has written upon it will be used without stint for the purposes of this

---

* 10 Otto, page 297, lines 8 *et seq.*

Essay. It is discussed in the fifth chapter of the third volume of his History of the Inquisition in the Middle Ages. Pages 298 *et seq.* relate especially to the suppression of the order in England.

The bull *Pastoralis praeeminentiae* was made by Pope Clement V., on November 22d, 1307.[*] It recites what Philip the Fair, king of France, had done, at the requisition of the papal inquisition for France, in order to bring the Templars in that country to the judgment of the church, and orders all other sovereigns to do likewise in their respective dominions. The bull was received the following month by Edward II, king of England. Although the commands of the bull conflicted with the king's previously expressed opinions, he proceeded at once to obey them. On December 15th, royal orders were sent to all the sheriffs in England, giving instruction to capture all Templars on January 18th, 1308,[†] together with directions for the sequestration and disposition of their property. These were followed by corresponding commands for Ireland, Scotland and Wales. The seizure was made accordingly. The Templars were kept in honourable durance, and not in prison, awaiting the action of the pope. Delays then occurred until the arrival of the papal inquisitors in England in September, 1309. Further instructions were then sent out to arrest all Templars not previously seized and to produce them at London, Lincoln or York. It apparently was not easy to obtain official obedience to these orders. In the following December it was necessary to instruct all the sheriffs to seize the Templars wandering abroad in secular habits, and the sheriff of York was at later dates twice taken to task for permitting those in his custody to be at large.

At length on October 20th, 1309, the papal inquisitors together with the Bishop of London sat judicially in the bishop's palace to examine the Templars collected in London. Interrogated singly on all the numerous articles of accusation, they all asserted the innocence of their order. Most of the outside witnesses declared their belief to the

[*] Lea, III. 278.

[†] Lea, III. 298.

same effect, although some gave expression to the vague popular rumours and scandalous stories suggested by the secrecy of the proceedings within the order. The inquisitorial process seemed a sterile one in England. "The inquis- "itors were nonplussed. They had come to a country whose "laws did not recognize the use of torture, and without it "they were powerless to accomplish the work for which "they had been sent."* They finally applied to the king, and on December 15th obtained from him an order to the custodians of the prisoners to do with the bodies of the Templars what they pleased "in accordance with ecclesiastical "law," that term meaning the use of torture. Difficulties must have been interposed by those receiving the orders, for a second command was given on March 1st, 1310, and repeated on March 8th, with instructions to report the cause, if the first had not been obeyed. Little evidence of any importance was however obtained until May 24th, when three recaptured fugitive Templars made confessions such as were desired and which, it is easy to guess, were made under torture. Pope Clement "grew impatient at this lack of result. "On August 6th, *he wrote to Edward that it was reported* "*that he had prohibited the use of torture as contrary to* "*the laws of the kingdom and that the inquisitors were thus* "*powerless to extract confessions. No law or usage, he said,* "*could be permitted to overrule the canons provided for such* "*cases, and Edward's counsellors and officials who were* "*guilty of thus impeding the inquisition were liable to* "*the penalties provided for that serious offence,* while the "king himself was warned to consider whether his posi- "tion comported with his honour and safety, and was "offered remission of his sins if he would withdraw from "it."† Similar letters were at the same time sent to all the English bishops, who were taken to task for not having already removed the impediment, as their ecclesiastical duty required them.‡ "Under this impulsion Edward, August "26, again ordered that the bishops and inquisitors should

* Lea, III. 299.

† Lea, III. 300.

‡ Lea, III. 300.

" be allowed to employ ecclesiastical law, and this was re-
" peated October 6 and 23, November 22, and April 28, 1311,
" in the last instances the word torture being used, and in
" all of them the king being careful to explain what he does
" is through reverence for the Holy See.   August 18, 1311,
" similar instructions were sent to the sheriff of York.
" Thus for once the papal inquisition found a foothold in
" England, but apparently its methods were too repugnant
" to the spirit of the nation to be rewarded with complete
" success."*

There can be no doubt that the torturing of the Templars
by the king's officials at his command on ecclesiastical requisition was then *contrary to the law of the land of England*.   It was also certainly *a violation of Magna Charta*,
which was an act of parliament that had been re-enacted
over and over again.   The pope writing officially to the
king as aforesaid declared the binding and the ecclesiastical
law to be that the temporal law and statutes of England
forbidding the use of torture could not overrule the canons
of the church to the contrary.   That is to say, within the
limitations of ecclesiastical right, the law of the church was
binding on the king and his subjects and the law of the land
was not binding.   The temporal laws preventing trial by
torture, including Magna Charta, were void in so far as contrary to the canons and because so contrary.

What the pope wrote to the king he repeated in official
letters to the bishops.   Like the king and other Englishmen concerned in the torture of the Templars, they were
deficient in alacrity.   The English bishops, proceeding as
ecclesiastical judges, were unaccustomed to the practice of
causing men to be tortured.   Their courts were called courts
Christian.

Thus the Templars' case was a clear case of conflict between the law of the land of England and the Canon law of
the Roman church, which was settled upon the basis that
the former was void in so far as contrary to the latter and
because so contrary.

---

* Lea, III. 300, 301.

To this law of laws the king of England submitted and executed the Canon law. Thereby he refused to execute the 39th article of Magna Charta, which guarantees every freeman a trial according to the law of the land. He also refused to execute the various acts of parliament which re-enacted Magna Charta. The tortured Templars did not receive a trial according to the law of the land but a trial according to the law of the church.

DIVISION D.

Of the English law before the Reformation concerning temporal legislation contrary to ecclesiastical right and liberty.
Of the case of the Prior of Castlaker *v.* the Dean of St. Stephens in the Year Book of 21 Henry VII.

In division A. of this chapter, it has been shown, on the authority of Lindwood, that the English Canonists held that the Canon law rule concerning temporal statutes was in vigour in Roman Catholic England. Lindwood held that an act ordained by the temporal power, affecting ecclesiastical right and liberty, would not be valid (*non valeret*), except in so far as made upon the previous requisition, or confirmed by the subsequent approbation, of the church. Important as such legal doctrine was, it was still more important that its application in actual practice can be proved to have been made by men who were not doctors of Canon law but Common law jurists. Language applying such doctrine is reported as used at the bar and on the bench of the Court of Common Pleas, the very home of the learning of the Common law. This will be seen from a case in that court, reported in the Year Book of 21 Henry VII., pp. 1 to 5.

In it a question arose whether a certain act of parliament, being an act of the temporal power, could make the king, being a temporal man, the parson of a certain church. If the act did so, it gave spiritual jurisdiction to a temporal man without the consent of the spiritual power.

The correct answer to this question is shown by the report to be in the negative. The discussion of the question, furthermore, shows that, by the then English law, parliament had not unlimited power in ecclesiastical matters. Judge Blackstone could say so in a later time, but English judges could not say so before the Reformation.

It may seem strange to many of Blackstone's readers that parliamentary power should be spoken of as limited ; but it would have seemed stranger to Englishmen before the Reformation for any one to say that the temporal parliament could legislate with unlimited power in ecclesiastical matters regardless of the pope's wishes and authority. It required the Reformation, that is to say, an ecclesiastical revolution, for parliament to obtain its modern plenitude of power in matters ecclesiastical.

The case referred to was this. The Prior of Castlaker brought an action of annuity against the Dean of St. Stephens.* In making his title, the plaintiff claimed that all his predecessors had been seized of the annuity by the hands of a certain A., Parson of the Church of N. and all his predecessors *de temps dont memory ne court*, and that the annuity was in arrear. The defendant claimed that the parsonage was and had been appropriated to the Priors of B. *devant temps de memory*. Their priory was a cell of the Abbey of Caen in Normandy. In time of war King Edward III. seized all lands which were temporalties of Alien Priors. This was the state of things until 2 Henry V., in which year it was ordained by authority of parliament that all the lands so seized by the king should remain *in sa possession a luy et ses successors* forever.† Edward IV. granted the parsonage to the Deans of St. Stephens, by letters patent, which were produced by the defendant, who claimed that it was thereby given as it existed in the king's hands and so discharged of the annuity.

One of the questions involved in the case was this : Whether or not the king could be made parson by the act of parliament, (*si le Roy puit estre parson per l'acte de*

---

* The spelling *Castlaker* is that of the Year Book. Viner spells the word Castle-acre : See his head of Statutes, D. 5.

† For this act see Rolls of Parliament, vol. 4, page 22 (2 Henry V.). The enrolled words are : *demurrer en voz mains, a vous, et a voz heirs pur toutz jours.*

Parlement). If the king had been made Parson of the Church of N. by the Alien Priors act of 2 Henry V., the plaintiff could not recover, because the annuity was determined for reasons of prerogative. But if the king had not been parson, then no reason of prerogative existed for the determining of the annuity.

The following passages relating to the question whether the king had been parson or not, are translated from the report. The proceedings reported are those of two separate days. The case was considered at much length.

It was said by Palmes at the bar: "It seems that the "king can not be called parson by the act of parliament: "for no temporal act can make it that temporal act can "make temporal man have spiritual jurisdiction. For if it "was ordained by act, etc., that such a one should not "tender tithes to his curate, *the act would be void* (*le Act* "*sera void*), for concerning such thing as touches merely "the spiritualty, *such temporal act can make no ordinance* "(*tiel temporal'acte ne puit faire ascun ordinance*): the "law is the same (*meme la Ley*) if it was enacted that one "parson should have the tithes of another. So by this act, "which is merely one of a temporal court, the king can not "be made to have any spiritual jurisdiction."

Coningsby, in argument on the other side, maintained that the king could be parson and asserted as a fact that "the king had divers benefices in Wales which are contin-"ually in his hand."

Kingsmill, Justice, said: "The act of parliament can not "make the king to be parson: for we can not by our law* "make any temporal man to have spiritual jurisdiction, for "no one can do this except the Supreme Head [of the "Church]."

Fisher, Justice, said: "The king can not be parson by "this act of parliament, neither can any temporal man be "called parson by this act."

---

* "Our law" (*nostre Ley*) means the temporal law, the Common law, the law of the land, in opposition to the spiritual law, the Canon law, the law of the holy church. The expression was a usual one. *Cf.* Year Book of 12 Henry VII., p. 23.

On the other hand Vavasor, Justice, observed : "Whether "the king can be parson or not : and it seems to me "that he can. And as to this I shall first put to you "several precedents. I know of divers lords who have par-"sonages in their own use (and he gave their names and "places), so that it is not impertinent (*impertinent*) that the "king should be called parson ; and especially by the act "of parliament. For in the time of king Richard II., there "was division for the pope in time of vacation, as it was "afterward, and because it was certified to the king and his "council, that certain priests in England had offended in "divers points, they were deprived of their benefices by act "of parliament : so you can see how spiritual things were "taken by act of parliament from them who were spiritual "men. Those things were, indeed, mixed with the tempor-"alty : for if they were purely spiritual, perhaps it would "be otherwise."

The proceedings were terminated by Chief Justice Frowick's opinion in which he said : "As to the other matter, "whether the king can be parson by act of parliament ; as "I understand, it is not a great matter to argue : for I have "never seen that any temporal man can be parson without "the agreement of the Supreme Head [of the Church]. "And in all those cases which have been put, namely, those "of the benefices in Wales, and the benefices which laymen "have in their own use, I have seen to the matter ; the king "had them by the assent and agreement of the Supreme "Head [of the Church] ; *and so a temporal act can not,* "*without the assent of the Supreme Head [of the Church],* "*make the king parson (issint un acte temporel sans le* "*assente del' Supreme Teste ne puit faire le Roy parson).*"

From the foregoing extracts, it is maintained that the Canon law concerning the invalidity of temporal statutes affecting ecclesiastical right and liberty was received by the Common law and in the Common law courts to an extent which is of great legal moment. It is clear that before the Reformation parliament had not legally an unlimited power in ecclesiastical matters.

An act of parliament could not legislate in purely spiritual

matters without the pope's consent. His consent was absolutely necessary. Vavasor, the dissenting judge, claimed
validity for acts of parliament only in cases of mixed things,
or those in which the spiritualty was mixed with the temporalty. He reserved his opinion as to things purely
spiritual.

It will be observed that the dissenting judge's opinion is
answered by the chief justice. The former refers to certain
cases in which acts of temporal power were valid although
affecting the spiritualty and cites them as authority for his
opinion. This is controverted by the chief justice, who
holds that those cases are authority for the counter-opinion.
The said acts of temporal power were valid because the pope
gave his consent thereto.

Parliament could not therefore actually make statutes extending to two classes of matters. The first class included all
purely spiritual matters. The second class included some but
not all spiritual matters which were mixed with the temporalty. Without the pope's consent, acts of parliament extending thereto had no legislative vigour. So far the temporal law in England received the Canon law concerning the
nullity of temporal statutes contrary to ecclesiastical right
and liberty.

It will also be observed that the report of the argument of
Serjeant Palmes states that he applied the adjective *void* to
an act of parliament which legislated concerning a matter
merely affecting the spiritualty.

Lastly, it may be added that when the English acknowledged the supremacy of the pope as head of the church, the
notion that parliament had unlimited power in ecclesiastical
matters was an absurdity in or out of any court. Blackstone's doctrine of the absolute and uncontrolled power of
parliament in ecclesiastical matters could only have originated after the Reformation. At the same time, it should be
pointed out that the case of the prior of Castlaker *v.* the
Dean of St. Stephens was a very exceptional one, as will be
enlarged upon in the next division of this chapter.

DIVISION E.

Further reflections suggested by the case of the Prior of Castlaker *v.* the Dean of St. Stephens.

Such a case as this was exceptional in the courts of Common law. The judges of those courts were not persons to whom the church looked especially for the vindication of ecclesiastical rights. On the contrary, English judicial history* shows that the church would naturally expect them often to be unwilling to give it the measure of ecclesiastical right claimed by the Canon law.

The natural play of the spiritual and temporal powers was normally one of negotiation between the authorities of the church and those of the state. Whenever parliament met, the lords spiritual and the lords temporal could negotiate in the same chamber, while the commons were assembled near by in another, ready to unite in action with the other temporal estate.

From the time when a parliament of three estates first took part in legislation, the bishops and other prelates headed by the primate (who was the pope's legate in England) were real representatives of the church. The liberty of the elections at which they were chosen and the liberty of their parliamentary action as lords spiritual were realities.† The great Canonical principle of the liberty of the church was practically applied in parliament. The prelates were actually free to criticise and oppose proposed legislation objectionable to the church. Moreover, led by the primate, they could in divers cases give or pledge such ecclesiastical consent as would exempt statutes from the Canon law rule against temporal legislation affecting the church. As a rule the canons enacted by the convocations of the church and the statutes enacted by the parliament of the state did not conflict. Bishop Stubbs in a passage quoted and endorsed by Prof. Gneist observes :

---

* See Stubbs : History, III. 351, (library ed.) on the safeguards of the Common law.

† Gneist : *Verfassung* 196 ; Ashworth, Constitution, I. 240.

" Almost all the examples, however, in which the clergy
" went beyond their recognized rights in regulating the con-
" duct of the laity, come under the head of judicial rather
" than of legislative action. . . . . . Any direct conflict
"between the two legislatures is extremely rare. In the
"normal state of English politics, the prelates, who were
" the real legislators in convocation and also formed the ma-
" jority in the house of lords, acted in close alliance with
" the crown, and, under any circumstances, would be strong
" enough to prevent any awkward collision ; if their class
" sympathies were with the clergy, their great temporal es-
"tates and offices gave them many points of interest in
"common with the laity. Thus, although, as the judicial
" history shows, the lines between spiritual and temporal
" judicature were very indistinctly drawn, England was
" spared during the greatest part of the middle ages any
" war of theories on the relations of the church to the state."*

DIVISION F.

Further consideration of the connection between the Canon law and the English law. Of the case in Fitzherbert's Abridgment, Annuity 41, or Rous v. an Abbot.

In the case of the Prior of Castlaker v. the Dean of St.
Stephens, a question concerning the exercise of spiritual
power by the temporal legislature was undoubtedly involved. Another and a previous case will now be examined,
which may perhaps have involved a like exercise of spiritual
power, for it certainly affected both ecclesiastical persons
and ecclesiastical property. Designated by the names of
the parties it is that of Rous v. an Abbot, but it is best
known as the case in Fitzherbert's Abridgment, Annuity
41. It is found entered also in the earlier Abridgment of
Statham under Annuity in Easter 27 Henry VI., who gives
the names of the parties as above mentioned. Neither of

---

*Stubbs : History, III. 351, (library ed.). Gneist : *Verfassung*, p. 405,
note 6. *Cf*. Ashworth, Constitution, II. 56 .

these brief statements contains any reference to the Canon law and it may therefore be wholly erroneous to conjecture that the decision of the court had any connection with that law. On the other hand it is certain that the case was one affecting both ecclesiastical persons and ecclesiastical property and that in it a temporal court held a whole chapter of a temporal statute to be void because judicially ascertained to be "impertinent to be observed" and to legislate into existence certain irremediable evils connected with certain ecclesiastical seals.

This case arose under the statute of Carlisle, *de asportatis religiosorum*, 35 Edward I., which prohibited the payment of taxes and the transportation of things by English monasteries to foreign ecclesiastical superiors.* Its 4th chapter legislates concerning the seals of certain monasteries and came under judicial consideration in the Court of Common Pleas in Easter term, 27 Henry VI. Fitzherbert's entry is translated as follows, from the text of his first edition, folio 50*b*., Annuity, 41 :

"27 Henry VI. Note that the statute of Carlisle pro-
"vides of the orders of Cistercians and Augustinians, which
"have convent and common seal, that the common seal shall
"be in the keeping of the prior who is under the abbot
"and of four others of the wisest of the house, and that
"every deed sealed with the common seal, when not so
"kept, shall be void ; and the opinion of the court was that
"the statute is void, for it is impertinent to be observed
"(*que cest estatut est void quar es inpartinent destre ob-*
"*serve*), for the seal being in their keeping, the abbot can
"seale nothing with it, and when it is in the hands of the
"abbot, it is out of their keeping *ipso facto*, and if the statute
"be observed every common seal will be defeated by a simple
'surmise which cannot be tried, etc."

The above phrase, "*cest statut est void quar es inparti-*
'*nent destre observe*," is Englished by Coke differently in
different places. At the end of 118*a* of 8 Reports, the
statute is stated to be void, because "impertinent to be ob-

---

*Statutes of the Realm, I. 150.

"served," a very literal translation. In 2 Institutes, 588, however, he renders the French words less literally and says that the statute was void, "because impossible to be "observed." In the general proposition at the beginning of the same folio 118a concerning acts of parliament adjudged to be void, he prefers the words, "impossible to be performed." In this latter form of words the law of the case has been generalized and has found permanent lodgement in the books: See Bacon's Abridgment, Ed. Bouvier, vol. 9, p. 217; Viner's Abridgment, Statutes, E. 6, No. 15; Blackstone's Commentaries I., 91; Varnum's Trevett against Weeden, 30.

Coke does not mention Statham, but he doubtless had used the latter's entry of the case. It is Coke who asserts that the court was the Common Pleas.

Statham's entry of the case is thus translated:

"Easter: 27 Henry VI. One *Rous* brought writ of an-
"nuity against an abbot and showed deed of the annuity,
"made by the predecessor of the same abbot and sealed with
"the convent seal, and that the annuity was for certain
"loaves, ale and gowns and other things, etc. *Pole:* the
"statute of Carlisle willed that the Cistercians, *Premonsta-*
"*tenses* and Austins, who have convent and common seal,
"that the common seal shall be in keeping of the prior who
"is under the abbot, etc., and of four others the most wise
"of the house, and that any deed sealed with the common
"seal, that is not so in keeping, shall be void. And we
"say that at the time that this deed was sealed the seal was
"out of their keeping. And the opinion of the court was
"that this statute is void, for it is impertinent to be observed
"(*que ces estatute est voide qar il est impartinent destre*
"*observe*); for the seal being in their keeping, the abbot can
"seal no thing with it, for when it is in the abbot's hands,
"it is out of their keeping *ipso facto.* And if the statute
"should be observed, each common seal would be defeated
"by a simple surmise that can not be tried, etc. *Vide* that
"it was well disputed and several exceptions were taken to
"the plea, etc."

A collation of the foregoing texts of the two Abridgments

shows that every thing in Fitzherbert is copied from the previous work of Statham. The opinion of the court is in identical language in both entries. Certain things mentioned by Statham are, however, omitted by Fitzherbert. The plaintiff was named Rous. The defendant was an abbot. The action was brought for an annuity. Pole (whom Foss states was then a serjeant) was counsel for the defendant. The deed to Rous for the annuity from the abbot's predecessor was impeached as void by Pole, because made against the statute. In holding the statute void, it is clear that the court held the deed good. There was much discussion and there were several exceptions in the case.

In both Fitzherbert and Statham, the court is stated to say that "the statute is void." These words must be understood to mean that a part of the statute was void, *viz.*, the 4th chapter, relating to the convent seals. This point is of importance, for the whole statute of Carlisle was at one time maintained to be "no act of parliament." The reason alleged therefor was that the statute was made by the king, the lords temporal and the commonalty only, in the absence of the bishops and the other lords spiritual. The answer to this objection was that the lords spiritual were summoned by writs of summons as regularly as the temporal lords, but absented themselves from the parliament. In 2 Institutes, on the Statute of 35 Edward I., 585, 586, (ed. 1642), Coke examines this objection to the whole statute, and holds that it was a valid act of parliament. On the shortly following page 588 of the same work, however, he holds the seals chapter of the statute to be void, for the reasons given by the court in Fitzherbert.

It should be pointed out that there was only a limited period during which the vigour of the whole statute was by any possibility questionable on the ground of the absence of the spiritual lords. The statute was made in 35 Edward I., and was confirmed by the statute 4 Edward III., cap. 6.* At the parliament of the latter date the lords spiritual must have been present and uniting in the confirmation.*

Neither Fitzherbert nor Statham say any thing suggest-

* Statutes of the Realm, I. 263.

ing the idea of the seals chapter of the statute being void because legislating concerning ecclesiastical persons and property without the pope's consent. It certainly did so legislate and, according to the Canon law, it was *ipso facto et ipso jure* null, without his consent. Any temporal court holding it void for want of his consent would bring in the Canon law with full vigour. There is, however, no mention of anything Canonical in either of the Abridgments. *Prima facie*, it seems therefore inadmissible to conjecture that the decision of the case was in any way based on the Canon law. Nevertheless, further consideration may show it to be reasonable to assert that the remarkable language of the decision, as to the statute being void, had some sort of connection with the Canon law.

The case was certainly one affecting ecclesiastical persons and property, which arose under a temporal statute. The chapter of the statute, which was drawn in question, was so framed as to produce manifest wrongs to the church, and to laymen dealing with the church, in certain important matters. The temporal court did not attempt to strain the resources of interpretation in dealing with the objectionable text, but boldly confronted the issue of this part of the statute being void or valid. It held the 4th chapter void for matter of substance contained therein, not for any defect of form in the method of its enactment. This temporal court actually used and applied to this unrepealed statute the word, "*void*," which is the precise equivalent in Law French and in English for the Canon law terms, "*nullum*," and, "*non valet*." It can not be denied that this jurisdictional application of the word "void" to an unrepealed statute is remarkable language in a Common law court at any date. It was then very remarkable, because the case is the first on record in which English speaking temporal judges proceeding *jurisdictionaliter* applied the word *void* to an unrepealed statute for cause ascertained by themselves. It can not be denied that the like application of like language to temporal statutes by ecclesiastical judges was then and had been long before well known in the Canon law. In the case of the constitutions of Clarendon, the Pri-

mate Becket had declared most important temporal legislation to be null or void, and had done so successfully.
Neither can it be doubted that the ecclesiastical courts would
have declared the seals chapter of the statute to be void,
whenever they had an opportunity and were free to declare
the Canon law.

While it is not contended that the decision of the court
was made in formal obedience to any of the canons of the
church, it is contended that it is reasonable, under the circumstances, to conjecture that the decision had some sort
of connection with the Canon law.

Among such circumstances, not yet fully dwelt upon, is
the brevity of Statham's entry, which Fitzherbert curtails
in repeating. Some things were certainly omitted. Statham expressly says that the case was well disputed and
several exceptions were taken to the plea. It may, therefore, be possible that some of the things omitted might, if
known, serve to connect the decision in some direct or indirect way with the Canon law doctrine concerning temporal statutes affecting ecclesiastical right and liberty.

The conjecture now made, it is contended, is reasonable
from the point of view of the legal state of things existing
in England before the Reformation, when there was a partition of power between church and state, and when each
organization had courts and laws of its own. This general conclusion is in harmony with the particular conclusion to be reached by a consideration of the Canon law
then in local vigour in England on the subject of ecclesiastical seals. This will now be considered.

Be the law of the case what it may, the fact is that the
seals chapter of the statute of Carlisle flatly conflicted with
the express written law of the church in England, to wit,
the third part of the penultimate constitution made at the
Pan-Anglican Council held at London in 1236. This lega-
tine constitution begins by stating that the use of tabellions
did not obtain in the kingdom of England, on which account it was the more necessary to have recourse to authentic seals. It then enacts that archbishops, bishops, abbots,
priors and other clerical persons named, should have seals.

The third part of the constitution prescribes that in order to diligent care being had concerning the custody of seals, each of the persons aforesaid should keep his own seal or commit it to *one single person*, of whose faith he felt confident, to be kept by him ; and moreover that such person should swear that he would faithfully keep it, that he would not give it to any one to seal any thing, and that he would not seal any thing therewith, from which prejudice might be caused to any one, except what his lord had previously diligently read and seen to, and so had commanded to be sealed : *Sane de custodia sigillorum curam habere diligentem Praecipimus, ut unusquisque per se illud custodiat, vel uni soli, de cujus fide confidat, custodiendum committat, qui etiam juret, quod illud fideliter custodiet, nec ad sigillandum aliquid alicui concedet, nec ipse etiam aliquid sigillet inde, ex quo possit praejudicium alicui generari, nisi quod dominus ejus prius legerit et viderit diligenter, et sic praeceperit sigillari.** The ecclesiastical authority of this constitution can not be questioned. It was enacted at an English council presided over by a Cardinal Legate *a latere*.

There is certainly nothing "impertinent to be observed" in the legislation of the constitution as to ecclesiastical seals. If such was the binding law of keeping and using them before the statute of Carlisle, it was so after it, supposing the fourth chapter of the statute to be void. According to the constitution, abbots and priors must act in regard to them in one way, and according to the statute in another. If the law of the constitution was in vigour and observation in monasteries when the statute was made, the Court of Common Pleas must have known that law and have known that the statute was contrary thereto, even if it did not say so. Assuming these premises to be true when the court held the seals chapter of the statute to be void and decided the first abbot's deed to be valid against his successor, it not only used the Canon law language, but also tacitly, or otherwise, caused a Canon law constitution to be followed in its place.

---

* *Constitutiones Legatinae :* Oxon. 1769 (bound with Lindwood), page 69.

At the bottom of the case, there was thus an actual conflict between the law of the church and the law of the
statute.

These remarks upon the possible relation of the case in
question to the Canon law are submitted to the reader for
what they are worth. Even if they be wholly rejected, the
case is one of the very highest interest. It is unnecessery
to assume that it had anything to do with the Canon law,
to increase its claims to attentive consideration. Its importance is of the first magnitude, Canon law, or no Canon
law. In the first place, it is the earliest case in which a Common law court used the word "void" in holding an unrepealed statute to be void for a cause ascertained and decided by itself. In the second place, the Law-French of the
case, as transformed into English by Coke in the beginning
of 118a of 8 Reports, has secured a permanent place in
the English law on the head of statutes being "void" because "impossible to be performed," regardless of any differences of doctrine among those using that phraseology.*
In the third place, Coke's language and doctrine, while connected with the previous case of the convent seals, became
connected with the subsequent case of Trevett v. Weeden,
which is the first reported suit in America in which a statute
was judicially rejected as void because unconstitutional.
See chapter 25, *post*, and also end of chapter 16, *post*.

DIVISION G.

Of the Reformation and the restrictions which it re-moved from the power of parliament.

By the Reformation, a fundamental change was made in
the English constitution. The partition of power between
the English state and the Roman church was abolished. In
ecclesiastical matters, the prerogative of the king, and the
authority of parliament were no longer restricted by anything said or done by a power seated outside of England.
By the statute of 26 Henry VIII., c. 1. the pope was de-

---

*See Chapter 16, No. 10.

posed from the supreme headship of the church of England and the king substituted in his stead.*

By a *nonobstante* clause in the statute, derogation was made to the Canon law in England under the terms " foreign laws." These changes were followed by the well-known controversies concerning the limits of the perogative in ecclesiastical matters, by the abolition of the crown and of the king's supreme headship of the church, and by the restoration of both after an interregnum. Then came the revolution of 1688 giving parliament a plenitude of power in both ecclesiastical and temporal matters, which was so absolute that no king could dispute it in the name of prerogative.

How real this plenitude of power is, may be seen from the words of Blackstone (Com., I. 160), which have been previously quoted. According to them, parliament has a power which is absolute and without control, and has a sovereign and absolute authority in making, repealing and expounding laws, "concerning matters of all possible de-" nomination *ecclesiastical* or temporal."

It will be observed that, according to the foregoing passage, there is no restriction upon the vigour and scope of an act of parliament in ecclesiastical matters. This is very different from the legal state of things before the Reformation, under the partition of powers between the Roman church and English state. Then, as shown by Lord Chief Justice Frowick's words in the case in the Year Book of 21 Henry VII., the power of parliament was restricted in ecclesiastical matters. Parliament could not legally enact the ecclesiastical measure mentioned by him, if the pope did not consent thereto.

---

* Statutes of the Realm, III. 492.

CHAPTER XIV.

Conclusions as to conflicts between the laws of the church and the laws of the state from the point of view of the division into spiritual and temporal powers and the jurisprudence of the Canon law.

Comparison of the Canon law with the constitutional law of the United States and the several states on the head of conflicts of laws.

This chapter will contain statements of certain propositions concerning the Canon law, which, it is contended, are sustained by the foregoing investigation in chapters 12 and 13. They will be stated in connection with certain other propositions concerning the constitutional law of the United States and the several states. Both series of propositions bear upon the subject of this Essay. They will be stated in connection with each other under six several heads, as follows :

1. It is the ancient doctrine of the Canon law that temporal, lay, or civil statutes are null for certain Canonical cause. It is the received doctrine of lawyers throughout the United States that an act of Congress or a state statute may be void or null for constitutional causes.

2. Such canonical cause aforesaid is defect of lay power to enact temporal statutes contrary to ecclesiastical right or liberty. Here and now, it is the received doctrine of lawyers that, under a written constitution, there can exist no legislative power of making laws which are contrary to such constitution and in conflict therewith.

3. A Canon law court will, upon fitting judicial opportunity, proceed as competent to inquire and decide concerning

such Canonical cause and such defect of power and (they being found) to hold the questioned temporal statute to be null, *ipso facto et ipso jure.* This is shown by the Rotal case of the Roman lands and Genoese testament, decided in 1648, in which the Roman Rota expressly held that every temporal statute ascertained and decided to be contrary to ecclesiastical liberty is *ipso facto et jure nullum ex defectu potestatis laicorum statuentium.*

It was therefore neither a novelty nor an inelegancy in point of jurisprudence for the framers of an American constitution so to frame it that there should exist thereunder a judicial competency of deciding questioned legislation to be constitutional or unconstitutional and of holding it void or valid accordingly.

4. The Canon law contains a division of spiritual and temporal powers between a church, or religious organization, and a state, or political organization. The constitution of the United States contains a division of delegated and reserved powers between the United States and the several states, and a further division of such delegated powers between Congress and other vestees. Each of the constitutions of the several states contains a division of powers between the legislative, executive and judicial departments of the government of the state. The constitution of each state proceeds upon the basis that there is a division of federal and municipal powers between the Union and the state.

The Canon law shows that according to the principles of law and the doctrines of jurisprudence, defect of power in a system of division of powers, is legal and rightful cause for a temporal statute being null, and that the question of the existence of such cause may be a judicial one.

There is therefore precedent for saying that it accords with the principles of law and the doctrines of jurisprudence for a written constitution to be so framed that defect of legislative power, resulting from its system of divisions of powers, shall be a legal and constitutional cause for a statute being void, and that the question of the existence of such cause may be a judicial one.

5. Thus the idea of a judicial competency of deciding

a questioned statute to be contrary to binding right and holding it therefore null and void can be traced as far back as the Canon law. Furthermore, the use of the word "null" and the word "void" to express the absence of legislative vigour in an *unrepealed* statute, is not a new Americanism in speech. The Rotal judgment above mentioned holds part of a temporal statute to be "null" for the Canonical cause specified and shows what the Canon law had been for a long period of time.

The case of the Prior of Castlaker *v.* the Dean of St. Stephens in the reign of Henry VII. is a Common law case having relation to the Canon law, and the report of the argument at the bar shows that the word "void" was actually used as legally applicable to temporal statutes legislating on matters merely affecting the spiritualty. The case of Rous *v.* an Abbot in the reign of Henry VI. may or may not be connected with the Canon law, but certainly was one affecting ecclesiastical persons and property. In it the court applied the word "void" to a whole chapter of an unrepealed statute.

6. In any of the medieval states throughout which the division into spiritual and temporal powers was fundamental law under the sanction of spiritual coercion, the nullity of a temporal statute must have been merely an effect. The cause of that effect was the contrariety of the statute to ecclesiastical right or liberty. Controversies between the spiritual and temporal powers, must, therefore, have generally turned on questions concerning what was or was not contrary to ecclesiastical right or liberty, rather than on any question of the validity or invalidity of a temporal statute conceded to be so contrary. Similarly, here and now, there are numerous differences of opinion as to what is or is not constitutional. It is exceptional to hear the doctrine maintained that a law should be deemed obligatory, although pronounced by a competent court to be unconstitutional.

CHAPTER XV.

Of the English law concerning parliamentary legislation in certain temporal cases before the Revolution of 1688.

No. 1. *Of acts of parliament restricting the royal prerogative before 1688.*

No. 2. *Of the case of* Godden v. Hales *in the reign of* James II.

No. 3. *Of the sheriff's case in the Year Book of 2 Henry VII. p. 6*

This chapter will consider the English law concerning parliamentary legislation in certain cases affecting the royal prerogative, which arose before the Revolution of 1688. As is well known, that revolution divides the history of the law of prerogative into two parts, which differ as to the king's relations to acts of parliament.

No. 1.

Of acts of parliament restricting prerogative before 1688.

While it is true that since the Revolution of 1688 an English court would never think of holding an act of parliament to be void because it conflicted with the royal prerogative, a like assertion can not be made for the time before that date. In the case of Godden *v.* Hales, in 1686, the Court of King's Bench actually held that important provisions of the statute of 25 Charles II. cap. 2, were

void because conflicting with the king's rightful prerogative. It, moreover, gave judgment accordingly, there being
no other question in the cause.*

No. 2.

Of the case of Godden v. Hales.

The decision in this case is celebrated in English history
as intimately connected with the causes of the revolution of
1688. The abolition of the royal power of dispensing with
any statute, made in the 1st year of William and Mary,
was caused by the existence of this decision. The case is
discussed at length by Macaulay, who criticises both the
decision and the motives of the court with great severity.
The second paragraph of the bill of rights in the statute of
1 William and Mary, sess. 2. cap. 2., formally declares to
be illegal what the decision declared to be legal.

It is thus matter of authority that the decision was erroneous not only after the Revolution but also when it was
made. This does not, however, prevent it from being of
the highest interest to every one investigating the origin of
a judicial competency of deciding a questioned statute to
be contrary to binding right and holding it to be therefore
void. In this remarkable decision the court regarded it as
a judicial question whether or not a statute could bind the
king in certain cases of prerogative right and regarded it as
a judicial obligation to hold the statute to be invalid after
answering that question in the negative. According to now
prevalent American ideas, if the constitution of England
had been written, and such a prerogative right had been
constitutional, the court ought to have done precisely what
it did. Moreover, had the decision been one in favour of a
popular right instead of a prerogative right, the assertion
of a judicial competency of deciding a questioned statute
to be contrary to binding right, might have been, perhaps,

---

* Godden v. Hales is reported in Shower, 475 ; Comberbach, 21 ; Cobbett's
State Trials, IX. 1167. It is discussed in Macaulay's History, Ed. 2, vol. 2,
ch. 6, p. 84.

very differently regarded. Such, indeed, was precisely what happened in Rhode Island in 1786 as to the case of Trevett *v*. Weeden, which will be fully considered hereinafter and need only be briefly referred to here.

Trevett *v*. Weeden was a case in which a statute, made under an *unwritten* constitution, and destroying the popular right of trial by jury, was judicially rejected as unconstitutional and therefore void. In the interest of popular rights, an American court flatly refused to obey a clearly worded statute. Godden *v*. Hales was a case in which an English court, also proceeding under an *unwritten* constitution, did likewise in the interest of royal prerogative. Animated by different motives and striving for different objects, both courts, nevertheless, performed like judicial acts in regard to questioned legislation. The American court is celebrated in history for the success of its action not only in its own state, but throughout a "growing world," for Trevett *v*. Weeden is the first reported case of its kind on this continent. The English court is memorable in history for the failure of its action on the eve of a revolution which it helped to provoke. This historical contrast must strike all who consider it. That illustrious man of science, Joseph Henry, taught his students at Princeton to record their failures as well as their successes in making experiments. What is true of physical science, is as true of legal science. Let the failures be studied in history as well as in the laboratory.

The following extracts from Shower's report of the case of Godden *v*. Hales will be sufficient for the present purpose :

" Debt for five hundred pounds upon the statute of 25 "Car. II. c. 2, for accepting and exercising the office of "colonel, etc., not having taken the oaths, and subscribed "the declaration ; and set forth an indictment, and conviction for the same, *per quod actio accrevit.*

" The defendant pleads in bar, that after his admission, "and before three months expired, the king, by his letters "patent, had pardoned, released, and *dispensed* with said "oaths. The plaintiff demurs.

"Mr. Northey for the plaintiff. . . . . The king
"can not control an act of parliament that disables a
"man . . . .

"Glanville, serjeant [for defendant]. . . . .   . There
"is a great distinction between the laws of property and
"those of government . . . ."

The opinion of the court is as follows: "The Lord Chief
"Justice took time to consider of it, and spake with the
"other judges, and three or four days after, declared that
"he and all the judges (except Street and Powell who
"doubted) were of opinion, that the kings of England
"were absolute sovereigns; that the laws were the king's
"laws; that the king had a power to dispense with any of
"the laws of government as he saw necessity for it; that
"he was the sole judge of that necessity; *that no act of
"parliament could take away that power; that this was
"such a law;* that the case of Sheriffs in the second year
"of Henry the Seventh, was law, and always taken as law;
"and that it was a much stronger case than this. And
"therefore gave judgment for the defendant."

Thus the court held the statute invalid because it was judicially ascertained to deprive the king of a part of his
rightful prerogative.

No. 3.

*Of the Sheriff's case in the Year Book of 2 Henry VII.,
p. 6.*

The Sheriff's case alluded to by Lord Chief Justice Her-
bert was that of the shrievalty of Northumberland in the
Year Book of 2 Henry VII. (p. 6 and Index under *Roy*). An
interpretation of the report of this case, different from that
given in the opinion of the court in Godden *v.* Hales, is to
be found in the argument of Northey for the defendant.
Northey's argument is reported at much greater length in 8
Bacon's Abridgment, 70–79 (ed. Bouvier) than in Shower,
Comberbach or the State Trials. Northey disputed the authority of the Sheriff's case for any thing. Macaulay re-

gards Northey's argument in Godden *v.* Hales as insincere. This imputation, if true, does not however necessarily affect the correctness of his view of the Sheriff's case.

Lord Bacon's understanding of the report of the case is found in his Maxims Reg. 19, p. 38 of the Law Tracts, 2d. Edition. It accords with the subsequent opinion in Godden *v.* Hales, and is as follows:

" So if there be a statute made that no sheriff shall con-"tinue in his office above a year, and if any patent be made "to the contrary, it shall be void ; and if there be any " *clausula de non-obstante* contained in such patent to dis-"pense with this present act, that such clause also shall be " void ; yet nevertheless a patent of the sheriff's office made " by the king for term of life, with a *non-obstante* will be good "in law contrary to such statute, which pretendeth to ex-" clude *non-obstante's ;* and the reason is, because it is an " inseparable prerogative of the crown to dispense with po-"litic statutes, and of that kind ; and then the derogatory " clause hurteth not." The marginal note quotes for this the case in the Year Book of 2 Henry VII., p. 6.

Lord Bacon thus was of opinion that a statute taking away the king's prerogative power of dispensing with laws in certain cases was not binding upon the judges, and re-garded the case in 2 Henry VII. as judicial authority for that proposition.

The following account of the Sheriff's case is in part translated and in part abridged from the report in the Year Book of 2 Henry VII., p. 6 :

" In the Exchequer Chamber before all the justices, it was " shown for the king, how King Edward IV., by his letters "patent had ordained that the Earl of N. be sheriff of the " same county, and had granted the office of the aforesaid "county to the said Earl for the term of his life, with all "the other offices appurtenant thereto, rendering therefor "to the king at his exchequer annually one hundred "pounds, without any account, or without rendering any "other thing therefor, etc. Now whether the patent was "good ; and also how the patent should be understood. " And as to the first point the justices held the patent good ;

"for it is such a thing as can well be granted for term of
"life, or for inheritance, since divers counties have sheriffs
"by inheritance, and such begin by grant of the king.
"Then was shown a resumption, and then a proviso for H.
"Earl of N. was shown, so that the patent remains in its
"force.

"Radcliff showed the statutes of 28 Edward III. c. 7.
"and 42 Edward III. c. 5.,* whereby there should be no
"sheriff for more than a year, etc. ; and showed how there
"was a *non-obstante*. And this *non-obstante* the king
"always had upon his prerogative as well concerning the
"value and contents of lands, other things granted by the
"king, abandoned ships, and charters of murders, and sev-
"eral other cases in which there are statutes providing that
"patents which do those things should be void. Neverthe-
"less the patents of the king are good with a **non-obstante**,
"but without a *non-obstante* the patents are void because
"of the statutes. So here the patent is with a *non-obstante*.
"Wherefore, etc. But as to the second point several of the
"justices held," etc.

The second point was as to how the patent should be construed. It was discussed at considerably greater length
than the first point. The report ends with the following
words, the precise meaning of which is important:

"But because this was the first time, the justices and ser-
"jeants and attorney of the king agreed that they should
"study well as to the matter, and they should be heard,
"and what they had said was for nothing, for they wished
"to be at their liberty to say what they wished and to think
"for nothing what they had now said."

If this language is to be applied to the whole report, then
Northey's assertion that the case was no authority for anything, is strongly supported by it. If, however, it applies
only to the discussion of the second point, the authority of
the decision on the first point can not be attacked except
on the general ground of error. That part of the report,
which is concerned with the first point, has in itself no

---

* *Cf.* statute 1 of 14 Edward III. cap. 7 ; Statutes of the Realm, I. 283.

obscurity. It purports to give the common opinion of all the king's judges assembled in the Exchequer Chamber. That opinion was to the effect that royal letters patent doing certain things were prohibited and made void by statute, but that the king had the prerogative of derogating to such statute by a *nonobstante* clause in such letters patent, which then were good.

CHAPTER XVI.

Of the doctrine concerning void statutes from which Blackstone dissents in his tenth rule of interpretation.

No. 1. *Of Blackstone's tenth rule for construing statutes.*

No. 2. *Of Coke's doctrine upon the invalidity of statutes in certain cases.*

No. 3. *Of the case of the Mayor and Commonalty of London* v. *Wood.*

No. 4. *Of Bonham's case and Coke's opinion therein.*

No. 5. *Of Tregor's case.*

No. 6. *Of the case in Fitzherbert's Abridgment, Cessavit, 42.*

No. 7. *Of two cases* temp. *Elizabeth relating to the statute of 1 Edward VI. Cap. 14.*

No. 8. *Of Coke on* iniquum est aliquem suae rei esse judicem.

No. 9. *Coke's view of the seals case in Fitzherbert's Abridgment, Annuity 41, or Rous* v. *an Abbot.*

No. 10. *Of the effect of Coke's view of the seals case in English and American legal history.*

This chapter will be devoted to the consideration of the doctrine concerning the invalidity of acts of parliament in certain cases, from which Blackstone dissents in his tenth rule for the construing of statutes.

No. 1.

Of Blackstone's tenth rule for construing statutes.

Blackstone's tenth rule for construing statutes must be repeated :

" Lastly, acts of parliament that are impossible to be per-
"formed are of no validity ; and if there arise out of them
"collaterally any absurd consequences, manifestly contra-
" dictory to common reason, they are, with regard to those
"collateral consequences, void*." He immediately adds that he lays down this rule with these restrictions, although he knows that it is generally laid down more largely, to the import that " acts of parliament contrary to reason are void."

No. 2.

Of Coke's doctrine upon the invalidity of statutes in cer-
tain cases.

The larger laying down of the rule, thus referred to by Blackstone, requires examination. It is a matter upon which he thought one way, and Coke another.

The following observation of Bowyer's may here conven-
iently be quoted : †

" We must receive with considerable qualifications what
"Lord Coke said, in *Doctor Bonham's case* (8 Rep. 118),
"in which he declared that the Common Law doth control
"Acts of Parliament, and adjudges them void when against
"common right and reason.   And Lord Chief Justice Holt,
"in *The City of London* v. *Wood* (12 Mod. 687), adopted
"this dictum of Lord Coke, which is supported by Lord

---

* Commentaries, I. 91.

† Readings in the Middle Temple in 1850, pages 84, 85.

"Chief Justice Hobart, in *Day* v. *Savage* (Hob. Rep. 87),
" who insisted that an Act of Parliament made against
" natural equity, so as to make a man judge in his own
" cause, was void."

No. 3.

Of the case of the Mayor and Commonalty of London v.
*Wood.**

This case was an action of debt brought before the court
holden before the mayor and aldermen of London. The question arose whether the very man (the Lord Mayor) who, as
the head of the city, presided over the court, was not also
a party to the suit. The action was brought in the court in
the name of the mayor and commonalty of London and it
was held to be error.† Holt, C. J., said : " What my Lord
" Coke says in *Bonham's case*, in his 8 Co., is far from any
" extravagancy, for it is a very reasonable and true saying,
" that if an act of parliament should ordain that the same
" person should be party and judge, or which is the same
" thing, judge in his own cause, it would be a *void* act of
" parliament ; for it is *impossible* that one should be judge
" and party, for the judge is to determine between party and
" party, or between the government and the party ; and an
" act of parliament can do no wrong, though it may do sev-
" eral things that look pretty odd ; for it may discharge
" one from his allegiance to the government he lives under,
" and restore him to the state of nature ; but it cannot make
" one who lives under a government judge and party. An
" act of parliament may not make adultery lawful, that is,
" it cannot make it lawful for A. to lie with the wife of B.:
" but it may make the wife of A. to be the wife of B., and
" dissolve her marriage with A."‡
Coke's decision was made long before the Revolution of

---

* 12 Modern Reports, 669, 687.

† 12 Modern, 687, reports the case as the City of London *v.* Wood, but the
opinion states that the plaintiffs were as above mentioned.

‡ On this case compare Bank of U. S. *v.* Deveaux, 5 Cranch, page 90.

1688. Holt's decision was made after, but shortly after, that event. Blackstone was born in 1723 and his Commentaries were written much later. These dates are of importance in connection with the doctrine of Blackstone's tenth rule. That doctrine was intimately connected with the omnipotence of parliament, which was secured by the Revolution of 1688. The difference between the views of Holt and Blackstone indicates that a portion at least of the influence of the revolution on judicial minds was but gradual in its operation. Time was required to reach the position taken by Blackstone. His tenth rule, indeed, is not in every case uniformly applied. As will be pointed out in the next chapter, there is a relaxation of it, or an exception to it, in the case of an act of parliament conflicting with the law of nations.

No. 4.

Of Bonham's case and Coke's opinion therein.

In Coke's opinion in Bonham's case * he says :

" And it appears in our books, that in many cases, the " common law will control acts of parliament, and some- "times adjudge them to be utterly void : for when an act " of parliament is against common right and reason, or re- "pugnant, or *impossible to be performed*, the common law " will control it, *and adjudge such act to be void.*"

The cases which Coke adduces in support of these views are the following.

No. 5.

Of Tregor's case.

The earliest is Tregor's case in the Year Book of 8 Edward III. p. 30, in which Herle, J., said " that some statutes "are made against law and right, which, when those who "made them perceiving, would not put them in execution."

---

* 8 Reports, 118a.

No. 6.

Of the case in Fitzherbert's Abridgment, Cessavit, 42.

In 33 Edward III., Fitzherbert's Abridgment, Cessavit, 42, and *Natura Brevium*, 209 F., the case was this : There were two coparcener lords, and a tenant by fealty and certain rent. One coparcener had issue and died. It was decided that the aunt and niece shall not join in Cessavit for a cesser made before the title accrued to the niece, because the heir shall not have Cessavit for the cesser in the time of his ancestor. For in a Cessavit the tenant may tender arrears and damages and retain his land. This he can not do when the heir brings a Cessavit, for the arrears incurred in the ancestor's life do not belong to the heir. This decision was directly contrary to the statute of Westminster the second, chapter 21, which expressly gave the heir a *cessavit*, and, says Coke, "because it would be against common right and " reason, the Common law adjudges the said act of parlia- " ment as on that point void.*"

No. 7.

Of two cases relating to the statute of 1 Edward VI., Cap. 14.

In two cases in Queen Elizabeth's time relating to the statute of 1 Edward VI., cap. 14, it is said by Coke that the Common law controlled the statute and adjudged it void. The act gave certain chauntries to the king, reserving all rents and services to the donors. It was held that the donors should have the rent as a rentseck, etc., for " it " would be against common right and reason that the king " should hold of any, or do services to any of his subjects."

---

* Northey's opinion as to the statute and the writ of Cessavit in the colony of New York will be found in Chalmers's Opinions, Ed. 1, vol. 1, page 130 ; Ed. 2, page 149.

No. 8.

Of Coke on iniquum est aliquem suae rei esse judicem.

Coke lays down the following, without citing any authority except a general maxim: "So if any act of parlia-"ment gives to any to hold, or to have conusance of, all "manner of pleas arising before him within the manor of "D., yet he shall hold no plea, to which he himself is a "party: for, as hath been said, *iniquum est aliquem suae* "*rei esse judicem.*"

No. 9.

Coke's view of the seals case in Fitzherbert's Abridgment, Annuity, 41, or Rous v. *an Abbot.*

Coke enlarges on the important case in Fitzherbert, Annuity 41, relating to the convent seals, in which the 4th chapter of the statue of Carlisle was held void. Citing Fitzherbert, he says:

"The statute of Carlisle, made *anno* 35 E. 1., enacts "that the order of Cistercians and Augustines, who have a "convent and common seal, that the common seal shall be "in the keeping of the prior, who is under the abbot, and "four others of the most grave of the house, and that any "deed sealed with the common seal, which is not so in "keeping shall be void: and the opinion of the court (*in* "*an.* 27 H. 6. Fitzherbert, Annuity 41.) was, that this "statute was *void*, for it is *impertinent to be observed*, for "the seal being in their keeping, the abbot can not seal any-"thing with it, and when it is in the abbot's hands, it is "out of their keeping *ipso facto;* and if the statute should "be observed, every common seal shall be defeated upon a "simple surmise, which cannot be tried."

It is historically and legally important to point out that Fitzherbert's words "*inpartinent destre observe*," are here translated by Coke by the literal words, "impertinent to be observed."

In 2 Institutes 588, however, in commenting upon the statute of Carlisle, he translated them by, "impossible to be observed." In the general proposition quoted above from 118a of 8 Reports, he prefers the words, "impossible to be performed." So modified the language of the case in Fitzherbert, Annuity 41, on the 4th chapter of the statute of Carlisle has found a permanent place in the English law.*

No. 10.

Of the effect of Coke's view of the seals case in English and in American legal history.

Coke's phrase, "impossible to be performed," is adopted by Blackstone in his tenth rule above mentioned, although that rule differs from Coke's doctrine. Coke's doctrine was laid down more largely than Blackstone's. Blackstone's view has prevailed in England, and not Coke's. Coke's doctrine received much attention in America during the colonial period and was a subject of discussion in the seventeenth as well as in the eighteenth century.†

The difference in the legal history of American and English judiciaries has not been due exclusively to written constitutions. The first reported American case in which a judicial judgment rejected a legislative act as void because unconstitutional, was Trevett v. Weeden, which arose in Rhode Island, where the then constitution was not written. The statute of Rhode Island, which then came under judicial criticism, prescribed that offenders against paper money legislation should be criminally tried without a jury and according to the laws of the land. Coke's doctrine was quoted with important effect. Counsel argued that statutes "impossible to be performed" were void, and that such was the statute in question.‡ A statute prescribing a trial without a jury according to the laws of the land was as-

---

* *Cf.* Chapter 13, Division F, paragraph 4.

† See Gray's Treatise on Writs of Assistance in Quincy's Reports page 527, note 28 ; pages 520 to 530.

‡ Varnum's Case of Trevett against Weeden, 30, 31.

serted to be one "impossible to be executed." The court must have adopted this doctrine. Although there was no united written opinion of the court, the whole bench spoke by deeds as strong as words in the memorable judgment rendered. In the brief remarks of the judges individually in voting upon the judgment, one of them expressly said that the statute was impossible to be executed and voted accordingly.*

According to Coke's view of the convent seals case and of the 4th chapter of the statute of Carlisle, " impertinent to " be observed," and, "impossible to be performed," are words of the same meaning. According to Trevett v. Weeden, " impossible to be performed," and, "impossible to be executed," are words of the same meaning. There are thus links connecting these two historic cases. The possibility that the English case has a connection with the Canon law doctrine of temporal statutes being null for ecclesiastical cause, thus becomes of additional interest to American lawyers.

CHAPTER XVII.

Results of the foregoing examination of the history of the English law in England.

The present doctrine of the English law is that judges are bound by all statutes in all cases according to the clear and clearly expressed intention of the legislature. The foregoing investigation, it is contended, shows that the following distinctions as to different periods in the life of the English constitution must be made, in order to under-

---

* See *post* Chapter 25, which contains a review of the case of Trevett *v* Weeden.

stand the place which that doctrine occupies in English legal history.

First. Before the Reformation a real partition of power between church and state and a real division into temporal and spiritual powers existed. That "the English church "shall be free," *quod Anglicana ecclesia libera sit*, was written in the very first article of Magna Charta. This was no novel legislation. It was a declaration of the ancient law. In consequence of the then constitution of England, the legislative power of parliament was essentially different from what it was after the Reformation. Parliament could not then destroy the rights and liberty of the church in two classes of matters. The first class included all purely spiritual matters. The second class included some but not all spiritual matters that were mixed with the temporalty. If the parliament made a statute so extending, it was *ipso facto* and *ipso jure* void *ex defectu potestatis*. Such temporal legislation in such ecclesiastical matters did not bind either the subjects, the officials or the judges of the king.

Second. Before the revolution of 1688, there were the first developments of a doctrine that courts were competent to decide upon the rightfulness or wrongfulness, and ascertain the validity or invalidity, of statutes, when it was necessary to defend the royal prerogative against the encroachments of parliamentary power.

Third. Subsequently to the revolution of 1688, the doctrine became generally accepted that the judiciary are bound by all acts of parliament in all cases in which the intention of the legislature is clear and clearly expressed. Neither ecclesiastical rights, nor royal prerogative, can resist the vigour of any contrary act of parliament. Any relaxation of this doctrine, relating to statutes impossible to be performed, must be laid down in the terms of Blackstone's tenth rule.

Fourth. Coke's larger doctrine as to the invalidity of statutes, from which Blackstone dissents, is not accepted as law. Some further consideration of this negative result should be made.

It may, perhaps, be true that the rejection of Coke's rule

was necessary merely because it could not have been accepted without changing the form of government. If this be so, the acceptance of Blackstone's rule was not due to its internal excellence as a rule of interpretation but to its harmony with the form of government. This view of Blackstone's rule is to a certain extent encouraged by the prevailing doctrine concerning the interpretation of statutes conflicting with the law of nations, which is a relaxation of Blackstone's rule, if it be not an exception to it. This doctrine is laid down by Lord Stowell as follows in the case of the Le Louis, on page 239 of 2 Dodson's Admiralty Reports:

" Neither this British act of parliament, nor any commis-
" sion founded on it, can affect any right or interest of
" foreigners, unless they are founded upon principles and
" impose regulations that are consistent with the law of
" nations. That is the only law which Great Britain can
" apply to them; *and the generality of any terms em-*
" *ployed in an act of parliament must be narrowed in con-*
" *struction by a religious adherence thereto.**

Thus, to avoid a conflict between the law of nations and an act of parliament, an English judge will strain so hard that he will resort to a forced construction of the statute. So doing does not affect the form of government, for it does not affect the power of parliament to derogate to the law of nations. But if parliament wishes to derogate to that law, it is compelled to say expressly that it proceeds in derogation thereof, for if it do not do so, the judges will certainly presume that it proceeds otherwise and will interpret its act according to such presumption. Such interpretation is not an application of Blackstone's tenth rule, but a relaxation of it, or an exception to it. Without affecting the form of government, Stowell's doctrine occupies really an intermediate place between Blackstone's and Coke's.

---

* Compare Murray *v.* the Charming Betsey, 2 Cranch, page 118.

CHAPTER XVIII.

Of the relation of acts of parliament to the colonies before 1776.

No. 1. *Of the extension of acts of parliament to the colonies and their trade.*

No. 2. *Of the statute of 7 and 8 William III., cap. 22.*

No. 3. *Of the statutes relating to stranded ships.*

No. 4. *Of the case of the Canary wine trade and the statute of 15 Charles II., cap. 7.*

No. 5. *Of the law of statutes extending to the colonies before 1776.*

No. 6. *Of the modern English law of statutes extending to the colonies.*

In the foregoing pages the law concerning acts of parliament in England has been discussed. The present chapter will consider the relation of acts of parliament to the colonies and the trade thereof before 1776.

No. 1.

Of the extension of acts of parliament to the colonies and their trade.

Parliament maintained that it could bind the colonists in America as much as the inhabitants of England, whenever it saw fit to pass an act extending to the colonies or any of them. Thus arose an important branch of English law comprehending questions whether particular acts of parliament did or did not extend to the American colonies and their trade. In the administration of the government the practice was to settle such questions by reference to crown counsel. While a crown counsel could not hold an act of parliament to be void because contrary to constitutional right, he did say that an act was void of effect in the colonies when he decided that it did not extend to them or their trade. While the importance of this legal conception should not be exaggerated, it must not be ignored. The colonists claimed as a great constitutional right to which they were entitled, that acts of parliament should not extend to the government of the colonies except in certain exceptional constitutional cases.* As a matter of fact, the acts of parliament expressly mentioning the colonies, though of grave importance, were few in number. Other acts were not deemed to extend to the government of the colonies, if trained lawyers did not professionally so decide. These considerations have their place in the development of those constitutional ideas, which were carried out in written constitutions establishing judiciaries competent to criticise legislation under such constitutions.

On this, as on other heads of constitutional law concerning the English Colonies, Chalmers's collection of opinions of crown counsel is the most familiar book of reference. Forsyth's more recent collection, entitled : Cases and Opinions on Constitutional Law (London, 1869), contains also valuable matter relating to colonies.

No. 2.

Of the statute of 7 and 8 William III., cap. 22.

The statute of 7 and 8 William III., cap. 22, contained provisions of fundamental importance relating to the colonies. Its eighth section reads thus :

" And it is further enacted and declared by the authority "aforesaid, that all laws, by-laws, usages or customs at

---

* See Declaration of Rights of 14 October, 1774, in Journals of Congress, I. 26, last edition.

"this time or which shall hereafter be in practice, or en-
"deavoured or pretended to be in force or practice, in any
"of the said plantations, which are in any wise repugnant
"to the before mentioned laws, or any of them [12 Car. II.
"cap. 18; 15 Car. II. cap. 7; 22 & 23 Car. II. cap. 26, and
"25 Car. II. cap. 7.], so far as they do relate to the said
"plantations or any of them, or which are [any] ways re-
"pugnant to this present act, or to any other law hereafter
"to be made in this kingdom, so far as such law shall re-
"late to and mention the said plantations, are illegal null
"and void to all intents and purposes whatsoever."*

According to the foregoing legislation, every colonial law,
usage or custom, of any of the plantations, is thereby made
illegal null and void, (1) if it be repugnant to the said
statute of 7 and 8 William III., or (2) if it be repugnant to
the four said statutes of Charles II., "*so far as they do re-
"late to the said plantations or any of them*," or (3) if it
be repugnant to any future law of parliament "so far as
"such law shall relate to and mention the said plantations."

How far a statute of parliament related to, mentioned, or
extended to, any colony or colonies, might be a delicate
question of law. The two following examples will illustrate this last proposition.

No. 3.

Of the statutes relating to stranded ships.

In 1767 these acts required interpretation. Two crown
counsel were officially of the opinion that the act of 12
Anne stat. 2. cap. 13, relating to stranded ships and goods,
and so much of the act of 4 George II. cap. 12, as declared
the former act to be perpetual, extended to the American
colonies. But they "were inclined to think" that the 3d
clause of the latter act, relating to a newly introduced
crime, did not extend to those colonies (Chalmers's Colonial Opinions, Ed. 2, 212).

---

* See Statutes of the Realm, VII., 105.

No. 4.

Of the Canary wine trade and the statute of 15 Charles II., cap. 7.

Under the statute of 15 Charles II., cap. 7, no wine or other product of Europe could be transported to the American colonies, unless shipped in Great Britain. For many years Canary wine was shipped directly from the islands to New England and New York. In 1737 the legality of the trade was questioned upon the ground that the Canaries were geographically part of Europe.

Fane, the crown counsel, to whom the question was referred, thought that the geographical evidence showed that the Canaries were not European. He added that, if there should be any doubt upon the subject, the long usage of the trade itself was of great weight. He was officially of opinion that the trade was lawful. Thus the act of parliament did not relate to the wine trade of New England and New York with the Canaries. In so far as this, there was no repugnancy between the commercial customs of those colonies and the provisions of the act (Chalmers's Colonial Opinions, Ed. 2, p. 572).

No. 5.

Of the law of statutes extending to the colonies before 1776.

From a consideration of the statute of 7 and 8 William III. cap. 22 and the cases in Chalmers, it appears that when the question was whether or not a colonial law was illegal null and void because of repugnancy to a parliamentary law, the following legal proposition was correct, according to English views in the middle of the last century.

It was not sufficient to ascertain whether a colonial law was repugnant to a law of parliament in order to know whether the former was or was not illegal null and void. In all cases in which the act of parliament did not expressly legislate as to its own vigour in the colony, it was necessary to ascertain whether it was within the limitation of 7 & 8 William III. cap. 22. If it was not, it had no countervailing vigour against the repugnant colonial law. It must be ascertained whether the parliamentary law extended to the colony or not. If it did extend thereto, it must further be ascertained whether it did so wholly or only partially.

The American views, expressed in the Declaration of Rights of 1774,* as to the cases in which parliament was entitled to legislate for the colonies, of course restricted the rightful opportunities for applying the above principles. In the particular cases, however, in which it was generally admitted in the colonies that parliament was entitled to legislate for them, those principles could be fully applied without any objection on the part of any colonists

No. 6.

Of the modern English law of statutes extending to the colonies.

Although the statute of 28 & 29 Victoria, cap. 63, belongs to a date posterior to the declaration of independence, it may usefully be referred to in elucidation of the law of the British empire. It is an act to remove doubts as to the validity of colonial laws. The 2d section enacts that :†

" Any colonial law which is or shall be in any respect re-
"pugnant to the provisions of any Act of Parliament ex-
" tending to the colony to which such law may relate, or re-
"pugnant to any order or regulation made under authority
"of such Act of Parliament, or having in the colony the
" force and effect of such Act, shall be read subject to such
" Act, order, or regulation, and shall, to the extent of such
"repugnancy, but not otherwise, be and remain void and
" inoperative."

Under this statute, it appears that in every judicial case involving both a colonial law and an act of parliament, there

---

* Journals of Congress, Ed. 1800, vol. 1, p. 26.

† Tarring's law relating to the Colonies, 21.

are, besides the question of actual repugnancy of the former
to the latter, two other questions, which a court must decide:

First, the extent of the repugnancy, for, within it, but not
beyond it, the colonial law is derogated to by 28 & 29 Victoria, cap. 63 ;

Second, the question whether the act of parliament actually extends to the colony that made the colonial law.

How important the latter question might be is well known
in literary circles throughout the United States.   In Low *v.*
Routledge, L. R. 1 Ch. App. 42, the case depended upon
whether an act of parliament extended to Canada: "An
"alien friend, residing in Canada during the publication in
"England of a work composed by her, was adjudged en-
"titled to copyright under the Imperial Copyright Act, 4 &
"5 Vict. c. 45, although she was not so entitled by the
"Canadian Copyright Act,—the Imperial Act, by ss. 2 and
"29, extending to all colonies, settlements and possessions
"of the Crown now and hereafter."   (Tarring's Law relating to the Colonies, p. 21.)

It therefore does not now suffice to ascertain the extent to
which a colonial law is repugnant to an act of parliament,
in order to ascertain how far it is void and inoperative.   It
is true that the extent of the repugnancy in the colonial
law is a condition of the extent of its invalidity and inop-
erativeness, but this is only one of the conditions of the
limitation.   There is also another condition, *viz.*, one limiting the vigour of the contradicted act of parliament in
countervailing the repugnant colonial act.   If the act of
parliament does not extend to the colony, it has no countervailing vigour against a colonial law, which is repugnant to
it.   This extending question is one, which a judicial court
is competent to decide, as is proved by the case of Low *v.*
Routledge.

It thus appears that according to the express written law
of England it is now true, that judges can decide for themselves whether and how far an act of parliament extends to
a colony, and, in accordance with such decision, must hold,
that it does or does not countervail a colonial law repugnant
to it.

CHAPTER XIX.

Of legislation for the colonies by act o. prerogative.

DIVISION A.

Of the relation of the colonies to legislation by act of prerogative.

DIVISION B.

Of the case of Guernsey and Jersey.

DIVISION C.

Of the case of Campbell *v.* Hall or that o. the Island of Grenada.

The foregoing is a sufficient discussion of the topic of legislation for the colonies by act of *parliament.* The next head to be considered will be that of legislation for the colonies by act of *prerogative*, that is to say, bv the king in council, and not by the king in parliament.

DIVISION A.

Of the relation of the colonies to legislation by act of prerogative.

No branch of constitutional learning was more important for the colonial law of the thirteen colonies than the law of legislation by act of prerogative. Their charters, patents and forms of government were made by legislative acts of prerogative. Their legislatures were organized under such legislative acts, which were passed by the king in council and written in letters patent issued under his great seal. In so far as the laws of colonial legislatures derived their vigour from the metropolitan government and not from the consent of their colonial constituents, they were enacted by virtue of powers given by such acts of prerogative and not by incorporating acts of parliament.*

Such was the rule. An exception to it existed in the case of the colony of the Lower Counties upon Delaware. Although such an exception existed, the organization of the separate legislature of that colony was not connected with any act of parliament. Assuming it to be true that that legislature usurped power, such usurpation was made upon the prerogative of the king, not upon the authority of parliament.

The legislative power of the prerogative in colonial matters was part of the legislative power of the prerogative *abroad* as distinguished from the prerogative in England. The term prerogative *abroad* is found frequently used in the pages of Chalmers's Colonial Opinions. But the addition of the word *abroad* was not obligatory. In the great case of Campbell *v.* Hall upon the prerogative abroad, Lord Mansfield uses the simple term "prerogative" only.† The prerogative was always more limited in its exercise at home than abroad. This difference was increased by the revolu-

---

* See the charters, patents and commissions themselves, *passim ;* also Chalmers's Opinions and Chalmers's Colonies, *passim.*

† Cowper's Reports, ed. 1794, p. 204. See Division C. of this Chapter on the case.

tion of 1688. But there never was any question of the existence of the king's power of legislating by prerogative
abroad, either before or after 1688. Questions, however, relating to the limits of the power make an important branch
of English constitutional law. Whether the king's order in
council, proclamation, charter, commission, or letters patent,
should be deemed legislative, executive, judicial or mixed,
might sometimes be itself a question.*

The leading case of the Proclamations in 1610 is well
known as making an era in the whole history of the prerogative. King James I. had legislated by proclamations against
building houses in London, in order to prevent a so-called
overgrowth of the capital, and against using wheat to make
starch, in order to confine its uses to food. Coke was consulted. He and his three associates delivered a formal
opinion before the privy council, so defining the limits of
the prerogative, that it was made clear that the above proclamations could create no new offences and were contrary to
the law of the land. That is to say, the king had legislated
beyond the right of his power. His proclamation was null
and void as a law, and every court must so hold it to be, whenever it was pleaded. See 12 Reports, 74; Gardiner's History of England (1603–1642) II.. 104; 2 Cobbett's State
Trials, 723.

Blackstone, writing after the revolution of 1688, declares
that the king acting by prerogative and without his parliament had no legislative power: Commentaries I. 271. This
must, however, be understood of the prerogative at home
and not abroad: see his previous page 107. Chalmers's
Colonial Opinions, generally, show the same to be true.
The Guernsey and Jersey case, therein mentioned, p. 89, is
peculiarly clear as to the king having a legislative capacity
of making laws for those islands by order in council.

---

‡ See Chapter 20, No. 8, *post*.

DIVISION B.

Of the case of Guernsey and Jersey.

The following opinion of crown counsel shows that the king could by his prerogative alone, and without his parliament, act in a legislative capacity in rightful cases and make laws for a dependency or colony abroad.

On August 12th, 1737, Ryder and Strange, crown counsel, gave an official opinion, containing, among other things, the following. Debts due to the crown in Guernsey and Jersey could not be recovered through the medium of the courts of Exchequer and King's Bench. The only remedy which the crown had for the recovery of debts in those islands according to the existing law, was "by proceeding "upon proper suits, to be instituted in the courts there, ac- "cording to the course of those courts, and sending thither "the proper evidence of the debt, unless his majesty shall "think fit to interpose, *in his legislative capacity, and, by* "*an order in council, make a new law*, concerning the "method of recovering the crown debts against the inhab- "itants there." See Chalmers's Opinions, 89.

It will be observed that the date of this opinion is subsequent to the Revolution of 1688. If such a thing could be done after that date by prerogative, *a fortiori* it could be done previously.

DIVISION C.

Of the case of Campbell *v.* Hall, or that of the Island of Grenada.

The decision in the cause of Campbell *v.* Hall, otherwise called the case of the Island of Grenada, will be the next topic for consideration. This was an all-important case in the law of legislation for the colonies by act of prerogative. On November 22d, 1774, the unanimous opinion of the Court of King's Bench was delivered by L. C. J. Mansfield. The case is reported in Cowper, 204, and 20 Cobbett's State Trials, 239. It is referred to by C. J. Marshall in 8 Wheaton, 597.

In Campbell *v.* Hall, the royal act held to be void was an act of legislation made by the king proceeding upon his prerogative in council and not in parliament. The court, at the same time, held that the said royal act would have been valid, had it been issued previously to a certain date not long before. In so doing it considered both the right and the limitation of the king's power of legislating by his prerogative abroad.

The great importance of the principles involved in this case to the public law of the American colonies can not be enlarged upon here. It need only be repeated that it was under acts of legislation made by the king proceeding upon his prerogative exclusively, that colonial legislatures and governments, as a rule, were organized. To such acts of prerogative, as a rule, colonial laws owed their vigour in so far as that vigour was not derived from the consent of the constituents of the colonial legislatures. This was as true of Georgia, which was established after the Revolution of 1688, as of the twelve older colonies.

The case was very elaborately argued four several times and the opinion of the court was unanimous. The action was brought by the plaintiff James Campbell, a natural born British subject, who in 1763 had purchased a plantation in the island of Grenada. The defendant was William Hall, who had been a king's collector of a duty of four and a half per cent. upon all dead commodities and sugars exported from the island of Grenada. The action was brought to recover back a sum of money which was paid, as the said duty of four and a half per cent., on sugars, by and on account of the plaintiff. The action was one for money had and received. It was brought on the following ground, namely, " that the money was paid to the defendant with- " out any consideration ; the duty for which, and in respect " of which he had received it, *not having been imposed by* "*lawful and sufficient authority to warrant the same.*" That money then still remained in the hands of the defend- ant and had not been paid over to the use of the king ; so remaining " with the privity and consent of his majesty's " attorney-general, for the express purpose of *trying the* "*question as to the validity of imposing this duty.*"

The facts stated in the opinion were derived from a special verdict of elaborate detail.

The island of Grenada was conquered by the British arms from the French king in the war determined by the treaty of peace, dated February 10th, 1763. It was surrendered upon the same terms of capitulation as the island of Martinique; which surrender was followed by the cession made in the treaty. On October 7th, 1763, a proclamation under the great seal of Great Britain was issued, in which, among other things, the king published and declared that he had by letters patent under the great seal constituted certain governments, of which Grenada was one; that he had given the governor of each colony express power and direction, with the advice and consent of the king's council therein, to summon a general assembly of representatives of the people; and had given such governor, council and assembly power to make laws, statutes and ordinances for their colony such as were usual in like royal governments of America. On March 26th, 1764, another proclamation of the king under the great seal was issued relating, among other things, to the survey of the island and the allotment of lands, and inviting purchasers to purchase such lands. On April 9th, 1764, letters patent were issued containing the commission of Melville as governor of Grenada, with power to summon a colonial assembly competent to make laws with the consent of the governor and council according to the custom of like colonies. Under, the same, during 1765, an assembly was summoned and met the governor in the island.

On July 20th, 1764, an instrument containing letters patent under the great seal was issued, upon the validity of which the whole disputed question turned. By it, the king in council levied a duty of four and a half per cent. upon sugar and all dead commodities produced in and exported from the island and abolished the old French customs and import duties. By this act, the taxation of the colony was assimilated to that of the neighbouring British islands of the Leeward group.

The general question that arose from the facts found by the special verdict is stated to be this:

" Whether the letters patent under the great seal, bearing
" date 20th July, 1764, are good and valid to abolish the
" French duties ; and in lieu thereof impose the four and a
" half per cent. duty above mentioned, which is paid in all
" the British Leeward islands."

It was contended at the bar that the letters patent were
void on two points. The first point was, that even if they
had been made before the proclamation of October 7th,
1763, yet the king, of himself and without the concurrence
of parliament, could not exercise such a legislative power
over a conquered country. After an elaborate discussion,
this point was decided to be erroneous. It was held to be
unquestioned and unquestionable that the king had such
a right to legislative authority over a conquered country.

The second point, upon which it was contended that the
letters patent levying the duty were void, was as follows,
namely :

" That though tne king had sufficient power ana author-
" ity, before the 7th October, 1763, *to do such legislative*
" *act*, yet before the letters patent of 20th July, 1764, he
" had *divested* himself of that authority."

This second point was decided to be correct. The opinion states that " upon the second point we are of opinion
" that *before* the letters patent of the 20th July, 1764, the
" *king* had *precluded* himself from the exercise of a legis-
" lative authority over the island of Grenada. The first
" and most material instrument is the proclamation of the
" 7th October, 1763. See what it is that the king there
" says, with what view, and how he engages himself and
" pledges his word. ' For the better security of the liberty
" ' and property of those who are or shall become inhabi-
" ' tants of our island of Grenada, we have declared by this
" ' our proclamation, that we have commissioned our gov-
" ' ernor (as soon as the state and circumstances of the col-
" ' ony will admit) to call an assembly to enact laws, etc.'
" With what view is this made ? Is it to invite settlers and
" subjects : and why to invite? That they might think
" properties, *etc.*, more secure if the legislation was vested
" in an assembly, than a governor and council only. Next,

"having established the constitution, the proclamation of
"the 20th of March, 1764, invites them to come in as pur-
"chasers ; in further confirmation of all this, on the 9th of
" April, 1764, three months before July, an actual commis-
"sion is made out to the governor to call an assembly as
"soon as the state of the island will admit thereof. You
" observe, there is no reservation in the proclamation of any
"legislature to be exercised by the king, or by the gov-
"ernor and council under his authority in any manner,
"until the assembly should meet ; but rather the contrary :
"for whatever construction is to be put upon it, which may
"be very difficult through all the cases to which it may be
"applied, it alludes to a government *by laws in being*, and
"by courts of justice, *not by a legislative authority*, until
"an assembly should be called. There does not appear
" from the special verdict, any impediment to the calling of
" an assembly immediately on the arrival of the governor.
"But no assembly was called then or at any time after-
"wards, till the end of the year 1765.

" We therefore think, that by the two proclamations and
"the commission to Governor Melville, the king had imme-
"diately and *irrevocably* granted to all who were or should
" become inhabitants, or who had, or should acquire property
" in the island of Grenada, or more generally, to all whom
" it might concern, that the subordinate legislation over the
"island should be exercised by an assembly with the con-
"sent of the governor and council, in like manner as the
"other islands belonging to the king. Therefore, though
"the abolishing the duties of the French king and the sub-
"stituting this tax in its stead ; which according to the
"finding in this special verdict is paid in all the British
"Leeward islands, is just and equitable with respect to
"Grenada itself, and the other British Leeward islands,
"yet, through the inattention of the king's servants in in-
"verting the order in which the instruments should have
" passed, and been notoriously published, *the last act is
"contradictory to and in violation of the first, and is
"therefore void*. How proper soever it may be in respect
"to the object of the letters patent of the 20th July, 1764,

"to use the words of Sir Philip Yorke and Sir Clement
"Wearg, 'it can only now be done by the assembly of the
"'island, or by an act of the parliament of Great Britain.'

"The consequence is, judgment must be given for the
"plaintiff."

It is thus clear that the king legislating by prerogative
had established a constitution for the island of Grenada
and that another subsequent act of legislation by prerogative was judicially decided to be contrary to a colonial constitution binding the king and therefore was held void.

According to the decision of the English judges in Campbell *v.* Hall the king's prerogative power of legislation over
the colonies was limited by positive law. The American
colonies likewise maintained that that power was so limited.
American and English opinions were thus agreed upon the
principle of limitation by law, however much they might
differ in drawing the line defining the legal limits binding
the king in so legislating. As to the legislative power of
parliament over the colonies, the state of opinions was different. When the troubles before the American revolution
began, English opinion maintained that the said power of
parliament was unlimited and held that whether it legislated rigorously or rightfully, the colonies were equally
bound in all cases by all statutes actually made for them.
Summo jure parliament could enact *jus iniquum* for the
colonies as well as for England. On the other hand, American opinion maintained that parliamentary legislative power
over the colonies was, of right, limited by the colonists' constitutional rights. This limitation by constitutional right,
it will be observed, is distinctly different from a limitation
by positive law. This difference was especially obvious in
relation to the form of government as distinguished from the
matter of government. This is exemplified by the relation
of the judiciary to the two kinds of legislation. A challenged act of prerogative legislation could be decided unlawful and held therefore void by the judiciary, as was done
in Campbell *v.* Hall. But at that very date no court could
decide a challenged act of parliament to be contrary to constitutional right and hold it therefore void. Every court

must therefore hold such act of parliament to be binding, regardless of its being truthfully or untruthfully challenged on the ground of constitutional right.

These distinctions are of importance for the purposes of this Essay.   They show that, if prerogative legislation should exist under an American written constitution, and the state judiciary should decide wrongful and hold void an act thereof, so doing would merely be following the example of the British constitution in the reign of George III. But it would not be following that example for the state judiciary to decide unconstitutional and hold void a statute of the state legislature.   No American constitution could establish such a judicial competency, without differing from the British constitution as it was when Blackstone wrote his Commentaries.   At the same time the American idea of such an enlarged competency must have an historical relation to the English idea of the more restricted competency in Campbell *v*. Hall.

CHAPTER XX.

Of acts of colonial legislatures repugnant to the laws of England and of the nullity thereof consequent upon such repugnancy.

Of the exercise of the prerogative concerning colonial acts questioned or doubted for such repugnancy.

Of the case of Winthrop v. Lechmere "appealed home" from the colony of Connecticut.

No. 1. *Of the principle that the laws of a colony should not be repugnant to the laws of England.*

No. 2. *Of the distinction between a colonial act repugnant to the laws of England and one conflicting with an act of parliament legislating for the colonies.*

No. 3. *Further considerations concerning the word "repugnant."*

No. 4. *Of the nature of the exercise of the prerogative, when the king declared in council that a colonial act was null and void because repugnant to the laws of England.*

No. 5. *Of the colonies which transmitted, and those which did not transmit, the acts of their legislatures to the king in council for his approval or disapproval.*

No. 6. *Of the* modus procedendi *in disapproving laws in three different classes of cases before the king in council.*

No. 7. *Of the case of Winthrop* v. *Lechmere,* temp. *George I. and George II.*

No. 8. *Whether the order in council determining Winthrop* v. *Lechmere was purely judicial, or partly judicial and partly legislative.*

No. 9. *Of certain appeals to the king in council from Canada since 1867.*

The acts of colonial legislatures were null and void, when they were repugnant to the laws of England. In so far as the subject of this Essay makes it needful, this chapter will consider the legal requirement that the laws of a colony should not be repugnant to the laws of England.

No. 1.

Of the principle that the laws of a colony should not be repugnant to the laws of England.

In the charters and other letters patent, which as a rule organized the various colonies, it was always expressed or implied that the laws made by their respective legislatures should be agreeable to the laws of England, or not contrary to the laws of England, or not repugnant to the laws of England. All these three phrases were used, but the last, that of *not being repugnant*, may be considered the most characteristic of the three. It is laid down by Story as the received doctrine of the English law that the laws of a colony should not be repugnant to the laws of England. In his Commentaries (ed. 1, vol. 1, p. 144), he observes that the colonial "assemblies had the power of making local "laws and ordinances, not repugnant to the laws of Eng- "land, but as near as may be agreeable thereto subject to "the ratification and approval of the crown."

In Massachusetts, Rhode Island, Pennsylvania and Maryland respectively the charter or patent prescribed that the colonial laws should be neither repugnant nor contrary to the laws of England. In Connecticut, the charter prescribed that the laws should not be contrary to the laws of England. The word, "repugnant," was not used therein, but the word, "contrary," was deemed to have an identical meaning with it, and the two words were used interchangeably. This is shown by the following joint opinion of the attorney general and solicitor general which was given in 1730 upon the charter of Connecticut :

"To the right honourable the lords commissioners ior "trade and plantations. May it please your lordships,—

"In obedience to your commands, signified to us, by two
"letters, from Mr. Popple, transmitting to us copies of the
"charter of the colony of Connecticut, and of the memorial
"of John Winthrop, Esq., hereunto annexed, and desiring
"our opinion in point of law, whether the said colony have
"thereby any power vested in them of making laws, which
"affect property, or, whether that power is not confined to
"the making of by-laws only, and whether, if they have
"not the power of making laws affecting property, they
"have not forfeited their charter, by passing such laws;
"we have considered the said charter, and memorial, and
"are of opinion, that, by the said charter, the general as-
"sembly of the said province have a power of making laws,
"which affect property; but it is a necessary qualification,
"of all such laws, that they be reasonable in themselves,
"and not contrary to the laws of England; and, if any
"laws have been there made, repugnant to the laws of
"England, they are absolutely null and void.*

"P. YORKE,
"C. TALBOT.

"Aug. 1, 1730."

In the colonies under the immediate government of the
king the constitutions of the place depended as a rule upon
letters patent containing the king's commissions or delega-
tions of powers to persons appointed his governors there.

Thus in the commission of the first royal governor of New
Jersey, who was appointed upon the reunion of the two
Jerseys, it was provided that the laws and statutes made
by the governor, council and assembly should "not be re-
"pugnant, but as near as may be, agreeable unto the laws
"and statutes of this our kingdom of England."†

So too in the draft of Governor Sloughter's commission
as governor of New York, which is dated 31 January, 1690.
This was the instrument under which the first representative legislature in that colony was held. It was therein
prescribed that the laws made by the governor, council and

---

* Chalmers : Opinions, ed. 2, pp. 341, 342.

† Smith's History of New Jersey, p. 224.

assembly were to be, "as near as may be, agreeable unto "the laws and statutes of this our kingdom of England."*

In North Carolina the earliest royal commission for the office of governor is dated January 15th, 1729–30, the proprietary governor having held over some time after the surrender. It was granted to Governor Burrington. The clauses relating to legislation contain the following restriction :

"Which said laws, statutes and ordinances are not to be "repugnant but as near as may be agreeable to the laws and "statutes of this our kingdom of Great Britain."†

But it was not necessary for the royal letters patent to express the truth that the laws of the colony should not be repugnant to the laws of England. It was implied by the unwritten constitution of the empire of which the colony was a part. This is shown by Story's general observation above quoted and by the following English authority.

In 1775, Lord Mansfield, when Attorney General Murray, was officially asked his opinion whether the legislature of Maryland had authority to pass a certain act. His response shows that it was a universal requirement that the laws of a colony should not be repugnant or contrary to the laws of England. He held that neither Maryland nor any other colony could make such a law. This he laid down, although no statement of the legislative power of the assembly of Maryland had been submitted to him. "The charter of "Maryland," he said, "and the power thereby given to "make laws is not stated. *There is always a restriction* "*that they should not be contrary to the laws of England.*"‡

It may here be well to make some reference to the colony of the Lower Counties upon Delaware. It was not under the immediate government of the king and its legislature was not organized by any royal letters patent. These circumstances did not, however, prevent it from being bound by the unwritten law of the empire which prohibited colonial legislatures from enacting laws repugnant to those of

---

* Broadhead's Colonial Documents of New York, III. p. 624.

† See Saunders's Colonial Records of North Carolina, III. p. 68.

‡ Chalmers : Opinions, ed. 2, p. 336.

England. Besides too, the historical relations of the colony of the Lower Counties to the second patent of the Duke of York for New York was such that its legislature was specially bound not to enact laws so repugnant. That patent contained a clause requiring that the laws of New York should not be contrary but as near as may be agreeable to to the laws of England.*

No. 2.

Of the distinction between a colonial act repugnant to the laws of England and one conflicting with an act of parliament legislating for the colonies

It should be observed with attention that the repugnancy of an act of a colonial legislature to the laws of England was not as precise a contrariety as that raised by a conflict between a colonial act and an act of parliament legislating for the colonies. A conflict between a colonial act and such an act of parliament came within the terms of the rule and limitation written in the statute of 7 and 8 William III., cap. 22, which has been previously discussed on pages 182 and 183. But it was by the unwritten law and constitution of the empire that colonial legislation was null and void when repugnant to the laws of England. It was sometimes easy to ascertain the contrariety involved in such repugnancy. Sometimes, however, it was by no means an easy thing to ascertain it precisely. While colonial laws were required to be agreeable to the laws of England, such requirement was not measured by a cast-iron rule. As some of the letters patent above referred to expressed the idea, such acts were to be as agreeable *as may be* to the laws of England. These cases of repugnancy between colonial and parliamentary statutes must not be confounded. A case of such repugnancy and one of such conflict must be regarded as distinctly different things. They differed not only in the respects already mentioned but also in others equally important.

* See Poor's Charters, p. 786.

When the acts of colonial legislatures were submitted to the attention of the king in council, the royal approval or disapproval was declared after due examination and consideration. Among the grounds for disapproving a colonial act was its ascertained repugnancy to the laws of England. The acts of the respective colonial legislatures had vigour until the king's disapproval was declared. Such exercise of the prerogative operated as a repeal and was frequently called by that name. On the other hand, the king's approval operated as a confirmation and was frequently so termed.*

The royal discretion in approving and disapproving colonial acts had a varied scope, but was not unlimited. An act of parliament was necessary to enable the king to approve colonial acts conflicting with acts of parliament. The statute of 10 & 11 Victoria, cap. 71, is such an act. It was passed in order that the queen might give her assent to a certain Canadian act: See Bowyer's Readings in 1850, page 84.

No. 3.

Further considerations concerning the word "repugnant."

As has been said, the word *repugnant* may be considered the most characteristic of the terms used in this part of the law of prerogative abroad. It is not found in the constitution of the United States, but is selected by C. J. Marshall in Marbury *v.* Madison to express the idea of contrariety thereto, or conflict therewith. The words in which he puts the question initiating his constitutional discussion in that case are: "whether an act, repugnant to the constitution, "can become the law of the land."

It may therefore seem to some natural to expect that cases can be found in which colonial courts decided acts of colonial legislatures to be repugnant to the laws of England and held them therefore void.

---

* *Cf.* Chalmers: Opinions, ed. 2, pp. 337, 338, 339, 340, 341.

No such cases are extant. It is true that there is a case in South Carolina in which a colonial act was decided to be contrary to Magna Charta and common right and was held therefore *ipso facto* void: Bowman *v.* Middleton, 1 Bay, 254. This decision, however, was not made by a judicial tribunal of the colony but by one of the state.

No. 4.

Of the nature of the exercise of the prerogative, when the king declared in council that a colonial act was null and void because repugnant to the laws of England.

While an act of a colonial legislature was null and void, if it were repugnant to the laws of England, the question of such repugnancy before the king in council was not a judicial one. It was a legislative question and was so decided by the king proceeding in council in his legislative capacity.

That such was and is the English opinion is shown by the following passage on page 84 of Bowyer's Readings in the Middle Temple in 1850:

"The power which the crown has of disallowing acts "passed by colonial legislatures, after they have received "the assent of the governour, and of refusing its assent when " they have not received that of the representative of the " crown in the colony, practically fulfils the purposes of the "extraordinary jurisdiction of the American supreme court. " It has lately been proposed to distinguish by legislative "enactments between colonial and imperial matters, en-"trusting the former only to the colonial legislatures, and " to erect a court for the determination of the validity of "colonial laws. But the difficulty of defining the distinc-"tion has not yet been overcome."

The following passage of Madison's shows that it was the American opinion that the king exercised his prerogative legislatively and not judicially, when he approved or disapproved the acts of colonial legislatures. In it Madison is alluding to certain letters of his to Jefferson, Randolph and Washington, which were written shortly before the meeting of the Framers' convention and contained a sketch of a constitutional government of the United States. He observes :*

"The feature, in these letters which vested in the gen-"eral authority a *negative on the laws of the States, was* "*suggested by the negative in the head of the British Em-*"*pire*, which prevented collisions between the parts and "the whole, and between the parts themselves. It "was supposed that the substitution of an elective and "responsible authority, for an hereditary and irrespon-"sible one, would avoid the appearance even of a de-"parture from republicanism. But although the subject "was so viewed in the convention, and the votes on it "were more than once equally divided, it was finally and "justly abandoned, as, apart from other objections, it was "not practicable among so many States, increasing in num-"ber, and enacting, each of them, so many laws. *Instead* "*of the proposed negative*, the objects of it were left as "finally provided for in the constitution."

These observations show the received opinion of Madison's colleagues in the Framers' convention as to the nature of the act of prerogative by which the king negatived a colonial act for repugnancy or other reason. The evidence thus shows that in America as well as in England the king was held to proceed legislatively and not judicially in declaring the act of a colonial legislature to be null and void because repugnant to the laws of England. Indeed, it is hardly possible that any one will deny that such was the rule. But whether that rule had exceptions is a question which some readers may think should be raised in an investigation such as this.

The consideration of this latter question requires some reference to the *modus procedendi* in different classes of cases before the king in council. At least three classes of such cases must be discriminated. These arose under a distinction between the thirteen colonies, which divided them into two kinds from a legislative point of view, *viz.*, those

---

* Gilpin : Madison Papers, II. 714, 715.

which transmitted, and those which did not transmit, the acts of their legislatures to the king in council for his approval or disapproval. This distinction must receive attention before answering the above question.

No. 5.

Of the colonies which transmitted, and those which did not transmit, the acts of their legislatures to the king in council for his approval or disapproval.

From the point of view of the exercise of the prerogative now under consideration there were two classes of colonies : (1) those in which it was required that the colonial laws should be transmitted to the king in council : and (2) those in which such transmission was not required.

Nine of the thirteen colonies finally belonged to the first class.

The charter of Connecticut did not require the transmission of the laws. Neither did that of Rhode Island.

By the patent of Maryland, the proprietary government was not required to transmit the laws enacted thereunder. For a considerable number of years the government of the colony was taken into the king's hands and out of those of the lord proprietor. During those years a different system must have been applied. As in other colonies immediately under the government of the king transmission must have been required.*

The colony of the Lower Counties upon Delaware was not required to transmit the laws enacted by its legislature. This assertion is based upon the fact that no evidence has been found showing that any act of that legislature was ever transmitted to the king in council and upon the great

---

* See Bacon's Laws of Maryland for the acts of 1692, June 9th, cap. 17 ; 1696, July 9th, cap. 18 ; 1706, April 19th, cap. 14 ; 1707, April 15th, cap. 16, and 1708, December 17th, cap. 3. These acts were transmitted to, and disallowed by, the king in council. They were enacted in the name of the king. Normally, in Maryland, the laws were enacted and the writs ran in the name of the lord proprietor.

improbability that any evidence to that effect remains un-
discovered.*

It should be borne in mind that a colony might belong to
both classes for different periods of its existence.   This was
the case with the two Carolinas.   During the first period of
their colonial existence they were under proprietary government.   During the second, they were colonial under the
immediate government of the king.   In the former period
transmission was not required : in the latter it was.

In those colonies in which the transmission of the laws
to the king in council was required, the acts of the respective legislatures had vigour until the king's disapproval was
declared.   Such disapproval had the effect of a repeal and
was frequently called by that name.   On the other hand
the king's approval had the effect of a confirmation and
was frequently called so.†   After acts of legislation were
enacted in a transmitting colony, the regular procedure required them to be transmitted within fixed terms to the
king in council in order there to be passed upon by him *in
his legislative capacity* in the due course of public business.   This procedure was dilatory.   The actual delays were
of much historical importance, but do not require discussion here.

As to those four colonies, which were not required to
transmit their laws to the king in council for approval or
disapproval, the procedure was different.   If a law repugnant to the laws of England was enacted in any of those
colonies, it was void, just as much as if enacted in any of

---

* In this matter I have not relied upon any researches of my own concerning the legislature of the Lower Counties upon Delaware.   I have been so for-
tunate as to be able to consult the most erudite of our historical scholars in
matters of colonial legislation, Mr. C. R. Hildeburn of the Laws Commission
of Pennsylvania.   In Appendix No. 3 to this Essay, I have inserted Mr. Hildeburn's opinion upon the state of the evidence concerning the question whether
the Lower Counties upon Delaware were a transmitting or a non-transmitting
colony.

I avail myself of this opportunity to express my gratitude to Mr. Hildeburn
for his invaluable assistance on numerous occasions in matters relating to the
history of colonial legislation on both sides of the Atlantic.

† See Chalmers : Opinions : ed. 2, pp. 337, 338, 339, 340, 341.

the other nine. The attention of the king was not, however, given to it, as of course, in the regular routine of public business before him in council. The royal attention was called to such act by its being challenged on the motion of some interested party other than the colony itself, in connection with some accidental affair involving its validity. When a colonial act was thus successfully impeached before the privy council, the king proceeding in his legislative capacity on his prerogative abroad, decided it to be repugnant to the laws of England and declared it to be void for that reason. This was done by an order in council.*

No. 6.

Of the modus procedendi *in disapproving laws in three different classes of cases before the king in council.*

The two classes of colonies above mentioned gave rise to three classes of cases, so far as the *modus procedendi* in the disapproval of colonial laws was concerned. These were as follows:

1. Cases in which the king in council had disapproved, or disallowed, or repealed, or declared null and void, the acts of colonial legislatures which had been transmitted according to the colonial charters or other letters patent.

2. Cases in which the king had done likewise concerning the acts of colonial legislatures which had not been transmitted as aforesaid and which had been brought before the royal attention in proceedings *not judicial.*

In both the foregoing classes of cases the king unquestionably proceeded in his legislative capacity in so exercising his prerogative.

3. The third class of cases consisted of those in which a colonial act was successfully challenged by the appellant in an appeal to the king in council from the *judicial* courts of a *non-transmitting* colony. In such a case, as the colony had not transmitted the challenged law, the royal attention

---

* See Chalmers · Opinions, ed. 2, p. 336.

was for the first time called thereto by the appellant and so in connection with a judicial proceeding. Was such a case an exception to the rule that when the king declared a colonial act to be null and void, his act was a legislative exercise of his prerogative? The answer to this question requires a consideration of the great case of Winthrop *v.* Lechmere.

No. 7.

Of the case of Winthrop v. *Lechmere,* temp. *George I. and George II.*

This case was an appeal from the Superior Court of Connecticut to the king in council. The order in council determining it in favour of the appellant was dated February 15th, 1727-8.

This appeal belonged to a class of judicial cases, which was important but not numerous. At the same time such appeals were familiar enough for an interesting and peculiar phrase to be used in connection with them. In them the appellants from colonial courts to the king in council were said to have "appealed home."*

The case of Winthrop *v.* Lechmere was this.† General Wait Winthrop of Boston in Massachusetts, died intestate leaving a son John Winthrop, Esq., of New London, in Connecticut, and a daughter, Anne, wife of Thomas Lechmere, merchant, of Boston. The real estate in Connecticut, which General Winthrop had owned, was valuable. By the colonial statute for settling intestate estates, it was in this case divided into three shares, two of which went to the son and one to the daughter. By this statute the common law right of primogeniture was abolished and the real estate of a decedent was divided equally among his children, except in the case of the eldest son, who was given the prerogative of a double share.

---

* See appellant's breviate or case in the Appeal of Phillips *v.* Savage in the Proceedings of the Historical Society of Massachusetts for 1860-2, pages 66, 67.

† See Public Records of the Colony of Connecticut, vol. 7, pp. 571–579 ; Massachusetts Historical Society Collections, Series 6, vol. 5, pp. 436–511.

One of John Winthrop's contentions was that this colonial statute was void, because repugnant or contrary to the laws of England. He invoked the charter of incorporation granted to the colony, by which its legislature was empowered to make only such laws as should be wholesome and reasonable and not contrary to the laws of England. He maintained that all other laws were not warranted by the charter.

John Winthrop claimed the whole of his father's real estate, as eldest son and heir according to the rule of the English law. Mr. and Mrs. Lechmere disputed this claim and contended that she was entitled to one-third of the real estate. Two series of litigations arose, one before and the other after May, 1726. In the litigations before that date Mrs. Lechmere failed to obtain any remedy for her rights, which had certainly been violated, if the colonial statute was valid. This failure was not because the colonial courts refused to obey that statute, but because it was either imperfect in its remedial dispositions or had been erroneously interpreted by the judges. Additional legislation was deemed necessary by the Assembly to secure Mrs. Lechmere her statutory rights aforesaid. This was accordingly provided for by the Assembly in May, 1726. A second series of litigations then ensued, the result being that Mr. and Mrs. Lechmere were successful on every point in dispute. In these litigations the judicial acts and decisions of the colonial courts were numerous. The following require special mention, viz., four sentences of the Superior Court of the colony, the first of June 29th, 1725, the second of September 28th, 1725, the third and fourth of March 22d, 1725–6. Throughout the whole of this second series of litigations the colonial courts fully recognized and applied the above mentioned colonial statutes as good, binding and valid, viz., the act for the settlement of intestate estates, and the act of May, 1726, remedying the imperfections of the former.

From the Superior Court of the colony John Winthrop "appealed home" to the king in council. His petition and appeal were referred by an order in council of May 13th,

1727, to the Lords of the Committee of the Privy Council for hearing Appeals from the Plantations. The Committee, after hearing the parties through their legal counsel, made a report on December 20th, 1727. This report was favourable to the appellant on every point in dispute. His contentions as to both the judicial acts and the legislative acts in question were fully sustained. This report was considered by the king when he met his council at a court held on February 15th, 1727-8. By the advice of the privy council, he approved and confirmed the report in every particular.

Inter alia the committee decided that the abovementioned four judicial sentences of the colonial Superior Court ought to be reversed and set aside by the king and that the two acts of the colonial legislature aforesaid ought to be declared null and void by him. Thus in the same report four judicial acts and two legislative acts were condemned. It should be observed that the question of the validity and repugnancy of the two colonial acts respectively was a new one before the king in council, because Connecticut was one of the colonies, which was not required to transmit the acts of its legislature for approval or disapproval.

The order in council recites *in extenso* the report of the committee, and, referring thereto, proceeds to say: "His "Majesty, taking the same into his royal consideration, is "pleased, with the advice of his Privy Council, to approve "of the said report and confirm the same in every particu- "lar part thereof; and pursuant thereunto, to declare, that "the aforementioned act, entituled, An Act for the settle- "ment of intestate estates, is Null and Void; and the same "is hereby accordingly declared to be null and void, and "of no force or effect whatever. And his Majesty is hereby " further pleased to order that all the aforementioned sen- "tences of the 29th June, 1725, of the 28th September, "1725, and of the 22d March, 1725-6, and every of them, "be and they are hereby reversed and set aside. . . . . . " And his Majesty does hereby further order, that the afore- "mentioned [other] sentence of the 22d of March, 1725-6, " . . . . . be also reversed and set aside; . . . . . . "and that all acts and proceedings done and had under the

"said sentences, all, every, or any of them, or by virtue or
"pretence thereof, be and they are hereby discharged and
"set aside, and declared null and void. And his Majesty
"is further pleased to declare, that the aforementioned act
"of Assembly, passed in May, 1726, empowering the said
"Thomas Lechmere to sell the said lands, is null and void ;
"and also that the said order made by the said superior
"court, bearing date the 27th of September, 1726, pursuant
"to the said act of Assembly, ... is likewise null
"and void ; and the said act of Assembly and order of the
"said superior court are accordingly hereby declared null
"and void, and of no force or effect whatever."

No. 8.

*Whether the order in council determining Winthrop v.
Lechmere was purely judicial, or partly judicial and
partly legislative.*

The foregoing extracts from the order in council, determining the case of Winthrop *v.* Lechmere, show that that act
of prerogative did, *inter alia*, the following things:

It reversed and set aside four judicial sentences of the
Superior Court of Connecticut ;

It declared null and void one judicial order of the same
court ;

It declared null and void two acts of the legislature of
Connecticut.

It is self-evident that the king's action concerning the
sentences and the order of the court was judicial. So far
then the order in council was certainly a judicial act of prerogative. Unless, therefore, an order in council can be
partly judicial and partly legislative, the king exercised
his prerogative judicially and not legislatively, when he
declared the two acts of the colonial legislature to be null
and void. That is to say, appeals like Winthrop *v.* Lechmere, questioning colonial laws as well as colonial judgments, furnish exceptions to the rule that the king pro-

ceeded legislatively in declaring a colonial act to be null and void because repugnant to the laws of England.

If appeals like Winthrop *v.* Lechmere furnished such exceptional cases, they are of great importance for the subject of this Essay. If the king proceeding judicially in council ever decided a challenged act of a colonial legislature to be repugnant to the laws of England and therefore declared it to be null and void, an English model existed in the last century for the American judicial competency which is the subject of this Essay.

If, however, an order in council could be of a mixed nature, that is to say, could exercise the prerogative legislatively, judicially and executively at the same time, then Winthrop *v.* Lechmere furnishes no exception to the rule that the king proceeded legislatively in declaring colonial acts to be null and void for repugnancy.

In the writer's opinion the order in council determining the appeal of Winthrop *v.* Lechmere was actually of a mixed nature. He deems it partly judicial and partly legislative. It was no mere judicial judgment. That part of it was judicial, which reversed and set aside the four sentences and declared the order of court to be null and void. That part of it was legislative, which declared the two acts of the colonial legislature to be null and void.

The writer understands this view to be supported by authority. In an order in council, dated April 10th, 1730, the order in council determining Winthrop *v.* Lechmere is referred to. The action therein taken concerning the Connecticut act for settling intestates' estates, is expressly called "a repeal" of that act. See the Talcott Papers in Collections of the Connecticut Historical Society, vol. 4, page 201.

An order in council was an act of prerogative. The prerogative was not divided into departments, like an American government under a written constitution. It could do things which required the acts of two or more departments under such an American government. Whether an order in council was legislative, judicial, executive or mixed, could only be determined by inspecting its text and considering how the prerogative was exercised by the king in making it.

If the writer err in this view, then the important consequence follows that the king proceeded judicially in declaring the said two acts of legislation to be null and void.

In order that the learned reader may judge for himself in this matter the order in council has been inserted in full in Appendix No. 4. It recites *in extenso* the report of the Committee on appeals from the plantations. Other sources of information concerning Winthrop *v.* Lechmere are referred to in that Appendix. The joint opinion of the Attorney general and Solicitor general, which is printed *ante* page 199, relates to the case.

No. 9.

Of certain appeals to the king in council from Canada since 1867.

In connection with this chapter, it is well to mention cases arising under the present constitution of Canada, which involve the question whether a colonial law be or be not constitutional. Such cases since 1867 are judicially determined in last instance by the queen in council. The present constitution of Canada is "the British North American act, "1867." It is a statute enacted by the British parliament at the wish of the colonies now composing the Dominion of Canada. It is both imperial legislation and a colonial constitution. Under it, the courts of the dominion and of the several provinces are competent to pronounce upon the constitutionality of laws enacted by the general and the provincial legislatures. In such cases the appeal in final instance is to the queen in council. In determining such appeals the queen certainly proceeds in her judicial capacity. The queen declares judicially whether the questioned legislation be constitutional or unconstitutional and valid or void accordingly.

For further information on this interesting branch of Canadian constitutional law, see Appendix No. 5 to this Essay.

CHAPTER XXI.

Conclusion of the investigation of the English law.

It has been previously remarked that the English constitution is not a written but a consuetudinary constitution
and one of great antiquity. Therefore it was surmised that
what was the law on a given matter at one period might not
be the law at another. This surmise may now be changed
into a positive assertion as to the matter in question. The
foregoing investigation shows that in the process of time
the English constitution has varied upon the law of legislation. It must especially be recollected that when the Roman
church was established in England, and power and jurisdiction were partitioned between pope and king, the legislative
power of the state was fundamentally different from what
it became after the Reformation.

It is now contended that the foregoing discussion of the
relation of the judiciary to acts of parliament in England
supports the truth of the following propositions:

(1). When George III. ascended the throne of Great
Britain and the American colonies, it was the settled law of
the British constitution, that no judicial court could decide
an act of parliament to be contrary to any superior rule of
binding right. Then as now all judges were bound by all
statutes in all cases by the clear and clearly expressed meaning of parliament. No court could therefore then question
the validity of an act of parliament upon any such ground.

(2). In England before the Reformation acts of parliament could not legislate contrary to ecclesiastical right and

liberty in any case affecting the church in things purely
spiritual and in some cases affecting it in spiritual things
mixed with the temporalty.   In such cases the Canon law
was in actual vigour in England and there was no conflict
between the law of the church and the law of the land.
Acts of parliament contrary to ecclesiastical right and liberty in these cases did not bind either the clergy or the
laity.   Neither were the king's judges bound thereby.

(3). Shortly before the revolution of 1688, an English
court held a statute void because judicially ascertained and
decided to be contrary to the king's prerogative.   The best
opinion is that this decision was error when made.   If it
was not then error, the law was changed by the revolution
of 1688.   Since that date any such decision must certainly
be error.

(4). At a time subsequent to the Reformation and antecedent to the Interregnum, Lord Chief Justice Coke endeavoured to develop a doctrine by which the judiciary
would have a certain competency of criticising statutes and
would be competent to decide the same to be contrary to
common right and reason, which statutes when so decided
would not be binding upon the judges but must by them
be held null.   This endeavour of Coke's failed to succeed in
England.   It had, however, an interesting effect in America,
if the case of Trevett v. Weeden be deemed from its early
date to be the most influential American example of a judicial competency to criticise legislation as unconstitutional.

It is further contended that the foregoing discussion supports the truth of the following :

Legislation by act of prerogative, made by the king in
council and not in parliament, was of the greatest importance in and for the American colonies.   Both before and
after the revolution of 1688, it was an unquestioned exercise
of his prerogative abroad for the king so to legislate.   While
the scope of such legislation was wide, the law limited that
scope.   It was a judicial question whether an act of such
legislation was or was not lawful (or constitutional) and
valid or void accordingly.   This is proved by the case of
Campbell v. Hall, reviewed on pages 190–196 ante.

CHAPTER XXII.

Conclusion of the investigation of foreign laws made in Part I. of the Historical Commentary.

The foregoing investigation of foreign laws shows that when Americans invented written constitutions, they did not create an unprecedented novelty in framing them upon the principle that judiciaries might decide questioned legislation to be contrariant to a constitutional or other rule of right and hold it therefore void : that is to say, that a written constitution might without unprecedented novelty make it a judicial and not an extrajudicial question whether such legislation was so contrariant or not. On the contrary, there were then important precedents in Europe for such an institution. Legal history makes it clear that long before American independence there were in Europe unwritten systems of public law, according to which legislation might sometimes be decided to be contrariant to a binding right of superior strength to the legislative power exercised. Under them, whether challenged legislation was accordant or contrariant to binding right, and whether legislators had or had not proceeded *secundum jus potestatis suae*, might sometimes be judicial and not extrajudicial questions.

The examination of the older English law, the English law of the prerogative abroad, the older French law, the older German law, the Roman law, and the Canon law support the propositions just laid down.

Actual cases from the older French law were adduced. Two of these were the regency cases in the reigns of Lewis

XIV. and Lewis XV., that is to say, purely temporal cases in which a temporal court decided temporal legislation to be contrary to binding right and held it therefore void. Another class of cases related to the division of powers between church and state in France. In them a temporal court for fifty years repelled royal legislation concerning ecclesiastical affairs as wrongful and invalid. In the end, this court failed, but it did not overrule itself. It yielded only to *vis major*. The king compelled it to register the concordate of 1517, but the registration was made under protest.

In the older German law, the example of the court of the Imperial Chamber was adduced. It was shown, on the authority of Bluntschli, that that court provided for the legislative authorities of the several states of the Old German Empire being restricted within certain limits by judicial means.

The investigation of the Roman law of legislative rescripts in Justinian's time showed that judges could decide whether such a rescript had or had not been made according to the law of such legislation and must reject the same when ascertained by them to be contrary thereto. The emperor laid down the *jus potestatis suae* as legislator, and made it obligatory upon his judges to apply it. He had no idea that the *deus ex machina* of his plenitude of power should be dragged into every case of private legislation.

Justinian's principles were adopted by the Canonists. This is shown by the case of the Bolognese mill in Chapter 12, No. 4. In it two acts of temporal legislation made by two popes, as temporal princes, were decided not good and were rejected by the court of the Rota Romana. Although that court was an ecclesiastical one, it had a certain temporal jurisdiction in Bolognese and other cases. As the case was a purely temporal one, it does more than show the doctrines of the Canonists. It may be held also to show the doctrines of the modern Civil law on the continent of Europe before the end of the last century, that is to say, at a time when private legislation was made by the rescripts of absolute princes and not by acts of assemblies or parliaments.

The Canon law, in cases affecting the division of powers between church and state, furnishes the most important of the results ascertained by this investigation. In No. 1 of Chapter 12, these results are carefully stated and need not be repeated.

The important results ascertained by the investigation of the English law are stated in the previous chapter and need not be repeated.

Part II. of this Historical Commentary relates to American laws in the same way that Part I. does to foreign laws. Conclusions relating to the subject of this Essay, which are drawn from a consideration of both Parts, will be found in the final chapter of Part II.*

---

* It will be observed that no mention has been made of the office of the Justice of Aragon in the foregoing investigation of foreign laws. This omission is not due to inadvertence. After the able and learned discussion of this office of the Justice of Aragon by Prescott, it is not an easy task to add any thing important to what is already written in English. The writer is not now prepared to attempt to do so nor does he now think that the attempt is actually necessary, as far as the subject of his Essay is concerned. The following references to the Justice of Aragon have been consulted : Dickinson's remarks in the Framers' convention in 5 Elliott's Debates 429 ; Prescott's Ferdinand and Isabella, pages *civ et seq.* ; Sergeant's Life of Lieber, 384, 385 ; C. W. F. Breyer de *Justitia Aragonum*, (Jena, 1800) ; *Actos de Cortes del Reyno de Aragon*, (Saragossa, 1664), folios 1, 5, 54, 55, 58, 59, 60 ; and Article on Aragon in Ersch and Grueber.

PART II.

INVESTIGATION OF THE LAWS OF CERTAIN OF THE STATES ON
THE RELATION OF JUDICIAL POWER TO UNCONSTITUTIONAL
LEGISLATION BEFORE AND DURING THE CONFEDERATION.

The next branch of this investigation will be purely American and will be confined to the time between the declaring
of independence and the writing of the constitution. It
will be concerned with the laws of certain of the old states
and especially with the laws of New York, Rhode Island
and North Carolina. The judicial annals of those states
are of especial importance to the subject of this Essay. In
each a great historical case was decided, which here requires particular attention.

CHAPTER XXIII.

**Of the states in which the judiciary claimed to be
competent to decide legislation to be constitutional
or unconstitutional, either during or before the
confederation.**

On June 6th, 1787, Gerry said in the Framers convention:
"In some of the states the judges had actually set aside
"laws, as being against the constitution."*

* 5 Elliot's Debates, 151.

The purpose of this chapter is to ascertain, as far as possible, what cases Gerry alluded to. It is possible, indeed, that the knowledge of some of his cases is lost beyond recovery.

One of the two most important cases for Gerry's purposes may not have been known to him when he spoke. This was Bayard *r.* Singleton, which was decided in North Carolina so late in May that the news of the decision may not have reached Philadelphia on June 6th.

In 1885 a learned and important paper was published by Mr. Meigs of Philadelphia on "the Relation of the Judici-"ary to the Constitution."* Although covering less than thirty pages, it is peculiarly rich in materials obtained by historical research. They belong both to the time before and that after the writing of the constitution. The present investigation is not concerned with the researches connected with the latter period.

Seven cases in five states have been presented by Mr. Meigs, which require discussion in this chapter. They are all older than the U. S. constitution. Two of these are, of course, the well known historical cases of Trevett *v.* Weeden in Rhode Island, and Bayard *v.* Singleton in North Carolina. Three cases belong to Virginia, one to New Jersey and one to Massachusetts. These seven cases will now be enumerated in chronological order with proper observations.

1778, Virginia. Case of Josiah Philips. In May, 1778, Philips was attainted by a bill of attainder passed by the Assembly of Virginia. According to this act he was guilty of devastating and marauding within the state. In the autumn of the same year, he was captured, indicted, tried and convicted of highway robbery. The act of attainder was not enforced or acted upon in any way. "Unfortu-"nately," says Mr. Meigs, "it seems now impossible to as-"certain whether this was the voluntary action of the at-"torney general, as stated by Girardin,† or whether the "court declined to recognize the act and directed the pris-

---

* American Law Review for March and April 1885, pages 177–203: On the Relation of the Judiciary to the Constitution, by William M. Meigs.

† Burk's History of Virginia, IV. 305, 306.

"oner to be tried, as is intimated by Prof. Tucker.* If the
"latter, the case is undoubtedly the first of the kind in the
"country."

1782, Virginia. Commonwealth v. Caton, Hopkins and
Lamb, 4 Call's Reports, 135. The prisoners had been convicted of treason under the act concerning treason passed by
the legislature in 1776. This act deprived the executive of
the power of granting pardon in cases of treason. In June
1782, a resolution pardoning the prisoners was adopted by
the house of delegates and rejected by the senate. The following October, the attorney general moved that execution
of the judgment might be awarded. The prisoners pleaded
the resolution of the house of delegates as a good pardon,
claiming that that house had power to pardon in cases of
treason and impeachment. The attorney general denied the
validity of the resolution as a pardon, because the senate
had not concurred in it. "The general court," says the reporter, "adjourned the case, for novelty and difficulty, to
"the court of appeals."

The judges of the court of appeals were of opinion that
the treason act of 1776 was not an infringement of the constitution. It was decided that the pardon by resolution of
the house of delegates, which had been pleaded by the prisoners, was invalid. On page 20 of the report it is said:
"Chancellor Blair and the rest of the judges were of opinion,
"that the court had power to declare any resolution or act
"of the legislature, or of either branch of it, to be unconsti-
"tutional and void."

The reporter adds in a N. B.: "It is said, that this was
"the first case in the United States, where the question rel-
"ative to the *nullity* of an unconstitutional law was ever
"discussed before a judicial tribunal."

It should be observed that in this case no law was decided
unconstitutional. A resolution of one house was declared
a nullity because the other had not concurred. The only
law questioned was the treason act, the constitutionality of
which was affirmed by the judges.

---

* Tucker's Blackstone, Appendix, Vol. I, p. 293.

1786, Rhode Island. Trevett v. Weeden. This case is discussed at length in Chapter 25, *post*.

1786? or 1787? New Jersey. Holmes v. Walton. This case "is said to have decided that a provision of one of the "seizure acts for the trial of certain cases by a jury of six was "unconstitutional; but, further than this, we have been "able to discover nothing; both searches and inquiries have "been in vain." Mr. Meigs adds that it is not clear when the case was decided, except that it was between 1779 and 1789 when Judge Brearly was Chief Justice.

Mr. Meigs is inclined to think that the nature of the case indicates its date to be not long after the close of the Revolutionary war. The writer conjectures that the latter part of 1786 or the earlier part of 1787 had best be taken as the date of the decision of the case. It is most prudent to assume that it was one of the cases alluded to by Gerry on June 6th, 1787. On the other hand, the conjecture that the case was decided after Trevett v. Weeden seems to be the safest. These considerations result in a period covering the latter part of 1786 and the earlier part of 1787.

Holmes v. Walton is referred to in the State v. Parkhurst, 4 Halstead, 444.

1786? or 1787? Massachusetts. Anonymous case. It is mentioned in a letter of J. B. Cutting to T. Jefferson, dated 11 July, 1788. Cutting says that this case "occurred in "Massachusetts where, when the legislature trespassed "upon a barrier of the constitution, the judges of the Su-"preme Court solemnly determined that the statute was un-"constitutional. In the very next session, there was a "formal and unanimous repeal of the law, which was per-"haps not necessary."

Mr. Meigs observes that he has been unable to discover any thing more concerning this case, than what is said by Cutting in his letter. For that letter, see Bancroft's History of the Constitution, II. 473. The same date is assigned to this as to the previous case and for the same reasons.

1787, May North Carolina. Bayard v. Singleton. This case is discussed at length in Chapter 26, *post*. It is there shown that the constitutional decision in the case was made at Newbern so late in May that Gerry may not have known of it when he made his speech on June 6th. The decision must, however, have been known in Philadelphia soon after that date.

As has been intimated above, the loss of documents may have destroyed the knowledge of some of the cases known to Gerry. Thanks to Mr. Meigs, however, a satisfactory answer has been given to the question to which this chapter is devoted.

CHAPTER XXIV.

Of the law of New York and of the case of Rutgers v. Waddington.

The date of this case was 1784, on August 27th of which year the judgment was delivered.

Although the suit was begun and ended in the Mayor's Court of the City of New York, the inferiority of the jurisdiction did not prevent the decision from being regarded as a matter of great federal importance throughout the United States. The writer of the elaborate and carefully pondered opinion of the court was James Duane, well known as a lawyer and political leader, who had been selected for mayor at the critical time following the evacuation of the city. Upon the fate of this suit depended many other like litigations. It was elaborately argued on both sides. Among the counsel were the attorney general and Hamilton, the former for the plaintiff and the latter for the defendant. It was generally feared that a conflict between a recent statute of the state and the recent treaty of peace would result, and that one or other must give way. If a federal conflict should arise between the union and the state concerning the execution of the treaty of peace as a consequence of the litigation, not only private suitors, but the state of New York and the United States would be gravely affected by the decision of the court.

Such a conflict the court strove to avoid. It held that if the statute were properly interpreted, no conflict could arise between it and the law of nations, and consequently that a conflict between the statute and the treaty was out of all question. To understand the statute otherwise would be reading it according to a literalness which killed not only public rights but also certain most just rights of individuals. Thus by interpretation the court succeeded to its own satisfaction in avoiding a federal crisis. It did not do so, however, to the satisfaction of the House of Assembly, which at its next session passed resolutions condemning the decision.*

While the court did not directly pass upon the nature of conflicts between state statutes and the state constitution, it felt compelled to lay down the law of legislation in terms fully securing the supremacy of the legislature and the subordination of the judiciary. If its exposition of the law was correct, it was certainly a necessary consequence that no court could hold any statute void, because judicially ascertained by it to be unconstitutional.

A contemporary report of the case of Rutgers v. Waddington was published. It has been the principal source of the information in the account following. It is entitled: Arguments and Judgments of the Mayor's Court of the City of New York in a cause between Elizabeth Rutgers and Joshua Waddington: New York, printed by Samuel Loudon, 1784.†

In Rutgers v. Waddington, the action was one of trespass brought upon a statute of New York, dated March 17th,

---

* Dawson, page xlv.

† The above report is reprinted in facsimile in the following: The Case of Elizabeth Rutgers *versus* Joshua Waddington with an historical introduction by Henry B. Dawson, Morrisania, 1866. Upon the case see also Alexander Hamilton's letter, dated April 19th, 1792, in the American State Papers, vol. I, p. 232 ; J. C. Hamilton's Republic, III. 11–21.

1783, for the occupation of the plaintiff's brewhouse and malthouse in the city of New York during the military possession of that city by the British army.*

On June 10th, 1778, the commissary general of the British army took possession of the two houses by virtue of authority from his commander-in-chief. From September 28th, 1778, to April 30th, 1780, the defendant occupied the property under a license and permission from the commissary general. From the last date to March 17th, 1783, the defendant's occupation was under a license and permission of the said commander-in-chief himself at a rent of £150 per annum.†

These military orders were pleaded by the defendant as justifications for his occupancy during the two said periods respectively. The defendant further pleaded in bar of any action brought under the statute, that by the treaty of peace all right or claim which British subjects or American citizens might otherwise have had to any retribution or indemnity for things done in consequence of the war, or in relation thereto, were relinquished, renounced and released.‡

To this the plaintiff replied that the statute provided, *inter alia*, that no defendant should be admitted to plead any military order or command of the enemy in justification of any such occupation of property as that in question.§

As to the defendant's plea concerning the first period of his occupancy, the court decided that the order of the commissary general was unlawful, because he had by the law of nations no right to make it, and furthermore that the occupancy thereunder had no relation to the war.‖ As to the plea concerning the second period, the court decided that the order of the commander-in-chief was lawful according to the law of nations, he having thereunder the

---

* Pamphlet Report, pp. 1, 5 *et seq.*

† Same, p. 9.

‡ Same, pp. 10 *et seq.*

§ Same, pp. 11 *et seq.*, 37.

‖ Same, pp. 18, 19, 20.

right to raise military contributions by renting the property
to the defendant at £150 per annum *

As to the defendant's plea concerning the treaty of peace,
it was decided that the only benefit therefrom, concerning
which he could raise a question before the court, was an
implied, and not an express, amnesty. The only express
indemnity found in the treaty had relation to cases plainly
and certainly different from that before the court † The
implied amnesty claimed by the plaintiff was "made out
"by reasoning from the law of nations to the treaty "‡
The occupancy of the property during the first period
under the unlawful order of the commissary general had no
relation to the war, and no amnesty implied by the law of
nations upon the fact of the treaty making a peace, covered
any wrongful acts that had no relation to the war.

As has been said, the second period of the occupancy, or
that under the order of the commander-in-chief, was decided
to be a thing having a relation to the war.   This, however,
made no conflict between the treaty and the statute.   The
only conflict, of which there could be any question, was one
between the statute and the law of nations.   To the defendant's pleading the military order of the British commander-
in-chief, the plaintiff had answered that the statute prohibited the military orders of the enemy from being pleaded
against any action brought under it. She had previously
pleaded that the statute comprehended in terms her whole
case and gave the remedy demanded.   All this was true, if
the statute was to be taken according to the full latitude of
its language and according to a rigorously literal meaning
which conflicted with the law of nations.   Such literal meaning could not, however, be the true meaning, unless the
statute repealed so much of the law of nations as might conflict with itself.   It was, says the court, a much debated
question in the argument, "whether the courts of justice
"ought to be governed by the statute, where it clearly mil-
"itated against the law of nations.   Here it is material to

---

* Same, pp. 30, 36.

† Same, p. 37.

‡ Same, p. 44.

"observe that the description of persons, who are subject
"to be sued by this statute is general; extending to all who
"occupied or injured the real or personal estate of the
"exiles, within the power of the enemy. The counsel for
"the defendant, by stating a number of pointed cases,
"shewed clearly, from the nature of things, that the statute
"must admit of exceptions. Mr. Attorney General, one of
"the counsel for the plaintiff, ... admitted that
"many cases may be out of the statute, though the plain-
"tiff's is not of the number.*

"Thus then, it seems to be agreed, on both sides, that
"the provision in the statute, being general, can not ex-
"tend to all cases : and must therefore receive a reasonable
"interpretation according to the intention and not according
"to the latitude of expression of the legislature: It follows
"as a necessary consequence, that the interpretation is the
"province of the court, and, however difficult the task, that
"we are bound to perform it."†

. . . .

After due consideration the court came to the following
conclusions : Properly interpreted, the statute contained
nothing repugnant to any thing in the treaty of peace:
properly interpreted, it contained nothing repealing any
part of the law of nations. Consequently it could contain
no provisions, with which the subsequent treaty of peace
conflicted, on the ground that they repealed some part of
the law of nations.

The court observed :

"The repeal of the law of nations, or any interference
"with it, could not have been in contemplation, in our
"opinion, when the legislature passed this statute; and we
"think ourselves bound to exempt that law from its opera-
"tion : First, because there is no mention of the law of
"nations, nor the most remote allusion to it, throughout the
"whole statute : Secondly, because it is a subject of the
"highest national concern and of too much moment to have

---

* Same, pp. 39, 40.

† Same, p. 40.

"been intended to be struck at in silence ; and to be con-
"trolled implicatively under the generality of the terms of
"the provision : Thirdly, because the provision itself is so
"indefinite, that without any control, it would operate in
"other cases unreasonably, to the oppression of the inno-
"cent, and contrary to humanity ; when it is a known
"maxim* ' that a statute ought to be so construed, that no
"'man who is innocent be punished or endamaged :'
"*Fourthly, because the statute under our consideration*
"*does not contain even the common* NONOBSTANTE *clause,*
"*though it is so frequent in our statute book—'and it is*
"*'an established maxim that where two laws are seem-*
"*'ingly repugnant, and there be no clause of* NONOB-
"*'*STANTE *in the latter, they shall, if possible, have such*
"*' construction, that the latter may not repeal the former*
"*'by implication :'*† Fifthly, because, although it is a true
"rule that *posteriores leges prioribus derogant,* to use the
"language of Sir Thomas Powis in the Dutchess of Hamil-
"ton's case—‡ ' at the same time, it must be remembered,
"'that repeals by implication are disfavoured by law, and
"'never allowed of but where the inconsistency and repug-
"'nancy are plain, glaring and unavoidable : for these re-
"'peals carry along with them a tacit reflexion upon the
"'legislature, that they should ignorantly, and without
"'knowing it, make one act repugnant to and inconsistent
"'with another : and such repeals have ever been inter-
"' preted so as to repeal as little of the precedent law as
"'possible.'§

. . .   .

"Whoever then is clearly exempted from the operation

---

* I Inst. 360.

† The marginal note in the court's opinion cites Dyer's Reports, 348, at the
bottom. In Dyer 347 b., it is said : " When there are two statutes, the one
"in appearance crossing the other, and no clause of *nonobstante* is contained
"in the second statute, so that one may stand with the other, the exposition
"ought to be that both should stand in force," &c. The quotation in the
court's fourth head is from a comment on this passage, the source of which is
not mentioned.

‡ 10 Modern, 118.

§ Same, pp. 44, 45.

"of this statute by the law of nations, this court must take
"for granted, could never have been intended to be com-
"prehended within it by the legislature."*

[It is here in point to quote the following from the opinion
of the U. S. Supreme Court in Murray *v.* the Charming
Betsey, delivered by C. J. Marshall : "An act of Congress
"ought never to be construed to violate the law of nations if
"any other possible construction remains :" 2 Cranch, 118.]

This conclusion was not reached without much anxiety,
for the court was marching between the wolves and the prec-
ipice. Rarely has a political situation in a civil society,
free from fear of military power, been more strained than
that then existing in New York. If the court made an in-
considerate step on one side, a conflict between the judiciary and the legislature would ensue. If it shrunk from a
necessary step on the other, a conflict between the union and
the state would ensue ; for the state would then refuse execution to a treaty made by the union. Stone and iron,
therefore, struck fire, when the plaintiff's counsel objected
that Congress could not make a treaty of peace reaching the
internal police of the state of New York.

To this objection the opinion made answer that the operation and effect of the treaty, within the state of New York,
were proper subjects for judicial inquiry and decision. The
judgment of the court must be determined by its spirit and
true meaning. A fair and reasonable construction must be
given to it, and no man should be deprived of any benefit
which such a construction would give him.

The authority of the treaty was a matter distinct from
its operation. Its authority was the confederation, which,
as far as the court had power, it would never suffer to be
violated. The union of the states had been legalized in the
state constitution of 1777 and had been adopted as a fundamental law in the first act of the legislature of the state.
By the confederation, the Congress had full and exclusive
powers of making peace and war. The obligation of the
treaty of peace made by Congress was perpetual.

* Same, p. 45.

Read by the light of the present day and excluding the light of history, such views may seem to some to lead directly to an expectation that the court was on the eve of declaring itself not bound by any state statute violating the confederation or the treaty. This, however, would be an anachronism. From a constitutional point of view, both in civil and religious matters, the New York of to-day is a different place from the New York of the first year of independent peace. Such a judicial declaration as the above, made by a New York court in 1784, could have a different legal meaning from that imported by like words used by a like tribunal in 1892.

What follows the foregoing exposition of federal right is nothing like any claim for judicial competency to hold legislation void because ascertained to be contrary to federal or to constitutional right. The modest claim made on behalf of the judiciary was merely to a judicial discretion within the limits of Blackstone's tenth rule for construing statutes. This was consequently a claim to a judicial discretion confined to matters collateral to the principal matters of a statute in cases unforeseen. In such cases, as the intention of the legislature was not clear, a reasonable judicial presumption concerning the same was rightful. The discretion, which Blackstone claimed for an English court, was asserted for a New York court, but nothing more. Every thing more was disclaimed.

Closely following Blackstone's words and ideas, the court observed : " *The supremacy of the Legislature need not* " *be called into question ; if they think fit positively to en-* " *act a law, there is no power which can controul them.* " *When the main object of such a law is clearly expressed,* " *and the intention is manifest, the Judges are not at lib-* " *erty, altho' it appears to them to be unreasonable, to re-* " *ject it : for this were to set the judicial above the legisla-* " *tive, which would be subversive of all government.*

" *But when a law is expressed in general words, and* " *some collateral matter, which happens to arise from* " *those general words is unreasonable, there the judges* " *are in decency to conclude, that the consequences were*

" *not foreseen by the legislature; and therefore they are*
" *at liberty to expound the statute by equity, and only*
" QUOAD HOC *to disregard it.*

" *When the judicial make these distinctions, they do*
" *not controul the legislature; they endeavour to give their*
" *intention its proper effect.*

" This is the substance of the authorities, on a compre-
"hensive view of the subject ; this is the language of Black-
"stone in his celebrated commentaries,* and this is the
"practice of the courts of justice, from which we have
"copied our jurisprudence, as well as the models of our
"internal judicatories."†

Blackstone's tenth rule for construing statutes in England under an *unwritten* constitution was thus adopted
bodily by a court of New York under a written constitution.

The court applied the foregoing doctrine in interpreting
the statute and came to the decision that collateral matter
arose out of its general words, which was unreasonable. It
held itself bound to conclude that such unreasonable consequence was not foreseen by the legislature. It was bound,
therefore, to explain the statute by equity and to disregard
it in so far only as it would operate thus unreasonably as
to such unforeseen consequence. The statute, therefore,
did not comprehend the cases of American prisoners in the
power of the enemy nor those of enemies clearly exempted
by the law of nations.

After this interpretation, the court held itself in a position to declare, that the questions whether the statute re-
voked the law of nations, and whether any part of the
statute was repealed by the subsequent treaty, were foreign
to the circumstances of this case.

The bearing of the law of the opinion upon the case of a
conflict between a state statute and the state constitution
is obvious. If Blackstone's doctrine was the law of New
York, no court could ever reject a statute in order to obey
the constitution, although the latter was written. If a court
could do so, the law of legislation would be based upon a

---

* Blackstone's Commentaries, I. p. 91.

† Pamphlet Report, p. 41.

denial of Blackstone's doctrine. Thus, if the opinion be correct, the question whether a statute be constitutional or not, could never be a judicial, and must always be an extrajudicial question. All courts must be bound by all statutes of the legislature. It has previously been shown that such is the law of legislation under the written Swiss federal constitution and under all the written German state constitutions.

And, indeed, in the opinion of some lawyers of 1784, the claim of the court to a limited Blackstonian discretion might have rather been impaired than strengthened by the written constitution of New York. By its third article, a Council for revising acts of the Senate and Assembly was established. This consisted of three or more members, *viz.*, the governor and two or more of the highest judicial magistrates (the chancellor and judges of the Supreme Court). If an act was approved by the Council, it became a law. If not, a majority of two-thirds of both houses was required to repass it. According to the article, the Council, proceeding by the rule of majority, could object to any proposed law deemed improper by them. Improper proposed laws were such as were "inconsistent with the spirit of this con-"stitution, or with public good "* The Council had approved the statute in question. In their judgment it was consistent with the spirit of the constitution and with the public good. The majority of the Council consisted always of judicial members and the attorney general seemed to the court to regard the determination of the Council upon the statute in the light of a judicial decision by which the court ought to be guided for the sake of uniformity in the dispensation of justice. The court declined to take any such view. The determination of the Council was not a judicial one. The court did not believe that the judicial members of the Council "would in the seat of judgment always be "precluded, even by their own opinion given in the Coun-"cil of Revision." Thus was decided the question whether the third article of the constitution interfered with the lim-

---

* Poor, Charters and Constitutions, II. 1332, article 3 of the Constitution of New York.

ited discretion claimed for the judiciary. Such a decision on one part of Blackstone's rule confirms what the writer has observed above on the whole rule as the law of the opinion in cases of conflict between statutes and the constitution.

On the whole matter of the case of Rutgers v. Waddington, it is, therefore, correct to say that according to the law of the opinion, no court could decide a questioned statute unconstitutional and hold it therefore void.

Before dismissing the consideration of Rutgers v. Waddington, an additional observation is necessary for further reference.

The opinion of the court is the means of now introducing the head of the *nonobstante* clause, which will play a most important part in the exposition of the law of the subject of this Essay.

The opinion points out that, if the statute had contained a clause of *nonobstante* to the law of nations, there would have been an express repeal of any part of that law contrariant to the statute. The absence of such a clause or of other express language of like import excluded the possibility of such a repeal, because the notion of any repealing by implication must be rejected. Contrariety between the statute and the law of nations could not be presumed. It must be expressed. This exposition of the law of the *nonobstante* clause was most opportune. It fell on the fruitful soil of 1784 and before long the seed produced a harvest. In the spring of 1787, the United States in Congress assembled moved federally the several states to enact identical laws with clauses of *nonobstante* to all their respective statutes and parts of statutes containing anything contrariant to the treaty of peace. Not only the year 1787, but the years 1788, and 1789, were memorable in the long American history of the legal institution known as the *nonobstante* clause. That history begins with the bull of Alexander VI., in 1499, and is not yet ended, as will hereinafter fully appear.

CHAPTER XXV.

Of the law of Rhode Island and of the case of Trevett v. Weeden.

The next subject for consideration will be the historical case of Trevett v. Weeden, heard and adjudicated by the Superior Court of Judicature of Rhode Island, at Newport, on September 25th and 26th, 1786.

Judge Cooley observes that this was the first American case in which a law "was declared unconstitutional and "void."*

The general assembly of Rhode Island, by an act of May session, 1786, provided for the emission of certain paper money. By an act of June session, 1786, the same body enacted that any person who should refuse to receive the said paper money in exchange for goods on sale at the value of the face of the bills, or who should make two prices for such goods, one in paper and the other in silver, etc., should upon conviction thereof be fined one hundred pounds for the first offence, and for the second be fined the same amount and become incapable of electing, or being elected, to any office of honour.

By act of special August session, 1786, the assembly provided for offences against the previous act being tried by special courts, each of which should proceed in the following way : "that the said court, when so convened, shall "proceed to the trial of said offender ; and they are hereby

---

* Constitutional Limitations, 5th Ed., page 194 footnote.

"authorized so to do, *without any jury*, by a majority of "the judges present, *according to the laws of the land*, and "to make adjudication and determination ; and that three "members be sufficient to constitute a court."* It was further enacted that there should be no appeal from the judgment of the court, etc.

The cause of Trevett *v*. Weeden was a *qui tam* action "brought by John Trevett, informer, against John Weeden, "butcher, for refusing to take, of the said John Trevett, for "meat, the bills of credit emitted by an act of the general "assembly of said state."†

To the plaintiff's complaint the defendant made answer by the following plea :

"The said John Weeden comes into court and prays the " honourable court here will not take cognizance of the com- "plaint of the said John Trevett ; because he saith, that it "appears by the act of the general assembly, whereon said "information is founded, that the said act hath expired, " and hath no force: Also, for that by the said act the " matters of complaint are made triable before special " courts, incontrollable by the supreme judiciary court of "the state : And also, for that the court is not authorized " or empowered by said act, to impanel a jury to try the "facts charged in the information, *and so the same is un- "constitutional and void :* All which the said Weeden is " ready to verify. Wherefore he prays judgment of the " court here, *that they will not take further cognizance of* "*the said information.*" ‡

What the counsel for the prosecution said is not extant, but it must have consisted only of brief and ordinary obser- vations. General James M. Varnum, member of the federal Congress from Rhode Island, was the senior counsel for the defence. Some time after the hearing of the cause, he printed his argument in a pamphlet published at Providence by John Carter, in 1787.

* Varnum, p. 59.

† Providence Gazette, October 7th, 1786 ; American Museum, vol. 5, p. 36.

‡ Gazette as cited ; Museum as cited ; Varnum, p. 2,

Varnum was the leading spirit of the cause. In his remarkable argument he sought to show :*

(1) That the act, upon which the information was founded, had expired ;

(2) That, by the act, special jurisdictions were created, uncontrollable by the supreme or superior court of judicature ;†

(3) That, by the act, the court was not authorized or empowered to impanel a jury to try the facts contained in the information ;‡

(4) That the trial by jury was a fundamental constitutional right, was a part of the legal constitution of Rhode Island, had always been claimed as such, had always been ratified as such, and had always been held most dear and sacred ;§

(5) That the legislature derived all its authority from the constitution, that it had no power of making laws but in subordination to the constitution and that therefore it could not infringe or violate the constitution, as was done by enacting an act depriving citizens of the constitutional right of trial by jury ;‖

(6) "That therefore the act is unconstitutional and void ;¶

(7) "That this court has power to judge and determine "what acts of the general assembly are agreeable to the "constitution;**

(8) "That this court is under the solemn obligations to "execute the laws of the land, and therefore can not, will "not consider this act as a law of the land."††

Before going further it may be remarked that the act of the general assembly in the quotations from the defendant's plea abovequoted is said to be "unconstitutional and void." In the quotation in Varnum, page 3, line 3, the language is identical. That language, however, is not accurate. The

---

* Varnum, p. 35, 5.
† 　Ib. 　　" 　" 　7.
‡ 　Ib. 　　" 　" 　10.
§ 　Ib. 　　" 　" 　11.
‖ 　Ib. 　　" 　" 　20 *et seq.*
¶ 　Ib. 　　" 　"
** 　Ib. 　　" 　"
†† 　Ib. 　　" 　"

precise words were that the act was "unconstitutional and "so void." This is proved by Varnum, page 37 line 10 from the bottom and page 38, line 2 from the bottom. Judge Howell's observations on the latter page are decisive on this important point.

The first of Varnum's contentions was that the act in question had expired. The defence did not, however, place their principal reliance upon this objection, which appears to have hung upon the unskillfulness of the penman of the act. As Varnum feared the injustice of the legislature to the judges, in the event of the court's doing justice to his client, it might become a useful shield for the latter. It was probably thought so by the court, judging from the speech defending its action and judgment which was made by Judge Howell before the legislature. Every thing said both by Varnum and the judges in court must be read in the light of their common expectation that the legislature would proceed in some hostile way against the latter, if they refused to obey the act.

The argument upon the second point, viz., that, by the act, special jurisdictions were created uncontrollable by the supreme court of judicature, does not go to the question whether or not the act was unconstitutional and so void. It was, however, one of much moment in moving the court to consider whether the act was so or not on other points.

Proof of this is found in paragraph 2 page 10, which holds that at most the Supreme Court could, under the act, correct only the errors of a special court composed of three or more of its own members, but could not correct the error of any of the five special courts composed of members of the courts of Common Pleas.

The next head of Varnum's argument was an inquiry whether the legislature of the state "can deprive the citi- "zens of their constitutional right, the trial by jury."

It must here be recalled by the reader that the constitution of Rhode Island was, in 1786, an *unwritten* constitution ascertained from history, not from the inspection of a written fundamental law denominated a constitution.*

---

* *Cf.* Luther *v.* Borden, 7 Howard, page 35.

It is of the essence of Varnum's whole argument that there was a continuity in the constitution of Rhode Island from the foundation thereof in the reign of Charles II. down to the then year 1786. The Revolution had changed only certain parts of the constitution. The legislature of the state was identical with the legislature of the colony, and was not a new legislature put in the place of an old one which had been destroyed. The knowledge of what the constitution of the state was, and the legal vigour and validity thereof were derived from the same source, *viz.*, the custom and usage of the people. This custom and usage of the people began far back in colonial times and extended from one generation to another down to the then present year of 1786. There was no break in the continuity of that custom and usage at the Revolution.*

In Connecticut, it may be injected, a like unwritten constitution existed in a like way.† An act had been passed there in 1776, declaring that the old colonial charter of Charles II. should have vigour under independence. That act, however, was not made by any constitutional convention, but by the ordinary legislature. It was the common custom of the people of Connecticut that gave vigour to the colonial charter as part of the constitution of that state.

Although the colonial charter of Rhode Island lost all vigour at the Revolution, as an act of the late sovereign, it was, *mutatis mutandis*, continued in vigour a part of the unwritten constitution of the new state by the custom and usage of the people and was law by virtue of their custom and usage, as it was formerly law by virtue of the king's prerogative lawfully and rightfully exercised.

The charter had been granted by the king upon the petition of the people. It was conclusive evidence of the intention of the king and of the compact of the people. The powers of the legislature were clearly created and as clearly limited by it. They had power and authority to make laws, provided such laws were not contrary and not repug-

---

* *Cf.* Varnum, pp. 22, 23, 25.

† *Cf.* Calder *v.* Bull, 3 Dallas, 386, and Poor's Charters and Constitutions, under Connecticut.

nant to the laws of England. The laws of England included the common law, Magna Charta, and the trial by jury.[*]

The people of the state, at the Revolution, might have met in solemn convention in order to annul the old constitution and make a new one by a written instrument. They had not done so, nor any thing like it. Neither had the people entrusted their legislators with the power of altering the constitution. They had continued the ancient constitution, *mutatis mutandis*, by their unbroken custom. The old legislature was continued with the old constitutional limitations upon its power. The colonial legislature could not have abolished the trial by jury, and therefore the state legislature could not abolish it. The state had a constitution as much as the colony.[†]

"If we have not a constitution, by what authority doth "our general assembly convene to make laws and levy "taxes? Their appointment by the freemen of the towns, "excluding the idea of a social compact, cannot separately "give them power to make laws compulsory upon the other "towns. They could only meet, in that case, to form a "social compact between the people of the towns. But "they do meet by the appointment of their respective "towns, at such times and places, and in such numbers, "as they have been accustomed to from the beginning. "When met, they make laws and levy taxes, and their "constituents obey those laws, and pay those taxes. Con-"sequently they meet, deliberate and enact, in virtue of a "constitution, which, if they attempt to destroy, or in any "manner infringe, they violate the trust reposed in them, "*and so their acts are not to be considered as laws, or* "*binding upon the people.*"[‡]

The above reflections upon the constitution of Rhode Island are confined to matters of historical law and positive right. Varnum does not, however, speak only of such considerations. As was usual, perhaps unavoidable in the

---

* Varnum, pp. 22, 23.

† *Cf.* Varnum, pp. 30, 25, 23, *cf.* 34.

‡ Varnum, pp. 25, 26.

eighteenth century, his argument goes into reasoning from an abstract philosophy of law. He quotes freely from Locke and Vattel. With much originality, he adapts their abstract views of infant society and social compacts to the actual facts of the settlement and history of the towns (or townships) of the colony of Rhode Island and the Providence Plantations. Space precludes further disquisition of this portion of the discussion except upon one point. A quoted passage from Vattel holds that the legislature of any state having a constitution can not alter the fundamental constitutional laws, without having in express terms the power to change the same as part of their commission. This passage concludes : " In short, these legislators derive their " power from the constitution ; how then can they change " it, without destroying the foundation of their authority."

This view of Vattel's as to a constitution of a state in the abstract is deemed by Varnum to support his own view of the concrete constitution of Rhode Island. Both, indeed, regard every act of any legislature made in violation of the constitution of their state to be void because made beyond their commission, mandate or appointment. Vattel maintains that this is so because the legislature can not destroy the constitution without destroying that which is the only foundation of their legislative power or authority. Varnum approves this doctrine as an abstract one, but his pamphlet does not clearly assert it to be true of the concrete constitution of Rhode Island. According to the report of his spoken words he did clearly make such an assertion.* It is of much importance to observe that the philosophic law, which Varnum quotes from Vattel, is identical with the actual law of North Carolina, as laid down by the Superior Court of that state in the case of Bayard *v.* Singleton in 1787, the next year following. That court held that the legislature of North Carolina could not make a law which altered the constitution of the state, without destroying the foundation of their own legislative authority. The great difference between the cases of Trevett *v.* Weeden and

---

* See Providence Gazette and American Museum.

Bayard *v.* Singleton was that the former arose under an unwritten, and the latter under a written, constitution. Both related to the denial of the trial by jury, as will be seen when the latter case is fully examined.

Varnum's next contention was that it was a *judicial* question whether or not the legislature had violated the constitutional rights of the people in enacting the law referred to. " As the legislative is the supreme power in government, who " is to judge whether they have violated the constitutional "rights of the people ? I answer, their supremacy (consist- "ing in the power of making laws, agreeable to their "appointment) is derived from the constitution, is subor- " dinate to it, and therefore, whenever they attempt to en- " slave the people, and carry their attempts into execution, " the people themselves will judge, as the only resort in the "last stages of oppression. But when they proceed no " farther than merely to enact what they may call laws, and " refer those to the judiciary courts for determination, then, " (in the discharge of the great trust reposed in them, and " to prevent the horrors of civil war, as in the present case,) "the judges can, and we trust Your Honors will, decide " upon them."*

[That is to say, when the legislature enact a law abolishing the constitutional rights of the people, prevent all judicial action concerning it, and execute the act themselves, the people must then submit, or resort to civil war as the only remedy. But when the legislature enact such a law and do not attempt to execute it themselves, but direct the judiciary to carry it into execution, the duty of the judges is this : they must examine such legislation and determine whether it deprives the people of their constitutional rights or not, and if it do so, then, they must say so, and hold it to be therefore no law of the land. If the judges do otherwise, they unite with the legislature in compelling the people to resort to civil war as the only remedy left. If, however, the judges furnish a peaceful remedy to the people for their wrongs, they are not acting *extrajudicially*, but *judicially*.

* Varnum, p. 26.

It is a fundamental object in establishing courts of justice and civil society to prevent every kind of war except foreign war, by furnishing judicial remedies for legal wrongs.]

In a despotism the judges are not independent, according to Varnum. There all officials are merely ministerial. Where political freedom exists, the judges are free and independent administrators of justice. With such judges only can a real judiciary exist.*

The power which Varnum asked the court to exercise was, he maintained, a judicial one. It was not an extra-judicial one. The judges would assume no legislative power in exercising it. Its rightfulness is based upon the separation, not upon the confusion, of the powers of government. In a tyranny, all the public powers are lodged together in one hand, whether it be the government of a single tyrant, or a body of tyrants, as the legislature of Rhode Island would be, if that body possessed judicial, executive and legislative powers combined. "The true distinction "lies in this, that the legislative have the uncontrollable "power of making laws not repugnant to the constitution. "The judiciary have the sole power of judging those laws, "and are bound to execute them ; but cannot admit any "act of the legislative as law, which is against the "constitution."†

The judges had sworn an oath of office to execute the laws and also an oath of allegiance to the state. Rhode Island became a state in order to support its fundamental constitutional laws. The trial by jury is a fundamental constitutional law and therefore is binding upon the judges by a double oath.‡ There were no laws of the general assembly distinct from the laws of the state. Laws made by the general assembly under the powers thereof derived from the constitution "become the laws of the land and as such "the court is sworn to execute them. But if the general "assembly attempt to make laws contrary hereunto, the "court can not receive them." If the judges should do so,

---

* Varnum, p. 26.
† Ib. " 27.
‡ Ib. " 28.

they would violate both their oaths. " There is no middle
" line. The legislative hath power to go all lengths, or not
" to overleap the bounds of its appointment at all. So it is
" with the judiciary ; it must reject all acts of the legisla-
" tive that are contrary to the trust reposed in them by the
" people, or it must adopt all."*

There is certainly verisimilitude in the idea that this passage of Varnum's had much to do in suggesting the following passage of Marshall's in Marbury v. Madison :

" Between these alternatives there is no middle ground.
" The constitution is either a superior, paramount law, un-
" changeable by ordinary means ; or it is on a level with
" ordinary legislative acts, and, like other acts, is alterable
" when the legislature shall please to alter it.

" If the former part of the alternative be true, then a leg-
" islative act contrary to the constitution is not law ; if the
" latter part be true, then written constitutions are absurd
" attempts on the part of the people to limit a power in its
" own nature illimitable."†

Just as all men and all judges were bound by the laws of
nature in preference to any human laws, because they were
ordained by God himself anterior to any political institutions, so the judges of the state were bound by the principles of the constitution of the state in preference to any
acts of the general assembly, because those principles were
ordained by the people anterior to the powers of the general
assembly and because those principles created those powers.‡

Varnum quotes Bacon's Abridgment for the proposition
that " if a statute . . . . be repugnant, or impossible to
" be performed, the Common law shall control it, and ad-
" judge it to be void."§ He maintains that the act of the
general assembly is repugnant when it authorizes the judges
to " proceed to trial without any jury, according to the laws
" of the land." The laws of the land constitute the jurors
the triers of facts, and the judges the triers of law only.

---

* Varnum, pp. 29, 28,

† See page 56, *ante*, and 1 Cranch, 176–180.

‡ Varnum, p. 29.

§ Ib. " 30.

It was impossible that judges should try a man, without a jury, and at the same time try a man "according to the "laws of the land," which certainly secured to every freeman a trial "by the lawful judgment of his peers." Contraries could not exist and be executed at the same time. "This act therefore is impossible to be executed."*

What Varnum here says directly connects Trevett *v.* Weeden with the traditional language of the English lawbooks on statutes that are impossible to be performed. It has been previously pointed out that that language is to be traced to the case of the convent seals and the 4th chapter of the statute of Carlisle in Fitzherbert, Annuity, 41. That Varnum used the said language with important effect upon the court is proved by Judge Howell's speech to the legislature of the state hereinafter quoted, in which he maintained that the statute was "unconstitutional, had not the force of "law, and could not be executed."† Thus, links exist connecting Trevett *v.* Weeden with the case of the convent seals and the fourth chapter of the statute of Carlisle, which was the first case in which a Common law court said that an unrepealed statute was "void" for cause judicially ascertained. The possibility that such a use of the word "void" may have an origin in the Canon law has therefore increased interest to Americans. See *ante* pages, 176–178.

The constitution of Rhode Island was in Varnum's opinion an extremely liberal and popular system in which all the officers of government were elected by the two houses of the general assembly in grand committee. Before the revolution the king, as supreme executive, formed the balance. Since then, the executive power had become blended with the legislative, for, Rhode Island had not, like other states in the Union, adopted any substitute for that defect.‡ Hence, to save the existence of the constitution, to prevent the dissolution of government under it, and to keep political liberty from coming to an end, the judiciary must hold itself independent of the legislature. If it did not do so, all three

---

* Varnum, pp. 31, 30.

† Ib. p. 38.

‡ Ib. pp. 33, 34.

powers, legislative, executive and judicial, would be blended in the general assembly. He had previously pointed out that this was a distinctive mark of every tyranny. In other words, as the result of a revolution made for liberty there was no free government at all in Rhode Island.

Varnum's argument was not replied to by the plaintiff's counsel, who avoided any discussion of constitutional points. Merchant, the junior counsel for the defence, said but little in closing.* Channing, the attorney general, was in court, but took no part in the proceedings.† He stated, however, before the legislature that he approved the action and conduct of the judges and believed that "their determination "was conformable to the principles of constitutional law."‡ It is evident that the weight of the bar of the state was on the side of the court and its judgment.

The judgment of the court was "that the information "was not cognizable before them."§ These terms do not say that the statute was "unconstitutional and so void," as is pointed out by Judge Howell on pages 38 and 39 of Varnum. The judgment, however, plainly rejected and repelled the challenged statute. The bar, the legislature and the public all understood the reason why the court rendered such a judgment, viz., because the statute was, as the defendant's plea asserted, "unconstitutional and so "void."

The following constitutes the whole of the brief extant report of what was said by them.‖

"The court adjourned to next morning, upon opening of "which, Judge Howell, in a firm, sensible and judicious "speech, assigned the reasons which induced him to be of "the opinion that the information was not cognizable by "the court—declared himself independent as a judge—the "penal law to be repugnant¶ and unconstitutional—and

---

* Providence Gazette, as cited,

† Varnum, p. 51.

‡   Ib.   "   "

§ Such was the recorded judgment : See Varnum, page 38, last paragraph.

‖ Providence Gazette as cited : Compare American Museum as cited.

¶ "Unjust," in the Museum's text.

"therefore gave it as his opinion that the court could not
"take cognizance of the information ! Judge Devol was of
"the same opinion. Judge Tillinghast took notice of the
"striking repugnancy of the expressions of the act, ' With-
"'out trial by jury, according to the laws of the land '—
"and on that ground gave his judgment the same way.
"Judge Hazard voted against taking cognizance. The
"Chief Justice declared the judgment of the court* with-
"out giving his own opinion."

As throwing further light upon the views of the judges,
the following additional matter may be gained from the
proceedings in the case of the judges before the general assembly. Soon after their decision, the judges were summoned by both houses of that body to attend them in order
"to render their reasons for adjudging an act of the gen-
"eral assembly to be unconstitutional and so void."† Judge
Howell, in his speech before the legislature, "pointed out
" the objectionable part of the act upon which the informa-
" tion was founded, and most clearly demonstrated by a
"variety of conclusive arguments, that it was *unconstitu-*
"*tional, had not the force of a law, and could not be exe-*
"*cuted.*"‡ Judge Tillinghast said, in his remark to the as-
"sembly that he felt himself perfectly independent while
"moving in the circle of his duty."§ Judge Hazard, in
his remarks to the same body, said that his sentiments were
the same as those which his brethren had declared and that
the opinion which he gave at the trial was that which he
thought right, and that he still thought it so.‖

The foregoing proceeding before the legislature was in
October, 1786. The proceeding was adjourned to the next
month. On November 4th, Judges Hazard, Tillinghast and
Howell made a written protest to the legislature against the
apprehended design of dismissing the judges by a summary
vote. They acknowledge liability only to a proper and

---

* The words, "against the informer," are here found in the Museum's text.
† Varnum, p. 37.
‡   Ib.   " 38.
§   Ib.   pp. 42, 43.
‖   Ib.   p. 43.

legal tribunal upon certain and specific charges, in other words, to formal impeachment. They state that their communication was made after "having appeared before both "houses in grand committee, and made full communication "of all the proceedings of the court, relative to the case in "which said judgment was rendered; and having entered "into a full and free examination of the several parts and "principles of the penal law in question, and compared "them with the constitution, or fundamental laws of the "state, and all other laws operating thereon, which secure "the citizens thereof their rights and privileges; and hav-"ing established their observations thereon by many of the "most approved authorities in law, as well as by the con-"stitution of the federal union, and the members thereof, "since the revolution in this country."*

The effect of this protest was to stop the pending proceeding of the legislature against the judges. No proceedings in impeachment were initiated. The judges held their offices uninterruptedly until the end of their annual terms. In the following spring, however, the general assembly had their opportunity for revenge, and at the annual election for judges chose other persons to succeed the brave and prudent magistrates, who had vindicated the right to trial by jury by treating a law against it as "unconstitutional "and so void."

Varnum's pamphlet gives no report of what the judges said in court, although it contains some statement of what three of them said before the legislature. The opinions of the judges are to be found in the account in the American Museum. Until recently Varnum's pamphlet and the Museum contained the only contemporary accounts practically accessible. Five contemporary newspaper accounts have, however, been brought to light by Prof. McMaster's note in his History, vol. 1, p. 339. One of these, that in the Providence Journal of October 27th, 1787, has been followed in this chapter. The account in the American Mu-

---

* Varnum, 44, 45.

seum is evidently copied from that in the Providence Gazette.   It only differs as to some omissions, which are of
secondary importance.   The statements of the judges' opinions in the Gazette and the Musuem are identical, except
as to one word which has been noted in the footnote.

CHAPTER XXVI.

Of the law of North Carolina and the case of Den on the dem. of Bayard and Wife *v*. Singleton.

No. 1. *Rehearsal of the case of Bayard* v. *Singleton according to the report in Martin's Reports.*

No. 2. *Further information concerning the case derived
from other sources.*

No. 3. *Text of Iredell's letter of an Elector printed in
Newbern on August 17th, 1786.*

No. 4. *Text of the letter of James Iredell to Richard
Dobbs Spaight dated August 26th, 1787.*

No. 5. *Further reflections upon the case of Bayard* v.
Singleton.

No. 6. *Of the date when the decision in Bayard* v. *Singleton became known to the Framers' convention.*

The cause of Den on the dem. of Bayard and wife *v*. Singleton is the first reported case in which an act of a legislature was decided to be contrary to a *written* constitution.
It arose in North Carolina before the Superior Court of that
state.   The date of the decision was in May Term, 1787.
May Term comprehended the last ten working days of the
month of May.

No. 1.

Rehearsal of the case of Bayard v. *Singleton according to the report in Martin's Reports.**

This cause was an action of ejectment for the recovery of a lot of ground with a house and a wharf, in the town of Newbern in North Carolina. The defendant held under a title derived from the state of North Carolina, by a deed from a superintendent commissioner of confiscated estates. Nash for the defendant moved that the suit be dismissed according to an act for securing and quieting the possession of the purchasers of property sold by the commissioners of forfeited estates. This act required the courts, in all cases in which the defendant made affidavit that he held the disputed property under a sale from a commissioner of forfeited estates, to dismiss the suit on motion. Such an affidavit had been filed by the defendant.

The plaintiffs claimed title under a deed from Cornell, who was the father of Mrs. Bayard, and whose estates had been confiscated. The plaintiffs were not citizens of North Carolina, but of another state of the Union. Cornell had been a colonist of North Carolina, who refused to become a citizen of the state, and lived and died a British subject.

Nash's motion brought on "long arguments from the "counsel on each side, on constitutional points."

The court made a few observations on the constitution and system of government, and wished to be advised. Numerous like suits were involved in the fate of this.

The foregoing proceedings took place at Newbern in May, 1786. In May, 1787, at the same place, Nash's motion was resumed and a very lengthy debate from the bar took place. Whereupon the court recommended the parties to consent to "a fair decision of the property in question, by a jury "according to the common law of the land." This recommendation, however, was without effect. Another mode was proposed for putting the matter in controversy on "a "more constitutional footing for a decision," than that of

---

* Martin's Reports (first division) pp. 48–52. Second Edition, I. pp. 42–48.

a motion under the aforesaid act. This proposal also must have failed.

"The court then, after every reasonable endeavour had "been used in vain for avoiding a disagreeable difference "between the legislature and the judicial powers of the "state, at length with much apparent reluctance, but with "great deliberation and firmness, gave their opinion sepa-"rately, but unanimously for overruling the aforemen-"tioned motion for the dismission of the said suits.

"In the course of which the judges observed, that the "obligation of their oaths, and the duty of their office re-"quired them in that situation, to give their opinion on "that important and momentous subject; and that not-"withstanding the great reluctance they might feel against "involving themselves in a dispute with the legislature of "the state, yet no object of concern or respect could come "in competition or authorize them to dispense with the "duty they owed the public, in consequence of the trust "they were invested with under the solemnity of their "oaths.

"That they therefore were bound to declare that they "considered, that whatever disabilities the persons under "whom the plaintiffs were said to derive their titles, might "justly have incurred, against their maintaining or prose-"cuting any suits in the Courts of the state; yet such dis-"abilities in their nature were merely personal, and not by "any means capable of being transferred to the present "plaintiffs, either by descent or purchase; and that these "plaintiffs being citizens of one of the United States, are "citizens of this state, by the confederation of all the states; "which is to be taken as a part of the law of the land, un-"repealable by any act of the General Assembly.

"That by the constitution every citizen had undoubtedly "a right to a decision of his property by a trial by jury. "For that if the legislature could take away this right, and "require him to stand condemned in his property without "a trial, it might with as much authority require his life "to be taken away without a trial by jury, and that he "should stand condemned to die, without the formality of

"any trial at all: that if the members of the General As-
"sembly could do this, they might with equal authority,
"not only render themselves the legislators of the state
"for life, without any further election by the people, from
"thence transmit the dignity and authority of legislation
"down to their heirs male forever.

" But that it was clear, that no act they could pass, could
"by any means repeal or alter the constitution, because if
"they could do this, they would at the same instant of
"time, destroy their own existence as a legislature, and dis-
"solve the government thereby established. Consequently
"the constitution (which the judicial power was bound to
"take notice of as much as any other law whatever), stand-
"ing in full force as the fundamental law of the land, not-
"withstanding the act on which the present motion was
"grounded, *the same act must of course, in that instance,*
"*stand as abrogated and without effect.*"

In consequence of this decision, there was a trial by jury
in the cause in November Term, 1787, in which the jury
found a verdict for the defendant

No. 2.

*Further information concerning the case derived from
other sources.*

The senior counsel for the plaintiff, the party in whose interest the statute was rejected as unconstitutional, was Iredell, afterwards judge of the Supreme Court of the United
States. Another of the plaintiff's counsel was William R.
Davie, one of Framers of the constitution, who was actually attending the convention in Philadelphia when the
above decision was made at Newbern in May, 1787.

The report in Martin's Reports was made by Judge Spencer, who sat in the case. He does not report the arguments
of counsel. There is, however, no difficulty in ascertaining
what must have been said by Iredell, who was leading
spirit in the litigation and in the great question involved
therein. It was he, who the year before had prepared the

way for such a litigation by an elaborate public letter discussing the great question, which was published at Newbern on August 17th, 1786.

Thus the doctrine of the case has a history previous to the decision in May Term, 1787. It had also a subsequent history which caused Iredell to write a second important paper concerning it. The decision of the Superior Court was an act of great civic courage. It created much excitement and was received with severe adverse criticism in North Carolina, where it was known in public discussion as the Newbern case. The three courageous magistrates who composed the court were Samuel Ashe, Samuel Spencer, and John Williams. President Battle in his history of the court observes : *

" These, our earliest judges, are entitled to the eminent
" distinction of contesting with Rhode Island the claim of
" being the first in the United States to decide that the
" courts have the power and duty to declare an act of the
" legislature, which in their opinion is unconstitutional, to
" be null and void. The doctrine is so familiar to us, so
" universally acquiesced in, that it is difficult for us to rea-
" lize that when it was first mooted, the judges who had the
" courage to declare it were fiercely denounced as usurpers
" of power. Spaight, afterwards governor, voiced a com-
" mon notion when he declared that 'the state was subject
" 'to the three individuals, who united in their own persons
" 'the legislative and judicial power, which no monarch in
" 'England enjoys, which would be more despotic than the
" 'Roman triumvirate and equally insufferable.' . . . As I
" have mentioned, the action of the court was the founda-
" tion of one of the charges brought by Hay [in the legisla-
" ture]. He accused them with dispensing with a law—the
" 'Newbern case.' . . . The judges were eventually sus-
" tained by public opinion."

One of the most important of the adverse critics of the decision was Richard Dobbs Spaight, who opposed it from Philadelphia, where he was attending the Framers' conven-

* 103 North Carolina Reports, pp. 472, 473.

tion. To him there and then Iredell addressed an elaborate letter in defence of the decision and its doctrine.

Iredell's public letter of August 17th, 1786, and his letter to Spaight of August 26th, 1787, are legal arguments and historical papers of great ability and grave importance. They are printed in his biography. As that work is so rare as to be obtainable only with difficulty and delay, these documents are printed in full. From them what Iredell said in argument before the court may easily be inferred.

No. 3.

*Text of Iredell's Letter of an Elector printed at New-bern on August 17th, 1786.**

"To the Public : As the question concerning the power "of the Assembly deeply concerns every man in the State, " I shall make no apology for delivering my sentiments upon " it. They are indeed only the sentiments of an obscure " elector, but one who, he trusts, has rights that he as much "values, though with less ability to defend them, as the " proudest member of Assembly whatever.

" I have not lived so short a time in the State, nor with so " little interest in its concerns, as to forget the extreme " anxiety with which all of us were agitated in forming the " constitution, a constitution which we considered as the " fundamental basis of our government, unalterable, but by " the same high power which established it, and therefore " to be deliberated on with the greatest caution, because if "it contained any evil principle, the government formed "under it must be annihilated before the evil could be cor-"rected. It was, of course, to be considered how to im-" pose restrictions on the legislature, that might still leave " it free to all useful purposes, but at the same time guard " against the abuse of unlimited power, which was not to " be trusted, without the most imminent danger, to any

---

* Reprinted from the Life and Correspondence of James Iredell, by G. J. McRee, vol. 2, pp. 145–149.

"man or body of men on earth. We had not only been
"sickened and disgusted for years with the high and almost
"impious language of Great Britain, of the omnipotent
"power of the British Parliament, but had severely smarted
"under its effects. We felt in all its rigor the mischiefs of
"an absolute and unbounded authority, claimed by so weak
"a creature as man, and should have been guilty of the
"basest breach of trust, as well as the grossest folly, if in
"the same moment when we spurned at the *insolent des-*
"*potism* of Great Britain, we had established a *despotic*
"power ourselves. Theories were nothing to us, opposed
"to our own severe experience. We were not ignorant of
"the theory *of the necessity of the legislature being abso-*
"*lute in all cases*, because it was the great ground of the
"British pretensions. But this was a mere speculative
"principle, which men at ease and leisure thought proper
"to assume. When we were at liberty to form a govern-
"ment as we thought best, without regard to that or any
"theoretical principle we did not approve of, we decisively
"gave our sentiments against it, being willing to run all the
"risks of a government to be conducted on the principles
"then laid as the basis of it. The instance was new in the
"annals of mankind. No people had ever before deliber-
"ately met for so great a purpose. Other governments have
"been established by chance, caprice, or mere brutal force.
"Ours, thank God, sprang from the deliberate voice of the
"people. We provided, or meant to provide (God grant
"our purpose may not be defeated), for the security of every
"individual, as well as a fluctuating majority of the people.
"We knew the value of liberty too well, to suffer it to de-
"pend on the capricious voice of popular favor, easily led
"astray by designing men, and courted for insidious pur-
"poses. Nor could we regard, without contempt, a theory
"which required a greater authority in man than (with
"reverence be it spoken) exists even in the Supreme Being.
"For His power is not altogether absolute—His *infinite*
"*power* is limited by His *infinite wisdom*.

"I have therefore no doubt, but that the power of the
"Assembly is limited and defined by the constitution. It

"is a *creature* of the constitution. (I hope this is an ex-
"pression not prosecutable.) The people have chosen to
"be governed under such and such principles. They have
"not chosen to be governed, or promised to submit upon
"any other ; and the Assembly have no more right to obe-
"dience on other terms, than any different power on earth
"has a right to govern us ; for we have as much agreed to
"be governed by the Turkish Divan as by our own General
"Assembly, otherwise than on the express terms prescribed.

"These are consequences that seem so natural, and in-
"deed so irresistible, that I do not observe they have been
"much contested. The great argument is, that though the
"Assembly have not a *right* to violate the constitution, yet
"if they *in fact* do so, the only remedy is, either by a
"humble petition that the law may be repealed, or a uni-
"versal resistance of the people. But that in the meantime,
"their act, whatever it is, is to be obeyed as a law ; for the
"judicial power is not to presume to question the power of
"an act of Assembly.

"To these positions, not unconfidently urged, I answer :—

"1. That the remedy by petition implies a supposition,
"that the electors hold their rights by the *favour of their*
"*representatives.* The mere stating of this is surely suffi-
"cient to excite any man's indignation. What ! if the As-
"sembly say, we shall elect only once in two years, instead
"of electing annually, are we to petition them to repeal
"this law ? to request that they will be graciously pleased
"not to be our tyrants, but to allow us the benefit of the
"government we ourselves have chosen, and under which
"they alone derive all their authority ?

"But 2. The whole people may resist. A dreadful ex-
"pedient indeed. We well know how difficult it is to ex-
"cite the resistance of a whole people, and what a calami-
"tous contingency, at best, this is to be reduced to. But
"it is a sufficient answer, that nothing can be powerful
"enough to effect such a purpose in a government like
"ours, but *universal oppression.* A thousand injuries
"may be suffered, and many hundreds ruined, before this
"can be brought about. A majority may see A. B., C. D.,

"and E. F., and hundreds of others quietly injured one
"after another, and not stir a step towards a civil war.
"Let any man then ask himself, Suppose a law is passed
"by which I am ruined! Have I interest enough to over-
"turn the government of my country? If I have, we still
"may be a ruined people, and myself ruined among the
"rest. If I have not, upon what footing do my liberties
"depend? The pleasure of a majority of the Assembly?
"God forbid! How many things have been done by ma-
"jorities of a large body in *heat* and *passion*, that they
"themselves afterwards have repented of! Besides, would
"the *minority* choose to put themselves in the power of a
"majority? Few men, I presume, are always in a *major-*
"*ity*. None, therefore, could have even a chance of being
"secure, but sycophants that will for ever sacrifice reason,
"conscience, and duty, to the preservation of a temporary
"popular favor. Will this not put an end to all freedom
"of deliberation, to all manly spirit, and prove the utter
"extinction of all real liberty?

" But this resource is evidently derived from the princi-
"ple of *unbounded legislative power*, that I have noticed
"before, and that our constitution reprobates. In England
"they are in this condition. In England, therefore, they
" are less free than we are. Every parliament in that coun-
"try chosen for *three* years, continued itself for seven.
" This is an absolute fact, that happened long within the
"present century. Would this be a fit precedent for us?
" May our Assembly do so, because their Parliament did?
" May our governor have a negative on the laws, because
"he has a faint image of monarchial power? As little, I
" trust, is the government of Great Britain to influence in
" other things, equally inconsistent with our condition, and
" equally preposterous as these.

"These two remedies then being rejected, it remains to
"be inquired whether the judicial power hath any author-
" ity to interfere in such a case. The duty of that power,
" I conceive, in all cases, is to decide according to the *laws*
"*of the State*. It will not be denied, I suppose, that the
" constitution is a *law of the State*, as well as an act of As_

"sembly, with this difference only, that it is the *funda-*
"*mental* law, and unalterable by the legislature, which de-
"rives all its power from it. One act of Assembly may re-
"peal another act of Assembly. For this reason, the latter
"act is to be obeyed, and not the former. An act of As-
"sembly cannot repeal the constitution, or any part of it.
"For that reason, an act of Assembly, inconsistent with
"the constitution, is *void*, and cannot be obeyed, without
"disobeying the superior law to which we were previously
"and irrevocably bound. The judges, therefore, must take
"care at their peril, that every act of Assembly they pre-
"sume to enforce is warranted by the constitution, since if
"it is not, they act without lawful authority. This is not
"a usurped or a discretionary power, but one inevitably
"resulting from the constitution of their office, they being
"judges *for the benefit of the whole people*, not *mere ser-*
"*vants of the Assembly.* And the danger, about which
"there is so much alarm, attending the exercise of this
"power is, in my opinion, the least that can be imagined
"to attend the exercise of any important power whatever.
"For the judges, besides the natural desire which must be
"entertained by every man living in a popular government,
"of securing the favor of the people, are in fact dependent
"on the Assembly; for though their duration in office is
"permanent, at least as long as the act is in being which
"establishes their court, *their salaries are precarious;*
"and in fact are they only nominally independent in point
"of station, when the Assembly may every session deter-
"mine how much they shall have to subsist upon. Did
"any man in England, previous to the Revolution, appre-
"hend any injury to the prerogative from the judges of
"those days? They depended indeed, both for salary and
"place, on the breath of the crown. But the dependence
"here, I am persuaded, will in general be found equally
"effectual, at least to prevent a wanton abuse of power,
"and, it is much to be feared, may in some instances pro-
"duce an actual bias the other way, which, in my humble
"opinion, is the great danger to be apprehended. It may

"also be observed, that if the judges should be disposed to
"abuse their power, merely for the sake of the abuse, they
"have means enough of doing so, for every act of Assem-
"bly may occasionally come under their judgment in one
"shape or other, and *those acts may be wilfully miscon-*
"*strued as well as the constitution.*

" But it is said, if the judges have this power, so have the
"county courts. I admit it. The county courts, in the
"exercise of equal judicial power, must have equal autho-
"rity. But every argument in respect of the judges (ex-
"cept their dependence for salary), and other obvious ones,
"occur in great force against this danger, besides the liberty
"of appeal, which ultimately rests everything, almost,
"with the superior courts. The objection, however, urged
"by some persons, that sheriffs and other *ministerial*
"officers must exercise their judgment too, does not apply.
"For *if the power of judging rests with the courts*, their
"decision is final as to the subject matter. Did ever a
"sheriff refuse to hang a man, because he thought he was
"unjustly convicted of murder?

"These are a few observations that have occcured to me
"on this subject. They are given by a plain man, unambi-
"tious of power, but sincerely and warmly interested in
"the prosperity of his country; feeling every respect for
"the constitutional authority of the legislature, which, in
"his opinion, is great enough to satisfy an ambitious, as
"well as to support the efforts of a public spirited mind,
"but a determined enemy on all occasions to arbitrary
"power, in every shape whatsoever; and reverencing, be-
"yond expression, that constitution by which he holds all
"that is dear to him in life.

"AN ELECTOR."

No. 4.

*Text of Iredell's Letter to Richard Dobbs Spaight dated August 26th, 1787.**

" August 26th, 1787. . . . In regard to the late decision at
" Newbern, I confess it has ever been my opinion, that an
" act inconsistent with the Constitution was void ; and that
" the judges, consistently with their duties, could not carry
" it into effect. The Constitution appears to me to be a
" fundamental law, limiting the powers of the Legislature,
" and with which every exercise of those powers must,
" necessarily, be compared. Without an express Constitu-
" tion the powers of the Legislature would undoubtedly
" have been absolute (as the Parliament in Great Britain is
" held to be), and any act passed, *not inconsistent with*
" *natural justice* (for that curb is avowed by the judges
" even in England), would have been binding on the people.
" The experience of the evils which the American war fully
" disclosed, attending an absolute power in a legislative
" body, suggested the propriety of a real, original contract
" between the people and their future Government, such,
" perhaps, as there has been no instance of in the world but
" in America. Had not this been the case, bills of attain-
" der, and other acts of party violence, might have ruined
" many worthy individuals here, as they have frequently
" done in England, where such things are much oftener the
" acts of a party than the result of a fair judicial inquiry.
" In a republican Government (as I conceive) *individual*
" *liberty* is a matter of the utmost moment, as, if there be
" no check upon the public passions, it is in the greatest
" danger. The majority having the rule in their own hands,
" may take care of themselves ; but in what condition are
" the minority, if the power of the other is without limit ?
" These considerations, I suppose, or similar ones, occa-
" sioned such express provisions for the personal liberty of

---

* Reprinted from Life and Correspondence of Iredell, vol. 2, pp. 172–176.
Compare Spaight's Letter to Iredell, which is printed on pages 169, 170 of the
same volume, and reprinted in Appendix No. 6 of this Essay.

" each citizen, which the citizens, when they formed
" the Constitution, chose to reserve as an unalienated
" right, and not to leave at the mercy of any Assembly
" whatever. The restriction might be attended with
" inconvenience ; but they chose to risk the inconve-
" nience, for the sake of the advantage ; and in every trans-
" action we must act in the same manner : we must choose
" between evils of some sort or other : the imperfection of
" man can never keep entirely clear of all. The Constitu-
" tion, therefore, *being a fundamental law*, and a law *in*
" *writing* of the solemn nature I have mentioned (which is
" the light in which it strikes me), the judicial power, in the
" exercise of their authority, must take notice of it as the
" groundwork of that as well as of all other authority ;
" and as no article of the Constitution can be repealed by a
" Legislature, which derives its whole power from it, it fol-
" lows either that the *fundamental unrepealable* law must
" be obeyed, by the rejection of an act unwarranted by and
" inconsistent with it, or you must obey an act founded on
" an authority not given by the people, and to which, there-
" fore, the people owe no obedience. It is not that the
" judges are appointed arbiters, and to determine as it were
" upon any application, whether the Assembly have or have
" not violated the Constitution ; but when an act is neces-
" sarily brought in judgment before them, they must, un-
" avoidably, determine one way or another. It is doubted
" whether a subsequent law repeals a former one, in a case
" judicially in question ; the judges must decide this ; and
" yet it might be said, if the Legislature meant it a repeal,
" and the judges determined it otherwise, they exercised a
" *negative* on the Legislature in resolving to keep a law in
" force which the Assembly had annihilated. This kind of
" objection, if applicable at all, will reach all judicial power
" whatever, since upon every abuse of it (and there is no
" power but what is liable to abuse) a similar inference may
" be drawn ; but *when once you establish the necessary*
" *existence of any power*, the argument as to abuse ceases
" to destroy its validity, though in a doubtful matter it
" may be of great weight. Suppose, therefore, the Assem-

"bly should pass an act, declaring that in future in all
" criminal trials the trial by jury should be abolished, and
" the court alone should determine.   The Attorney-General
" indicts ; the indictment is found ; the criminal is arraigned,
" and the Attorney-General requires the trial to come on.
" The criminal objects, alleging that by the Constitution all
" the citizens in such cases are entitled to a trial by jury ;
" and that the Assembly have no right to alter any part of
" the Constitution; and that therefore the act appointing the
" trial by the court is void.   Must not the court determine
" some way or other, whether the man shall be tried or not ?
" Must not they say whether they will obey the Constitu-
" tion or an act inconsistent with it ?   So—suppose a still
" stronger case, that the Assembly should repeal the law
" naming the day of election, (for that is not named in the
" Constitution,) and adjourn to a day beyond it, and pass
" acts, and these acts be attempted to be enforced in the
" courts.   Must not the court decide they will obey such
" acts or no ?   And would it be approved of (except by a
" majority of the *de facto* Assembly) if they should say ;
" ' We cannot presume to declare that the Assembly, who
" ' were chosen for one year, have exceeded their authority
" ' by acting after the year expired.'   It really appears to
" me, the exercise of the power is unavoidable, the Constitu-
" tion not being a mere imaginary thing, about which ten
" thousand different opinions may be formed, but a written
" document to which all may have recourse, and to which,
" therefore, the judges cannot wilfully blind themselves.
" This seems also to have been the idea of some of the early
" Assemblies under the Constitution, since, in the oath of
" allegiance are these expressions :   ' I, A. B., do sincerely
" ' promise and swear, that I will be faithful and bear true
" ' allegiance to the State of North Carolina, and to the
" ' powers and authorities which are or may be established
" ' for the government thereof, *not inconsistent with the*
" ' *Constitution.*'   (Act of Nov. 1777.)   In any other light
" than as I have stated it, the greater part of the provisions
" of the Constitution would appear to me to be ridiculous,
" since in my opinion nothing could be more so than for the

"representatives of a people solemnly assembled to form a
"Constitution, to set down a number of political dogmas,
"which might or might not be regarded ; whereas it must
"have been intended, as I conceive, that it should be a sys-
"tem of authority, not depending on the casual whim or
"accidental ideas of a majority either in or out of doors for
"the time being ; but to remain in force until by a similar
"appointment of deputies specially appointed for the same
"important purpose ; and alterations should be with equal
"solemnity and deliberation made.   And this, I apprehend,
"must be the necessary consequence, since surely equal au-
"thority is required to repeal as to enact.   That such a
"power in the Judge may be abused is very certain ; that
"it *will* be, is not very probable.   In the first place, in a
"democratical government like ours, it is the interest of
"every man ambitious of public distinction to make him-
"self pleasing to the people.   This is so much the case, that
"there is great danger of men sacrificing their honor to
"their popularity, if their principles and firmness of mind
"are not of a texture to keep them steady in an honorable
"course.   It can be no man's interest certainly to make
"himself *odious* to the people by giving unnecessary and
"wanton offence.   It is also to be considered, that though
"the judges are permanent in station (at least as long as
"the Act of their appointment is in force*), yet, as their
"salaries are during pleasure, they are in fact dependent on
"the Assembly, few men likely to be judges being rich
"enough to consider them as a trifle.   Besides, if they are
"disposed by a gross abuse of power (for the mere pleasure
"of abusing it) to put their *negatives* on our laws by giv-
"ing them a false construction, cannot they do this every
"day with other Acts of Assembly (few of which I believe
"are more exempt from cavil than any article of the Consti-
"tution)?   So that it really seems to me, the danger is the
"most chimerical that can be supposed of this power being
"abused ; and if you had seen as I did, with what infinite
"reluctance the judges came to this decision, what pains
"they took by proposing expedients to obviate its necessity,

---

* I mean the Act constituting their courts.

" you would have seen in a strong light how little probable
" it is a judge would ever give such a judgment, where he
" thought he could possibly avoid it. But whatever may
" be the consequences, formed as our Constitution is, I can-
" not help thinking they are not at liberty to choose, but
" must in all questionable instances decide upon it. It is a
" subject indeed of great magnitude, and I heartily lament
" the occasion for its discussion. In all doubtful cases, to
" be sure, the Act ought to be supported : it should be un-
" constitutional beyond dispute before it is pronounced such.
" I conceive the remedy by a new election to be of very
" little consequence, because this would only secure the
" views of a majority ; whereas every citizen in my opinion
" should have a surer pledge for his constitutional rights
" than the wisdom and activity of any occasional majority
" of his fellow-citizens, who, if their own rights are in fact
" unmolested, may care very little for his.—I believe many
" think as you do upon this subject, though I have not
" heard much said about it, and I only speak on the general
" question, independent of an application to any case
" whatever. Most of the lawyers, I believe, are of my
" opinion in regard to that. The power of the judges, take
" it altogether, is indeed alarming, as there is no appeal
" from their jurisdiction, and I don't think any country
" can be safe without some Court of Appeal that has no
" original jurisdiction at all, since men are commonly care-
" ful enough to correct the errors of others, though seldom
" sufficiently watchful of their own, especially if they have
" no check upon them.

"Jas. Iredell."

No. 5.

Further consideration of the decision of Bayard v. *Singleton.*

The foregoing decision is of the greatest constitutional moment not only from its inherent value, but also from its connection with both previous and with subsequent history.
Its several points must therefore be restated with some of

their relations to other points of law discussed elsewhere in this Essay.

I. In the first place it must be precisely understood that the law of the land, that is so all important in the decision, was the law of the land of North Carolina, just as in Trevett *v.* Weeden it was the law of the land of Rhode Island that was all important. This is clear from the language of the court in speaking of the constitution of the state "as "the fundamental law of the land" and also in speaking of "a fair decision of the property in question by a jury, "according to the common law of the land." The confederation is called by the court "a part of the law of the "land," that is to say the confederation of the United States was a part of the law of the land of North Carolina, which was one of the United States.

II. In the next place it will be observed that the court was of opinion that by the constitution of North Carolina every citizen of the state had undoubtedly a right to the trial by jury, and that the legislature of the state could not take away this right by any act they might pass.

This position coincides perfectly with that taken by Varnum in Trevett *v.* Weeden and approved by the court in that case. The sole difference between Trevett *v.* Weeden and Bayard *v.* Singleton is that the former case arose under an unwritten constitution, and the latter under a written one. In both cases the trial by jury was regarded as the sole trial according to the law of the land. In North Carolina the court recommended the parties to consent to a decision of the property "by a jury according to the common law of the land." In Rhode Island Judge Tillinghast held that a trial without a jury was not a trial according to the laws of the land.*

III. In the third place, the court was of opinion that the constitution of North Carolina stood " in full force " as the fundamental law of the land of North Carolina and that the legislature of the state could not repeal or alter the said constitution.

---

* See page 246, *ante.*

IV. The reason in the opinion of the court, why the legislature of the state could not pass any act repealing or altering the constitution of the state, was this : If the legislature could pass such an act, they would, *eo instante*, destroy their own existence as a legislature, and dissolve the government established by the constitution.

The position is so identical with that taken by Varnum in Trevett *v.* Weeden, that it must be assumed to have been taken from his argument. That Varnum's position on this head was approved by his court can not be doubted. Thus the Superior Courts of North Carolina and Rhode Island agreed on this head within a year of each other.

V. The court distinctly was of opinion that the judicial power was bound to take as much notice of the constitution of the state as any other law whatever. This is precisely the doctrine which Marshall elaborates in Marbury *v.* Madison at great length.

IV. The court decided that the act of the general assembly was made in alteration of the constitution, that it was the ground upon which the motion before the court was made, and that it must "in that instance, stand as abro-"gated and without any effect."

The action of the Superior Courts of North Carolina and Rhode Island were in singular agreement under different kinds of constitutions. Both refused a trial without a jury.

VII. The court decided that the confederation was part of the law of the land of North Carolina and could not be repealed by any act of the general assembly of North Carolina. As will be shown hereafter the constitution of the United States is part of the law of the land of North Carolina. The relation between these two propositions is of great importance.

VIII. The court decided that the plaintiffs "being citizens "of one of the United States, are citizens of this state, by the "confederation of all the states," and so had the same right to a trial by jury in North Carolina as the citizens of that state.

Thus a trial by the law of the land of North Carolina was

in that state the right of the citizens of every other state, because the confederation was to be taken as part of the law of the land of North Carolina.

No. 6.

Of the date when the decision in Bayard v. Singleton became known to the Framers' convention.

It is, perhaps, an open question whether the constitutional decision in Bayard *v.* Singleton was known in Philadelphia on June 6, 1786. If it was not then known, the case can not be one of those alluded to by Gerry in his speech above mentioned.*

The decision could not have been rendered earlier than Monday, May 21st, or later than Thursday, May 31st. These dates are based on the then existing legislation concerning the May Term of the Superior Court, which was held at Newbern and comprised the last ten working days of the month of May. See Iredell's Laws of North Carolina, Edenton, 1791, page 528.

With southerly winds and other favorable circumstances, communication by water between Newbern and Philadelphia may have been made in seven or eight days. Communication by land must have taken a good deal more time. On August 12th, 1787, Spaight in Philadelphia wrote his letter to Iredell in North Carolina. Iredell's answer is dated fourteen days later, on August 26th. See Iredell's Life, vol. 2, pages 168, 172.

There are two arguments in favour of no time being lost in sending the news of the decision to Philadelphia. Davie, who was Iredell's colleague as counsel for the plaintiffs, was attending the Framer's convention as a member from North Carolina. Spaight was another member from that state, who had the keenest interest in the case and who became a leading opponent of the decision.

If the decision was not known in Philadelphia on June

---

* See page 219, *ante.*

6th, it must have become so soon after, that is to say, a good while before the critical date of July 17th., On that day the convention adopted *nem. con.* Martin's resolution which provided a judicial method of settling conflicts between the laws of the Union and those of the states. See 5 Elliot's Debates, page 322.

CHAPTER XXVII.

Further considerations connected with the foregoing cases and especially that of Rutgers *v.* Waddington.

Bayard *v.* Singleton and Rutgers *v.* Waddington are thus in direct contradiction as to the nature of written constitutions. The New York court decided in express terms that Blackstone's tenth rule for construing statutes applied in New York although the constitution was a written one. On the other hand, the North Carolinian court, because the constitution was written, gave a decision which made Blackstone's rule illegal and inapplicable in that state. Every statute conflicting with the constitution must be judicially held void in North Carolina, while legal right in New York was just the contrary. The two cases under written constitutions are in conflict. The case of Trevett *v.* Weeden can not turn the balance between them, because it arose under an unwritten constitution.

In 1787 conflicts between state laws and federal treaties were a source of the greatest difficulty to the federal Congress. At the same date future conflicts between state laws or constitutions and the new constitution laws or treaties of the United States were the subject of the deepest thought to the Framers' convention. At the first sight, therefore, Rutgers *v.* Waddington must have seemed a great discouragement to all members of both bodies who desired that state judges should be bound to hold state legislation to be void in so far as contrary to federal law under the old confederation or the new constitution. Further examination, however, must have shown anxious inquirers in 1787 that the decision in Rutgers *v.* Waddington suggested an excellent and a technical means of escape from such difficulties. The New York court had refused to presume that the legislature had intended to derogate to the law of nations and had decided that the statute did not derogate thereto. In doing this, it laid the greatest stress on the fact that the statute did not contain any *nonobstante* clause derogating to the law of nations. Had it done so, the whole case would, the court thought, have been an altogether different one. The will of the legislature would then have clearly bound the court to make a contrary decision. The court would have been compelled to interpret the treaty according to the will of the legislature and contrary to the law of nations.

The observations of the New York court upon the legal institution of the *nonobstante* clause, have been previously quoted. They show clearly that the repeal of things contrary, which is made by a *nonobstante* clause, is an express one, and that no court can use construction or interpretation to disregard it. It was the absence of an *express* repeal by such a *nonobstante* clause or otherwise, which enabled the court to say that no repeal existed, because it had no right to imply one.

The observations of the court upon the *nonobstante* clause contain nothing new as general principles of law and are expressly stated to be based upon authority. The application of the doctrine to the new state of things before the court is another matter and one furnishing much new food for thought.

The absence of a derogation made by a *nonobstante* clause enabled the court to interpret the statute to be in harmony with the law of nations and the treaty. The presence of such a clause would have compelled the court to interpret the statute to be in contrariety with the law of nations and the treaty. Thus in every case of conflict between laws of different kinds, a *nonobstante* clause, enacted by competent lawgivers, must govern judicial action, whether such exercise of legislative power be good or be evil. Had the state legislature used the *nonobstante* clause against the treaty, it would have been an evil use thereof. But why should not such a clause be well used in such a case, that is to say, used in favour of federal right when state statutes were federally wrongful? This, it is suggested, was a natural question to anxious inquirers in 1787, who were seeking solution for the problem of conflicts between federal and state laws. Certain it is that both the federal Congress and the constitutional convention actually proposed the use of *nonobstante* clauses for such purposes, as will be hereinafter particularly rehearsed. As the Congress was the first so to do, it is evident that it set the example to the convention. But who suggested the idea to Congress, that is to say, the idea of a new American application of an old English and European institution? In the writer's opinion, Rutgers *v.* Waddington is a very probable and the most probable source from which such a suggestion could have been taken. If this be so, the opinion in that case is an important historical monument in the constitutional law of the Union. It clearly defined the extreme of possible mischief in conflicts between the laws of the Union and those of the states and it led the way to the discovery of that remedy which the Framers, following the Congress, thought the best solution of the difficulty.

CHAPTER XXVIII.

Conclusions of the Historical Commentary.

The following propositions are contended to be correct statements of results ascertained and supported by the foregoing Historical Commentary on foreign and American laws.

I. It accords with the principles of law and with legal reasoning that a constitution should be of such a nature, that the judiciary thereunder should be *incompetent* to decide a questioned law to be unconstitutional or impeachable and hold it therefore void. This can be so when the constitution is either unwritten or written. Such an unwritten constitution was that of Great Britain in 1776 and long before. Such written constitutions are those now existing in nearly every German state. The various written constitutions which have existed in France, since the revolution of 1789, also afford examples of the truth of this proposition. So too did the written constitution of New York existing in 1784, if the opinion of Rutgers *v.* Waddington, dated in that year, was correct. Rutgers *v.* Waddington is older than the U. S. constitution, but the other cases referred to under written constitutions are junior thereto.

II. Nevertheless, it equally accords with the principles of law and with legal reasoning that a written or unwritten constitution should be of such a nature that the judiciary thereunder should be *competent* to decide a questioned law to be contrary to the constitution or to binding right of superior strength to the legislative power exercised, and, when it had so decided, to hold the same to be therefore void. Such can be the law when the constitution is either written or unwritten. Before the U. S. constitution was framed there were unwritten and written constitutions under which it might be a judicial and not an extrajudicial question whether challenged legislation was accordant or contrariant to constitutional or other binding right, and whether legislators had or had not proceeded *secundum jus potestatis suae* in enacting it. For unwritten European constitutions, this is shown by the cases adduced from the older French law, the older English law, the English law of the prerogative abroad, the Roman law of rescripts, and above all the Canon law. For an American unwritten constitution this is shown by the great case of Trevett *v.* Weeden in Rhode Island in 1786. For a written constitution the truth of the proposition is shown by the case of Bayard *v.* Singleton, in North Carolina in 1787, in which one of the counsel for the party challenging the law, was a Framer of the constitution. All the said cases are older than the constitution of the United States.

On the whole matter, therefore, the Framers of the constitution were at liberty to do what they deemed wisest and best in regard to the judicial competency in question, without danger of violating the principles of law or those of either civil or politic prudence. The judiciaries established or affected by the new constitution might be either enabled to exercise, or disabled from exercising, such a competency, without danger of a leap in the dark. Either course might be taken without being unprecedented.

The question, whether this judicial competency was ever heard of before it was established in America, has now been answered.

The next part of this Essay will discuss the question whether the Framers intended that the said judicial competency should belong to the federal judiciary established by the new constitution, or to the state judiciaries affected by it.

PART III.

OF THE HISTORICAL ANTECEDENTS OF THE CONSTITUTIONAL
TEXTS CONCERNED.

Part III. of the Historical Commentary will investigate the origin of the texts of the constitution, that are concerned and will discuss their historical relation to antecedent texts which existed under the confederation.

CHAPTER XXIX.

Of the historical antecedents of paragraph 2. VI. of the constitution.

No. 1. *Of the text of paragraph 2. VI.*

No. 2. *Of the treaty of peace with Great Britain.*

No. 3. *Of certain acts of the federal Congress concerning the treaty of peace and their historical relation to paragraph 2. VI.*

No. 4. *Of the relation of the judiciaries of the states to the treaty of peace, according to the federal letter of Congress dated April 13th, 1787.*

No. 5. *Of the resolutions of the federal Congress passed March 21st, 1787, and recited in the federal letter of April 13th.*

No. 6. *Of the scope of legislation concerning the treaty of peace then recommended to the states by Congress.*

No. 7. *Of state statutes posterior to the confederation and conflicting with federal treaties.*

No. 8. *Rehearsal of the federal law concerning conflicts between U S. treaties and state statutes, as laid down in the letter of Congress.*

No. 9. *Of the origin of the doctrine that a treaty may be part of the law of the land of a state.*

No. 10. *Of the origin of the doctrine that the legislature can not repeal some parts of the law of the land of a state.*

No. 11. *Of the meaning of the words, "the law of the "land," in the first resolution of Congress and in its federal letter.*

No. 12. *Of the origin of the pursuance clause of paragraph 2. VI.*

The texts of the constitution, with which this **Essay is** particularly concerned, are paragraph 2. VI. and the beginning of section 2. III. The first contains, among other things, a special address to the judges of the state courts. The last is part of an article, which specially concerns the courts of the United States.

This chapter will investigate the origin of the text of paragraph 2. VI. and examine its historical relation to antecedent texts under the confederation.

No. 1.

Of the text of paragraph 2. VI.

Paragraph 2. VI. reads thus :

" This constitution, and the laws of the United States " which shall be made in pursuance thereof ; and all treaties " made, or which shall be made, under the authority of the " United States, shall be the supreme law of the land ; and " the judges in every state shall be bound thereby, any thing " in the constitution or laws of any state to the contrary " notwithstanding."

The contents of the first two clauses of this paragraph include :

1st, the constitution ;
2d, the laws aforesaid ;
3d, the treaties aforesaid.

Of the first two clauses, that of treaties contains the only things capable of existing previously to the establishment of the constitution.

No. 2.

Of the treaty of peace with Great Britain

When the Framers met in convention the violation of the treaty of peace by certain of the states was one of the most pressing anxieties of the political situation of the Union. It was also an anxiety most fruitful of results in developing the frame of the constitution. The treaty of peace was intimately connected with the origin and form of paragraph 2. VI.

No. 3.

Of certain acts of the federal Congress concerning the treaty of peace and their historical relation to paragraph 2. VI.

Paragraph 2. VI. is in part modelled and in part developed from acts of the federal Congress relating to the treaty of peace with Great Britain. Those acts were passed in the March and April before the meeting of the Convention on May 14th, 1787. On the previous April 13th, the United States in Congress assembled unanimously recommended the several states to enact identical laws of the following frame : " Whereas certain laws or statutes made and passed " in some of the United States, are regarded and complained " of as repugnant to the treaty of peace with Great Britain, " by reason whereof not only the good faith of the United " States pledged by that treaty, has been drawn into ques-

" tion, but their essential interests under that treaty greatly
" affected. And whereas justice to Great Britain, as well as
" regard to the honour and interests of the United States,
" require that the said treaty be faithfully executed, and
" that all obstacles thereto, and particularly such as do or
" may be construed to proceed from the laws of this state,
" be effectually removed.

 " Therefore,

 " Be it enacted by . . . .
" and it is hereby enacted by the authority of the same,
" that such of the acts or part of acts of the legislature of
" this state, as are *repugnant to the treaty of peace* between
" the United States and his Britannic Majesty, or any arti-
" cle thereof, shall be, and hereby are repealed. And further,
" that *the courts of law and equity* within this state be,
" and they hereby are *directed and required* in all causes
" and questions cognizable by them respectively, and aris-
" ing from or touching the said treaty, to *decide and ad-*
" *judge* according to the tenor, true intent and meaning of
" the same, *any thing in the said acts, or parts of acts,*
" *to the contrary thereof in any wise notwithstanding.*" *

A federal letter of Congress to the several states upon the
subject of the treaty transmits and urges the above recom-
mendations with elaborate arguments of the highest interest.

No. 4.

*Of the relation of the judiciaries of the states to the
treaty of peace according to the federal letter of Congress.*

Among the arguments urged by Congress is the following
remarkable doctrine concerning the proper relation of the
state judiciaries to the treaty. It is contained in the latter
part of the following extract from the federal letter :

 " Such a general law would, we think, be preferable to
" one that should minutely enumerate the acts and clauses
" intended to be repealed : because omissions might acci-
" dentally be made in the enumeration, or questions might

---

* Journals of Congress, ed. 1801, vol. 12, p. 35, April 13th, 1787.

" arise, and perhaps not be satisfactorily determined, re-
" specting particular acts or clauses, about which contrary
" opinions may be entertained. *By repealing in general*
" *terms all acts and clauses repugnant to the treaty, the*
" *business will be turned over to its proper department,*
" *viz., the judicial; and the courts of law will find no*
" *difficulty in deciding whether any particular act or*
" *clause is or is not contrary to the treaty.*"*

This express declaration of the proper functions of the
judicial department of government concerning treaties, it is
here maintained, is the germ from which the Framers of the
constitution developed its provisions concerning the judiciaries of the states, as found in paragraph 2. VI. By the
prescriptions of that paragraph the judges in each state are
bound to use their judicial power, according to the rule and
limitation therein prescribed, whenever their duty requires
them to pass upon either constitutional or treaty questions
involving the validity of legislation of any kind.

No. 5.

*Of the resolutions of the federal Congress passed March
21st, 1787, and recited in the federal letter of April 13th,
1787.*

The federal letter of Congress to the states and the draft
of identical laws for their legislatures enclosed therein were
written in pursuance of three resolutions, which had been
passed on March 21st, 1787, as unanimous acts of that body.
The text of the third resolution was, *mutatis mutandis*, of
the same frame with that of the body of the draft of identical laws above quoted. All these resolutions were part
and parcel of the action of Congress in the matter and were
recited and commented upon in their federal letter. The
first of them reads :

" Resolved, That the legislatures of the several states
" cannot *of right* pass any act or acts, for interpreting, ex-
" plaining, or construing a national treaty or any part or

---

* Same volume, p. 36.

"clause of it; nor for restraining, limiting or in any manner
" impeding, retarding or counteracting the operation and exe-
" cution of the same, for that on being *constitutionally made,*
" *ratified and published,* they become in virtue of the con-
" federation, *part of the law of land,* and are not only in-
"dependent of the will and power of such legislatures, but
"also binding and obligatory upon them,"*

No. 6.

*Of the scope of the legislation concerning the treaty of
peace recommended to the states by the federal Congress.*

The federal letter of Congress moves each and all the
states to enact the proposed law, in order to avoid naming
the names of states violating the treaty.

It is to be observed that the state legislation proposed by
the federal letter of April 13th and the third federal resolution of March 21st, 1787, contained far reaching legislative
remedies against state statutes violating the treaty of peace
and so also the federal right of the Union. In spite of the
great scope of these provisions, the proposed legislation by
no means covered the whole difficulty of conflicts between
federal treaties and state laws. It did not settle the question whether or not a state could in strict rigour of law
enact statutes contrariant to treaties, which, nevertheless,
had legal vigour within the territorial limits of the state.
It also made no provision for the cases of *future* state laws
being enacted, which intentionally conflicted with the treaty
of peace. Such cases were intimately connected with the
question whether existing contrariant state laws made posterior to the treaty were on the same footing with like laws
made prior thereto.

---

*Journals of Congress, volume cited, page 24, March 21st, 1787.

No. 7.

Of state statutes posterior to the confederation and conflicting with the federal treaties.

One of the urgent problems requiring solution by the Framers of the constitution was that of preventing posterior as well as prior state laws from impeding the execution of federal treaties.　Under the confederation, the question of such posterior laws had been felt to be a very difficult and a very delicate one.　In the debate upon it, on March 21st, 1787, in the federal Congress, Madison said :

"" A distinction too might be started possibly between "laws prior and laws subsequent to the treaty ; a repealing "effect of the treaty on the former not necessarily imply-"ing the nullity of the latter.　Supposing the treaty to "have the validity of a law *only*, it would repeal all ante-"cedent laws.　To render succeeding laws void, it must "have more than the *mere* authority of a *law*.　In case "these succeeding laws, contrary to the treaty, should "come into discussion, before the courts [*i. e.* of the states], "it would be necessary to examine the foundation of the "federal authority, and to determine whether it had the "validity of a constitution paramount to the legislative "authority in each state.　This was a delicate question, "and studiously to be avoided, as it was notorious that, "although in some of the states the confederation was in-" corporated with, and had the sanction of, their respective "constitutions, yet in others it received a legislative ratifi-" cation only, and rested on no other basis.""*

These remarks should be compared with the solution of the treaties-problem made by paragraph 2. VI. of the constitution.　That solution was effected upon a system of constitutional law, one of the principles of which was that the derogation imported by the *nonobstante* clause of paragraph 2. VI. applies to future as well as past state laws contrariant to treaties, regardless of the maxim *lex poste-*

* Elliott, V. 99.

rior derogat legi priori. This will be fully commented upon when the whole text is considered. It is here, however, requisite to point out clearly that the origin of the notwithstanding or *nonobstante* clause of paragraph 2. VI. is to be traced directly to the said draft of identical laws of April 13th and third resolution of March 21, 1787. There, and there only, is to be found the original source of the idea of applying that ancient piece of legislative machinery to state laws contrariant to federal treaties. The constitution, it is true, makes a more comprehensive use of the *nonobstante* clause than the said draft of identical laws. It applies the clause not merely to past state laws and constitutions contrariant to past treaties, but to all state laws and constitutions contrariant to the constitution and the constitutional laws and treaties of the United States, regardless of priority or posteriority in date. Nevertheless the original idea of applying the *nonobstante* clause to the laws of a state, because conflicting with a written act of the United States, is derived from the draft of identical laws and resolution aforesaid.

No. 8.

Rehearsal of the federal law concerning conflicts between U. S. treaties and state statutes as laid down in the letter of Congress.

According to the letter of Congress, the three resolutions therein recited, and the draft of identical laws therein recommended, the principles of law asserted by federal authority concerning the treaty of peace appear to have been as follows :

Great Britain had claimed that infractions of the treaty of peace existed on the part of the United States of America. Too little attention, in the opinion of Congress, appeared to have been paid to the treaty in some of the states.

The confederation had committed to Congress the care of all rights which other nations ought to have, as against the United States, according to the law of nations and the faith of treaties. The treaty of peace was contracted with a pledge of the public faith to the King of Great Britain, which Congress, by the express terms of the confederation, could engage on behalf of each and every state.

In support of their jurisdiction in these respects, Congress cited as authority that part of the 9th article of the confederation, which related to matters belonging to the law of nations. This was the first paragraph of that article, containing delegation from the states, to the United States in Congress assembled, of certain exclusive power and right upon the subjects of war, peace, alliance, *treaties*, captures, letters of marque and reprisal, piracies, felonies on the high seas, and appeals in cases of captures.

The federal letter of Congress asserted that " when there-"fore a treaty is constitutionally made, ratified and pub-"lished by us, it immediately becomes binding on the whole "nation, and superadded to the laws of the land, without "the intervention of state legislatures."* The first resolu-tion of Congress asserted the following proposition of " a " national treaty or any part or clause of it," *viz.*, that " on " being constitutionally made, ratified and published, they " become by virtue of the confederation part of the law of " the land." While these positions were distinctly af-firmed, no authority was anywhere mentioned for the doc-trine that a treaty was in any land a part of the law of the land. The authority, which can, however, be adduced therefor, will be quoted upon a subsequent page. Neither was any authority referred to for the proposition that the confederation was the law of the land anywhere, a matter which is elsewhere referred to in this Essay.

Congress pointedly remarked that the parties to the treaty of peace were the king of Great Britain on the one side, and all the United States collectively on the other. The different states did not make the treaty separately but col-lectively. On this head, the position taken was identical with that tersely expressed by C C. Pinckney in the Janu-ary following, when he said in the assembly of South Caro-lina that " we do not enter into treaties as separate states,

---

* Journals of Congress, as cited, page 33.

"but as *united states*."* Thus, the legislature of a state could not make a federal treaty. Neither could it prevent a federal treaty, when made, from becoming part of the law of the land. The legislature of a state could not therefore "of right" pass any law either repealing a treaty or conflicting therewith, or interfering with the operation and execution thereof, or prescribing any other rule for the interpretation thereof than the law of nations. A statute which the legislature of a state could constitutionally enact, it could constitutionally repeal; but no treaty could under the confederation be altered without the consent of the United States in Congress assembled in pursuance thereof and given in accordance therewith. Nor, was their consent even sufficient to change a treaty. No treaty could be changed without the consent of both contracting parties, one of whom was the foreign sovereign contracted with under the law of nations.

No authority was mentioned by Congress for the doctrine or view that in any land there may be a part of the law of the land which the legislature thereof can not repeal. An authority therefor is, however, referred to elsewhere in this Essay.

While the legislature of a state could neither repeal, construe, nor otherwise interfere with any treaty, the judiciary of a state was asserted to have a different relation thereto. The letter observed: "In cases between individuals, all "doubts respecting the meaning of a treaty, like doubts "respecting the meaning of a law, are in the first instance "mere judicial questions, and are to be heard and decided "in the courts of justice having cognizance of the causes "in which they arise, and whose duty it is to determine "them according to the rules and maxims established by "the laws of nations for the interpretation of treaties."† Consequently the legislature of a state could not prescribe to the courts or citizens of the state any rule of interpretation different from the law of nations. A contrary doctrine would not only be irrational in theory but inconvenient in

---

* 4 Elliot's Debates. page 279.

† Journals of Congress. as cited. page 33.

practice, for according to it the same article of the same treaty might have different meanings in different states.

The then actual state of things was such in the opinion of Congress that the legislature of each state ought to enact a repeal of all acts and parts of acts repugnant to the treaty of peace in the form of the draft of law. According thereto, the treaty would be declared to be legally and explicitly binding and obligatory upon the "courts of law and equity" of the state "anything in the said acts or parts of acts to "the contrary thereof in any wise notwithstanding."*

It will be observed that the words "of right," make an avoidance of the question of strict rigour of law previously mentioned. This avoidance also appears in the federal letter of Congress in a peculiar shape. How far a state law repugnant to a treaty would be valid and obligatory within the mere limits of the enacting state, was a question which the federal Congress hoped that it would never be called upon to discuss. It was, however, expressly added, that no matter what might be the answer to the question, it was certain that such a repugnant law would not bind the contracting parties to any treaty. In the case of the treaty of peace, the contracting parties were the King of Great Britain, on the one side, and all the United States collectively on the other.†

It seems impossible not to be forcibly struck with the great resemblance to the features of the foregoing resolutions of Congress and the recommended draft of identical laws which is presented by the provisions concerning treaties in paragraph 2. VI. of the constitution. Those provisions of that section read:

"All treaties made, or which shall be made under the "authority of the United States, shall be the supreme law " of the land ; and the judges in every state shall be bound "thereby, any thing in the constitutions or laws of any state "to the contrary notwithstanding."

The law of the land, the binding of the judges in every

---

* Same volume, page 36.

† Same volume, page 24.

state by treaties, the *nonobstante* or notwithstanding clause, are thus all to be found in both the draft of identical laws recommended by Congress to the states in April, 1787, and in the constitution framed during the following summer and submitted to the same states in following September.

Such resemblances and repetitions can not have been accidental. There were too many members of the convention who were members of Congress at the dates and times concerned, for the action of the two bodies not to be related. Madison was a most assiduous member of both assemblies, and has preserved for posterity both the debates of the Congress on the treaty question and the debates of the Convention on the whole constitution. Gorham, another delegate in that Congress, was not only a Framer, but also a member of the first committee of five which reported the original draft of the constitution. All of the members of the second committee of five, which reported the revised draft, except G. Morris, represented their states in that Congress, *viz.*, Johnson the chairman, Hamilton, and King, besides Madison. The binding of state judges by treaties, and the *nonobstante* clause derogatory to state acts, were things written in the amended draft of constitution that was referred to the second committee of five. The words "law of the land" were not found therein, but were inserted by that committee in their revised draft. Instead of the previously existing words, "shall be the supreme law " of the several states and of their citizens and inhabitants," they substituted what is now the present text, "shall be "the supreme law of the land." As four members of the committee had been members of the Congress which had so applied the words "law of the land" to a treaty, it is easy to answer the question, where did the idea of their alteration come from.

The federal letter of April 13th and resolutions of March 21st, 1787, are of such importance in the history of the constitutional text, that the writer feels it requisite to insert them *in extenso* in Appendix No. 7 to his Essay.

Critical objections to the exposition of federal right made by the letter of Congress will be found in Judge Iredell's dissenting opinion in Ware *v.* Hylton, page 276 and end of page 279 of 3 Dallas.

See G. Dufour's *Droit Administratif Appliqué* (Paris, 1868), I. 5–9, for a view of the law of treaties, which is of interest in the present connection.

No. 9.

Of the origin of the doctrine that a treaty may be part of the law of the land of a state.

Other questions equally interesting may now be asked. Where did the idea come from, that a treaty is to be regarded as part of the law of the land? Upon what authority was this declared to the legislature of each state by the federal Congress?

Before answering these questions, it should be observed that the precise words of the draft of identical laws of April 13th and third resolution of March 21st are "*part* of "the law of the land." The word "part" in this phrase is the clue.

The lawyers and statesmen of 1787 were assiduous students of Blackstone. Those of Blackstone's present readers, who have collated his Commentaries with texts of the constitution and related documents, will have no difficulty in recognizing the passage upon which the draft for identical laws was modelled. The letter of Congress distinctly makes the law of nations and the faith of treaties parts of one subject; and Blackstone, IV. ch. 5, p. 67, thus speaks of the position of the law of nations in England :

"In arbitrary states this law (*i. e.* the law of nations), "whenever it contradicts or is not provided for by the mu-"nicipal law of the country, is enforced by the royal power : "but since in England no royal power can introduce a new "law, or suspend the execution of the old, therefore the law "of nations (whenever any question arises which is properly "the object of its jurisdiction) is here adopted in its full "extent by the common law and is held to be *a part of* "*the law of the land.*"

Thus in every state having the Common law, the law of nations is an adopted law and held to be part of the law of the land.

According to the letter of Congress exclusive power relating to subjects belonging to the law of nations was delegated to the United States in Congress assembled, among which was the making of treaties. Treaties were contracts between nations proceeding under the law of nations. Treaties could only be rightfully interpreted according to the law of nations. Treaties were part of the law of the land.

The doctrine of Blackstone concerning the law of nations being part of the law of the land, and the doctrine of Congress concerning a treaty being part of the law of the land, have thus self-evidently an intimate relation, and the latter must have been derived from the former.

In the next month (May, 1787), at Newbern, it was judicially decided that the confederation of the United States was part of the law of the land of North Carolina. See page 250, *ante.*

No. 10.

Of the origin of the doctrine that the legislature of a state can not repeal some parts of the law of the land of the state.

A further important question must now be asked. Upon what authority could the federal Congress, or any one, say to the legislature of a state that some part or parts of the law of the land could not be repealed by such legislature?

The authority which Congress had in mind could have been none other than the Rhode Island case of Trevett *v.* Weeden, which had been decided the previous autumn, as has been already rehearsed. That case had naturally attracted the marked attention of lawyers, statesmen and public men throughout the United States. The elaborate argument of Varnum, the counsel for defendant and the leading spirit of the cause, had been circulated by him in a printed pamphlet. *Varnum himself* was a member of the federal Congress and was present on March 20th and April 13th, 1787, when the treaty question was debated and acted upon.* Varnum's professional ability must have favourably impressed his colleagues in Congress, for they elected him one of the judges of the Northwest Territory in the October following.† There are therefore special, as well as general, reasons why the Congress of 1787 should have been duly impressed with the decision of the case of Trevett *v.* Weeden.

In Trevett *v.* Weeden the law of the land of Rhode Island was expressly involved. The clause of the state statute of August 22d, 1786, which the court repelled as void and refused to be bound by, reads thus: "That the said court, "when so convened, shall proceed to the trial of the said "offender, and they are hereby authorized so to do, *with-* "*out any jury*, by a majority of the judges present, *accord-* "*ing to the laws of the land*."

As has been mentioned, Tillinghast, J., in giving his opinion, said that he "took notice of the striking repug- "nancy of the expressions of the act 'without trial by jury "'according to the laws of the land,' and on that ground "gave the judgment the same way."

In Varnum's argument at the bar, one of the positions maintained is identical. He denies categorically that an act of the legislature abolishing the trial by jury would become " the law of the land," as certain ardent politicians in Rhode Island then maintained.‡

That in 1788 there was a law of the land of Rhode Island, superior and derogatory to any statute violating the citizens' right to trial by jury, was established by the judgment in the case of Trevett *v.* Weeden. Rhode Island was a land with a law of the land which in the opinion of the state judges protected the right of trial by jury from infringement by the state legislature. The federal Congress in April, 1787, moved the state to take another step in the

---

* Journals of Congress, Ed. 1801, vol. 12, pp. 22, 30, 33.

† The same, p. 138.

‡ See pages 236 et seq., *ante.*

same direction, when they wrote to Rhode Island and the other states that in each the law of the land protected the faith of treaties and the treaty of peace from infraction by any repeal of the state legislature. The answer of the legislature of Rhode Island to the letter of Congress was one of assent, for in its September session of the same year it passed a statute enacting "that the treaty of peace between "the United States of America and His Britannic Majesty "is fully binding upon all the citizens of this state, *as a* "*law of the land*, and is not in any respect to be receded "from, misconstructed, or violated." *

No. 11.

Of the meaning of the words, "the law of the land," in the first resolution and the federal letter of Congress.

The point has now been reached when, in order to avoid an important misapprehension, it must be pointed out with precision what is the distinctive meaning of the words, "the law of the land," as applied to treaties in the first resolution and in the letter of Congress on the treaty question. It is to these texts, and through them to the before quoted passage of Blackstone, that must be traced the original idea of the application of the words "law of the land" to treaties, as made in paragraph 2. VI. of the constitution. It will be found impossible to understand the intentions of the Framers in their final action upon the text of that section, if there be any misapprehension as to what they meant in saying that treaties shall be the supreme law of the land and that the judges in every state shall be bound thereby, any thing in the constitution or laws of any state to the contrary notwithstanding. In the proper place it will be shown that the fifth of their series of frames for that paragraph, the final result of careful and elaborate discussion and effort, can not be rationally accounted for, unless "the su-"preme law of the land" mean "the supreme law of the

---

American State Papers, I. 229. Foreign Affairs.

"several states," and not the supreme law of the United States.

In using the words, " the law of the land," the first resolution and the letter of Congress must have been understood by the states addressed as meaning the law of the land of each several state respectively. The Congress of the confederation, indeed, could not possibly have meant anything else in federally addressing the states individually. There was the highest authority for the fact that each state had a law of the land of its own. In each of eight states, the written constitution expressly mentioned the law of the land of the state, and in a ninth state the laws of the land thereof. In the two states with unwritten constitutions, it was certain that there was a law of the land of each respectively, as shown by the case of Trevett v. Weeden. It is a rightful presumption that that great case suggested, as it certainly supported, the peculiar form of action chosen by Congress, because it was then the only reported case recognizing that a fundamental part of the law of the land of a state was a matter of positive right superior to any enactments of the legislature of the state. The trial by jury was judicially recognized in Trevett v. Weeden to be such a fundamental part of the law of the land of Rhode Island, and so too, claimed Congress, were all treaties. What was true of one state was true of all. If true of a state like Rhode Island with an unwritten constitution, it was *a fortiori* true of those in which written constitutions existed. There was, indeed, very soon after a case which could be quoted as authority for the states with written constitutions. This was Bayard v. Singleton. It was not early enough to anticipate the action of Congress, but early enough for a prompt confirmation of that action. It was also early enough to anticipate the action of the legislature of North Carolina, which in December of the same year passed "an "act declaring the treaty of peace between the United States "of America and the King of Great Britain to be *part* "*of the law of the land.*"* As has been previously rehearsed, in that important case, in the May term following

---

* American State Papers, Foreign Affairs, I. 230.

the April letter of Congress, the Supreme Court of North Carolina rendered a decision holding that a certain act of the legislature was repugnant to the constitution of the state and that it therefore must be held void ; that the written constitution of the state was fundamental law of the land of North Carolina ; that the confederation was part of the fundamental law of the land of the state ; and that the confederation, like the state constitution, could not be repealed by the state legislature.*

That the confederation was part of the law of the land of a state and unrepealable by the legislature thereof, are points of the decision, that are important links in the chain of authorities, preceding the constitution, which support and confirm the position of the federal Congress upon federal treaties.

That the treaty of peace was superadded to, and became part of, the law of the land of each several state is shown by the following cases which were prior in date to the federal letter of Congress and were mentioned in the public debates upon the new constitution in the lower house of the legislature in South Carolina. On January 16th, 1788, Gen. C. C. Pinckney said, in speaking of the legal vigour of the treaty of peace in South Carolina : "The treaty had "been enrolled in the prothonotary's office by the express "order of the judges. It had been adjudged, in a variety "of cases, to be *part of the law of the land*, and had been "admitted to be so, whenever it was pleaded. If this had "not been the case, and every individual state had pos- "sessed the right to disregard a treaty made by Congress, "no nation would have entered into a treaty with us." Later in the same debate, Pinckney "rose to mention some "instances he had omitted of the treaty with Great Britain "being considered in our courts as *part of the law of* "*the land.* The judge who held the court at Ninety-six "discharged upwards of one hundred recognizances of per- "sons committed for different crimes, which fell within the "meaning of the treaty. A man named Love, accused of

---

* See *ante* Chapter 26.

"murder, was liberated.   It is true, the people, enraged at
"the enormity of his conduct, hanged him soon after ; but
"of this the judicial power knew nothing until after its
"perpetration.   Another murderer was allowed to plead the
"treaty of peace in bar, that had conducted General Pick-
"en's brother into the hands of the Indians, who soon
"after put him to death."   On the next day C. C. Pinckney remarked, " I contend that the article in the new con-
"stitution, which says that treaties shall be paramount to
"the laws of the land, is only declaratory of what treaties
"were, in fact, under the old compact.   They were as much
" the law of the land under that confederation, as they are
"under this constitution."*

The foregoing, it is contended, establishes the correctness
of the propositions (1), that when the Congress of 1787 sat
and the convention of 1787 met, the law of the land meant
the law of each several state, and not the law of the United
States, and (2), that the treaty of peace was superadded to,
and made part of, the law of the land of each several state.

No. 12.

*Of the origin of the pursuance clause of paragraph
2. VI.*

The origin of the pursuance clause of paragraph 2. VI remains to be traced.   In order to avoid repetition, this will
be done elsewhere.   The origin of that clause will be considered in Part IV. of the Historical Commentary and will
be reconsidered in the Textual Commentary.

---

* 4 Elliot's Debates, 266, 270, 278

CHAPTER XXX.

Of the federal text which is the historical antecedent of the beginning of section 2. III. of the constitution.

So much for the relation which the draft of identical laws, federal letter and the resolutions of Congress bear to paragraph 2. VI. of the constitution. It is next necessary to point out the relation which the same documents bear to another text of the constitution, *viz.*, the beginning of section 2. III.

The beginning of section 2. III. provides, *inter alia*, that "the judicial power shall extend *to all cases in law and* "*equity arising under . . . treaties* made, or which shall "be made, under their authority."

Except as to the word "under," the origin of this provision must be intimately related to the following part of the text of the draft of identical laws, *viz.*, that which proposed that "the courts of law and equity in *all causes and* "*questions* cognizable by them respectively, and *arising* "*from or touching the said treaty,* shall decide and adjudge "according to the true intent and meaning of the same." *

The causes and questions cognizable by courts of law and equity and arising from a treaty, which are found in this draft recommended to the state legislatures, are evidently precursors of the cases in law and equity arising under treaties, which are found in the constitution, except as to

---

* Journals of Congress, vol. 12, page 35.

the use of the word "under" instead of the word "from" after the word "arising."

The idea upon which both the antecedent and the subsequent texts are framed is evidently the same. It is the idea that judicial courts, in questions and cases of law and equity, arising before them from or under a treaty, should have the power and obligation of deciding and adjudicating according to the treaty as *lex juris*.

The above part of the draft of identical laws and the treaties portion of section 2. III. have thus directly this relation to each other : the former is the historical antecedent of the latter purely and simply.

Now the whole of the beginning oɪ section 2. VI. is framed upon one and the same system. Of that system the treaties portion is the key, the idea upon which it is framed being extended to the other portions, which are concerned with the constitution and the laws. Those other portions have, therefore, in a qualified sense, the same historical antecedent as the treaties portion. Consequently, in either an absolute or a qualified sense, all portions of the beginning of section 2. III. have an historical antecedent in the same text of the federal draft of identical laws for the several states.

From this and the preceding chapter it appears that paragraph 2. VI. and the beginning of section 2. III. have a common origin. This fact is of much importance in any commentary upon the constitution. It is especially important in this Essay, which makes the following contentions concerning those constitutional texts :

(1) In Part IV. of the Historical Commentary it is contended that the evidence makes it clear that the two texts were closely connected in the framing thereof and that the Framers intentionally framed them so as to be adapted to each other.

(2) In the Textual Commentary, it is contended that, independently of the extratextual evidence, the two texts can be shown to be so intimately related that they are *twin* texts.

PART IV.

Of the intention of the Framers of the Constitution on the relation of judicial power to unconstitutional legislation.

Part IV. of the Historical Commentary will be devoted to the investigation of the intentions of the Framers of the constitution concerning the relation of judicial power to unconstitutional legislation according to the constitution which they framed.

CHAPTER XXXI.

Preliminary.

No. 1. *Of the intentions of the Framers in so far as they concern the subject of this Essay.*

No. 2. *Of the public law existing during the sessions of the Framers' convention and of the importance thereof.*

No. 3. *Of the views of the Framers in convention concerning the constitutional history of the first eleven years of independence*

This chapter will first state what this investigation will seek to prove concerning the intentions of the Framers and then present historical considerations elucidating their position in beginning the task of framing the new constitution.

No. 1.

Of the intentions of the Framers of the constitution in so far as they concern the subject of this Essay.

In this and the following six chapters, it will be sought to prove that the Framers of the constitution actually intended,

First: that the courts of the several states should become competent and obliged in all litigations before them, to decide upon the questioned (federal) constitutionality of state laws and state constitutions, and to hold the same to be void in so far as contrary to the constitution and constitutional laws and treaties of the United States:

Second: that the right to decide upon the questioned constitutionality of U. S. laws and to hold them to be void, when unconstitutional, should be a right belonging to the courts of the several states in all litigations before them:

Third: that the U. S. Supreme Court should be competent in all litigations before it to decide upon the questioned (federal) constitutionality of state laws and state constitutions and to hold the same to be void in so far as contrary to the constitution and constitutional laws and treaties of the United States:

Fourth: that the U. S. Supreme Court should be competent in all litigations before it, to decide upon the questioned constitutionality of U. S. laws, and to hold the same to be void when unconstitutional.

The foregoing propositions in strictness cover the subject of this Essay, but the expressed intentions of the Framers can not be properly explained and elucidated without pointing out that they intended also,

Fifth: that whenever the judiciary of a state in any litigation should decide the question of (federal) constitutionality in favour of the state law or state constitution, impeached as being wholly or partially so unconstitutional, there should be a right of appeal to the U. S. Supreme Court upon that question :

Sixth : and that whenever the judiciary of a state in any litigation decided the question of constitutionality against a U. S. law impeached as unconstitutional, there should be a right of appeal to the U. S. Supreme Court upon that question.

These propositions are here asserted as part of the history of the constitution, but, according to the plan of this Essay, it must be subsequently proved that they also agree with the express meaning of the constitutional text independently of, and without reliance upon, the debates and proceedings of the convention. As historical propositions, merely, they depend upon a due consideration of the historical evidence, the principal part of which consists of the debates and journal of the convention.

No. 2.

Of the public law existing during the sessions of the Framers' convention and of the importance thereof.

The new constitution was framed under the old confederation. If it had failed to secure the ratification of nine states, the confederation would have remained in vigour as public law. The federal law of the Union and the municipal laws of the several states of the Union, as existing in the summer of 1787, together made the legal ground upon which the Framers met and from which they started in framing the new constitution. Their starting place is one of the points of view from which their work must be regarded by historical investigators.

During the eleven years previous to the meeting of the Framers' convention of May 14th, 1787, legal principles had been developing upon the subject of republican constitutions written and unwritten, in their relations to the *lex terrae* of each state and to the federal law of the United States.

After March 14th, 1781, federal rights were based upon the written Articles of Confederation.

In 1787, nine of the states possessed perfect written constitutions. Two other states, Virginia and New Jersey, were in a peculiar constitutional situation. Each had a written act of government, done in the name of the people, which had been established and put into operation in 1776 before independence, but in readiness for that event. Each of these instruments seems to have been generally regarded as a conditional written constitution, which became purged of the condition, when the colonies became states.

On the other hand, in Connecticut and Rhode Island, the state constitutions were unwritten or consuetudinary. As such they are of peculiar interest both inherently, and for comparison with the constitutions of the other states.

It is only necessary to read the Framers' debates upon the proposed modes of ratifying the new constitution to see how important had been the recent development of new ideas in public law and constitutional prudence during the previous eleven years. Such development was natural, indeed inevitable, in a period of wonderful activity in organizing governments upon the recently discovered principle of written constitutions. This new principle was an American creation. Now, it is a European as well as an American institution. In 1787, when the great majority of the several states had adopted written municipal constitutions, the Framers proposed to write a federal constitution for the United States. This resolution was the result of the history of the previous eleven years, during which public right, law and fact had so rapidly developed.

No. 3.

Views of the Framers in convention concerning the constitutional history of the first eleven years of independence.

The following remarks of Ellsworth in the convention, on July 23d, will first be quoted. In advocating ratifications of the new constitution by the legislatures and not by popular conventions, he remarked :

" It was said by Colonel Mason, in the first place, that the " legislatures had no authority *in the case.* . . . As to the " first point, he observed that *a new set of ideas has crept in* " *since the Articles of Confederation were established.* " *Conventions of the people, or with power derived ex-* " *pressly from the* people, were not then thought of. The " legislatures were then considered as competent. Their " ratification has been acquiesced in without complaint. To " whom have Congress applied on subsequent occasions for " further powers ? To the legislatures, not to the people."*

These observations are most important, for " the case" mentioned by Ellsworth was the case of the constitution itself. Randolph had previously asserted as a .matter of course that there had been a great development of ideas and knowledge upon such subjects, since the framing of the Articles of Confederation. On May 29th, in speaking of the defects of the confederation, he said that its authors had " done all " that patriots could do, in the then infancy of the science "of constitutions and of confederacies."†

That the period of eleven years between 1776 and 1787 had been one of new and original experience in polity, was Rutledge's opinion. In speaking of revenue bills on August 13th, he dwelt on " our own experience of eleven years." He asserted that the clauses in the state constitutions, relating to such bills, " had been put in through a blind adher-" ence to the British model. If the work was to be done "over now, they would be omitted."‡

Although no written constitution was then twelve years old, yet in the debate of June 4th, Gerry said distinctly, in speaking of the judiciary under the new constitution, " they " will have a sufficient check against encroachments of their " own department by their exposition of the laws, which " involved a power of deciding on their constitutionality. " In some states the judges had actually set aside laws, as

---

* Elliot V. 351.

† Ib. 126.

‡ Ib. 419.

" being against the constitution. This was done, too, with " general approbation." *

On July 17th Madison distinctly alluded with approval to the case of Trevett *v.* Weeden, saying: "In Rhode " Island, the judges who refused to execute an *unconsti-* " *tutional law* were displaced, and others substituted, by " the legislature, who would be the willing instruments of "their masters." †

It will be observed that Gerry's remark applies only to some of the states. It had not been proven in all that judicial courts could decide questioned statutes to be unconstitutional and hold them therefore void. Although there was a written constitution in New York, the law of that state was identical with the English law, as laid down by Blackstone, if the decision in Rutgers *v.* Waddington was correct.‡

CHAPTER XXXII.

Of the Framers' intentions in regard to the state courts.

That the Framers intended that the state courts should cease to be bound by the old confederation and become bound by the new constitution.

That they intended that the state courts should not be bound by unconstitutional acts of Congress and should be competent to decide whether any such act is constitutional or unconstitutional.

No. 1. *Of the Framers' ideas concerning the state courts.*

No. 2. *Of the Framers' ideas concerning state statutes posterior to the confederation.*

* Elliot V. 151.

† Ib. 321.

‡ See *ante* Chapter 26.

No. 3. *Of the Framers' ideas concerning the ratifications of the confederation.*

No. 4. *Of the old confederation as an obstacle to ratifying the new constitution.*

No. 5. *Of the pursuance of the confederation and the Framers' views thereupon.*

No. 6. *Of the pursuance of the confederation, the pursuance of the constitution, and the relation of both to acts of Congress which are not made in pursuance of the constitution. Of the Framers' intentions concerning such acts of Congress.*

No. 7. *Conclusion as to the Framers' intentions concerning the competency of the state courts in cases in which the validity of acts of Congress is questioned on the ground that they are not made in pursuance of the constitution.*

The first two of the series of propositions stated in chapter 31, No. 1, are concerned with the Framers' intentions in regard to the state courts. The first proposition is concerned with the relation of the state courts to state legislation questioned as federally unconstitutional. The second is concerned with the relation of the state courts to acts of Congress questioned as unconstitutional. In theory the foregoing is the proper order of stating those propositions. In practice, however, for the present historical purpose, the best method is to discuss the second proposition before the first; for, in an exposition of the Framers' intentions, the relations of the state courts to the old confederation, to the new constitution, and to the acts of the new Congress must go together. The consideration of the series of propositions laid down in chapter 31, No. 1, will therefore begin with the second, which runs as follows:

That the Framers of the constitution actually intended that the right to decide upon the questioned constitution-

ality of U. S. laws and to hold them to be void, when unconstitutional, should be a right belonging to the courts of
the several states in all litigations before them.

No. 1.

Of the Framers' ideas concerning the state courts.

In the opinion of Madison and the Framers generally *the
judicial difficulty to be met under the new constitution related to the courts of the several states, and not to those
of the United States.* As will be seen further on, there
was no opposition on August 27th to organizing the judicial power of the United States, so that the Supreme Court
could judicially decide acts of Congress to be unconstitutional and hold them therefore void. But how to establish
the validity of the constitution and the constitutional laws
and treaties of the United States, in the courts of the several states, was a matter of great perplexity, upon which
the Framers differed. How to prevent the state judges
from giving precedence to the constitution and laws of their
respective states when conflicting with those of the Union,
was a problem for which, not merely one, but several, so-
lutions were suggested in the convention.

No. 2.

*Of the Framers' ideas concerning state statutes poste-
rior to the confederation.*

As has been previously mentioned, it was in 1787 a grave
question of federal law whenever conflicts arose in the state
courts between state statutes and the confederation, whether
such of the former as were made posterior to the completion of the confederation were on the same footing as those
that were made prior thereto. Madison's remarks upon
this question in Congress on March 21st, have already been
referred to. His remarks on the same subject on June 5th,
in the convention, will now be quoted. In supporting popular ratifications of the constitution, in the debate of June

5th, Madison "thought this provision essential. The Ar-
"ticles of Confederation themselves were defective in this
"respect, resting, in many of the states, on the legislative
"sanction only. *Hence, in conflicts between acts of the*
"*states and of Congress, especially where the former are*
"*of posterior date, and the decision is to be made by state*
"*tribunals, an uncertainty must necessarily prevail;*
"*or rather, perhaps, a certain decision in favour of the*
"*state authority.*"*

No. 3.

*Of the Framers' ideas concerning the ratifications of
the confederation.*

It will be observed that Madison's observations comprehend many, but not all, of the states. As an example of a
state in which the Articles of Confederation did not rest
exclusively upon a legislative ratification, Massachusetts
may be mentioned. The constitution of Massachusetts was
made prior to the completion of the confederation, but after
that state had ratified that instrument. It was adopted in
1780, and was evidently framed in expectation of the confederation being completed. This venerable constitution,
now the oldest written constitution in the world, provides
in its Part I., Article 4, that "The people of this common-
"wealth have the sole and exclusive right of governing
"themselves as a free, sovereign, and independent State,
"and do, and forever hereafter shall, exercise and enjoy
"every power, jurisdiction, and right which is not, or may
"not hereafter be, by them expressly delegated to the
"United States of America in Congress assembled."†

From this provision it results that the tribunals of Massachusetts, in making decisions concerning conflicts between
state law and federal law, had in 1787 no embarrassment
caused by any mere legislative ratification. Whether the
act of the state legislature involved was prior or posterior

---

* Elliot V. 157.

† Poor's Charters and Constitutions, p. 958.

to the confederation, mattered not.   In all cases a judge of
Massachusetts was bound to proceed upon the basis that the
constitution as well as the legislature of his state had sanctioned the confederation.   Madison's criticism upon the
judicial operation of federal acts did not, therefore, apply
to Massachusetts.

But while the express sanction of the confederation by
the state constitution avoided the difficulty in question, it
raised another of great embarrassment to the Framers' convention.   This very sanction was an obstacle to the legislature of Massachusetts ratifying any new articles of union or
new federal constitution proposed to it otherwise than in
pursuance of the old confederation.

The case of the written constitution of New York will
throw further light on this point.   In the convention on
July 23d, King alluded to the refusal of that state to grant
to Congress the impost power as recommended by that body
on April 18th, 1783.   He remarked "that, among other ob-
"jections made in the state of New York to granting powers
"to Congress, one had been, that such powers as would
"operate within the states could not be reconciled to the
"constitution, and therefore were not grantable by the leg-
"islative authority."   See Elliot V. 355, and Journals of
Congress for August 11th and 23d, 1786.   This was one of
the reasons why King preferred a reference to popular conventions, as the most certain means of obviating "all doubts
"and disputes concerning *legitimacy of the new consti-*
"*tution.*"

No. 4.

*Of the old confederation as an obstacle to ratifying the
new constitution.*

It will thus be seen that the existing confederation was
to the Framers a lion in the way of the meditated constitution.   It was a languishing, perhaps even dying, but certainly not a dead lion.   Only the month before the convention met, the United States in Congress assembled had fed-

erally declared to all the states that the treaty of peace was the law of the land of every state by virtue of the confederation. In spite of this, as ratification by all the states could not be counted upon in a convention which represented less than all the states, the Framers had to find a way for the state judges to become unbound by the old confederation, while devising means for binding them by the new constitution.

What has been previously said relating to Trevett v. Weeden, Bayard v. Singleton, and Blackstone on the law of nations may here be recalled. In each state, the confederation, when ratified by the legislature, became part of the law of the land of the state. The treaty of peace was also part of the law of the land of each state. The legal position of the confederation before the state courts thus required the gravest consideration, if it was to be successfully changed. Captious criticism like impeaching the confederation as conflicting with the common law (*cf.* Elliot V. 353), was worse than useless.

On June 8th, Madison, as may be learned from Yates, supported an unlimited legislative power of negativing state laws. He held that the limited negative proposed by the resolution under consideration would be inefficient. " The " judges of the state must give the state laws their opera- " tion, although the law abridges the rights of the national " government." * This was before the existing constitutional provision had been moved, but it shows what would be the judicial difficulty in the several states, under the new constitution, which any constitutional provision would have to overcome.

In discussing the modes of ratification, on July 23d, Madison said that " he considered the difference between a " system founded on the legislatures only, and one founded "on the people, to be the true difference between a league " or treaty, and a constitution. . . . . A law violating a "treaty ratified by a pre-existing law might be respected by " the judges as a law, though an unwise and perfidious one. " *A law violating a constitution established by the people*

---

* Elliot I. 400, V. 171.

"themselves would be considered by the judges as null and "void." *

No. 5.

Of the pursuance of the confederation and the Framers' views thereupon.

In the debate of July 23d., on ratifying the new constitution, the great question was whether the ratification of the states should be made by the ordinary legislatures or by popular conventions.

Gerry said that "he considered the confederation to be "paramount to any state constitution. The last article of "it, authorizing alterations, must consequently be so as "well as the others ; and everything *done in pursuance* of "the article must have the same high authority with the "article."† It is here to be remarked that Gerry speaks of things done in pursuance of an article of the confederation. As to things done *not* in pursuance of the articles of confederation, Gouverneur Morris's remarks in the same debate are of great importance. According to him, it must have then been true in point of law, that a state court could decide an act of the Congress of the confederation to be null and void because not made in pursuance of the Articles of Confederation. Gouverneur Morris observed :

"If the Confederation be *pursued*, no alteration can be "made without the unanimous consent of the legislatures. "Legislative alterations not conformable to the federal com-"pact would clearly not be valid. The judges would con-"sider them null and void."‡

That is to say, an act of the Congress of the confederation promulgating an alteration of the Articles of Confederation confirmed by the legislatures of less than thirteen states could legally, and would certainly, be decided by the judges of the state courts to be contrary to the 13th Article of the Confederation, and therefore be held null and void.

---

* Elliot V. 356.

† Ib. 353.

‡ Ib. 355.

It is indisputable that the great majority of the convention held that popular ratifications of the constitution were indispensable, if a union of less than thirteen states, as well as a union of all, was to be provided for. A partial union, as well as a unanimous one, is foreseen by Article VII of the constitution, which reads:

" The ratification of the conventions of nine states shall " be sufficient for the establishment of this constitution be- " tween the states so ratifying the same."

This foresight had its effect, for an actually existing partial union of the states was the ladder by which a union of all was reached. Thus, after nine and before all the states had ratified the new constitution, each then existing ratification presented judicially a very peculiar case to the courts of its respective state. The question, *utrum hic casus ad jus antiquum aptandus sit*, could only be answered in the negative;* for it was impossible to adapt the case to the 13th article of the confederation requiring any alteration thereof to be agreed to by Congress and "con- "firmed by the legislatures of every state."

As a matter of fact, the constitution went into operation with only eleven states included within the union of the constitution. This was not accomplished by moving the legislatures of the several states to act *under* the confederation. Nothing of the sort was professed to be done. What was professed was to move the constituents of those legislatures to act *praeter* the confederation. In each state making a ratification of the new constitution, the judges were by that ratification commanded by the people thereof to hold it to be the supreme law of the land. Thereby the confederation was to cease to be the law of the land of that state and the constitution was to be substituted in its place.

---

* Compare *Dig. lib.* 28. *tit.* 2. *l.* 29. § 27.

No. 6.

Of the pursuance of the confederation, the pursuance of the constitution, and the relation of both to acts of Congress which are not made in pursuance of the constitution. Of the Framers' intentions concerning such acts of Congress.

It is of extreme importance to observe the signification of Morris's language: "if the confederation be *pursued.*" It is well known how important was Morris's influence upon the language of the constitution.* Shortly before he had spoken, Gorham had said : "if the last article of the Con-"federation is to be *pursued,* the unanimous concurrence "of the states will be necessary."†

Both Morris and Gorham pursued the confederation in applying the verb "pursue" to the execution thereof in the various *casus foederis,* and Gerry also did so in a like use of the noun "pursuance." Its 11th article speaks of the "assembling of the United States *in pursuance of* this Con-"federation." The intimate relation between this language and Morris's is unmistakable. The verb *pursue,* the adjective *pursuant,* and the noun *pursuance* are three forms of a technical term of law, the meaning of which will be discussed when the text of paragraph 2. VI. is critically examined. At the present moment, when the question is merely as to the intentions of the Framers, it suffices to point out that according to Morris an act of the Congress of the confederation in which the confederation was not pursued, or (to use the very words of its 12th article) which was not made "in pursuance of this confederation," must, under the confederation, legally be held null and void by the judges of the state courts. Morris's language was no mere personal opinion, but it was one representing both the opinion and action of the convention. He spoke thus on July 23d. Six days previously, on July 17th, the convention had applied the term, "in pursuance of," to the making of acts or laws of

---

* Bancroft's History of the Constitution, II. 207, and Spark's Life of Morris, III. 323.

† Elliot V. 354.

the United States by the future legislature or Congress in pursuance of the Articles of Union. This was done in a resolution which was the basis of paragraph 2. VI. of the constitution and which was in August and September three times reconsidered and twice amended by the convention. In this repeated action the application of the term was emphasized, the "constitution" being substituted for the "Articles of Union," and "*in pursuance thereof*" for "in "pursuance of." According to the clauses of paragraph 2. VI. of the constitution "the laws of the United States which "shall be made *in pursuance thereof*" bind the state judges, and withstand any state legislation to the contrary. A convention which thought that the acts of the Congress of the confederation must be made *in pursuance* of the confederation, and, if not so made, must *necessarily* be held null and void by the state judges, and which therefore proceeded *praeter* the confederation, must undoubtedly have intended a certain thing in framing the constitutional text upon such a model. They must have intended that the future laws of the United States, which were *not* made in pursuance of the new constitution, should *not* bind the state judges, but should by them be held therefore *null and void*.

No. 7.

Conclusion as to the Framers' intentions concerning the competency of the state courts in cases in which the validity of acts of Congress is questioned on the ground that they are not made in pursuance of the constitution.

Thus the Framers must actually have intended that the state courts should be competent to decide whether a questioned act of Congress be made or not made in pursuance of the constitution and to hold it valid or void accordingly.

In other words, namely in those of the second proposition contended for,* the Framers intended that the right to decide upon the questioned constitutionality of the U. S.

---

* On page 294, *ante*.

laws and to hold them void, when unconstitutional, should be a right belonging to the courts of the several states.

It should perhaps here be more fully stated why this second proposition as to the Framers' intention has been discussed before the first in the series laid down in chapter 31, No. 1.

In a critical commentary upon the text of the constitution, the second proposition should be considered after the first, for it relates to a right which is a limitation upon an obligation contained in the first. But in an explanatory view of the intentions of the Framers as to the new constitution, which involves the relation thereof to the old confederation, it has naturally and unavoidably come first into consideration. As will be seen from the foregoing, the present right of a state court to decide whether or not a U. S. law has been made *in pursuance of the constitution*, is historically inseparable from the previously existing right of the same court to decide whether or not a federal act was made *in pursuance of the confederation*. This previously existing right had to be fully considered by the convention in framing article VII. of the constitution, which related to the ratification thereof by the conventions of the states. In so doing, what they thought and intended concerning the present right aforesaid became manifest.

CHAPTER XXXIII.

Further consideration of the intentions of the Framers concerning the state courts. That they intended that the state courts should be competent and obliged to decide upon the questioned federal constitutionality of state legislation and to hold the same void in so far as so unconstitutional.

No. 1. *Of conflicts between the laws of the Union and*

those of the states and the relation thereof to the framing of the new constitution.

No. 2. *How the plans for a new union, which were presented to the convention, were affected by conflicts of the laws of the states with the confederation and federal treaties.*

No. 3. *Of the two principal plans of union, which were presented in the convention.*

No. 4. *Of the two methods proposed in the convention for settling conflicts between the laws of the Union and those of the states.*

No. 5. *Of the legislative method for settling conflicts between the laws of the Union and those of the states.*

No. 6. *Of the judicial method for settling conflicts between the laws of the Union and those of the states.*

No. 7. *Of the intentions of the Framers in rejecting the legislative method and adopting the judicial method.*

No. 8. *History of the proceedings of the convention in framing the text concerning the judicial method for settling conflicts between the laws of the Union and those of the states.*

No. 9. *Of the meaning of the words "law of the land" in the constitution, according to the intentions both of the committee and the convention.*

No. 10. *Conclusion as to the correctness of the first proposition concerning the Framers' intentions laid down in chapter 31, No. 1.*

No. 11. *Of the connection between the first and second propositions concerning the Framers' intentions laid down in chapter 31, No. 1.*

No. 1.

*Of conflicts between the laws of the Union and those of
the states and the relation thereof to the framing of the
new constitution.*

The intentions of the Framers will now be considered in
regard to the matter stated in the first proposition laid down
in chapter 31, No. 1, namely, that the Framers actually intended that the courts of the several states should become
competent and obliged in all litigations before them, to decide
upon the questioned (federal) constitutionality of state laws
and state constitutions, and to hold the same to be void in
so far as contrary to the constitution and constitutional
laws and treaties of the United States.

The Framers were agreed upon the prime necessity of
finding a proper method of settling conflicts between the
laws of the Union and those of the states, and well they
might be. Such conflicts of laws in a union of states are
not mere antinomies, such as may occur in the municipal
law of every state anywhere, and which a great jurist
teaches may be settled by purely scientific authority.* The
resemblance is rather to the former conflicts between the
laws of the state and those of the church which in Europe
shook society to its foundations.

No. 2.

*How the plans for a new union, which were presented
to the convention, were affected by conflicts of the laws of
the states with the confederation and federal treaties.*

Conflicts of the laws of the states with the confederation
and federal treaties were among the weightiest causes producing the meeting of the Framers' convention. Every
plan of union introduced to their consideration showed this
truth. The most important of those plans were the two

---

* Puchta : *Cursus der Institutionen,* Ed. 6, I. 44.

moved respectively by Randolph on behalf of Virginia and by Patterson on behalf of New Jersey. Both these plans will be so frequently referred to in this discussion that some observations upon them are now requisite.

No. 3

Of the two principal plans of union, which were presented in the convention.

Randolph's plan was one for Articles of Union, which would supersede the Articles of Confederation, and was regarded as being preferred by the large states. Patterson's was for new articles in alteration of, and addition to, the old confederation, and was regarded as preferred by the small states.

The resolutions of Randolph's plan were the starting point of the proceedings and debates of the convention. They had been carefully prepared in advance, and were in fact the only matured proposal ready for discussion. They were brought in by Randolph as the representative of the delegation from Virginia, among whom was Washington. To a large extent, the propositions of Randolph's plan were accepted and elaborated, sometimes with, and sometimes without, adaptation to dispositions derived from other sources. In some very important respects its propositions were, however, not accepted, and the constitution is very different from what it would have been, had the whole plan been followed. On the other hand, Patterson's plan was rejected as a whole. Subsequently to that rejection, however, part of it was taken as a basis for framing texts of the constitution, which adjusted fundamental relations between the Union and the states. The constitution is a very different instrument from what it would have been, had it contained nothing in common with Patterson's plan.

No. 4.

Of the two methods proposed in the convention for set-
tling conflicts between the laws of the Union and those of
the states in the new constitution.

The Framers were divided in their preferences for two
very different ideas concerning the settling of conflicts between the laws of the Union and those of the states. One
of these ideas was that of vesting in the legislative Congress
of the Union a negative power over state laws in certain
cases. This idea was brought before the convention as a
fundamental part in Randolph's plan. This legislative
negative power required a federal legislative discrimination
as to particular state laws.

The other leading idea was one requiring judicial discrimination in particular cases of conflict, in which a general rule of legislation, written in the constitution, would
receive specific application. The origin of this idea is to be
traced to the previously mentioned draft of identical laws
which the federal letter of Congress, dated April 10th, 1787,
recommended to the legislatures of the several states as the
means of settling conflicts between state laws and the treaty
of peace. This idea was preferred by the Framers and was
expanded in two ways. It was applied not merely to treaties
but also to the new constitution and to the laws made in
pursuance thereof. It was not only made a rule addressed
to the judges in every state, but was laid down in paragraph
2. VI. in such distinct legislative terms as to bind all persons, public and private, capable of being bound by legislative dispositions in the constitution.

No. 5.

Of the legislative method for settling conflicts between
the laws of the Union and those of the states.

The idea of the legislative negative was the one first
brought to the consideration of the convention. It was

fully considered at different times and was temporarily
adopted in the committee of the whole. On July 17th it
was, however, finally rejected, after an important debate.
This was done by a vote of seven states to three. This negative decision was made merely as a step towards further
positive action as to a different measure, for Luther Martin
instanter moved the following resolution, which was
adopted unanimously :

" Resolved, That the legislative acts of the United States,
"made by virtue and in pursuance of the Articles of Union,
"and all treaties made and ratified under the authority of
"the United States, shall be the supreme law of the re-
"spective states, as far as those acts, or treaties, shall re-
"late to the said states, or their citizens and inhabitants :—
"*and that the judiciaries of the several states shall be*
"*bound thereby in their decisions—anything in the re-*
"*spective laws of the individual states to the contrary,*
"*notwithstanding.*"*

No. 6.

*Of the judicial method of settling conflicts between the
laws of the Union and those of the states.*

Martin's resolution is self-evidently copied from the first of
the two paragraphs of the 7th resolution of the plan of confederation offered by Patterson on behalf of New Jersey.
The text of the resolution follows that of Patterson's said
paragraph almost word for word, except that the former
speaks of the Articles of Union and the latter speaks of
powers vested by the Articles of Confederation. The whole
of Patterson's 7th resolution will now be quoted. Both of
its paragraphs are intimately connected with the subject of
conflicts between the laws of the Union and those of the
states, as will be enlarged upon subsequently. Its first
paragraph, however, is here particularly in question. The
whole resolution contains two paragraphs and reads thus :†

* Journal, 183 ; Elliot V. 322.

† Journal, 126.

"7. Resolved, That all acts of the United States in Con-
"gress assembled, made by virtue and in pursuance of the
"powers hereby vested in them, and by the articles of the
"confederation, and all treaties made and ratified under
"the authority of the United States, shall be the supreme
"law of the respective states, as far as those acts or treaties
"shall relate to the said states, or their citizens ; and that
"the judiciaries of the several states shall be bound thereby
"in their decisions, anything in the respective laws of the
"individual states to the contrary notwithstanding.

"And if any state, or any body of men in any state, shall
"oppose or prevent the carrying into execution such acts
"or treaties, the federal executive shall be authorized to
"call forth the powers of the confederated states, or so
"much thereof as may be necessary, to enforce and compel
"obedience to such acts, or an observance of such treaties."

A comparison of the text of Patterson's first paragraph
with that of the draft of identical laws proposed by the
federal Congress to the several states on the previous April
13th can not fail to suggest itself to the reader of this Essay.* Such a comparison will show that so far as treaties
are concerned, they resemble each other as much as an article in a confederation can well resemble a draft for identical laws on the statute books of thirteen different states.

The draft of identical laws in every state in which the
legislature might enact it, would repeal all laws or parts of
laws, which conflicted with the treaty of peace, and would
bind the state courts of law and equity, in all cases and
questions before them that arose from the treaty, to decide
and adjudge according to the treaty, notwithstanding or
nonobstante anything in the said laws or parts of laws to
the contrary of the treaty. The draft was expressly declared, by the federal letter of Congress recommending it,
to be one of a law of general, not specific, repeal. It did
not make any enumeration of, or discrimination as to, particular laws conflicting with the treaty. Said Congress in
the letter : "By repealing in general terms all acts and

---

* See text of the draft on pages 274, 275, *ante.*

"clauses repugnant to the treaty, the business will be turned "over to its proper department, viz., the judicial ; and the "courts of law will find no difficulty in deciding whether "any particular act or clause is or is not contrary to the "treaty."*

There can thus be no doubt that a state court, under a law like the draft, could decide a state law to be wholly or partially contrariant to the treaty and hold it therefore so far void. This is precisely what Martin's resolution intended the state courts to do as to state laws conflicting with the federal treaties and laws of the United States. His resolution provided that the legislative acts of the United States made in pursuance of the Articles of Union, and treaties made under the authority of the United States, should be the supreme law of each state respectively, and then by a *nonobstante* clause derogated to every law of any state contrariant to such legislative acts and treaties, while expressly binding the judges of each state and their decisions by those legislative acts and treaties as against the state laws so derogated to.

What the Congress of the confederation proposed to secure by identical laws of the thirteen state legislatures, Martin's resolution proposed to accomplish by one legislative provision in the Articles of Union, which should be judicially applied to particular cases by the judges of each state.

No. 7.

Of the intentions of the Framers in rejecting the legislative method and adopting the judicial method.

It is therefore clear that in adopting Martin's resolution, the convention intended that the courts of a state should have the competency and obligation to decide the question whether or not a state law be contrariant to the constitutional laws and treaties of the Union and to hold the same derogated to or null in so far as so contrariant.

---

* Journals of Congress XII. 36.

Thus the convention, after rejecting the idea of a legislative negative power for settling conflicts between the laws of the Union and those of the states, substituted in the place thereof the idea of a judicial criticism for that purpose. To speak with more precision, a positive legislative rule of general import was inserted in the new constitution, which was to be judicially applied to particular cases or conflicts as they arose. Thereby, judicial was substituted for legislative discrimination. A further distinction must also be made. The discarded legislative discrimination was intended to be exclusively that of the proposed legislature of the Union. The judicial discrimination adopted was that of all judiciaries capable of being bound by legislation written in any new constitution or articles of union.

It is true that the state judges only are named and mentioned in Martin's resolution and the corresponding text of the constitution (paragraph 2. VI.), but the clauses of both are general legislative dispositions and as legislation bind the courts and judges of the Union as well as those of the states, as will be hereinafter more fully set forth. As has before been pointed out, the anxiety of the Framers related to the courts of the states, not to the courts of the Union. The judicial courts of the several states were intended to be legislatively bound by the new constitution to apply the laws of the Union and cause them to be executed in certain *casus foederis*, notwithstanding any acts of their respective state legislatures to the contrary. For this reason, it was necessary to mention the state judges expressly and specially. For this reason, as well as others, it was necessary to insert a *nonobstante* clause of derogation to state laws conflicting with the laws of the Union in any *casus foederis*.

No. 8.

History of the proceedings of the convention in framing the text concerning the judicial method of settling conflicts between the laws of the Union and those of the states.

Martin's resolution, like all others adopted by the con-

vention, was referred to the committee of five for the purpose of their reporting a constitution. This was the first
committee of five, of which Rutledge was chairman. It is
to be distinguished from the second committee of five, of
which Johnson was chairman. The first committee reported
the original draft of the constitution, which was amended
by the convention. The amended draft was referred to the
second committee, which reported the revised draft.

On August 6th., Rutledge's committee reported the draft
of a constitution, of which the 8th article reads as follows:
" The acts of the legislature of the United States made in
" pursuance of this constitution, and all treaties made under
" the authority of the United States, shall be the supreme
" law of the several states, and of their citizens and inhab-
" itants; and the judges in the several states shall be bound
" thereby in their decisions; anything in the constitutions
" or laws of the several states to the contrary, notwithstand-
" ing." (Journal, 222; Elliot V. 379.)

The alterations of Martin's resolution made in the above
by the committee require no comment, except (1) that the
substitution of the word, "Constitution," for the words,
"Articles of Union," resulted from the general instruction
of their appointment by resolution of July 23d,* and (2) that
state constitutions as well as state laws were written into
the derogation made by the *nonobstante* or notwithstanding
clause.†

On August 23d, Rutledge moved to amend Article 8th of
the draft so as to read as below given. This amendment
consisted in striking out the first fifteen words of the article
and substituting the following: "This constitution and the
"laws of the United States made in pursuance thereof."
Rutledge's motion was unanimously adopted, and article
8th then read thus: ‡

" This constitution and the laws of the United States made
" in pursuance thereof, and all treaties made under the
" authority of the United States, shall be the supreme law
" of the several states and of their citizens and inhabitants;

---

* Journal, 199, 201.

† *Cf.* Journal 183 and 222.

‡ Journal, 282, 283; Elliot V. 467.

"and the judges in the several states shall be bound thereby
"in their decisions; anything in the constitutions or laws
" of the several states to the contrary, notwithstanding."

" Which passed in the affirmative."*

It was Rutledge, the chairman of the committee that reported the draft of a constitution, who thus proposed to im-
prove the committee's work by an addition of the first magnitude. This addition expressly enacted that the constitution of the United States should become the supreme law
of the several states and of their citizens and inhabitants;
that the state constitutions and state laws conflicting therewith should be derogated to, and that in such conflicts the
judges of the several states should be bound by the former
and not by the latter.

Here should be pointed out the constitutional relation of
Rutledge's motion to the then very recent decision upon the
law of the confederation, which the Superior Court of North
Carolina had given in the case of Bayard v. Singleton. In
that case, as previously mentioned, that court had decided
that the confederation of the United States was the fundamental law of the land of North Carolina and was unrepealable by the legislature of the state, so that any law of the
state conflicting therewith would not be judicially held
valid. Thus the proposition which the Superior Court of
North Carolina decided to be the law of the confederation,
is *mutatis mutandis* identical with the legislative disposition which Rutledge moved should be inserted in the new
constitution as the express law thereof.

On August 25th, as stated by the Journal, p. 293,

" It was moved and seconded to amend the eighth article,
" to read,

" This constitution and the laws of the United States
" which shall be made in pursuance thereof, and all treaties
" made or which shall be made under the authority of the
" United States, shall be the supreme law of the several
" states, and of their citizens and inhabitants; and the
" judges in the several states shall be bound thereby in their

---

* The vote was unanimous according to Madison, Elliot V. 467.

"decisions, any thing in the constitutions or laws of the "several states to the contrary, notwithstanding."

This resolution passed in the affirmative.

Madison's debates give the following additional information concerning the foregoing resolution:*

"On motion of Mr. Madison seconded by Mr. Gouverneur "Morris Article 8 [of the draft] was reconsidered, and, after "the words, 'all treaties made' were inserted, *nem. con.*, "the words, 'or which shall be made.' This insertion was "meant to obviate all doubts concerning the force of treaties "pre-existing, by making the words, 'all treaties made' "refer to them, as the words inserted would refer to future "treaties."

These observations show that Madison was as anxious concerning the pre-existing treaty of peace, in the then convention, as he had been in Congress in the previous March and April. They also show that the *modus operandi* of paragraph 2. VI. was intended to be *unrestricted* by any rule of *lex posterior derogat legi priori*.

On September 8th, the convention appointed its second committee of five, to which was referred the amended draft of the constitution, and which, on September 12th, reported the revised draft of the constitution. It consisted of Johnson, chairman, Hamilton, G. Morris, Madison and King.†

The 2nd section of the 6th article of the committee's revised draft reads thus:

"This constitution, and the laws of the United States "which shall be made in pursuance thereof, and all treaties "made, or which shall be made, under the authority of the "United States, shall be the supreme law of the land; and "the judges in every state shall be bound thereby, anything "in the constitution or laws of any state to the contrary "notwithstanding."‡

It will be observed that the committee made the following changes of language:

(1) for the words, "the supreme law of the several states

---

* Elliot V. 478.

† Journal, 346, 347.

‡ Ib. 366.

"and of their citizens and inhabitants," they substituted the words, " the supreme law of the land ;"

(2) for the words, " the judges of the several states shall "be bound thereby in their decisions," they substituted the words, " the judges in every state shall be bound "thereby ;"

(3) for the words, " any thing in the constitutions or laws " of the several states to the contrary notwithstanding," they substituted the words, "anything in the constitution " or laws of any state to the contrary notwithstanding."

The words of the revised draft are now the words of the constitution, no subsequent changes in the text of paragraph 2. VI. having been made. The question therefore arises whether the foregoing modifications of language in any way modified the intentions of the Framers, either inadvertently or consciously.

The revised draft, as reported by the committee, was read by paragraphs in the convention and compared with the amended first draft. In some places it was corrected and amended, and where not amended and corrected was agreed to.* This consideration began on September 13th.

There is no record of any debate, criticism or motion upon the changes of language introduced by the committee into the paragraph which is now paragraph 2. VI. of the constitution.

There is no mention whatsoever of the subject in Madison's debates, in the Journal, in the sheets of yeas and nays, or in the addition made to the printed Journal either from Brearly's notes or upon Madison's authority. †

It is thus clear that without supposing some concealed intention on the part of the committee and an actual negligence of all other members of the convention, the foregoing changes or emendations made by the former could not have been consciously made contrary to the intentions of the latter. That is to say, in the modifications of language above mentioned, the committee meant, and was then under-

---

* Journal, p. 371, last ten lines, p. 375 lines 14 to 20.

† See Journal p. 371 to end, and especially p. 372, first paragraph, and p. 379, note.

stood by the convention to mean, to carry out and not to
change the intentions of the latter. The force of these considerations will probably be admitted by all as to the second
and third modifications of language. The writer will not,
however, assume that it will be admitted by all as to the
first modification. A particular examination will therefore
be made concerning the substitution of the words, "the
"supreme law of the land," for the words, "the supreme
"law of the several states, and of their citizens and inhab-
"itants." That the committee did not in fact intend to dis-
obey their instructions must be conceded, if the legal meaning of the words, "law of the land," in 1787 under the confederation, as hereinbefore explained, be correct. As has
been shown, those words then signified the law of each several state respectively, and not the law of the United States.

No. 9.

*Of the meaning of the words "law of the land" in the
constitution according to the intentions of both the committee and the convention.*

It is perfectly true that there have been lawyers as well
as laymen who have taken for granted that the words "law
"of the land" in paragraph 2. VI., mean law of the United
States and not law of each several state. Nothing short of
the clearest demonstration can, however, impose such a
meaning upon the text, for it destroys the whole legislative
point and legal sequence of the remainder of the sentence,
which does not say that the judges of the United States,
but that "the judges in every state," shall be bound by the
antecedents notwithstanding any thing to the contrary "in
"the constitution or laws of any state."

That the aforesaid misunderstanding of the words, "law
"of the land," is due to the inadvertence of others and not
to the inadvertence of the Framers, will be a task undertaken when the text of paragraph 2. VI. is critically
examined.

It is, however, here proper to insist, as part of the history of the text, that neither the committee nor the convention could have had any idea, intention or purpose of changing the words of the amended draft to any new text signifying the supreme law of the United States and not the supreme law of the several states. The reader knows how the committee got the words "law of the land." Four of its five members were delegates in the federal Congress which had in the spring previous applied them to treaties in the same way in which the application of them was in August made to treaties and extended to the new constitution and the laws made in pursuance thereof. Nor was the committee the first public body to extend this application of the words "law of the land" to other things of the Union besides treaties. As must be repeated, between April and August 1787 the Superior Court of North Carolina had decided that the confederation, like the state constitution, was part of the fundamental law of the land of North Carolina, which the state legislature could not repeal. The meaning of those words, under the new constitution, could only have been what it was under the confederation, that is to say, that the law of the land was the law of each several state respectively.

There is no record of the proceedings of the committee, but there is evidence relating to the ideas of one of its members upon the subject, which throws light upon the ideas of all. This member is Hamilton, one of the authors of the Federalist. Number 16 of that work was written by Hamilton. In it he discusses the possibility of a majority in a state legislature usurping authority in violation of the new constitution. In so doing, he speaks thus of the judges of the state courts :

"If the judges were not embarked in a conspiracy with "the legislature, they would pronounce the resolutions "of such a majority to be contrary to the supreme law "of the land, unconstitutional and void.   *   *   The "magistracy (*i. e.* the judges of the state), being equally "*the ministers of the law of the land, from whatever source* "*it might emanate, would doubtless be as ready to guard* "*the national as the local regulations from the inroads of* "*private licentiousness.*" (Federalist, Dawson's edition, pp. 105, 106.)

It is clear from the foregoing italicised passage that the writer understood that the words, "law of the land," in paragraph 2. VI. would, if the constitution became established, import that each state had a law of the land of its own ; that part of it emanated from the Union, and the remainder from the state itself ; and that the judges of the state were the ministers of all parts of this law of the land of the state. One part of the said law consisted of "na-"tional regulations" and the other of "local regulations." By local regulations were meant the constitution and laws of the state, written and unwritten, and by national regulations, the constitution and constitutional laws and treaties of the United States. The words "the supreme law of the "land" must have been understood by Hamilton and consequently by the other members of the committee to mean the supreme law of the land of each state, or of every state severally, and not the supreme law of one single land of the United States merged together.

It remains to speak of the ideas of the convention upon the subject. Although no remarks upon the words "law "of the land" were made by any of the Framers of the convention, C. C. Pinckney, one of their number, made important observations thereupon in another place, which have been previously quoted in this Essay.* These were addressed to the legislature of South Carolina, where he, as a member of the late convention, was expressly and publicly giving his constituents an account of his stewardship. By referring to the extracts hereinbefore given, it will be seen that the judicial cases cited by Pinckney show clearly that the treaty of peace was superadded to and became part of the law of the land of South Carolina (and consequently in the other states was superadded to and made part of the law of the land of each respectively). He affirmed in express terms that paragraph 2. VI. was declaratory and that the treaties were the law of the land as much

---

* See pages 289, 290, *ante.*

under the confederation as under the constitution. This he
said after Bayard *v.* Singleton, in a neighbouring state, had
proved that the confederation itself was part of the law of
the land of North Carolina, as must again be repeated.

Pinckney's remarks demonstrate that a competent and
prominent member of the Framers' convention had no idea
that any departure from the original intentions of the latter
body had been made by it, when it accepted the aforesaid
change of language made by their committee, that is to say,
the change from the words, "the supreme law of the sev-
"eral states and of their citizens and inhabitants," to the
words, "the supreme law of the land." His remarks do
more. They are so expressed that there can be no doubt
that C. C. Pinckney's opinion was not a mere personal opinion, but a representative one. They thus furnish positive
evidence as to the character of the opinions of the Framers
in general upon the committee's action.

The foregoing examination, it is maintained, shows that
the committee of five on the revised draft no more departed
from the previously expressed intentions of the Framers in
the first, than in the other two modifications of language,
introduced by them into the text of what is now paragraph
2. VI. of the constitution.

No. 10.

*Conclusion as to the correctness of the first proposition
concerning the Framers' intentions laid down in chapter 31, No. 1.*

It is also maintained that the foregoing history of the
framing of the said constitutional text establishes the truth
of the proposition that the Framers actually intended that
the courts of the several states should become competent
and obliged in all litigations before them, to decide upon
the questioned (federal) constitutionality of state laws and
state constitutions, and to hold the same to be void in so
far as contrary to the constitution and constitutional laws
and treaties of the United States: that is to say, that it is
correct to affirm proposition 1st on page 294.

No. 11.

*Of the connection between the first and second proposi-
tions concerning the Framers' intentions asserted in chapter 31, No. 1.*

It has been previously shown that the Framers intended
that the right to decide upon the questioned constitutionality of U. S. laws and to hold them to be void, when unconstitutional, should be a right belonging to the courts of
the several states in all litigations before them. It is here
proper to add that such a right of the state judges is necessarily, and must have been intended to be, a limitation
upon the obligation imposed upon them in cases of conflicts between the constitutions or laws of their states and
the laws of the United States. The skillful incorporation
of such a limitation in the express terms of the obligation
liberates them from the rule of paragraph 2. VI., whenever
U. S. laws are not made in pursuance of the U. S. constitution. Such laws are outside of the limits of the rule.

CHAPTER XXXIV.

**Of the Framers' intentions as to the competency of
the U. S. Supreme Court to decide upon the questioned (federal) constitutionality of state legislation
and to hold the same void in so far as so unconstitutional.**

No. 1. *Of the inferior courts of the United States.*

No. 2. *That paragraph 2. VI. was intended to be a legislative rule of judicial decision for all courts, both of the
United States and of the several states.*

No. 3. *Of the proposed and rejected legislative power of negativing state legislation, as showing the Framers' intentions concerning the relation of federal authority to conflicts between the laws of the Union and those of the states.*

No. 4. *Of the origin and purposes of the legislative negative method.*

No. 5. *Of the relation of paragraph 2. VI. to the beginning of section 2. III.*

No. 6. *The history of the legislative negative in the convention examined, in order to ascertain the intentions of the Framers concerning judicial competency in cases of conflict between the laws of the Union and those of the state.*

The 3d proposition laid down in Chapter 31, No. 3, will now be considered, *viz.*, that the Framers of the constitution actually intended that the U. S. Supreme Court should be competent in all litigations before it to decide upon the questioned (federal) constitutionality of state laws and state constitutions and to hold the same to be void in so far as contrary to the U. S. constitution.

No. 1.

Of the inferior courts of the United States.

Although the convention did not frame any constitutional clause ordaining any inferior courts of the United States, it did frame texts giving Congress power to constitute such inferior tribunals in the future. Whether such courts, when so constituted, were intended to have the same competency, is therefore here a proper question to ask. To that question an affirmative answer is given, for, it is maintained that they actually intended that all courts, past present and future, both state and federal, should be so competent.

No. 2.

That paragraph 2. VI. was intended to be a legislative rule of judicial decision for all courts, both of the United States and of the several states.

If what has been previously said be correct, it has been made clear that the Framers intended that the courts of the several states should be both competent and obliged to do what, it is now furthermore asserted, they intended all courts of the United States to be competent to do. This was done by paragraph 2. VI. That paragraph was four times considered in the convention without one negative vote being given against it. It was regarded as, and intended to be, a legislative disposition. As will be hereinafter fully commented upon, the final clause is a *clausula nonobstante*, that is to say, a legislative clause of the most express and technical nature. While this clause derogates to old and other laws of a certain sort, clauses preceding it enact new law of a different sort. Paragraph 2. VI. is therefore a legislative rule and limitation, which is particularly and especially addressed to "the judges in "every state." It is thus a *legislative* rule of decision for those judges, but being a *legislative* rule, it is one for all other courts capable of applying it and all other persons capable of obeying it As a legislative rule of judicial decision, it can be applied by the U. S. judges. The fact that the Framers regarded the rule in paragraph 2. VI. as legislation or written law is alone sufficient to prove that they actually intended that the rule of decision therein contained should bind the supreme and all future courts of the United States as well as all the courts of all other states.

Strictly speaking, it is therefore unnecessary to proceed further in investigating the intentions of the Framers as to proposition 3d. It would, however, be doing great injustice to the matter to stop here. It is, indeed, part of a greater matter.

The competency of any court to decide between conflicting federal and state laws is but a part of the constitutional system for securing the execution of the laws of the Union, either by federal or state agency, in the different *casus foederis*. Such securing of execution was, *par excellence*, the particular task of the Framers, for its absence was believed by them to be the greatest of all the defects of the confederation. At an early date they undertook the consideration of that part of this task which related to conflicts between the laws of the Union and those of the states. At an early date, as will be hereinafter more particularly mentioned, they resolved not to write in the new constitution any clauses of federal execution against a state by military process for violation of federal right. At an early date, however, they adopted a certain plan for settling conflicts between the laws of the Union and those of the states which they afterwards discarded. This temporary preference was the legislative negative power previously mentioned and for which the present system of paragraph 2. VI. was substituted.

No. 3.

Of the proposed and rejected federal legislative power of negativing state legislation, as showing the Framers' intentions concerning the relation of federal authority to conflicts between the laws of the Union and those of the states.

The history of the legislative negative is of much importance in connection with the history of the other measure which was a substitute for it. A comparative view of the history of both measures is necessary for ascertaining the full intentions of the Framers. It will show that, when they changed their minds as to one measure, and preferred another, they did not change their minds as to the object, which both measures were intended to secure. The legislative negative, that is to say, a congressional power of negativing all state laws conflicting with the laws of the Union, was self-evidently intended to secure the execution of the laws of the Union in all *casus foederis* in spite of the opposition of any state legislature to the contrary.

No. 4

Of the origin and purposes of the legislative negative method.

It was avowedly an imitation of the old colonial prerogative of the English crown by which the king had power to negative all colonial laws conflicting with the laws or policy of the metropolitan country. From a constitutional point of view, the proposed negative power was as much the means of securing the execution of the laws of the Union as the king's prerogative was a means of securing the execution of the laws of the British empire. Such a return to the old polity was ardently advocated by certain Framers, especially Madison and Charles Pinckney. It had that particular hold on its advocates, which an apparently feasible plan of political restoration often has on the best minds. But it was in the end found to be practically incapable of limitation and definition in a written constitution. It was held to be certain "to disgust the states," and well it might. In its place the plan of a judicial discrimination under a general *clausula nonobstante* was substituted. In accordance therewith, paragraph 2. VI. was elaborated by degrees and framed as now written in the constitution

No. 5.

Of the relation of paragraph 2. VI. to the beginning of section 2. III.

Now, it is true, as will be subsequently pointed out, that paragraph 2. VI. gravely affected the framing of a third or judicial article. The cases in law and equity in paragraph 1, section 2, article III, were intended to be adapted to the law of paragraph 2. VI. All the *casus* named in one text

were intended to be *aptati* to the *jus* of the other text.
More briefly, those two portions of the constitution were
intended to be twin texts. This important fact should not,
however, mislead students of the constitution into thinking
that the system of paragraph 2. VI. is to be exclusively regarded as part only of a mere judicial plan and as merely a
jure dicundo institution. It is something more than that.
It is not merely a judicial institution. It is also one for securing the execution of the laws of the Union in the different *casus foederis*. In this respect, it has the same object
as the legislative negative had. This, it is contended, is
shown by the historical evidence relating to the legislative
negative, its nature, its provisional adoption and final
rejection.

Before rehearsing that evidence, it is proper to give specific evidence showing that the Framers intended paragraph
2. VI. and the beginning of section 2. III. to be twin texts.

Article 8 of the draft corresponds to paragraph 2. VI. of
the constitution. On August 25th, Madison made a motion
that after the words, "all treaties made," in said article 8,
the further words, "or which shall be made," should be inserted. This motion passed *nem. con.**

The beginning of section 3. of draft article 11. corresponds
to the beginning of section 2. III. of the constitution. On
August 27th, on motion of Rutledge, certain words were
struck out of the said draft text, and "after the words
"United States were inserted, *nem. con.*, the words, 'and
" 'treaties made or which shall be made under their author-
" 'ity,' *conformably to a preceding amendment in another
"place.*"†

There is thus clear and direct evidence that the treaty
clauses in paragraph 2. VI. and the beginning of section 2.
III. respectively were avowedly made twin texts relating
to each other. If this be true of those clauses, it must be
true of the other portion of the texts as well, as the mere
collation thereof suffices to show. That is to say, that the
beginning of section 2. III. :

---

* Elliot V. 478.

† Ib. 483.

"The judicial power shall extend to all cases, in law and "equity, arising under this constitution, the laws of the " United States, and treaties made, or which shall be made, "under their authority "—and paragraph 2. VI. :

" This constitution, and the laws of the United States which "shall be made in pursuance thereof ; and all treaties made, "or which shall be made, under the authority of the United " States, shall," etc.,—are twin texts and relate to each other as such.

No. 6.

The history of the legislative negative in the convention examined, in order to ascertain the intentions of the Framers concerning judicial competency in cases of conflict between the laws of the Union and those of the states.

The evidence relating to the intentions of the Framers, which is derived from the history of the finally rejected legislative negative, will now be rehearsed.

In a paper written late in his life, Madison was of the opinion that the earliest written sketch of a " constitutional "government of the Union," which resembled the present one, was, perhaps, that given in his letters to Jefferson, Randolph and Washington, dated in 1787 on March 19th, April 8th, and 16th, respectively. In connection with this subject he observes that " the feature in these letters which "rested in the general authority, a negative on the laws of "the states, was suggested by the negative in the head of "the British empire, which prevented collisions between "the parts and the whole, and between the parts them- "selves. It was supposed that the substitute of an elective " and responsible authority, for an hereditary one, would "avoid the appearance even of a departure from republican- "ism. But although the subject was so viewed in the con- " vention, and the votes on it were more than once equally "divided, it was finally and justly abandoned, as, apart "from other objections, it was not practicable among so "many states, increasing in number, and enacting, each of "them, so many laws. *Instead of the proposed negative,* "*the objects of it were left as finally provided for in the* "*constitution.*"

It will here be observed that Madison thus held that "the "objects" of the negative, *viz.*, the preventing of collisions between the Union and the states, were not abandoned with that measure, but "were left as finally provided for in the "constitution." He says nothing about the constitutional provisions for such objects being incidental or merely incidental to the judiciary of the Union as a federal institution.

In the convention, on May 29th, Randolph presented his plan for the Articles of Union on behalf of Virginia. Its 6th resolution contained a clause providing that the national legislature "ought to be empowered to negative all laws "passed by the legislatures of the several states contraven-"ing, in the opinion of the national legislature, the Articles "of Union."* On May 31st, this clause was agreed to and enlarged so as to include a negative of state laws contravening "treaties subsisting under the authority of the Union."† On June 8th, the amended clause was reconsidered, and Charles Pinckney moved to alter it so as to give the national legislature power "to negative all the laws which to them "shall appear improper." ‡ This motion was lost by a vote of 7 to 3 with one state divided, after a prolonged debate. The matter thus was formally left as it stood before, that is to say, a limited negative was supported by the committee of the whole, while an unlimited negative was rejected.

The inherent difficulties of the negative had, however, shown themselves. Randolph's resolutions, as altered and added to, were on June 19th ordered by the committee of the whole to be reported to the house, which was accordingly done. Thus at that date the Framers were formally, though provisionally, committed to a limited negative. But the difficulty of "drawing the line of jurisprudence" limiting such a power had been discovered and had sapped the powerful support which it originally had. In the meantime

* Elliott V. 127.

† Ib. 139.

‡ Journal p. 109.

the plan of confederation, offered by Patterson on behalf of New Jersey, had been considered. Although rejected as a whole, part of that plan was subsequently the bridge by which the convention escaped from the legislative negative in every shape and reached what is now paragraph 2. VI.

On July 17th, the legislative negative was again considered, and, although it was not the last time at which its advocates secured a hearing, it was then finally rejected. By a vote of 7 states to 3, the convention rejected the clause of the 6th resolution of the committee of the whole empowering the national legislature " to negative all laws passed by " the several states contravening, in the opinion of the " national legislature, the Articles of Union, or any treaties " subsisting under the authority of the Union."

The debate was as important as it was decisive.

G. Morris, Sherman and L. Martin opposed the negative, Madison and Charles Pinckney advocated it.

Madison observed that "a power of negativing the im- " proper laws of the states is at once the most mild and cer- " tain means of preserving the harmony of the system. Its " utility is sufficiently displayed in the British system. " Nothing could maintain the harmony and subordination " of the various parts of the empire, but the prerogative by " which the crown stifles in its birth every act of every part " tending to discord and encroachment."

G. Morris said, that he "was more and more opposed to " a negative. The proposal of it would disgust all the " states. A law that ought to be negatived will be set aside " in the judiciary department, and, if that security should " fail, may be repealed by a national law."

Sherman said that "such a power involves a wrong prin- " ciple, to wit, that a law of a state contrary to the Articles " of Union, would, if not negatived, be valid and opera- " tive."*

In finally rejecting the legislative negative, and overruling its previous action, the convention took a step backwards, only to make a leap forwards. Luther Martin's motion in favour of the plan of what is now paragraph 2. VI.,

---

* Elliot V. 321, 322.

was, as before stated, immediately offered and adopted without opposition, and apparently without debate. Such action is incomprehensible, if the Framers intended to abandon what had been their avowed object, as well as abandon the measure by which they had intended previously to secure that object. In first adopting and then discarding a legislative negative to be applied with legislative discrimination, and substituting therefor a judicial discrimination applying a general clause of derogation, they intended only to change the means of accomplishing their object, and not to abandon that object itself.

The last observation does not, however, depend merely upon inference, for, subsequently the legislative negative secured a re-hearing in the proceedings on the draft constitution. This was on August 23rd, and the debate throws important light upon the point in question. On that day, shortly after Rutledge had carried his amendment inserting the words "this constitution" in article 8 of the draft (now paragraph 2. VI.), Charles Pinckney made a last effort in favour of the legislative negative. His motion to adopt it coupled it with a proviso requiring a two-thirds vote in both houses. This proposition was not intended to be a substitute for the plan of paragraph 2. VI., but to be an additional method of settling conflicts between the laws of the Union and those of the states.* Five speakers avowed themselves favourable to Pinckney's idea in some form, while five opposed it, and one doubted.†

Williamson "thought it unnecessary, and having already "been decided, a revival was a waste of time."

Wilson advocated the measure, saying that "the firmness "of judges is not, of itself, sufficient." This remark of Wilson, though brief, is decisive upon the point in consideration. The plan adopted and the plan rejected had both the

---

* The great point as to the judiciary of the constitution is that state execution was imposed on state judiciaries and them only by name, and that federal execution was carried out by the federal *judiciary par excellence*. That is to say, federal execution is normally judicially regulated and caused to be executed. Federal execution *sub judicibus per officiales executivos.*

† Elliot V. 468.

same object. Wilson does not speak of state judges, but of judges in general.

Madison favoured Pinckney's measure and moved to commit it, which motion was negatived by six states to five, when Pinckney withdrew his proposition.

Thus ended all chance of reviving the rejected plan of a legislative negative in the nature of the old royal prerogative. The place which such a plan had once temporarily held in the favour of the Framers was permanently occupied by another, *viz.*, the legislative rule of judicial decision, which paragraph 2. VI. now prescribes for settling conflicts between the constitution or other laws of the Union and any contradictory constitutions or laws of the states.

From the foregoing review, it is contended to be a true conclusion that the legislative rule of judicial decision prescribed by paragraph 2. VI. was intended by the convention to be a general disposition for settling the conflicts aforesaid and was not limited to the courts of the several states, but comprehended also the Supreme Court of the constitution and such future courts of the United States as Congress might constitute. If this be true, it is correct to affirm proposition 3d on page 294, *viz.*, that the Framers of the constitution actually intended that the U. S. Supreme Court should be competent in all litigations before it to decide upon this questioned (federal) constitutionality of state laws and state constitutions and to hold the same to be void in so far as contrary to constitution and constitutional laws and treaties of the United States

CHAPTER XXXV.

Of the Framers' intentions concerning the competency of the U. S. Supreme Court to decide upon the questioned constitutionality of acts of Congress and to hold the same void when unconstitutional.

The next matter for consideration is proposition 4th, on page 294, concerning the intentions of the Framers, *viz.*, that the U. S. Supreme Court should be competent in all litigations before it, to decide upon the questioned constitutionality of U. S. laws, and to hold the same to be void when unconstitutional.

The evidence of the truth of this will be found in the proceedings of the convention in framing the text of the clause, which is the beginning of section 2. III., which reads :

"The judicial power shall extend to all cases in law and "equity arising under this constitution, the laws of the "United States and treaties made, or which shall be made, "under their authority."

The history of the formation of this text may be begun by quoting Randolph's and Madison's motion, passed on June 13th, which reads :

"That the jurisdiction of the national judiciary shall ex-"tend to cases, which respect the collection of national "revenue, impeachments of any national officers, and ques-"tions which involve national peace and harmony." *

This resolution is repeated *verbatim* in the series of resolutions reported, June 19th, by the committee of the whole, being resolution the 13th.†

---

* Journal, 121.

† Ib. 137.

On July 18th, the clause of "impeachments of national "officers" was stricken out and it was then unanimously resolved to alter the said 13th resolution, so as to read : "That the jurisdiction of the national judiciary shall extend " to cases arising under laws passed by the general legisla- "ture, and to such other questions as involve the national "peace and harmony."*

This resolution is reported *verbatim* in the series of resolu- tions, stated by the Journal to be referred to the first com- mittee of five with instructions to report a constitution, be- ing resolution the 16th.†

On August 6th, that committee reported the draft of a constitution. The beginning of the 3d section of its 11th article reads :

"The jurisdiction of the Supreme Court shall extend to "all cases arising under laws passed by the legislature of "the United States."

On August 27th, when the 11th article of the draft con- stitution was under consideration, and the above text was reached, the following proceedings took place as reported by Madison : ‡

"Dr. Johnson moved to insert the words '*this constitu-* "'*tion and the*' before the word 'laws.' Mr. Madison "doubted whether this was not going too far, to extend the "jurisdiction of the court *generally to cases arising under* "*the constitution*, and whether it ought not to *be limited* "*to cases of a judiciary nature. The right of expounding* "*the constitution, in cases not of this nature, ought not* "*to be given to that department.* The motion of Dr. John- "son was agreed to, *nem. con., it being generally supposed* "*that the jurisdiction given was constructively limited to* "*cases of a judiciary nature.*

"On motion of Mr. Rutledge the words 'passed by the "'legislature,' were stricken out ; and after the words, "' United States,' were inserted, *nem. con.*, the words, 'and

---

* Journal, 188, 189.

† Ib. 212, 207, 199. On July 20th, the executive made removable by impeach- ment. 5 Elliot, 343.

‡ Elliot V. 483.

" 'treaties made or which shall be made under their author-
" 'ity,' conformably to a preceding amendment in another
" place."

The beginning of the section thus then read : " *The juris-*
"*diction of the Supreme Court* shall extend to all cases
" arising under this constitution and the laws of the United
" States and treaties made or which shall be made under
" their authority." In spite of the true construction of the
amended text being generally supposed in the convention
to mean that the jurisdiction of the Supreme Court, in
cases arising under the constitution, was extended to cases
of a judiciary nature and not extended to all cases generally
whether judicial or extrajudicial, Madison was not satisfied.
Not long after, while this section was still under consideration, he says : " Mr. Madison and Mr. Gouverneur Morris
"moved to strike out the beginning of the third section,
" 'The jurisdiction of the Supreme Court,' and to insert
" the words, ' the judicial power' which was agreed to *nem.*
"*con.*" The section thus then read : " *The judicial power*
" shall extend to all cases arising under," etc.

The constitution itself now reads : " The judicial power
"shall extend to all cases *in law and equity* arising
" under," etc.

"The judicial power," intended by the Framers when
making the said amendment was the judicial power of the
United States, both in law and equity, as mentioned in section 3, of article 11. of the draft, which, as previously
amended, thus read at that particular moment : " The judi-
" cial power of the United States, both in law and equity,
" shall be vested in one Supreme Court, and in such inferior
" courts as shall, when necessary, from time to time, be
" constituted by the legislature of the United States."

It is thus clear the Framers expressly intended that the
judicial power of the United States should *not* extend to
constitutional cases of an *extrajudicial* nature arising under
the new constitution. It is equally clear, however, that
they expressly intended that the said judicial power should
positively extend to constitutional cases of a judiciary or
judicial nature arising under the constitution. There was

no doubt or anxiety among the Framers upon this head. Their only anxiety was to prevent the jurisdiction of the Supreme Court from extending to constitutional cases of an extrajudicial nature. On that August 27th, it was twice provided that jurisdiction should extend to constitutional cases of a judicial nature. The first provision was the text of the draft as amended in Johnson's motion. This first provision gave rise to the first case of constitutional construing on record. The words, "the jurisdiction of the Supreme "Court shall extend to all cases arising under this consti-"tution," were construed by the Framers to mean that the jurisdiction was constructively limited to cases of a judicial nature, that is to say, expressly extended to cases of a judicial nature and not further to cases of an extrajudicial nature. On second thought, they were not satisfied with this merely constructive meaning for their words and substituted the other words, which were selected because expressly and not constructively importing their intended meaning. By this substitution the text read: "The *judi-*"*cial power* shall extend to all cases arising under this "constitution." The express meaning of the new text and the construed meaning of the old text thus perfectly coincided. This meaning was later in the day reaffirmed by the insertion of the words, "both in law and equity," upon a motion which could have occasioned no debate, for Madison does not mention it, although it is of course recorded in the Journal.*

It was thus generally assumed in the convention that all constitutional cases of a judicial nature were just as much extended to by the judicial power, as all statutory cases of a judicial nature. That is to say, cases of a judicial nature, which involved the constitutional validity of legislative acts enacted under the constitution, were just as much extended to, as judicial cases involving the statutory validity of executive acts performed under a statute.

From the foregoing it can not be doubted that the con-

---

* Journal, 300. Those words were incorporated in the revised draft reported on September 12th, from which the word "both" was struck out, by a motion of September 15th. Journal, 383, 384.

vention intended that the judicial power should comprehend competency to ascertain whether an act of Congress
be a law made under the constitution or not, and, if not so
made, to hold it to be no law thereunder. The propriety
of a judicial competency so to act was generally accepted.
The anxiety was to confine the Supreme Court to judicial
action and to prevent it from exercising a general jurisdiction in constitutional cases, whether of a judicial or extrajudicial nature.

The generation of 1876 and 1877 learned to its cost, how
well founded were Madison's fears of the judiciary ming-
ling in extrajudicial controversies. Righteous history records the wrongful termination of the presidential crisis of
1876 and 1877. The year of the hundreth anniversary of
independence began in hope and ended in fear. It closed
during the execution of a *coup d' état* by which military
force, under the control of the party in power, nullified the
election of a President. On the 4th of March, 1877, men
witnessed the triumph of the un-American conspiracy. On
that ill-omened day, the wrong was consummated by an in-
stallation of a President, which was made under such evil
auspices, that no augur could have called it an inaugura-
tion.

In the conflict between the two houses of Congress upon
the counting of the votes, the expedient of an electoral
commission as arbiter was resorted to. Although the commission was extrajudicial, three judges, being one-third of
a full Supreme Court, were made members thereof. The
commission was so constituted, that these judges had power
to turn the scale whichever way two of them might decide.
Thus one-third of the Supreme Court were brought into direct relation with the Senate and indirect relation with the
army. The army was behind the Senate.

The Senate was armed. The House of Representatives
was unarmed. Its only hope was in the mediation of the
judges. That hope failed it.

Two matters of the gravest moment here require consideration.

First : The case was avowedly an extrajudicial one. It

was a controversy between the two houses of Congress. It is, therefore, distinct from cases arising under the constitution to which the judicial power unquestionably extends. It is also distinct from those cases arising under the constitution, as to which it has been questioned whether the judicial power does or does not extend to them. The controversy between the Senate and the House was *avowedly* an extrajudicial one. It was necessarily so, according to the form of government.

Second : What the Framers thought the whole Supreme Court could not do, one-third of the court failed to do, *viz.*, intervene as mediators in an extrajudicial controversy to the satisfaction of both opposing parties. The foregoing pages of this chapter show that such an intervention of the judges of the Supreme Court in the extrajudicial controversy between the Senate and the House was made in direct contradiction to the express intentions of the Framers. They expressly intended that the Supreme Court should not have jurisdiction of extrajudicial controversies arising under the constitution.

Was this drawing of judges of the Supreme Court into an extrajudicial controversy an isolated case ? Or is it to be a precedent for the future, whenever elections fail to elect ? That Madison was indeed prescient, is proved by the dire event now known. Did he forsee others, like it, yet to come ? God forbid !

Before dismissing the present topic an additional remark is not improper. In striking out the words "the jurisdic-"tion of the Supreme Court," and substituting the words, "the judicial power," important consequences followed as to the context in the draft. The draft of the constitution contained a chain of four clauses, which were linked together by the iterative use of the word "jurisdiction." In the corresponding portion of the constitution that word is used twice only. The first of the four clauses has been changed as mentioned. The second and third retain the terms, "original jurisdiction," and "appellate jurisdic-"tion," respectively. The fourth clause of the draft related to the U. S. inferior courts and the nature of the "jurisdiction" which they might receive. This clause was struck out and no clause whatsoever was inserted in the constitution mentioning the jurisdiction of the U. S. inferior courts. Thus the frame of the whole judicial article of the draft was changed by the alteration of the first, and the omission of the fourth, of its jurisdiction clauses. From what has been said above, it seems that the fear of an extrajudicial jurisdiction of the Supreme Court had a good deal to do with breaking the chain of four jurisdiction clauses found in the draft. That fear has consequently a place in the history of the formation of the constitutional text, which deserves the fullest investigation.

In conclusion, it is contended that the foregoing shows that it is correct to affirm proposition 4th on page 294, namely, that the Framers actually intended that the U. S. Supreme Court should be competent in all litigations before it, to decide upon the questioned constitutionality of U. S. laws, and to hold the same void when unconstitutional.

CHAPTER XXXVI.

Of the intentions of the Framers concerning appeals from the state judiciaries to the U. S. Supreme Court.

No. 1. *Of the 5th and 6th propositions concerning the Framers' intentions.*

No. 2. *Examination of the debates and proceedings of the convention, in order to ascertain their intentions concerning the said propositions.*

No. 3. *Of certain views of Chief Justice Marshall on pages 376, 377 of 6 Wheaton.*

No. 4. *Further examination of the debates of the Framers made requisite by the said views of Marshall.*

Chapter 36. will be devoted to the two propositions concerning the intentions of the Framers still remaining for consideration.

No. 1.

Of the 5th and 6th propositions concerning the Framers' intentions.

These propositions maintain that the Framers actually intended,

Fifth : that whenever the judiciary of a state in any litigation should decide the question of (federal) constitutionality in favour of the state law or state constitution, impeached as wholly or in part so unconstitutional, there should be a right of appeal to the U. S. Supreme Court upon that question :

Sixth : and tha whenever the judiciary of a state in any litigation should decide the question of constitutionality against the U. S. law impeached as unconstitutional, there should be a right of appeal to the U. S. Supreme Court upon that question.

These propositions may be considered together. In a strict sense they are not within the limits of the subject of this Essay. If true, however, they elucidate the subject. If it also be true, that the law of the constitution on these heads accords with the intentions of those who framed its text, an edifying comparison with its law on the subject of this Essay will be furnished.

No. 2.

Examination of the debates and proceedings of the convention, in order to ascertain their intentions concerning the said proposition.

The debates and proceedings of the convention will now be examined in connection with the foregoing propositions.

The first clause of Randolph's ninth resolution provided,
" that a national judiciary be established, to consist of one or
" more supreme tribunals and of inferior tribunals." On
June 4th, the first part of this clause was agreed to by the convention unanimously. The second was amended so as to read,
"to consist of one supreme tribunal, and one or more
"inferior tribunals," and in that shape passed in the
affirmative.*

On the next day, June 5th, there was a reconsideration
of the clause when the following proceedings took place.†

" Mr. Rutledge having obtained a rule for reconsideration
" of the clause for establishing *inferior* ‡ tribunals under
" the national authority, now moved that that part of the
" clause in the ninth resolution should be expunged ; argu-
" ing *that the state tribunals might and ought to be left,*
" *in all cases, to decide in the first instance, the right of*
" *appeal to the supreme national tribunal being sufficient to*
" *secure the national rights and uniformity of judgment ;*
" that it was making unnecessary encroachments upon juris-
" diction of the states, and creating unnecessary obstacles
" to their adoption of the new system.

" Mr. Sherman seconded the motion.

" Mr. Madison observed, that, unless inferior tribunals
" were dispersed throughout the republic with *final* ‡ juris-
" diction in *many* cases, ‡ appeals would be multiplied to a
" most oppressive degree ; that, besides, in many cases an ap-
" peal would not be a remedy. What was to be done after im-
" proper verdicts, in state tribunals, obtained under the biased
" directions of a dependent judge, or the local prejudices of
" an undirected jury ? To remand the cause for a new trial
" would answer no purpose. To order a new trial at the
" supreme bar would oblige the parties to bring up their
" witnesses, though ever so distant from the seat of the
" court. An effective judiciary establishment, commen-

---

* Journal 97, 98.   Elliot V. 155.

† Elliot V. 158, 159, 160.

‡ Original italics.

" surate to the legislative authority, was essential. A gov-
" ernment without a proper executive and judiciary would
" be a mere trunk of a body, without arms or legs to act or
" move.

" Mr. Wilson opposed the motion on like grounds. He
" said, the admiralty jurisdiction ought to be given wholly
" to the national government, as it related to cases not with-
" in the jurisdiction of a particular state, and to a scene in
" which controversies with foreigners would be most likely
" to happen.

" Mr. Sherman was in favor of the motion. He dwelt
" chiefly on the supposed expensiveness of having a new
" set of courts, when the state courts would answer the same
" purpose.

" Mr. Dickinson contended strongly, that *if there was to*
" *be a national legislature, there ought to be a national*
" *judiciary, and that the former ought to have authority*
" *to institute the latter.*

" On the question for Mr. Rutledge's motion to strike out
" ' inferior tribunals,' it passed in the affirmative. Connec-
" ticut, New York, New Jersey, North Carolina, South
" Carolina, Georgia, ay, 6; Pennsylvania, Delaware, Mary-
" land, Virginia, no, 4; Massachusetts divided.

" Mr. Wilson and Mr. Madison then moved in pursuance
" of the idea expressed by Mr. Dickinson, to add to the
" ninth resolution the words following: 'that the national
" ' legislature be empowered to institute inferior tribunals.'
" They observed, that there was a distinction between es-
" tablishing such tribunals absolutely, and giving a discre-
" tion to the legislature to establish or not to establish them.
" They repeated the necessity of some such provision.

" Mr. Butler. The people will not bear such innovations.
" The states will revolt at such encroachments. Supposing
" such an establishment to be useful, we must not venture
" it. We must follow the example of Solon, who gave the
" Athenians, not the best government he could devise, but
" the best they would receive.

" Mr. King remarked, as to the comparative expense, *that*
" *the establishment of inferior tribunals would cost infin-*

" *itely less than the appeals that would be prevented by*
" *them.*

"On this question, as moved by Mr. Wilson and Mr.
" Madison,——Massachusetts, New Jersey, Pennsylvania,
" Delaware, Maryland, Virginia, North Carolina, ay, 8 ;
"Connecticut, South Carolina, no, 2 ; New York divided
" (in printed Journal, New Jersey, no)."

The foregoing debate and resolution are dated June 5th,
or five days after the convention had resolved that the legislature of the Union should have power to negative all
state laws contravening the articles, laws and treaties of the
Union.   On July 17th the project of such a legislative negative power was discarded and in its place was substituted
the present plan of judicial discrimination in applying the
general derogation of a *nonobstante* clause to state laws
contrariant to federal laws.

The precise date on which this change was made must
not be forgotten, for on the next day, July 18th, the following action and debate took place.*

" The twelfth resolution [of the committee of the whole]
" 'that the national legislature be empowered to appoint
" 'inferior tribunals,' being taken up,——

" Mr. Butler could see no necessity for such tribunals.
" *The state tribunals might do the business.*

" Mr. L. Martin concurred.   They will create jealousies
"and oppositions in the state tribunals, with the jurisdic-
" tion of which they will interfere.

" Mr. Gorham. There are in the states already federal
" courts, with jurisdiction for the trial of piracies, &c., com-
"mitted on the high seas.   No complaints have been made
"by the states or the courts of the states.   Inferior tribu-
" nals are essential to render the authority of the national
" legislature effectual.

" Mr. Randolph observed, that the courts of the states
"can not be trusted with the administration of national
"laws.   The objects of jurisdiction are such as will often
" place the general and local policy at variance.

" Mr. Gouverneur Morris urged the necessity of such a
" provision.

* Elliot V. 331.

" Mr. Sherman *was willing to give the power to the leg-*
" *islature, but wished them to make use of the state tribu-*
" *nal, whenever it could be done with safety to the gen-*
" *eral interest.*" [*This observation of Sherman's is deci-*
sive upon the question. If the legislature of the Union
could make use of the state tribunals instead of using in-
ferior U. S. tribunals, appeals from the former must have
been as much intended as appeals from the latter.]

"Col. Mason thought that circumstances might arise,
" which could not be now foreseen, which might render
" such a power absolutely necessary.

"On the question for agreeing to the twelfth resolution,
"empowering the national legislature to appoint inferior
"tribunals, it was agreed to, *nem. con.*"*

On August 27th, Dickinson moved to amend the draft by
providing that the judges might be removed by the executive on the application of both houses of Congress.† This
motion was defeated, only one state present voting for it.
In the debate, Rutledge, the chairman of the committee
whose draft of constitution was under discussion, said :

" *If the Supreme Court was the judge between the United*
" *States and the particular states, this alone would be an*
" *insuperable objection to the motion.*"

Rutledge's observation could not, of course, have alluded
to suits between the United States and any particular state,
whether the former sued or was sued by the latter. No
such suits were ever thought of by the Framers.‡ He could
only have referred to the U. S. Supreme Court judging decisively and differently from the judges of a particular state
as to conflicts between the laws of the Union and those of
such state. He must therefore have meant appeals to the
U. S. Supreme Court from the state courts, in which the
appellant claimed that the latter had decided such conflicts
adversely to the laws of the Union.

---

* Elliot V. 331.

† Ib. 481.

‡ The fact that the United States can not sue a state is one of great moment
in constitutional jurisprudence, to which the writer's attention was called
many years ago by a distinguished jurist of a past generation.

A consideration of the foregoing extracts, it is maintained, shows the following points to be correct,

First : that at one time the Framers decided that there should be only one judicial tribunal of the Union, to which as a supreme court appeals from the state judiciaries should be made in litigations of national cognizance, and that for the mass of such litigations state courts should be tribunals of first instance.   This would have been the judicial system of the constitution, if Rutledge's motion had been adhered to.

Second : that a jurisdiction of the U. S. courts, which would be absolutely exclusive of any jurisdiction of the state courts as to all possible federal questions, cases, causes, suits, processes, points and rights, would necessitate a positive and actual establishment of a full system of inferior courts of the United States in the body of the constitution itself ; a thing which the Framers expressly avoided.

Third : that the system actually adopted is a *media sententia* between the two foregoing ; which system is one by which every inferior court is ordained and established by legislation found in some act of Congress and not in the constitution itself.   *This system was originated by Dickinson and may be called by his name.**

Fourth : that whenever the judiciary of a state should adjudicate a litigation which is claimed to be within the terms of paragraph 2. VI., and should refuse to be bound by the constitutional text or by the U. S. law or treaty invoked, an appeal was intended to lie to the U. S. Supreme Court.

No. 3.

Of certain views of C. J. Marshall on pages 376, 377 of 6 Wheaton, which here require consideration.

If Chief Justice Marshall's views on pages 376 and 377 of 6 Wheaton be correct, what the Framers refused to do, as

---

* How much of the constitution may be traced to an origin in Dickinson's mind, is a most interesting question. Perhaps, a full answer may show that a very great part of it may be traced to such an origin.

well as what they resolved to do, ought to be considered, in order to fully appreciate their intentions concerning the appeals in question. On those pages of the opinion in Cohens *v.* Virginia, he lays great stress upon the first two points urged by the defence against the jurisdiction of the court. They were, first, that a state was defendant and, second, that no writ of error lies from the U. S. Supreme Court to a state court. He strenuously denies the correctness of these points and observes :

"The questions presented to the court by the two first "points made at the bar are of the first magnitude, and "may be truly said to affect the Union. They exclude the "inquiry, whether the constitution and laws of the United "States have been violated by the judgment which the "plaintiffs in error seek to review; and, maintain, that, "admitting such violation, it is not in the power of the gov-"ernment to apply a corrective. They maintain, that the "nation does not possess a department capable of restrain-"ing peaceably, and by authority of law, any attempts "which may be made, by a part, against the legitimate "powers of the whole ; and that the government is reduced "to the alternative of submitting to such attempts, or of re-"sisting them by force. They maintain that the constitu-"tion of the United States has provided no tribunal for the "final construction of itself, or of the laws or treaties of the "nation ; but that this power may be exercised in the last "resort by the courts of every state in the union. That the "constitution, laws, and treaties may receive as many con-"structions as there are states ; and that this is not a mis-"chief, or if a mischief, is irremediable."

Marshall thus asserts the existence of a dilemma. One horn is department of government proceeding peacefully in the cases in question. Practically this means under the constitution appeals from the state judiciaries to the U. S. Supreme Court in such cases. The other horn is the whole (*i. e.* the union) using force against a part (*i. e.* a state) in the cases in question.

If Marshall's view be correct, the Framers were substantially in such a dilemma as to the cases in question : that is

to say, a dilemma, one horn of which required them to decide
upon a department of government proceeding peaceably
either by legislative or by judicial power, while the other
horn required them to decide upon the union proceeding by
the use of force against a state. After the rejection of the
legislative negative, they were not merely substantially, but
formally, in it.

Cohens *v.* Virginia was decided in 1821, that is to say,
after the publication of the Journal of the Convention, but
prior to that of Madison's report of its debates. It is,
therefore, necessary to examine those debates in connection
with the journal for any light they may throw upon Marshall's dilemma.

No. 4.

*Further consideration of the Framers' debates and pro-
ceedings, made requisite by the said views of Marshall.*

The two measures for meeting the difficulty of conflicts
between the laws of the Union and those of the states, upon
which the Framers' views have been rehearsed, were the legislative negative power and that actually adopted in paragraph 2. VI. These two measures, however, by no means
cover the whole ground considered by the convention.
Neither Patterson's nor Randolph's plan relied simply on
one of the measures aforesaid. Each backed the operation
of its respective measure with another proposed institution
which was common to both. This institution was federal
execution by the Union against any state violating the new
Articles of Union in any *casus foederis.* That is to say, if
any state should oppose the judicial application of the legislative derogation in one plan, or the legislative exercise of
the negative power in the other, the Union could proceed
by federal execution against such state to secure the fulfil-
ment of its obligation as a member of the Union.

One of the clauses of Randolph's 6th resolution declared
that the national legislature ought to be empowered " to call
" forth the force of the Union against any member of the

" Union failing to fulfil its duty under the articles thereof."*
On May 31st., this clause was considered. Madison was
apparently the only speaker, saying that "he hoped that
"such a system would be framed as might render this re-
"source unnecessary, and moved that the clause be post-
"poned." † This motion was agreed to unanimously and
the measure was in substance, though not in form, definitely
rejected.

The Framers did not take long to act thus upon the head
of federal execution against a state. One reason for such
promptness was, undoubtedly, the fact that the proposal of
such an institution had been long before the country. The
origin of Randolph's federal execution clause is to be found
in the plan of a confederation of the United States, which
was submitted in 1778 to the legislature of South Carolina
by William Henry Drayton. The 8th article of Drayton's
plan prescribed that in case any state should in any respect
violate the proposed articles of confederation, "the Congress
"shall, within one year thereafter, declare such state *under*
"*the ban of the confederacy*, and by the utmost vigour of
"arms forthwith proceed against such state, until it shall
"have paid due obedience, upon which *the ban shall be ta-*
"*ken off.*"‡

The use of the term "ban" in the foregoing is alone sufficient to show that Drayton's model in drafting his 8th
article was the public law of the then German empire.
Reference by Madison in the convention to the ban of the
German empire will be found in Elliot V. 210.§ In the
present German empire a similar institution, that of federal
execution against a state, is expressly provided for. Article 19. of the existing constitution of that empire is thus
translated by the writer: "If the members of the federation
"do not fulfil their constitutional federal duties, they can
"be held thereto by way of *execution*. This execution is

---

* Journal, p. 68.

† Elliot V. 140.

‡ Niles : Principles and Acts of the Revolution, ed. 1876, p. 368.

§ *Cf.* Weiske's *Rechtslexikon*, I. 604.

"to be decreed by the federal council and done by the
"emperor." *

It may be added that the members of the federation are
the several states of the empire and that the execution is
frequently termed federal execution.†

In connection with the term "execution" thus used in a
constitution written in 1871, Mason's remarks on June 20th,
1787, (Elliot V. 217) in the Framers' convention upon the
subject of "military execution," may be referred to. Mason's remarks and Drayton's 8th article, taken together,
show that the words *ban* and *execution* have both been used
in America in the same federal sense as the corresponding
words *Acht* and *Execution* in Germany.‡ It may be added
that federal execution against a state is a well known German institution, of which other examples may be given. It
existed in the former Germanic Federation both in theory
and practice. Under the operation thereof was made "the
"Ordinance for Federal Execution" of August 3d, 1820
(*Bundes-Executionsordnung*). § It also existed in the
North German Federation, the predecessor of the present
federal empire. By the North German constitution "the
"execution can be extended unto sequestration of the par-
"ticular land and of its power of government." The date
of this provision was 1867.‖

Federal execution by armed process against a state in certain *casus foederis* was also proposed by Patterson's plan
of new articles of the old confederation. The 2d paragraph
of his 7th resolution relates thereto, and has been previously
quoted.¶ It provides that "if *any state*, or any body of
"men in any state," shall oppose or prevent the carrying
into execution of federal acts or treaties, the federal executive shall be authorized to call forth the power of the con-

---

* See the text of constitution in L. von Roenne's *Verfassung des Deutschen
Reiches*, ed. 5th, p. 84.

† See von Roenne's cited work, index, under *Bundesexecution* and *Bundes-
staaten.*

‡ *Cf.* Weiske : on *Acht*, in article *Bann*.

§ L. von Roenne : *Staatsrecht des Deutschen Reiches*, ed. 2, vol. I, p. 72, note.

‖ L. von Roenne's first cited work, note on p. 84.

¶ Page 314 *ante.*

federated states, to enforce and compel obedience to such acts, or an observance of such treaties. *

Now the 15th and 18th clauses of section 8. I. of the constitution prescribe that Congress shall have power "to pro-"vide for calling forth the militia to execute the laws of the "Union" and "to make all laws which shall be necessary "and proper for carrying into *execution* the foregoing" power. The similarity of these constitutional provisions to one branch of the dispositions of the 2d paragraph of Patterson's 6th resolution is obvious. This makes all the more marked the fact that the Framers did not frame a text following the other branch of those dispositions, *viz.*, that which prescribed the use of federal arms *against a state* because it opposed or prevented the *execution* of federal acts and treaties. These dispositions the Framers did not copy, while copying the others, and while also copying the immediately previous paragraph, which made federal acts and treaties the supreme law of such opposing state, binding the judiciary of the state, notwithstanding any state laws containing things to the contrary.

It is clear from the foregoing that the absence of clauses in the new constitution relating to a ban of the Union and prescribing federal execution against a state under that ban, can not be attributed to inadvertence or want of consideration on the part of the Framers. The intentional absence of such clauses and the deliberate rejection of the legislative negative power have the following result, if Marshall's dilemma be a true one. Some judicial measure for meeting a case arising under the express provision of paragraph 2. VI. must have been intended by the Framers, that is to say, the case of a state judiciary erroneously or intentionally refusing to hold itself bound by the constitution or other law of the Union and, in its stead, applying and causing to be executed a contrariant state law or state constitution. If no judicial measure for meeting such a conflict was intended by the Framers, there was, according to the dilemma, a manifest lacuna in their measures for getting the laws of the Union executed.

---

* Elliot V. 192.

If there was actually such a lacuna, paragraph 2. VI. shows it to have been intentional, because that text creates the cases without which the lacuna would not exist.

It should here be added that such a lacuna existed in the Articles of Confederation, except as to appeals in cases of captures.

It may also be added that in the then existing German Empire, the *privilegium de non appellando* was a recognized institution deviating from the common law. By it, a prince of the Empire might secure exemption from appeals from his own to the imperial judiciary. Frederick the Great secured this *privilegium* for all his territories within the Empire.

The Framers had thus ample notice of the consequences of non-appellation to a federal from state judiciaries, both in America and Europe.

Assuming it to be true that before the rejection of the legislative negative the Framers were substantially, and after it formally, in Marshall's dilemma, what they did not do concerning federal execution against a state, and what they did do concerning the U. S. Supreme Court and affecting the judiciaries of the states, unite in proving that they intended to provide for appeals from the latter to the former, whenever it should be claimed that the latter unconstitutionally prevented the execution of the laws of the Union.

In conclusion, this chapter, it is contended, shows that it is correct to affirm the 5th and 6th propositions as to the intentions of the Framers, as stated on pages 294 and 295, *ante.*

CHAPTER XXXVII.

Of appeals from the inferior courts of the United States to the Supreme Court as existing under the constitution and as intended by the original draft of that instrument.

A subject distinct from, but relating to, the foregoing is that of appeals from the U. S. inferior courts to the U. S. Supreme Court. Some observations thereupon will now be useful for subsequent reference.

The legal existence of the appeals in question has never been questioned. The idea generally entertained of the nature of such an appeal is that it comes from an inferior court, in which original jurisdiction is inherent, to a supreme court, to which appellate jurisdiction is inherent, that is to say, from one court of native or inherent jurisdiction to another. If this be true of the constitution, it is, nevertheless, true that a different sort of appeal was proposed in the original draft of the constitution.

If the convention intended that the present sort of appeals should exist, they must have differed from the committee that framed the draft of the constitution. That committee must have intended that there should be a different sort of appeals from the inferior courts to the Supreme Court. Whether the convention clearly intended to differ from, or agree with, the committee, or failed to have any clear intentions as to the nature of such appeals, are very interesting questions. They need not be answered here. Another question may, however, well be answered, namely : what must have been intended by the committ...

as to the nature of such appeals according to the draft of the constitution reported by them.

The draft of the constitution, like the constitution itself, established one Supreme Court, but no inferior courts. Both documents provided for inferior courts being established by Congress from time to time.

The scheme of the judicial article of the draft, however, differed considerably from that of the constitution. By that article of the draft, the jurisdiction of the Supreme Court, and not the judicial power of the United States, extended to certain cases (and controversies) mentioned, including cases of impeachment. In a select number of those cases (and controversies), including cases of impeachment, that jurisdiction was to be original, and in all the other cases (and controversies) mentioned it was to be appellate. Any part of the jurisdiction of the Supreme Court, except that relating to cases of impeachment of the President of the United States, might be assigned to the inferior courts of the United States by congressional legislation. The last of these dispositions is contained in a clause, which is simply wonderful to constitutional students. It is so, because it is one mentioning the jurisdiction of the inferior courts, while the constitution contains no clause whatsoever mentioning their jurisdiction. The text of the draft is the final sentence of a section of four sentences, the first of which defines the extending of the jurisdiction of the Supreme Court (not that of the judicial power as in the constitution). This remarkable text reads thus : *

" The legislature may assign any part of the jurisdiction "above mentioned (except the trial of the President of the " United States) in the manner, and under the limitations, "which it shall think proper, to such inferior courts as it " shall constitute from time to time."

Thus, the jurisdiction of the inferior courts was an assigned jurisdiction, which was not native to, or inherent in, them, but was part or parts of a jurisdiction native to, or inherent in, that Supreme Court to which they were inferior. The jurisdiction of the inferior courts was a dative, not a

* Journal, pp. 226, 227.

native, jurisdiction which they could only get as assignees of the Supreme Court under acts of Congress. The clause just quoted is deserving of the profoundest attention. Fully to appreciate its dispositions, it must be recalled that the first of the four jurisdiction clauses of the draft prescribed, *inter alia*, that " the jurisdiction of the Supreme Court" should extend " to all cases of admiralty and maritime ju- " risdiction " and that the men who drafted that provision were professional lawyers who understood the legal prin- ciples of judicial procedure in admiralty.

These principles of procedure are those of the modern Civil Law, that is to say, those of the Roman law modified by the Canon law. From the point of view of these prin- ciples, the proper construction to be put upon the inferior courts of the draft, as assignees of the jurisdiction of a su- perior court that was new and living and not ancient and defunct, is as follows, *viz.*, they could only have been prop- erly and scientifically constituted as delegate or commis- sioned tribunals inferior to a Supreme Court that was either actually or constructively the sole tribunal delegating juris- diction to them according to, and in execution of, the as- signments of Congress. By the distinct dispositions of the draft their jurisdiction could only be one assigned to them as assignees of the Supreme Court. Their jurisdiction was not one inherent in themselves, but was derived from the Su- preme Court through the legislative assignments of the Con- gress by whose acts they would be constituted from time to time. Under such assignments there must have been either an actual or a constructive delegation of parts of its inher- ent jurisdiction made by the Supreme Court to the inferior courts in the assigned cases. Appeals to the Supreme Court from such inferior courts must have been actually or con- structively appeals, that were made to a delegating tribunal from delegate tribunals in delegated cases. They must have been appeals to a court of native or inherent jurisdiction from courts of dative or non-inherent jurisdiction.

If this conclusion be correct, the jurisdiction of the inferior courts according to the draft differed greatly from that which they have always exercised under the constitution.

The existing inferior courts are not tribunals of delegated jurisdiction. They are tribunals, whose jurisdiction is inherent and not assigned.

It is perfectly true, that the clause under consideration was struck out of the draft by an express motion of August 27th.,* but it is also true that it was the sole text mentioning the jurisdiction of the inferior courts and that nothing whatsoever was substituted in its place. Thus it came to pass that the constitution contains no text mentioning the jurisdiction of the inferior courts. The Committee intended that there should be such text, and inserted it in the draft. The convention struck out that text and omitted to insert another on the same subject.

If the omission of such a text was an error, it was a grave one, for it must make much difficulty in understanding the judicial part of the frame of the constitution and structure of the government. If no such error was committed, such difficulty may not exist. But error or no error, the omission was actually made.

The foregoing conclusion as to appeals from the inferior U. S. courts has an important bearing upon the subject of appeals from the state courts. The appellate jurisdiction clause of the constitution mentions the Supreme Court as a tribunal *ad quod*, but does not mention any tribunals *a quibus*. The corresponding clause of the draft did likewise, but it was followed by a context relating to the jurisdictions of both the supreme and inferior courts and the relation between the same. This context is expressive of so peculiar a dependency of the inferior courts upon the Supreme Court, that their not being designated as tribunals *a quibus* in any text must have been a different circumstance according to the draft from what it was and is under the constitution.

When this context was stricken from the draft, the state courts and the inferior courts were put in similar, perhaps in identical, predicaments, as to any consequences resulting from the omission to mention tribunals *a quibus* in the appellate jurisdiction clause of the new constitution.

The constitution was reported to Congress and submitted

* Journal, page 300, line 11.

by it to the several states for ratification or rejection by their respective popular conventions. How could those conventions understand the appellate jurisdiction clause? They would certainly understand it to refer to some tribunals *a quibus*. In the subsequent commentary upon the text of the appellate jurisdiction clause, it will be contended that it would be natural in them to think that it referred to the existing state courts, as well as to the future inferior courts, as tribunals *a quibus*.

APPENDICES.

APPENDIX No. 1.
(See Page 5.)

(This appendix was not sufficiently completed by the author, to justify its publication.)

APPENDIX No. 2.
(See Page 123.)

Sacrae Rotae Romanae Decisionum recentiorum a Paulo Rubeo J. C. Romano selectarum, Pars Decima. Ab Anno M.DC.XLVII. usque ad totum Annum M.DC.XLIX. Venetiis, M.DCC.XVI. Apud Paulum Balleonium. Superiorum permissu, ac privilegiis.

Reverendiss. P. D. Cerro, Sacrae Rotae Decano. Romana, seu Januen. Locorum Montium. Veneris 26, Junii 1648.

ARGUMENTUM.

Conditum in Ecclesia testamentum subjaceat ne statuto laicorum circa solemnitates illius. Clerici licèt possint in favorabilibus uti statutis laicorum, in iis tamen, quae in eisdem statutis contra libertatem Ecclesiasticam reperiuntur, uti nullo modo possunt etiam volentes.

SUMMARIUM.

1. *Testamentum conditum cum solis quinque testibus est nullum.*
2. *Teste uno deficiente in testamento corruit testamentum.*
3. *Immissio conceditur haeredi, qui exhibet testamentum non abolitur:, neque in aliqua parte cancellatum.*
4. *Statutum potest minuere numerum testium in testamento requisitum.*
   Statutum Januae sub rubr. de testamentis solum numerum quinque testium exposcit in illis, num. 4.
5. *Testamentum conditum in Ecclesia subjaceat ne statuto laicorum circa numerum testium, & num. seqq.*
6. *Statutum requirens majores solemnitates, quàm requirantur de jure civili in testamentis, dicitur odiosum.*
   Statutum dicitur favorabile, si solemnitates juris civilis in testamento diminuit, num. 6.
8. *Statutum contra libertatem Ecclesiasticam est ipso jure nullum, & num. 16.*
9. *Statutum etiam Clericis, & Ecclesiae favorabile, conditum à laicis est ipso jure nullum.*
10. *Statutum laicale ut nullius sit roboris, & momenti, sufficit, quod etiam virtualiter, & indirectè ericos tangat, & laedat.*
11. *Laici non possunt neque directè, neque indirectè de personis Ecclesiasticis, eorumque bonis disponere.*
12. *Clerici uti possunt per modum privilegii statutis laicorum in quantum faciunt pro se ipsis, & non acceptare sed reiicere id, quod facit contra se.*
13. *Clericus utens statutis laicorum, cogitur eis uti cum omnibus suis qualitatibus.*
    Limita, ut num. seqq.
14. *Conditiones, & qualitates ubi sunt diversae, & separatae ex acceptatione unius, non cogitur quis acceptare alias.*
17. *Clericus licèt acceptar possit statutum in favorabilibus, quatenus tamen facit contra se, etiam volens acceptare non potest.*

18. Clerici abstinere tenentur à negotiis laicorum.

19. Laici statuere nequeunt super re spirituali.

*20. Dipositio concernens favorem salutis aeternae, & ani-
nae sublevamentum, dicitur ad pias causas.*

*21. Dispositio ad pias causas substinetur cum solo num-
ero duorum testium.*

Decisio CCXXXI.

Inter caetera bona haereditaria q. Antoniae Spinolae re-
perta fuerunt quamplura loca Montium, hodie detenta per
D. Franchum Spinolam illius fratrem, tanquam ejus
haeredem ab intestato: Ideô D. Joannes Baptista de Fran-
chis haeres scriptus in testamento, introducta causa coram
me petiit super immissionem, quam fore denegandam idem
D. Franchus duplici medio tuebatur.

Et primò, quia testamentum caret legitimo numero Testium,
tanquam conditum cum solis quinque testibus, licèt de jure
septem omninò requirantur, § *final. instit. de testam.* it aut
uno deficiente testamentum corruat, *l. si unus C. eodem.*

Secundò quia ex Statuto Januae *in rubric. de testam.
& ultim. volunt. lib. I. cap.* 12 prohibetur subditis relin-
quere Sacerdotem vel Clericum executorem testamentarium,
vel fideicommissarium sub pœna quo ad hoc nullitatis testamenti, undè cùm Jo: Baptista sit Clericus, testamentum
quoad ipsum est nullius roboris.

His tamen non obstantibus resolutum fuit eidem dandam
esse immissionem, quia non controvertitur loca Montium,
de quibus agitur, esse haereditaria Antoniæ, & exhibetur
testamentum non abolitum, neque cancellatum, nec in
aliqua parte suspectum, juxta dispositionem *l. final. C. de
edict. Div. Adr. toll.*

Primum autem objectum visum fuit cessare ex dispositione ejusdem Statuti sub eadem *rubr. de testam. & ultim.
volunt.* qua cavetur testamentum, seu ultimam voluntatem
probatam publico Instrumento, in quo descripti sint quinque Testes idonei, firmam esse, & validam. Undè dum
in Testamento, de quo agitur, quinque Testes fuerunt adhi-
biti, prout ibidem disponitur, utique illius validitas, &

subsistentia impugnari non valet, cùm Statutum possit minuere numerum testium à jure requisitum, ex theor. Bartol. *in leg. cunctos populos nu. 21. cum seqq. Cod. de Summ. Trinit.* quem sequuti fuerunt Angel. *consil.* 233. *num.* 1 *vers. & secundum formam,* Vasquez *de success. creat. lib.* I. *tit. de testamen. poten.* § 1. *num. 20.* firmans *in vers. quid dicendum,* hanc sententiam veriorem esse, & sequendam, prout etiam aliis relatis comprobat Crass. *de success.* § *testamentum qu.* 55. *num.* 23, & firmavit Rota *in Perusina relevationis testamenti* 7. *Maii* 1632 *coram bon. mem. Pirovano, quae est decis.* 126. *num.* 17. & 18. *part.* 7. *recent.*

Nec obstat, quòd cum fuerit conditum in Ecclesia Societatis JESUS à jurisdictione statuentium exempta, juvari non possit hujusmodi statutaria dispositione, ut fuit dictum *in Viterbien. Haereditatis* 4, *Martii* 1641. § *praetereà,* & 28. *Martii* 1642. §. *placuit etiam coram R. P. D. meo Ghisilerio,* & 1. *Junii* 1643. § *ex altero etiam coram R. P. D. meo Verospio.*

Hoc enim procederet, si ageretur de statuto odioso requirente majores solemnitates, quàm requirantur de jure Civili, in quibus terminis loquuntur omnes Auctoritates in contrarium allegatae, & ipsaemet decisiones *in dicta Viterbien. Haereditatis.* Secus autem ubi agitur, prout hic, de statuto favorabile, cùm ex eo minuantur solemnitates juris, ut post Bart. *in d. leg. cunctos populos* n 23 & Bald. *in l. si cum speciali sub num.* 5. *C. de testam.* respondit Rota *in Senen. Spoliorum* 5. *Junii* 1545. *coram recol. me Card. Hieronymo Pamphilio,* §. *non obstat;* tunc enim si nullam mentionem facit, ut in proposito, de Ecclesiis, & Ecclesiasticis personis, ipsemet Ecclesiae, & ad eas recurrentes, sive in ipsarum Claustris suas ultimas voluntates peragentes, & etiam Clerici, uti possunt, & juvantur ejus favorabili dispositione per modum privilegii, tanquam merè privilegiativa, ut probat Abb. *in cap. Ecclesia Sanctae Mariae num.* 37. ibique Felin. *num.* 81. & Dec. *num.* 276. *de Constit.* Bald. *in cap. cum venisset nu.* 6. *vers. oppono extra de eo, qui mitt. in possess.* Bursatt. *cons.* 93. *num.* 22. *lib.* I. Surd. *cons.* 301. *num.* 24. Car-

pan. *in praelud. ad Stat. Mediol. num.* 612. Capr. *concl.*
15. *nu.* 32 & 33. Alderan. Mascard. *de general. stat. inter-
petr. concl.* I. *num.* 192. *cum seqq.* Carol. de Grass. *de effect. Cler. effect.* 2. *num.* 43. Ciarlin. *contr. for. cap.* 45.
num. 5 & 6. Sperel. *dec. for. Eccles.* 10. *num.* 35. Rot.
dec. 438. *num.* 7. & 50. *par.* 8. *recent.* & in aliis relatis
per Add. ad sanct. mem. Gregor. *dec.* 279. *n.* 24. idemque
admisit *in Senogallien. Fructuum Census* 10. *Junii* 1644.
§. *denique non obstat, vers. & sic supradicta conclusio
cor. R. P. D. meo Ghisilerio.*

Corruit pariter secundum objectum, quia cum Statutum
in ea parte adimit Clericis facultatem, ipsis competentem
ex dispositione juris, tam civilis *in leg. Deo nobis,* §. *hoc
etiam cognitum, Cod. de Episc. & Cler.* quàm Canonici *in
cap. quia nos,et in cap. Joannes de testam.* & loquuntur
verbis arctativis, praescriptivis, & prohibitivis directis in
personas, expressam mentionem faciendo de Clericis, ibi,
*Nullusque Testator possit constituere, vel ordinare ali-
quem Clericum conditionis praefatae fideicommissarium
vel executorem testamentarium,* &c., tanquam contra libertatem Ecclesiasticam est nullum ipso facto, & jure, ex
defectu potestatis Laicorum statuentium, ut de statuto
tollente Clericis, quod ipsis à jure conceditur, decidit text.
in cap. eos de immun. Eccles. & in Auth. cassa, et irrita,
ubi Bart. *Cod. de sentent. excomm.* Felin *in dict. cap.
Ecclessia S. Mariae num.* 61. *de Const.* Innoc. *in cap.
noverit de sentent. excommun.* Alex. *cons.* 210. *n.* 12. *lib.*
2. Socc. sen. *cons.* 241. *num.* 3. *libr.* 3. Riminal. sen. *cons.*
483. *n.* 10. *versic. fortificantur predicta lib.* 3. Anchar.
cons. 61. *num.* 2. *vers. item. si Statutum,* Rimin. Jun.
cons. 85. *num.* 29. *lib.* 1. Ruin. *consil.* 23. *num.* 16.
lib. 2. Honded. *consil.* 3. *n.* 13. *cum. seqq. lib.* I. Surd.
cons. 2. *num.* 22. Carpan. *ubi supra num.* 578. *num.*
583. Marant. *disput.* 8. *num.* 2. *& 3.* Mart. *de jurisdict. part.*
4 *cent.* 1. *cas.* 5. *num.* 43. *cas.* 55. *num.* 6. & 7. *& cas.* 62. *num.*
9. Carol. de Grass. *d. effect.* 2. *num.* 68. Bellett. *disquis.
Cler. tit. de exempt. Cleric. à stat. saecul.* § 1. *num.* 9. De
Statuto praeceptivo, arctativo, & prohibitivo probant
Imol. *in cap. constitutus nu.* 7. *de restit. in integr.* Abb.

in cap. à nobis. num, I. & 4. *cum. seqq. de sentent. ex-comm. & in dict. cap. Ecclessia S. Mariae num.* 4. Alex. *dict. cons.* 210. *sub num.* 1. *in fin. vers. sive statutum lib.* 2. Bursatt. *d. cons.* 93. *nu.* 45. Honded. *d. cons.* 3. *num.* 23. *lib.* I. *& cons.* 20. *num.* 18. *libr.* 2. Lap. *allegat.* 101. *nu.* 14. *vers. quod aut sunt.*, Marant. *d. disput.* 8. *num.* 8. *usque ad* 12. Mart. *d. cent.* 1. *cas.* 21. *num.* 11. & 12. Sperell. *dict. dec.* 10. *nu.* 20. Et denique de Statuto ex-pressam mentionem faciente de Clericis, vel Ecclesiis, quan-tumvis favorabile, & privilegiativo, est text. apertus *in d. cap. Ecclesia S. Mariae*, ubi Abb. *num.* 5. & 14. *in fin.* Felin. *num.* 76. *aliique scribent. de Const.* Bald. *in d. l. cunctos populos num.* 10. *Cod. de Summ. Trinit.* Bart. *in l. fin. num.* 18. *C. de Sacrosanct. Eccles.* Butr. *in cap. quod Clericus de for. compet.* Surdus *consil.* 301. *num.* 13. & 14. Nevizan *consil.* 39. *sub numer.* 9. *vers. sed respon-detur*, Menoch. *de recuperan. remed.* 14. *num.* 56. Gail. *pract. observat. libr.* 2. *observat.* 32. *numer.* 2. cum aliis pluribus pleno calamo congestis per Carol. de Grass. *dict. effect.* 2. *num.* 45. & 46. & 488. & 489. Bellett. *dict. tit. de exempt. Cleric. à stat. saecul.* §. 4, *num.* 6. Sperell. *dict. decis.* 10. *num.* 30. &. 32.

Idque etiam si dicta verba activa, & prohibitiva non videantur directa in personas Clericorum, sed tantummodo Testatoris Laici : Quia praeterquod satis dicitur contra libertatem Ecclesiasticam, dum tollit Clericis beneficium ipsis de jure competens, vel dum de eis expressam men-tionem facit, *ex juribus allegatis*, sufficit quod virtualiter, & indirectè prohibendo exequutoriam in personas Clerico-rum illos tangat, & laedat, ut inde nullius sit roboris, & firmitatis, juxta distinctionem magistraliter traditam per Rim. sen. *dict. cons.* 483. *num.* 10. *vers. & benè facit lib.* 3. Soccin. jun. *cons.* 1. *num.* 11. *vers. quoniam licèt lib.* 2. quam egregiè expendit Marant. *d. disp.* 8. *sub num.* 44. *vers. ad. septimum respondeo*, sequitur Mart. *ubi supra d. cent.* 1. *d. cas.* 62. *num.* 10. Carol. de Grass. *dict. effect.* 2. *nu.* 11. and meliùs omnium Castropal. *oper. moral. par.* 2. *tit. de rever. deb. Eccles. disp. unic. punct.* 8. *num.* 7. Laici enim non possunt in specie statuere de personis Ecclesiasticis, neque de ipsorum bonis directè, aut indirectè cùm illorum jurisdictioni non subsint, ut articulo maturè discusso responsum fuit in *Ravennaten. haereditatis* 5. *hujus coram R. P. D. meo Otthobono, & signanter in § cujus verissima.*

Nec ex eo, quòd Joann. Baptista ˙utitur dispositione hujus statuti in ea parte, qua mandat validum esse testamentum cum quinque Testibus, intrat obligatio illud acceptandi etiam in altera parte, qua disponit Clericos non posse constitui fideicommissarios, nec executors Testamentarios. Quia speciale est in Ecclesiis, & personis Ecclesiasticis posse uti per modum Privilegii, Statutis, & Constitutionibus Laicorum, generalibus tamen, nullamque mentionem de ipsis facientibus, in quantum faciunt pro se ipsis, & concernunt eorum commodum, & favorem, & non acceptare, sed reiicere, in quantum faciunt contra ipsos, & sunt eis praejudiciales, ut notat gloss. *in cap. novit, verb. quicumque, versic. quod Ecclesia de judic.* Abb. *in d. cap constit. num.* 4. *de integr. restit. & in cap. ex litteris numer.* 6. *& 7. de vit. & honest. Cleric.* Soccin: sen. *consil.* 71. *num.* 19. *libr.* 4. Afflict. *de jure prothom.* §. 9. *num.* 17. P. Diana *resol. moral. tr.* I. *de immun. Eccles. resol.* 43. *per tot. tom.* 3. Mart. *ubi supradict. centur.* 1. *cas.* 5. *num.* 44. *& 45.* Bellet. *pariter ubi supra* §. 2: *numer.* 37.

Minùsve applicatur limitatio, quòd Clericus volens uti hujusmodi Statutis cogatur illis uti cum omnibus suis qualitatibus, clausulis, & conditionibus, ut tradit Bald. *in l. venditiones num.* 9. *C. de contrah. empt. & in l. omni novatione sub num.* 9 *C. de Sacros. Eccles.* cum aliis relatis per Tiraq. *de retract. lignag.* §. 1. *glos.* 13. *num.* 6. *& 7.*

Quia praeterquod non procedit in qualitatibus, & conditionibus diversis, & separatis, quarum una non tendit ad limitandum, extendendum, seu qualificandum alteram, ut doctè consulendo distinguit Honded. *consil.* 78. *n.* 111 *cum quatuor seqq. lib.* 2. Prout in effectu sunt in casu nostro, cùm Paragraphus minuens numerum testium sit omninò diversus, & separatus à Paragrapho prohibente executoriam, tam respectu materiae, quarum una nihil habet commune cum altera, quàm etiam respectu ordinis, & scripturae, ex quo licèt uterque contineatur sub eadem rubrica, Paragraphi tamen sunt prorsus separati, & unus valdè distat ab alio cum intermedio aliorum quatuordecim differentis materiae : Admitti potest in qualitatibus, conditionibus, seu clausulis validis, justis, & subsistentibus, atque generaliter favorabilibus, tam Clericis, quàm Laicis pro communi omnium Civium utilitate, in quibis terminis loquuntur, Bald. *loco allegato,* caeterique adducti per Tiraqu. *ut ipsemet se explicat sub dict. numer.* 7. *vers. neque enim hic diutius,* idemque probat Seraph. *de privil. juram. privil.* 77. *num.* 26. *vers. sed certè his non obstantibus.* Secus autem quando, prout hic, qualitas statuti est nulla, injusta, & odiosa, tendens expressè in damnum, & odium Clericorum. Ista enim tanquam principaliter contra libertatem Ecclesiasticam, & expressam mentionem faciens de Clericis, habetur perindè, ac si facta, & apposita non fuisset, ut ratiocinatur Socc. sen. *cons.* 122. *sub num.* 6. *vers. secunda, quia prima pars lib.* I. Castropal. *ubi supra par.* I. *tit. de leg. in commun. & ejus caus. tract.* 3. *disp.* I. *punct.* 24. § 6. *num.* 1. Carol. de Grass. *dict. effect.* 2. *num.* 28 *vers. tunc enim;* & consequenter acceptata parte valida, & favorabili tantùm abest, quòd Clericus uti debeat dicta parte nulla, & odiosa, quòd imò etiam volens illa uti non potest, ut concludit Sperell. *dec.* 11. *num.* 30.

Et pro justitia resolutionis duo ulteriùs Domini ponderabant : Alterum, quòd statutum excludit tantummodo Clericos ab executoria, firmo manente in reliquis Testamento, ideòque extendi non debet ad casum nostrum, quo Jo : Baptista fuit haeres institutus, ne aliàs corruat etiam ipsum testamentum contra mentem statuentium : Alterum, quòd ipsi statuentes intellexerunt de executore dando in prophanis, ne Clerici se immisceant in negotiis Laicorum, à quibus etiam de jure abstinere teneantur, *ut in Cap.* I. *& per tot.* 88. *distinct. & in cap. te quidem* 11. *q.* I. Non autem de executore, prout hic, operis pii, & relicto pro exoneranda conscientia defuncti, metiendo voluntatem à potestate, cum Laici statuere nequeant super re spirituali, *cap. tua de ordin. cognat. cap. lator, qui fil. sint legit.*

Soccin. sen. *consil.* 35. *n.* I. *lib.* 1. Carol. de Grass. *alleg. effect.* 2. *num.* 81.

Caeterùm dum Antonia Testatrix haeredem instituit Joan. Baptistam sub fide, quòd exoneraret conscientiam suam, ut legitur in ipsomet testamento, ibi, *Et hà eletto la persona di d. Sign. Gio: Battista, perche è certa, che per l' attinenza del sangue, e grado, che hà di Sacerdote, userà ogni diligenza, acciò la coscienza di d. Testatrice, della quale è in questa parte intieramente informato, resti pienamente sodisfatta*: Censetur principaliter contemplasse favorem salutis aeternae, & animae sublevamentum, proindeq ; dispositio dicitur ad pias causas, ex theor. Bald. *in auth. similiter n.* 2. *vers. & dicitur, C. ad. falc.* Bart. *in repetit. lib.* I. *num* 33. *C. de Sacros. Eccles.* Florian. de S. Petr. *in l. cum quidam,* § *dies n.* 2. *vers. dicitur autem, ff. de usur.* Ang. *in l. precibus num.* 5. *vers. idem, C. de impub. & aliis subst.* benè Jas. *cons.* 110. *num,* 7. *lib.* I. Crot. *cons.* 194. *num.* 4. *lib.* 2. Jo: Baptista de thor. in addit. ad Tiraquell. *de privil. piae caus. in praefat. vers. item relictum pro incertis cum seqq.* Rot. *dec.* 245, num. 29. *part.* 7. *recent.* Quae substinetur cum duobus solis Testibus, *cap. relatum de testam.* Rot. *divers. decis.* 74. *num.* 12. *cum seqq. part 2.*

Et ità conclusum utraque parte informante, &c.

APPENDIX No. 3.

(See Page 206.)

Opinion of Chas. R. Hildeburn, Esq., upon the question whether the lower counties upon Delaware were a transmitting or a non-transmitting colony.

The Historical Society of Pennsylvania.

1300 LOCUST STREET,
PHILADELPHIA, *February 25th, 1892.*

DEAR SIR: In reply to your question as to whether the acts passed by the Assembly of the Government of Newcastle, Kent and Sussex upon Delaware, commonly called the Three Lower Counties of Pennsylvania. were ever transmitted to England for approval or disallowance by the Crown, I think I am justified in answering in the negative.

The Public Record office in London contains more or less complete manuscript series of the acts passed by the "transmitting colonies," and much matter concerning their consideration and the action taken upon them by the Crown.

But there is no evidence to be found in that office that the acts of this Assembly were ever transmitted or considered. And the notes of the Crown's action, which are to be found in almost all the printed collections of acts of the transmitting colonies, are entirely absent from all the editions of the "Laws of the Government of Newcastle, Kent and Sussex upon Delaware."

Yours very truly,

(Signed)   CHAS. R. HILDEBURN.

BRINTON COXE, ESQ.

APPENDIX No. 4.

(See Page 213.)

Order of the King in Council, upon the appeal of John Winthrop against Thomas Lechmere, annulling the Law of Connecticut, entitled "An act for the settlement of Intestate Estates."

At the Court at St. James's, the 15th day of February, 1727.

[L. S.]

Present:
The King's Most Excellent Majesty,
Lord President,
Lord Privy Seale,
Lord Steward,
Lord Chamberlain,
Duke of Ancaster,
Duke of Newcastle,

Earl of Lincoln,
Earl of Westmoreland,
Earl of Berkeley,
Earl of Scarborough,
Earl of Loudoun,
Earl of Uxbridge,
Earl of Sussex,
Viscot. Cobham,
Viscot. Torrington,
Lord Berkeley of Stratton,
Lieut. General Wills,
Sr. Robert Sutton.

Upon reading this day at the Board a report from the Rt. Honorable the Lords of the Committee for hearing Appeals from the Plantations, dated the 20th day of December last, in the words following, viz:

In obedience to an Order in Council of the 13th of May last referring to this committee the humble petition and appeal of John Winthrop, of New London, in his Majesty's Colony of Connecticut, Esq., only son and heir at law of Major General Waite Winthrop, of Boston in New England, Esq., his late father, deceased (to which appeal the petitioner was admitted by his late Majesty's Order in Council of the 28th of March last), their Lordships this day took the said petition into consideration; which said petition sets forth (amongst other things), the charter of incorporation granted to the said Province by King Charles the second, on the 13th of April, in the fourteenth year of his reign, by which the lands of the said Colony are held of the Crown, as of the manor of East Greenwich in Kent, in free and common soccage, and the laws which they are empowered to make are to be wholesome and reasonable, and not contrary to the law of England; and that the petitioner was possessed of and entitled to a very considerable real estate in the said Province, as heir at law to his said father Waite Winthrop, and his uncle the Honourable Fitz John Winthrop, both deceased: That his said father Waite Winthrop dyed intestate, leaving issue only the petitioner and one daughter, Anne, who was preferred in marriage in her

father's life time to Thomas Lechmere, of Boston aforesaid, merchant; and that on his said father's death he became entituled to all his real estate whereof he dyed seized in
fee, as his heir at law; and that on the 21st of February,
171⅘, at the court of probates held for the county of New
London in Connecticut, letters of administration were
granted to the petitioner of the goods, chattels, rights and
credits of his said father, and he entered into bond to the
judge of the said court of probates in 3,000 _l._ penalty,
with condition for his making a true inventory of all and
singular the goods, chattels and credits of the said deceased, and exhibit the same into the registry of the said
court of probates, and truly to administer the same according to law. But the petitioner having paid and advanced more to and for and on account of the said Thomas
Lechmere than the said Anne his wife's share of the said
intestate's personal estate come to the petitioner's hands
amounted to, and the said Thomas and Anne Lechmere having possessed most part of the said Waite Winthrop's personal estate, and not having required the petitioner to exhibit any inventory or account of his administration, and
the petitioner having discharged all his said father's debts,
save o·ly one bond for 300 _l._ on which he duly discharged
all interest, and would have paid off the principal but the
obligee declined accepting the same, the petitioner did not,
for these reasons, think it necessary to exhibit any inventory or account of his said administration. But, in order
to ruin and oppress the petitioner, six years after the said
letters of administration so granted to the petitioner (viz):
in July, 1724, the said Thomas Lechmere applied to the
court of probates, insisting he was, in right of his wife, entitled to a proportion of the said Waite Winthrop's real estate, but that he was kept thereout by the petitioner's not
having inventoried and administred the same, and caused the
petitioner to be summoned by the court of probates, to
show cause why he neglected to inventory the intestate's
estate and finish his administration according to his bond;
upon which the petitioner exhibited an inventory of the
said intestate's personal estate in the said court of pro-

bates, and the petitioner at the foot thereof insisted, administrators had nothing to do with lands, they belonging to the heir at law, and that he was in possession thereof as his right of inheritance according to the law of England, and therefore he was not obliged to exhibit any account of the real estate, that not being cognizable by a Court of Probates, and which inventory the petitioner prayed might be accepted and recorded ; but the court declared they were satisfyed the same was not a true and perfect inventory of all the said intestate's estate within that county, and that the petitioner's objections were against law, and decreed that the said inventory should not be admitted, and refused to accept it as such an inventory of the intestate's estate as ought to be exhibited ; and the said Thomas Lechmere in the same July put the petitioner's said administration bond in suit against him, and at the same time, in his own name and the name of Abel Wally, brought another action against the petitioner, as they had been sureties for him in an administration bond for his duly administring the intestate's estate, in the county of Suffolk in the Massachusetts Bay, alledging such administration bond had been sued and recovered from them, on account of the petitioner's not having exhibited an inventory or brought in his administration accounts ; and the said Thomas Lechmere also, at the same time brought four several writs of partition in his own name and in the name of his wife Anne, stiling her only daughter and co-heir of the said Waite Winthrop, to recover from the petitioner one-third of the real estate in said writs mentioned, insisting the said Anne was co-heir thereto with the petitioner, and as such, by the law of the Province, she was entituled to one-third of the said real estate ; and that on full and fair hearings, the final judgments in all the said six actions were given for the petitioner.

That it thus appearing the petitioner's inheritance could not be split and tore to pieces by the common ordinary means of justice, as the law was then understood, some more irresistable way was to be found out to oppress the petitioner ; and for that purpose the said Thomas Lechmere preferred a petition to the General Assembly, in 1725, in the name of himself and his wife, setting forth the said several judgments given against him, and that they were never likely to recover of the petitioner one-third of the said real estate, though the same descended, as they alledged, to the said Anne and the petitioner as co-heirs of their father without the aid and relief of that Assembly, and that. either by reason of the insufficiency of the diction of the law of the Colony already made, or by the court's sense or exposition thereof; for they had no remedy by the common law, as appeared by the said judgments against them, nor could have any remedy by the court of probates, for that the petitioner refused to inventory the real estates; and, as the law of the Colony had given them a right to one-third the premises, it was not consistent with the honour of the Colony, but that the government would afford some indisputable method for their better obtaining their said right; and to that end they prayed the Assembly to set aside the said judgments and to grant a new tryal, wherein they might, notwithstanding the exposition of the superiour court upon the law, well support their said actions of partition, which petition, tho' of so very extraordinary nature, the Assembly received and ordered the petitioner to attend to answer the same. That the petitioner put in his answer, insisting there was nothing contained in the said petition that called for the interposition of the Assembly, or in which they ought or could give any relief, notwithstanding which, and without any hearing, the Assembly resolved that relief might and ought to be had in the probates in such like cases by a new grant of administration, exhibiting an inventory of the whole estate, and a distribution made according to the rules of law upon the whole, and at the same time, tho' they came to this resolve, they dismissed the said Lechmere's petition.

That the petitioner, by this very extraordinary resolve finding the danger he was in, again exhibited to the court of probates a full and true inventory of his father's personal estate come to his hands, valued and appraised, and again insisted in writing at the foot thereof, that administrators had nothing to do with lands, they belonging to him as heir at law and as his right of inheritance according to the law of England, and that no real estate ought by law to be exhibited not cognizable by a court of probates ; and the petitioner moved the court to have the same accepted as a full inventory of all the intestate's estate within that Colony proper for a court of probates by law to demand, and offered his oath that it was the whole personal estate of the deceased. But the court insisting on the petitioner's taking an oath that it was an inventory of the whole of the intestate's real as well as personal estate, which the petitioner refused to comply with, insisting he ought not to inventory any real estate. Whereupon the said court, by their sentence of the 29th of June, 1725, rejected the said inventory and refused to accept the same, from which sentence of denyal the petitioner appealed to the superior court. That after the said appeal, and before it came on to be determined, the said Lechmere commenced a suit in the court of probates to have administration granted to him of the said intestate's estate ; and the petitioner being summoned to show cause why administration should not be granted to the said Lechmere, for cause insisted on his said appeal being depending, and which cause the said court allowed, from which allowance the said Lechmere also appealed to the said superior court.

That on the 28th September, 1725, the superior court, on hearing the petitioner's appeal, declared that they were of opinion that real as well as personal estate were ordered to be inventoried by the law of that Colony, and that all courts of probates ought to be guided in their administrations thereby, notwithstanding the laws of England do not ordain that real estates should be inventoried ; and thereupon ordered that the petitioner should not be admitted to evidence to the said inventory by any other oath than that which was agreeable to the laws of the Province ; and affirmed the judgment of the court of probates, and condemned the petitioner in costs ; from which judgment the petitioner prayed, and was allowed, a review to the next superior court. And the said Lechmere's appeal coming on at the same time, the court also in that suit affirmed the judgment of the court of probates ; from which sentence the said Lechmere prayed, and was allowed, a review likewise.

That, on hearing the petitioner's said appeal on the review, on the 22d of March, 172⅝, the court affirmed their said former judgment and condemned the petitioner in costs ; and on the said Lechmere's review, which came on at the same time, the said superior court, forasmuch as the petitioner's said appeal was then determined, adjudged that the said letters of administration formerly granted the petitioner should be vacated, and the same was thereby vacated, and that the said Thomas Lechmere and Anne his wife, should have administration on the deceased's estate ; and the said superior court thereby granted power of administration to the said Thomas and Anne Lechmere on the said intestate's estate, and condemned the petitioner in costs ; from both which judgments of the superior court the petitioner prayed, but was in a very extraordinary manner denied, an appeal to his late Majesty in Council ; but which appeal he was admitted to, upon his petition to his late Majesty.

That the petitioner, finding his inheritance in this imminent danger of being torn in pieces, all application for relief to his Majesty being denied him : to prevent, if possible, anything being done in the premises till he could lay his case before his Majesty, entered and filed his protest, as heir at law to his father, against granting letters of administration to his father's estate to any other person whatever, the court having before lodged that power with the petitioner, and also against any division of any real estate pretended to belong to the petitioner's father, all such real estate being the petitioner's undoubted right of inheritance, who was seized and possessed of the same according to the laws of England, and which he was entituled to under the charter of the said Province, and, therefore, the petitioner protested against any proceedings of the said court contrary to the law of England : Notwithstanding which, the judges of the said superior court the same 22d of

March, granted letters of administration to the said intestate's estate to the said Thomas Lechmere and Anne, his
wife, and took the usual administration bond from the said
Thomas Lechmere and his sureties, which letters of administration and bond extend only to the goods, chattels,
rights and credits of the deceased, which the petitioner had
before duly administred.

That the said Thomas Lechmere under colour hereof, inventoried and appraised all the petitioner's real estate, and
exhibited an inventory thereof before a special superior
county court held for that purpose on the 29th of April,
1726, which the said court, notwithstanding the said Lechmere, either by his letters of administration or his administration bond, had nothing to do with real estates, took
upon them, contrary to law, to sit specially and receive the
said inventory, and by their acts of that date approved the
same, and ordered it to be received ; and the said Lechmere
also then exhibited to the court an account of 38l. 7s. 4d.
for charges and time spent in the administration, and of a
debt due to Robert Lattimore for 318l. silver money, which
was the bond the petitioner had offered to discharge as
aforesaid, and for which he had duly paid interest ; which
account the said court also allowed and ordered to be kept
on fyle ; and the 12th of May, 1726, the said Lechmere (being conscious he had no power over any real estate by virtue of the administration) petitioned the Assembly, setting
forth that no personal estate of the intestate had come to
his hands, the estate come to his hands being all real,
and finding there was due from the said estate 356l. 7s. 4d.,
being the two sums in his above account mentioned, and no
moveables to pay the same, he prayed the Assembly to enable him to pay the said debts by ordering him to sell and
dispose of so much of the said lands, thereby to defray the
said debts with other necessary charges.

That the petitioner being informed of this application,
that the Assembly might do nothing herein without the
fullest notice possible, the petitioner presented a memorial to the Governor and Company, agreeing in substance
with the above recited protest, and declaring that he, being

aggrieved with the aforementioned proceedings, should lay
the whole by appeal before his Majesty. But which re-
monstrance of the petitioner the Assembly the same day
dismissed, and immediately afterward, on the said Lechmere's petition, granted him a power to sell the said lands,
and ordered that a bill should be brought in for that end in
form ; whereupon the petitioner entered and fyled his protest with the said Governor and Company, to the effect
with that before mentioned, and further protesting against
their proceeding to grant power to any pretended adminis-
trator to sell any part of the petitioner's real estate under
colour of debts due from the said deceased, as they would
answer the same before his Majesty in Council, which protest, the Assembly declared, had in it a show of contempt to
the Governor and Assembly and the authority there established, and, therefore, on the 25th of the same May, they
ordered the sheriff to bring the petitioner to the bar of the
said Assembly to answer for the contempt manifested in
the said protest, and immediately afterwards passed an act
empowering the said Thomas Lechmere to sell so much of
the said lands as might be sufficient to discharge the said
debts and the necessary costs, the said Lechmere taking the
advice of the superior court in such sale, and enacting
such deed or deeds of sale to be good.

That the petitioner humbly lays the whole of these proceedings before his Majesty, by which the many extraordinary and unjustifiable steps may appear to have been taken
against him, in order to disinherit him of his inheritance,
and to set up his sister as co-heir with him, and to make a
division of his real estate between him and his sister, contrary to the common law of England and the royal charter
of the said Province ; and, in consideration thereof, and of
the many hardships of the petitioner's case, the petitioner
humbly prays his Majesty to reverse the said two sentences
of the superior court of the 22d of March, 172$\frac{5}{6}$, with
costs and damages to the petitioner, and to order the said
administration, so illegally and irregularly granted to the
said Thomas and Anne Lechmere, to be called in ; and also
to set aside and discharge all subsequent proceedings

grounded thereon ; and that his Majesty would repeal the said act passed by the Assembly empowering the said Thomas Lechmere to sell and dispose of the petitioner's said real estate ; and that his Majesty would be pleased to grant him all such further and other relief as the circumstances and nature of his case should require.

Their Lordships having heard all parties concerned, by their counsel learned in the law, on the said petition and appeal, and there being laid before their Lordships an act passed by the Governor and Company of that Colony, entituled an act for the settlement of intestate estates, by which act (amongst other things) administrators of persons dying intestate are directed to inventory all the estate, whatsoever, of the persons so deceased, as well moveable as not moveable, and to deliver the same upon oath to the court of probates ; and by the said act (debts, funerals and just expenses of all sorts, and the dower of the wife (if any) being first allowed) the said court of probates is empowered to distribute all the remaining estate of any such intestate, as well real as personal, by equal portions, to and amongst the children and such as legally represent them, except the eldest son who is to have two shares or a double portion of the whole ; the division of the estate to be made by three sufficient freeholders, on oath, or any two of them, to be appointed by the court of probates. Their Lordships, upon due consideration of the whole matter, do agree humbly to report as their opinion to your Majesty, that the said act for the settlement of intestate estates should be declared null and void, being contrary to the laws of England, in regard it makes lands of inheritance distributable as personal estates and is not warranted by the charter of that Colony ; and that the said three sentences of the 29th of June, 1725, of the 28th of September, 1725, and of the 22d day of March, 172⅚, rejecting the inventory of the said intestate's estates exhibited by the petitioner, and refusing to accept the same, because it did not contain the real as well as personal estate of the said intestate, and declaring real as well as personal estates ought to be inventoried, may be all reversed and set aside ; and that the petitioner be admitted to exhibit an inventory of the personal estate only of the said intestate; and that the court of probates be directed not to reject such inventory, only because it does not contain the real estate of the said intestate; and that the said sentence of the 22d of March, 172⅚, vacating the said letters of administration granted to the petitioner, and granting administration to the said Thomas and Anne Lechmere, should be also reversed and set aside; and that the said letters of administration, so granted to the said Thomas Lechmere and Anne, his wife, should be called in and vacated; and that the said inventory of the said real estate exhibited by the said Thomas Lechmere and Anne, his wife, should be vacated; and that the order of the 29th of April, 1726, approving of the said inventory and ordering the same to be recorded, should be discharged and set aside; and that the original letters of administration granted to the petitioner should be established and ordered to stand; and that all such costs as the petitioner hath paid unto the said Thomas Lechmere, by direction of the said sentence, may be forthwith repaid him by the said Thomas Lechmere; and that the suit brought by the said Lechmere and his wife, on which the said sentence was made, may be dismissed, and that all acts and proceedings done and had under the said sentences, or any of them, or by virtue or pretence thereof, may be discharged and declared null and void; and also that the said act of Assembly, passed in May, 1726, empowering the said Lechmere to sell the said lands, should be declared null and void. And it appearing to their lordships that the said superior court, by an order bearing date the 27th of September, 1726, and made pursuant to the said act of Assembly, allowed the said Thomas Lechmere to sell of the said real estate to the value of ninety pounds current money there, for his charges, and three hundred and eighteen pounds silver money, to answer the said bond debt due from the intestate, their lordships are of the opinion that the said order of the superior court should be declared null and void; and also that the petitioner should be immediately restored and put into the full and quiet possession of all such parts of the said real estate as may have been taken from him, under pretence of, or by virtue or colour of the said sentences, orders, acts and proceedings, or any of them ; and that the said Thomas Lechmere do account for and pay to the said petitioner the rents and profits thereof received by him or any one under him, for and during the time of such his unjust detention thereof.

His Majesty, taking the same into his royal consideration, is pleased, with the advice of his privy council, to approve of the said report, and confirm the same in every particular part thereof ; and pursuant thereunto, to declare, that the aforementioned act, entituled an act for the settlement of intestate estates, is Null and Void ; and the same is hereby accordingly declared to be null and void, and of no force or effect whatever. And his Majesty is hereby further pleased to order, that all the aforementioned sentences of the 29th June, 1725, of the 28th of September, 1725, and of the 22d March, 172$\frac{5}{6}$, and every of them, be and they are hereby reversed and set aside ; and that the petitioner, John Winthrop, be, and is hereby, admitted to exhibit an inventory of the personal estate only of the said intestate, and that the court of probates do not presume to reject such inventory because it does not contain the real estate of the said intestate. And his Majesty doth hereby further order, that the aforementioned sentence of the 22d of March, 172$\frac{5}{6}$, vacating the said letters of administration granted to the petitioner, and granting administration to the said Thomas and Anne Lechmere, be also reversed and set aside ; and that the said letters of administration, so granted to Thomas Lechmere and Anne, his wife, be called in and vacated ; and that the said inventory of the said real estate, exhibited by the said Thomas Lechmere and Anne his wife, be vacated ; and that the said order of the 29th of April, 1726, approving of the said inventory and ordering the same to be recorded, be discharged and set aside ; and that the original letters of administration granted to the petitioner be, and they are hereby, established and ordered to stand ; and that all such costs as the petitioner hath paid unto the said Thomas Lechmere by directions of the said sentences, all, every, or any of them, be

forthwith repaid to him by the said Thomas Lechmere;
and that the suit brought by the said Thomas Lechmere
and Anne his wife, on which the said sentences were made,
be and they are hereby dismissed ; and that all acts and
proceedings done and had under the said sentences, all,
every, or any of them, or by virtue or pretence thereof, be
and they are hereby discharged and set aside, and declared
null and void. And his Majesty is further pleased to declare, that the aforementioned act of Assembly, passed
in May, 1726, empowering the said Thomas Lechmere to
sell the said lands, is null and void ; and also that the said
order made by the said superior court, bearing date the
27th of September, 1726, pursuant to the said act of assembly, allowing the said Lechmere to sell of the said real
estate to the value of ninety pounds current money there for
his charges, and three hundred and eighteen pounds silver
money, is likewise null and void ; and the said act of Assembly and order of the said superior court are accordingly
hereby declared null and void, and of no force or effect
whatever.

And his Majesty doth hereby likewise further order, that
the petitioner be immediately restored and put into the full,
peaceable and quiet possession of all such parts of the said
real estate as may have been taken from him, under pretence of, or by virtue or colour of the said sentence, orders,
acts, and proceedings, or any of them; and that the said
Thomas Lechmere do account for and pay to the said petitioner the rents and profits thereof, and of every part
thereof, received by him or any one under him, for and
during the time of such his unjust detention thereof.

And the Governour and Company of his Majesty's Colony
of Connecticut for the time being, and all other officers and
persons whatsoever, whom it may concern, are to take
notice of his Majesty's royal pleasure hereby signified, and
yield due obedience to every particular part thereof, as
they will answer the contrary at their peril.*

EDWARD SOUTHWELL.

---

*The Public Records of the Colony of Connecticut, &c., Vol. vii, pp. 571-579.

APPENDIX No. 5.

(See Page 213.)

Of the relation of judicial power to unconstitutional legislaiion according to the constitution of the Canadian Dominion.

In connection with the subject, it will be useful to consider the present constitution of the Canadian dominion or union of colonial provinces. It dates from 1867, being the act of the parliament of Great Britain, known as "the British North America Act, 1867." This instrument is thus both imperial legislation and a colonial constitution. The legal results of thirteen years of constitutional history are exhibited in a valuable work by Mr. Doutre, Q. C., of Montreal. It is entitled:

"Constitution of Canada. The British North America "Act, 1867; its Interpretation, etc., by Joseph Doutre, Q. "C., of the Montreal Bar. (Montreal, 1880)."

The following extracts from the preface are of great interest to common law jurists in all parts of the world.

" The design of this work is not to be a commentary upon "the text of the Federal compact, but, to bring together, "by the side of the text, the decisions of the courts, with "the dicta of judges and statesmen; and to discover the "principles which will aid those engaged in framing fed- "eral or provincial laws, and the legal profession generally "in the interpretation of the constitution of the country.

" *Previous to 'The British North America Act, 1867,'* "*the provincial courts did not consider they possessed the* "*power of enquiring and deciding whether the laws of* "*their respective legislatures were constitutional or not.* " *Occasional attempts were made to test the validity of* " *statutes, but they were ineffectual in their results. It* " *has been and is quite different under the Federal act.*

" The Supreme Court of Canada and the privy council in "England, have both concurred in recognizing the right,

" assumed by the provincial courts of original and appellate
" jurisdiction, to pass upon the constitutionality of the laws
" enacted by the provincial legislatures and the Parlia-
" ment of Canada. This was anticipated by the framers of
" the act, as appears by the debates in the House of Com-
" mons.

" On the 4th of March, 1867, when the bill was under
" discussion, in the Imperial Parliament, Mr. Cardwell
" said : 'As matters now stand, if the Legislatures of
" Canada acted *ultra vires*, the question would first be
" raised in the colonial law courts, and would ultimately
" be settled by the privy council at home.'

" Important decisions of the privy council, of the Su-
" preme Court of Canada, and of the various provincial
" courts, have been already reported, pronouncing upon the
" validity of the Dominion and Provincial statute laws,
" and, on many points settling the principles that should
" be applied in the construction of the confederation act,
" and defining the limit and scope of Federal and pro-
" vincial legislation.

" It may be thought by some, inadvisable, to have noted
" so many decisions of the Federal Court of the United
" States, but it will be remarked, how frequently our judges
" have been compelled, in the absence of other precedents,
" to look to the decisions of the highest court of that Con-
" federacy ; for, that Republic also consists of a Federal
" Union of separate sovereign States with a written consti-
" tution prescribing the sphere of action of the central gov-
" ernment and of the local governments ; and this neces-
" sarily required continual appeals to the judiciary to
" define, determine and settle, the line of demarkation
" between these two jurisdictions. Several cases have been
" reported more at length than many may, at first sight,
" deem expedient or desirable for a work of this kind ;
" but it must be borne in mind that these are recent and
" important cases, involving many issues of great moment,
" which have been discussed with great ability by the
" judges of the court of last resort in this Dominion.

"But, for those who do not lose sight of the fact that we "are on the threshold of a new system of national exist- "ence, and from want of an experience that time alone can "give, are deprived of any great number of judicial de- "cisions, no apology will be necessary.

"The Quebec resolutions of 1864, and the Constitution of "the United States have been added, for the reason, that a "ready reference to them is useful, if not necessary, in the "study of the constitutional act of Canada."

APPENDIX No. 6.

(See page 259.)

Letter of Richard Dobbs Spaight to James Iredell.

PHILADELPHIA, *August, 12th, 1787.*

DEAR SIR: * * *' The late determination of our judges at Newbern, must, in my opinion, produce the most serious reflections in the breast of every thinking man, and of every well-wisher to his country. It cannot be denied, but that the Assembly have passed laws unjust in themselves, and militating in their principles against the Constitution, in more instances than one, and in my opinion of a more alarming and destructive nature than the one which the judges, by their own authority, thought proper to set aside and delare void. The laws I allude to are the *tender laws*, and the laws for increasing the jurisdiction of the justices of the peace out of court; the latter they have allowed to operate without censure or opposition; the former they have openly and avowedly supported, to the great disgrace of their characters. I do not pretend to vindicate the law, which has been the subject of controversy; it is immaterial what law they have declared void; it is their usurpation of the authority to do it, that I complain of, as I do most positively deny that they have any such power; nor can they find anything in the Constitution, either directly or impliedly, that will support them, or give them any color of right to exercise that authority. Besides, it would have been absurd, and contrary to the practice of all the world, had the Constitution vested such powers in them, as they would have operated as an absolute negative on the proceedings of the legislature, which no judiciary ought ever to possess, and the State, instead of being governed by the representatives in General Assembly would be subject to the will of three individuals, who united in their own persons the legislative and judiciary powers, which no monarch in Europe enjoys, and which would be more despotic than the Roman Decemvirate, and equally insufferable. If they possessed the power what check or control would there be to their proceedings? or who is there to take the same liberty with them that they have taken with the legislature, and declare their opinions to be erroneous? None that I know of. In consequence of which, whenever the judges should become corrupt, they might at pleasure set aside every law, however just or consistent with the Constitution, to answer their designs; and the persons and property of every individual would be completely at their disposal. Many instances might be brought to show the absurdity and impropriety of such a power being lodged with the judges. ᵗ

It must be acknowledged that our Constitution, unfortunately, has not provided a sufficient check to prevent the intemperate and unjust proceedings of our legislature, though such a check would be very beneficial, and, I think, absolutely necessary to our well-being; the only one that I know of, is the annual election, which, by leaving out such members as have supported improper measures, will in some degree remedy, though it cannot prevent, such evils as may arise. I should not have intruded this subject upon you, but as it must certainly undergo a public discussion, I wish to know what is the general opinion on that transaction. * *

RICHARD DOBBS SPAIGHT.

*Life and Correspondence of James Iredell, by G. J. McRee, Vol. 2 pp. 169–70.

APPENDIX No. 7.

(See Page 283.)

Wednesday, March 21, 1787.

Congress assembled : Present as yesterday.

On the report of the Secretary of the United States for the department of foreign affairs, to whom was referred a letter of 4th March, 1786, from Mr. J. Adams, minister plenipotentiary of the United States of America at the court of London, together with the memorial of the said minister, dated the 30th November, 1785, and presented by him on the 8th of December following, to his Britannic Majesty's Secretary of State ; and the answer received by Mr. Adams to the said memorial, and contained in a letter from the said Secretary of State, dated at "St. James's, February 28, 1786," and other papers accompanying the same :

Congress unanimously agreed to the following resolutions:

Resolved, That the Legislatures of the several states cannot of right pass any act or acts, for interpreting, explaining, or construing a national treaty or any part or clause of it ; nor for restraining, limiting or in any manner impeding, retarding or counteracting the operation and execution of the same, for that on being constitutionally made, ratified and published, they become in virtue of the confederation, part of the law of the land, and are not only independent of the will and power of such legislatures, but also binding and obligatory on them.

Resolved, That all such acts or parts of acts as may be now existing in any of the States, repugnant to the treaty of peace, ought to be forthwith repealed, as well to prevent their continuing to be regarded as violations of that treaty, as to avoid the disagreeable necessity there might otherwise be of raising and discussing questions touching their validity and obligation.

Resolved, That it be recommended to the several States to make such repeal rather by describing than reciting the said acts, and for that purpose to pass an act declaring in general terms, that all such acts and parts of acts, repugnant to the treaty of peace between the United States and his Britannic Majesty, or any article thereof, shall be, and thereby are repealed, and that the courts of law and equity in all causes and questions cognizable by them respectively, and arising from or touching the said treaty, shall decide and adjudge according to the true intent and meaning of the same, anything in the said acts or parts of acts to the contrary thereof in anywise notwithstanding.*

Friday, April 13, 1787.

Congress Assembled: Present, Massachusetts, Rhode Island, Connecticut, New York, Pennsylvania, Virginia, North Carolina and Georgia; and from New Jersey, Mr. Clark, from Delaware, Mr. Kearney, and from South Carolina, Mr. Huger.

The secretary for foreign affairs, having in pursuance of an order of Congress, reported the draught of a letter to the states to accompany the resolutions passed the 21st day of March, 1787, the same was taken into consideration and unanimously agreed to as follows:

Sir: Our secretary for foreign affairs has transmitted to you copies of a letter to him, from our minister at the court of London, of the 4th day of March, 1786, and of the papers mentioned to have been enclosed with it.

We have deliberately and dispassionately examined and considered the several facts and matters urged by Britain, as infractions of the treaty of peace on the part of America, and we regret that in some of the states too little attention appears to have been paid to the public faith pledged by that treaty.

Not only the obvious dictates of religion, morality and national honor, but also the first principles of good policy, demand a candid and punctual compliance with engagements constitutionally and fairly made.

---

*Journals of Congress, ed. 1801, Vol. xii, pp. 23-4.

Our national constitution having committed to us the management of the national concerns with foreign States and powers, it is our duty to take care that all the rights which they ought to enjoy within our jurisdiction by the laws of nations and the faith of treaties, remain inviolate. And it is also our duty to provide that the essential interests and peace of the whole confederacy be not impaired or endangered by deviations from the line of public faith, into which any of its members may from whatever cause be unadvisedly drawn.

Let it be remembered that the Thirteen Independent Sovereign States have, by express delegation of power, formed and vested in us a general, though limited, sovereignty, for the general and national purposes specified in the confederation. In this sovereignty they cannot severally participate (except by their delegates) nor with it have concurrent jurisdiction ; for the ninth article of the confederation most expressly conveys to us the sole and exclusive right and power of determining on war and peace, and of entering into treaties and alliances, &c.

When, therefore, a treaty is constitutionally made, ratified and published by us, it immediately becomes binding on the whole nation, and superadded to the laws of the land, without the intervention of State legislatures. Treaties derive their obligation from being compacts between the sovereign of this and the sovereign of another nation; whereas laws or statutes derive their force from being the acts of a legislature competent to the passing of them. Hence it is clear that treaties must be implicitly received and observed by every member of the nation ; for as State legislatures are not competent to the making of such compacts or treaties, so neither are they competent in that capacity, authoritatively to decide on or ascertain the construction and sense of them. When doubts arise respecting the construction of State laws, it is not unusual nor improper for the State legislatures, by explanatory or declaratory acts, to remove those doubts. But, the case between laws and compacts or treaties is in this widely different ; for when doubts arise respecting the sense and meaning of a treaty, they are so far from being cognizable by a State legislature, that the United States in Congress assembled, have no authority to settle and determine them ; for as the legislature only, which constitutionally passes a law, has power to revise and amend it, so the sovereigns only, who are parties to the treaty, have power by mutual consent and posterior articles, to correct or explain it.

In cases between individuals, all doubts respecting the meaning of a treaty, like all doubts respecting the meaning of a law, are in the first instance mere judicial questions, and are to be heard and decided in the courts of justice having cognizance of the causes in which they arise, and whose duty it is to determine them according to the rules and maxims established by the laws of nations for the interpretation of treaties. From these principles it follows of necessary consequence, that no individual state has a right by legislative acts to decide and point out the sense in which their particular citizens and courts shall understand this or that article of a treaty.

It is evident that a contrary doctrine would not only militate against the common and established maxims and ideas relative to this subject, but would prove no less inconvenient in practice than it is irrational in theory ; for in that case the same article of the same treaty might by law be made to mean one thing in New Hampshire, another thing in New York, and neither the one nor the other of them in Georgia.

How far such legislative acts would be valid and obligatory even within the limits of the State passing them, is a question which we hope never to have occasion to discuss. Certain, however, it is that such acts cannot bind either of the contracting sovereigns, and consequently cannot be obligatory on their respective nations.

But if treaties and every article in them, be (as they are and ought to be) binding on the whole nation, if individual States have no right to accept some articles and reject others, and if the impropriety of State acts to interpret and decide the sense and construction of them, be apparent, still more manifest must be the impropriety of State acts to control, delay or modify the operation and execution of these national compacts.

When it is considered that the several States assembled by their delegates in Congress, have express power to form treaties, surely the treaties so formed are not afterwards to be subject to such alterations as this or that State legislature may think expedient to make, and that too without the consent of either of the parties to it; that is in the present case without the consent of all the United States, who collectively are parties to this treaty on the one side, and his Britannic Majesty on the other. Were the legislatures to possess and to exercise such power, we should soon be involved as a nation, in anarchy and confusion at home, and in disputes which would probably terminate in hostilities and war with the nations with whom we may have formed treaties. Instances would then be frequent of treaties fully executed in one State and only partly executed in another; and of the same article being executed in one manner in one State, and in a different manner, or not at all in another State. History furnishes no precedent of such liberties taken with treaties under form of law in any nation.

Contracts between nations, like contracts between individuals, should be faithfully executed, even though the sword in one case and the law in the other, did not compel it. Honest nations, like honest men, require no constraint to do justice; and though impunity and the necessity of affairs may sometimes afford temptations to pare down contracts to the measure of convenience, yet it is ever done, but at the expense of that esteem, and confidence and credit which are of infinitely more worth than all the momentary advantages which such expedients can extort.

But although contracting nations cannot, like individuals, avail themselves of courts of justice to compel performance of contracts; yet an appeal to Heaven and to arms is always in their power, and often in their inclination.

But it is their duty to take care that they never lead their people to make and support such appeals, unless the sincerity and propriety of their conduct affords them good reason to rely with confidence on the justice and protection of Heaven.

Thus much we think it useful to observe, in order to explain the principles on which we have unanimously come to the following resolution, viz:

"*Resolved*, That the legislatures of the several States cannot of right pass any act or acts for interpreting, explaining or construing a national treaty, or any part or clause of it, nor for restraining, limiting or in any manner impeding, retarding or counteracting the operatien and execution of the same; for that on being constitutionally made, ratified and published, they become in virtue of the confederation part of the law of the land, and are not only independent of the will and power of such legislatures, but also binding and obligatory on them."

As the treaty of peace, so far as it respects the matters and things provided for in it, is a law to the United States which cannot by all or any of them be altered or changed, all State acts establishing provisions relative to the same objects which are incompatible with it, must in every point of view be improper. Such acts do nevertheless exist; but we do not think it necessary either to enumerate them particularly, or to make them severally the subjects of discussion. It appears to us sufficient to observe and insist, that the treaty ought to have free course in its operation and execution, and that all obstacles interposed by State acts be removed. We mean to act with the most scrupulous regard to justice and candour towards Great Britain, and with an equal degree of delicacy, moderation and decision towards the States who have given occasion to these discussions.

For these reasons we have in general terms,

" *Resolved*, That all such acts or parts of acts as may be now existing in any of the States, repugnant to the treaty of peace, ought to be forthwith repealed; as well to prevent their continuing to be regarded as violations of that treaty, as to avoid the disagreeable necessity there might otherwise be of raising and discussing questions touching their validity and obligation."

Although this resolution applies strictly only to such of the States as have passed the exceptionable acts alluded to, yet to obviate all future disputes and questions, as well as to remove those which now exist, we think it best that every State without exception should pass a law on the subject. We have therefore,

"*Resolved*, That it be recommended to the several states to make such repeal, rather by describing than reciting the said acts ; and for that purpose to pass an act declaring in general terms that all such acts, and parts of acts repugnant to the treaty of peace between the United States and his Britannic Majesty, or any article thereof, shall be, and thereby are repealed ; and that the courts of law and equity in all causes and questions cognizable by them respectively, and arising from or touching the said treaty, shall decide and adjudge according to the true intent and meaning of the same, anything in the said acts, or parts of acts, to the contrary thereof in anywise notwithstanding."

Such laws would answer every purpose, and be easily formed. The more they were of the like tenor throughout the states the better, they might each recite that,

Whereas, Certain laws or statutes made and passed in some of the United States, are regarded and complained of as repugnant to the treaty of peace with Great Britain, by reason whereof not only the good faith of the United States pledged by that treaty, has been drawn into question, but their essential interests under that treaty greatly affected, *And whereas*, justice to Great Britain, as well as regard to the honor and interests of the United States, require that the said treaty be faithfully executed, and that all obstacles thereto, and particularly such as do or may be construed to proceed from the laws of this State, be effectually removed. Therefore,

Be it enacted by
and it is hereby enacted by the authority of the same, that such of the acts or parts of acts of the legislature of this State, as are repugnant to the treaty of peace between the United States and his Britannic Majesty, or any article thereof, shall be, and hereby are repealed. And further,

that the courts of law and equity within this State be, and they hereby are directed and required in all causes and questions cognizable by them respectively, and arising from or touching the said treaty, to decide and adjudge according to the tenor, true intent and meaning of the same, any thing in the said acts, or parts of acts, to the contrary thereof in anywise notwithstanding.

Such a general law would, we think, be preferable to one that should minutely enumerate the acts and clauses intended to be repealed, because omissions might accidentally be made in the enumeration, or questions might arise, and perhaps not be satisfactorily determined, respecting particular acts or clauses, about which contrary opinions may be entertained. By repealing in general terms all acts and clauses repugnant to the treaty, the business will be turned over to its proper department, viz: the judicial, and the courts of law will find no difficulty in deciding whether any particular act or clause is or is not contrary to the treaty. Besides, when it is considered that the judges in general are men of character and learning, and feel as well as know the obligations of office and the value of reputation, there is no reason to doubt that their conduct and judgments relative to these, as well as other judicial matters, will be wise and upright.

Be pleased, sir, to lay this letter before the legislature of your State, without delay. We flatter ourselves they will concur with us in opinion, that candor and justice are as necessary to true policy as they are to sound morality, and that the most honorable way of delivering ourselves from the embarrassment of mistakes, is fairly to correct them. It certainly is time that all doubts respecting the public faith be removed, and that all questions and differences between us and Great Britain be amicably and finally settled. The States are informed of the reason why his Britannic Majesty still continues to occupy the frontier posts, which by the treaty he agreed to evacuate; and we have the strongest assurances that an exact compliance with the treaty on our part, shall be followed by a punctual performance of it on the part of Great Britain.

It is important that the several legislatures should, as soon as possible, take these matters into consideration ; and we request the favor of you to transmit to us an authenticated copy of such acts and proceedings of the legislature of your State, as may take place on the subject and in pursuance of this letter.

By order of Congress.

(Signed)   ARTHUR ST. CLAIR,
President.*

---

* Journals of Congress, ed. 1801,Vol. xii, pp. 32-36.

INDEX.